CASES IN

COMPARATIVE

POLITICS FOURTH EDITION

CASES IN

COMPARATIVE

POLITICS FOURTH EDITION

PATRICK H. O'NEIL
KARL FIELDS | DON SHARE

W. W. NORTON & COMPANY
New York • London

W. W. Norton & Company has been independent since its founding in 1923, when William Warder Norton and Mary D. Herter Norton first published lectures delivered at the People's Institute, the adult education division of New York City's Cooper Union. The firm soon expanded its program beyond the Institute, publishing books by celebrated academics from America and abroad. By mid-century, the two major pillars of Norton's publishing program—trade books and college texts—were firmly established. In the 1950s, the Norton family transferred control of the company to its employees, and today—with a staff of four hundred and a comparable number of trade, college, and professional titles published each year—W. W. Norton & Company stands as the largest and oldest publishing house owned wholly by its employees.

Editor: Ann Shin
Associate Editor: Jake Schindel
Manuscript Editor: Barney Latimer
Project Editor: Diane Cipollone
Electronic Media Editor: Lorraine Klimowich
Electronic Media Assistant Editor: Jennifer Barnhardt
Editorial Assistant: Caitlin Cummings
Marketing Manager, Political Science: Sasha Levitt
Production Manager: Eric Pier-Hocking
Photo Editor: Michael Fodera
Permissions Manager: Megan Jackson
Permissions Assistant: Bethany Salminen
Text Design: Faceout Studio
Art Director: Hope Miller Goodell, Chris Welch
Composition: Jouve North America—Brattleboro, VT
Manufacturing: Quad Graphics—Taunton, MA

Library of Congress Cataloging-in-Publication Data

O'Neil, Patrick H., 1966-
   Cases in comparative politics / Patrick H. O'Neil, Karl Fields, and Don Share. — 4th ed.
      p. cm.
   Includes bibliographical references and index.
   ISBN 978-0-393-91279-1 (pbk.)
1. Comparative government—Case studies.   I. Fields, Karl J.   II. Share, Donald.   III. Title.
JF51.O538 2012
320.3—dc23
                                                                                    2012020082

W. W. Norton & Company, Inc., 500 Fifth Avenue, New York, N.Y. 10110
www.wwnorton.com
W. W. Norton & Company Ltd., Castle House, 75/76 Wells Street, London W1T 3QT
1 2 3 4 5 6 7 8 9 0

BRIEF CONTENTS

CONTENTS

ABOUT THE AUTHORS

PATRICK H. O'NEIL is Professor of Politics and Government at the University of Puget Sound in Tacoma, Washington. He has a Ph.D. in Political Science from Indiana University. Professor O'Neil's teaching and research interests are in the areas of democratization, conflict and political violence. His publications include the books *Revolution from Within: The Hungarian Socialist Workers' Party and the Collapse of Communism* and *Communicating Democracy: The Media and Political Transitions* (editor).

KARL FIELDS is Professor of Politics and Government and Director of Asian Studies at the University of Puget Sound in Tacoma, Washington. He has a Ph.D. in Political Science from the University of California, Berkeley. Professor Fields' teaching and research interests focus on East Asian political economy, including government-business relations, economic reform, and regional integration. His publications include *Enterprise and the State in Korea and Taiwan*.

DON SHARE is Professor of Politics and Government at the University of Puget Sound in Tacoma, Washington. He has a Ph.D. in Political Science from Stanford University. He teaches comparative politics and Latin American politics, and has published widely on democratization and Spanish politics. His books include *The Making of Spanish Democracy* and *Dilemmas of Social Democracy*.

PREFACE

Cases in Comparative Politics can be traced to an ongoing experiment undertaken by the three comparative political scientists in the Politics and Government Department at the University of Puget Sound. Over the years the three of us spent much time discussing the challenges of teaching our introductory course in comparative politics. In those discussions we came to realize that each of us taught the course so differently that students completing our different sections of the course did not really share a common conceptual vocabulary. Over several years we fashioned a unified curriculum for Introduction to Comparative Politics, drawing on the strengths of each of our particular approaches.

All three of us now equip our students with a common conceptual vocabulary. All of our students now learn about states, nations, and different models of political economy. All students learn the basics about nondemocratic and democratic regimes, and they become familiar with characteristics of communist systems and advanced democracies. In developing our curriculum, we became frustrated trying to find cases that were concise, sophisticated, and written to address the major concepts introduced in Patrick H. O'Neil's textbook, *Essentials of Comparative Politics*. Thus, we initially co-authored six cases adhering to a set of criteria:

- Each case is concise, making it possible to assign an entire case, or even two cases, for a single class session.
- All cases include discussion of major geographic and demographic features, themes in the historical development of the state, political regimes (including the constitution, branches of government, the electoral system, and local government), political conflict and competition (including the party system and civil society), society, political economy, and current issues. This uniform structure allowed us to assign specific sections from two or more cases simultaneously.
- The cases follow the general framework of *Essentials of Comparative Politics*, but could also be used in conjunction with other texts.

After the publication of the initial six cases (the United Kingdom, Japan, China, Russia, Mexico, and South Africa), we received positive feedback from teachers of comparative politics. Drawing on their comments and suggestions, we wrote new cases to accommodate individual preferences and give instructors more choice. We subsequently added cases on Brazil, France, India, Iran, the United States, and Nigeria. Based on feedback from instructors, the third edition added Germany, bringing the total number of cases to thirteen.

Selecting only thirteen cases is, of course, fraught with drawbacks. Nevertheless, we believe that this collection represents countries that are both important in their own right and representative of a broad range of political systems. Each of the thirteen cases has special importance in the context of the study of comparative politics. Five of our cases (France, Germany, Japan, the United States, and the United Kingdom) are advanced industrial democracies, but they represent a wide range of institutions, societies, political economic models, and relationships with the world. Japan is an important instance of a non-Western industrialized democracy and an instructive case of democratization imposed by foreign occupiers. While the United Kingdom and the United States have been known for political stability, France and Germany have fascinating histories of political turmoil and regime change.

Two of our cases, China and Russia, share a past of Marxist-Leninist totalitarianism. Communism thrived in these two large and culturally distinct nations. Both suffered from the dangerous concentration of power in the hands of communist parties and, at times, despotic leaders. The Soviet Communist regime imploded and led to a troubled and incomplete transition to capitalism and democracy. China has retained its communist authoritarian political system but has experimented with a remarkable transition to a largely capitalist political economy.

The remaining six cases illustrate the diversity of the developing world. Of the six, India has had the longest history of stable democratic rule, but like most countries in the developing world, it has nevertheless struggled with massive poverty and inequality. The remaining five have experienced various forms of authoritarianism. Brazil and Nigeria endured long periods of military rule. Mexico's history of military rule was ended by an authoritarian political party that ruled for much of the twentieth century through a variety of nonmilitary means. South Africa experienced decades of racially based authoritarianism that excluded the vast majority of its population. Iran experienced a modernizing authoritarian monarchy followed by its current authoritarian regime, a theocracy ruled by Islamic clerics.

In writing the cases we have incurred numerous debts. First, and foremost, we wish to thank our wonderful colleagues in the Department of Politics and Government at the University of Puget Sound. By encouraging us to develop a common curriculum for our Introduction to Comparative Politics offering, and by allowing us to team-teach the course in different combinations, they allowed us to learn from each other. These cases are much stronger as a result. The university has also been extremely supportive in recognizing that writing for the classroom is as valuable as writing scholarly publications, and in providing course releases and summer stipends toward that end. Student assistants Brett Venn, Jess Box, Liz Kaster and Céad Nardi-Warner proved extremely helpful in conducting research for our various cases; Irene Lim has, as always, supported us with her amazing technical and organizational skills. Our colleague Bill Haltom and David Sousa provided very helpful input throughout the project. Debby Nagusky contributed valuable copyediting assistance.

We very much appreciate the many helpful comments we have received from fellow instructors of comparative politics, including Emily Acevedo (California State University, Los Angeles), Josephine Andrews (University of California, Davis), Jason Arnold (Virginia Commonwealth University), Alex Avila (Mesa Community College), Caroline Beer (University of Vermont), Marni Berg (Colorado State University), Prosper Bernard, Jr. (College of Staten Island), Jeremy Busacca (Whittier College), Robert Compton (SUNY Oneonta), Bruce Dickson (George Washington University), Kenly Fenio (Virginia Tech), Sarah Goodman (University of California at Irvine), Ivy Hamerly (Baylor University), William Heller (Binghamton University), Yoshiko Herrera (University of Wisconsin at Madison), Robert Jackson (University of Redlands), Tamara Kotar (University of Ottawa), Brian Kupfer (Tallahassee Community College), Ricardo Larémont (Binghamton University), Peter H. Loedel (West Chester University), Mary Malone (University of New Hampshire), Pamela Martin (Coastal Carolina University), Mark Milewicz (Gordon College), Michael Mitchell (Arizona State Univerity), John Occhipinti (Canisius College), Anthony O'Regan (Los Angeles Valley College), Paul Rousseau (University of Windsor), Steve Sharp (Utah State University, Logan), Emmanuel J. Teitelbaum (George Washington University), José Vadi (Cal Poly, Pomona), and Stacey Philbrick Yadav (Hobart & William Smith Colleges).

Many thanks to all the folks at Norton—Peter Lesser, Ann Shin, Roby Harrington, and Aaron Javsicas among others—who have contributed to the success of this project. For this Fourth Edition we especially appreciate the hard work and attention of Jake Schindel. Finally, we thank our students at the University of

Puget Sound who inspired us to write these cases and provided valuable feedback throughout the entire process.

Don Share
Karl Fields
Patrick H. O'Neil
Tacoma, WA 2012

A note about the data: The data that are presented throughout the text in numerous tables, charts, and other figures are drawn from the *CIA World Factbook* unless otherwise noted.

CASES IN

COMPARATIVE

POLITICS

FOURTH EDITION

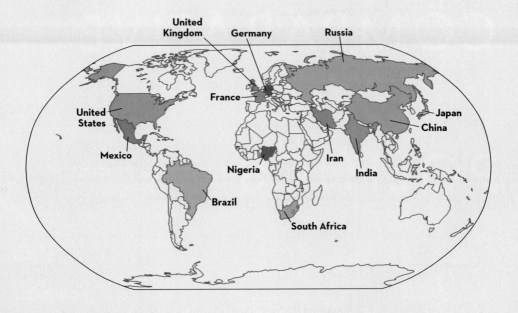

INTRODUCTION

What Is Comparative Politics?

Comparative politics is the study and comparison of politics across countries. Studying politics in this way helps us examine major questions of political science; for example, why do some countries have democratic regimes whereas others experience authoritarianism? Why and how do regimes change? Why do some countries experience affluence and growth, but others endure poverty and decline? In this volume, we describe and analyze the political systems of 13 countries. We focus on their major geographic and demographic features; the origins and development of their state; and their political regimes, patterns of political conflict and competition, societies, political economies, and relationships with the world. This brief introduction seeks to familiarize students with the very basic vocabulary of comparative politics. The concepts and terms described here will be extremely useful in an examination of any of the 13 country cases contained in this book. Moreover, this vocabulary is an essential tool for making comparisons *among* the cases.

Comparing States

States are organizations that maintain a monopoly of violence over a territory. The term *state* can be confusing because it sometimes refers to a subnational government (for example, any of the 50 states in the United States). Political scientists, however, use *state* to refer to a national organization. In this book, *state* is used in the latter, broader sense. Still, the concept of state is narrower than the notion of country, which encompasses the territory and people living within a state. As illustrated by our collection of cases, states can differ in many ways, including in origin, length of existence, strength, and historical development.[1] Political scientists also distinguish between the state and the **government**, considering the government to be the leadership or elite that administers the state.

Two of the most obvious differences among states are their size and population (see "In Comparison: Total Land Size" and "In Comparison: Population," pp. 4 and 5). The 13 countries included in this book vary considerably in both respects. States also vary in their natural endowments, such as arable land, mineral resources, navigable rivers, and access to the sea. Well-endowed states may have advantages over poorly endowed ones, but resource endowments do not necessarily determine a state's prosperity. Japan, for example, has become one of the world's dominant economic powers despite having relatively few natural resources. Russia and Iran, in contrast, are rich in natural resources but have struggled economically.

States also differ widely in their origins and historical development.[2] Some countries (for example, China, France, and the United Kingdom) have long

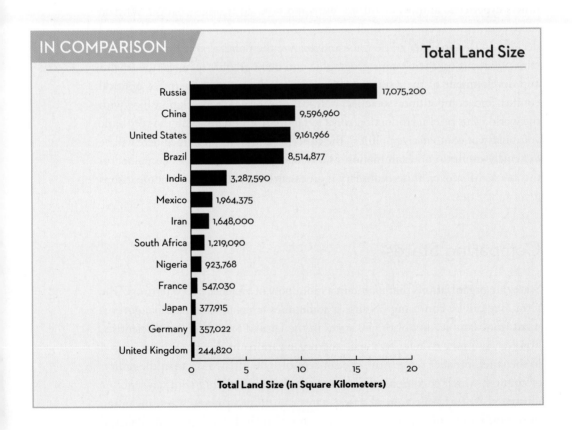

IN COMPARISON   Total Land Size

Country	Total Land Size
Russia	17,075,200
China	9,596,960
United States	9,161,966
Brazil	8,514,877
India	3,287,590
Mexico	1,964,375
Iran	1,648,000
South Africa	1,219,090
Nigeria	923,768
France	547,030
Japan	377,915
Germany	357,022
United Kingdom	244,820

Total Land Size (in Square Kilometers)

histories of statehood. Other political systems, such as Germany, experienced the creation of a unified state only after long periods of division. Many countries in the developing world became states after they were decolonized. Nigeria, for example, became an independent state relatively recently, in 1960. With the end of the Cold War in 1989 and the collapse of the Soviet Union two years later, a number of states emerged or reemerged. At the same time, Germany, which had been divided into two states during the Cold War, became a single state in 1990. It is important to point out that in today's world we continue to witness both the erosion of existing states (for example, Somalia) and the emergence of new ones (for example, the Republic of South Sudan—see "South Sudan, The World's Newest State," p. 6).

States differ, too, in their level of organization, effectiveness, and stability. The power of a state depends in part on its **legitimacy**, or the extent to which its authority is regarded as right and proper. Political scientists have long observed

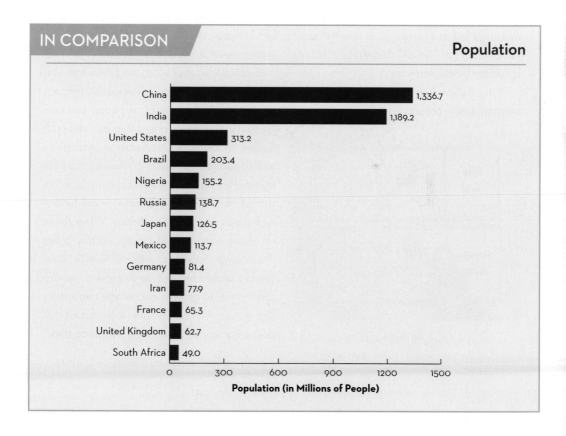

IN COMPARISON   Population

China — 1,336.7
India — 1,189.2
United States — 313.2
Brazil — 203.4
Nigeria — 155.2
Russia — 138.7
Japan — 126.5
Mexico — 113.7
Germany — 81.4
Iran — 77.9
France — 65.3
United Kingdom — 62.7
South Africa — 49.0

Population (in Millions of People)

APPLYING THE VOCABULARY OF COMPARATIVE POLITICS: SOUTH SUDAN, THE WORLD'S NEWEST STATE

The Republic of South Sudan became the world's newest state in July 2011, after a decades-long armed struggle to secede from the Republic of Sudan. A series of civil wars launched by southern Sudanese, who consider themselves ethnically distinct from those in the north, challenged the legitimacy and sovereignty of the government located in the north. The protracted conflict, which killed millions of South Sudanese and destroyed much of the south's economy, was finally halted by a peace agreement that led to a referendum in which over 98 percent of South Sudanese citizens opted for independence.

Along with a new state, South Sudan has adopted a new constitution, which outlines a

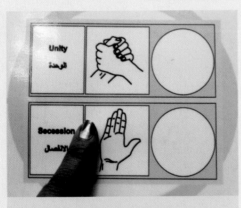

Voters in South Sudan were asked to decide between unity with the north or independence.

new political regime. It calls for a presidential system with a directly elected president, and a new bicameral national legislature. New states face many daunting challenges, and South Sudan is no exception. Decades of war have destroyed much of the economy, and South Sudan is among the very poorest states in the world. Most South Sudanese citizens are subsistence farmers. Only about a quarter of the state's roughly 8 million citizens are literate. South Sudan is also ethnically diverse, with more than 60 different languages spoken. It has a contentious relationship with the more powerful Republic of Sudan.

South Sudan may have one advantage as it builds its new state, though: about 80 percent of the large oil reserves of Sudan are now located in the independent Republic of South Sudan. However, South Sudan is landlocked and depends on the north's infrastructure for transporting oil. The peace accords that led to the referendum on independence call for the two states to split oil revenues. While these revenues may benefit South Sudan, other developing countries with oil wealth have found that overreliance on oil exports can distort economic growth, encourage corruption, and weaken democratic rule, a syndrome that political scientists often call a "resource trap."

that there are different sources of a state's legitimacy. State authority may draw on **traditional legitimacy**, in which the state is obeyed because it has a long tradition of being obeyed. Alternatively, a state may be considered legitimate because of **charismatic legitimacy**, that is, its identification with the magnetic appeal of a leader or movement. Finally, states may gain legitimacy on the basis of **rational-legal legitimacy**, a system of laws and procedures that becomes highly institutionalized. Although most modern states derive their legitimacy from rational-legal sources, both traditional and charismatic legitimacy often continue to play a role. In Japan and the United Kingdom, for example, the monarchy is a source of traditional legitimacy that complements the rational-legal legitimacy of the state. Some postcolonial states in the developing world have had considerable trouble establishing legitimacy. Often colonial powers created states that cut across ethnic boundaries or contain hostile ethnic groups, as in Nigeria and Iran.

States differ in their ability to preserve their sovereignty and carry out the functions of maintaining law and order. **Strong states** can perform the tasks of defending their borders from outside attacks and defending their authority from internal nonstate rivals. **Weak states** have trouble carrying out those basic tasks and often suffer from endemic internal violence, poor infrastructure, and the inability to collect taxes and enforce the rule of law. High levels of corruption are often a

MONARCHIES AS A SOURCE OF TRADITIONAL LEGITIMACY IN MODERN DEMOCRACY

By definition, monarchies are not democratic institutions, because monarchs are usually determined according to ascriptive criteria (most often ancestral lineage, seniority, and gender). Among the 13 cases in this volume, however, two vibrant democracies (Japan and the United Kingdom) have retained monarchs as heads of state. How can a democracy justify having a hereditary monarch as head of state? In both Japan and the United Kingdom, the monarch serves as not only a significant link to the past but also a reminder of the traditions that are cherished in each society. More important, both monarchs are bound by constitutions that limit their power almost entirely to symbolic functions. The monarchy has its critics in both countries, but most citizens support the presence of a head of state who is completely divorced from partisan politics.

symptom of state weakness. Taken to an extreme, weak states may experience a complete loss of legitimacy and power and may be overwhelmed by anarchy and violence. Political scientists refer to those relatively rare cases as **failed states.**[3]

Finally, states differ in the degree to which they centralize or disperse political power. **Unitary states** concentrate most of their political power in the national capital, allocating little decision-making power to regions or localities. **Federal states** divide power between the central state and regional or local authorities (such as provinces, counties, and cities). Unitary states, such as the United Kingdom and South Africa, may be stronger and more decisive than federal states, but the centralization of power may create local resentment and initiate calls for a **devolution** (handing down) of power to regions and localities. Federal states, such as Brazil, Germany, Mexico, Nigeria, Russia, and the United States, often find that their dispersal of power hampers national decision making and accountability.

IN COMPARISON   Freedom House Rankings, 2011

On a scale of 1 to 7, 1 = free; 5 = partly free; 7 = not free.

COUNTY	RANKING
United Kingdom	1
Germany	1
France	1
United States	1
Japan	1.5
South Africa	2
Brazil	2
India	2.5
Mexico	3
Nigeria	4
Russia	5.5
Iran	6
China	6.5

Source: Freedom House, www.freedomhouse.org/images/File/fiw/FIW_2011_Booklet.pdf (accessed 9/8/11).

Comparing Regimes

Political regimes are the norms and rules regarding individual freedoms and collective equality, the locus of power, and the use of that power. It is easiest to think of political regimes as the rules of the game governing the exercise of power. In modern political systems, regimes are most often described in written constitutions. In some countries, however, such as the United Kingdom, the regime consists of a combination of laws and customs that are not incorporated into any one written document. In other countries, such as China and Iran, written constitutions do not accurately describe the extra-constitutional rules that govern the exercise of power.

Democratic regimes have rules that emphasize a large role for the public in governance, protect basic rights and freedoms, and attempt to ensure basic transparency of and accountability for government actions. **Authoritarian regimes** limit the role of the public in decision making and often deny citizens' basic rights and restrict their freedoms. In the past quarter-century, the world has witnessed a dramatic rise in the number of democratic regimes.[4] Over half the world's population, however, is still governed by nondemocratic regimes, which one leading research organization defines as either "partly free," sometimes called illiberal (meaning that some personal liberties and democratic rights are limited while others are protected), or "not free," sometimes called authoritarian (meaning that the public has very little individual freedom).[5] Freedom House, a U.S research organization, regularly measures the amount of freedom in different

---

A SPECTRUM OF REGIMES: FROM AUTHORITARIANISM TO DEMOCRACY

Our 13 cases exemplify the broad spectrum of regime types. China has the most clearly authoritarian regime of them all, since it tolerates only one political party and does not convene democratic elections. Iran allows elections, but its unelected religious authorities severely circumscribe political parties and political institutions. Russia today is formally a democracy, but the power of state authorities makes it effectively a semi-authoritarian system, or illiberal democracy. The remaining cases in this volume more easily (if imperfectly and only recently in some instances) satisfy the criteria for being liberal democracies.

---

political systems, and the "In Comparison" table on p. 8 provides those measures for the 13 cases included in this volume.

COMPARING DEMOCRATIC POLITICAL INSTITUTIONS

Most political regimes, whether democratic or not, establish a number of political institutions. Students of comparative politics must learn to identify and distinguish these institutions precisely. The **executive** is the branch of government that carries out the laws and policies of a given state. We can think of the executive branch as performing two separate sets of duties. On the one hand, the **head of state** symbolizes and represents the people, both nationally and internationally, embodying and articulating the goals of the regime. On the other hand, the **head of government** deals with the everyday tasks of running the state, such as formulating and executing policy. The distinction between those roles is most easily seen in, for example, France, Germany, India, Japan, and the United Kingdom, which have separate heads of state and heads of government. Other regimes, such as those of Brazil, Mexico, Nigeria, South Africa, and the United States, assign the two roles of the executive branch to a single individual.

The **legislature** is the branch of government formally charged with making laws. The organization and power of legislatures differ considerably from country to country. In some political regimes, especially authoritarian ones such as China and Iran, the legislature has little power or initiative and serves mainly to rubber-stamp government legislation. In other systems, such as those of Germany and India, the legislature is relatively powerful and autonomous. **Unicameral legislatures** (often found in smaller countries) consist of a single chamber; **bicameral legislatures** consist of two legislative chambers. In the latter systems, one chamber often represents the population at large and is referred to as the **lower house**, and the other chamber (referred to as the **upper house**) reflects the geographical subunits.

The **judiciary** is the branch of a country's government that is concerned with dispensing justice. The **constitutional court** is the highest judicial body to rule on the constitutionality of laws and other government actions; in most political systems, the constitutional court also formally oversees the entire judicial structure. The power of a regime's judiciary is determined in part by the nature of its power of **judicial review**, the mechanism by which the court reviews laws and policies and overturns those seen as violations of the constitution. Some regimes give the judiciary the power of **concrete review**, allowing the high court to rule on constitutional issues only when disputes are brought before it. Other regimes give the judiciary the power of **abstract review**, allowing it to decide questions that do not arise from legal cases, sometimes even allowing it to make judgments on legislation that has not yet been enacted. In France, the Constitutional Council has the power of abstract review, whereas in the United States the Supreme Court has the power of concrete review. The highest courts in the United Kingdom, by contrast, do not have power to overturn legislation passed by the national legislature under any circumstances.

The powers of these political institutions and the relationships among them vary considerably across regimes. The most important variation concerns the relationship between the legislature and the executive. There are three major models of **legislative-executive relations** within democratic regimes: parliamentary, presidential, and semi-presidential. The **parliamentary system** (seen among our cases in Germany, India, Japan, and the United Kingdom) features an executive

DON'T JUDGE A LEGISLATIVE CHAMBER BY ITS NICKNAME

Two of the most common and potentially confusing terms in comparative politics referring to modern legislatures are *upper house* and *lower house*. The term *upper house* originally referred to the legislative chamber representing the most powerful classes in society (the aristocratic class), and in pre-democratic England that house wielded the most power. The "lower house" represented the less powerful merchant classes. With the emergence of democracy in many countries, the two houses remained, as did their nicknames, but their powers changed dramatically over time. Today, the lower house is the most representative of the population at large (this is the case in most of the democracies described in this book), and is therefore vested with more power. In modern democracies, upper houses tend to represent not the aristocracy but geographical subunits such as states, provinces, and regions. Upper houses tend to have fewer powers. However, like all things in comparative politics, there are exceptions. The U.S. upper house (the Senate) and lower house (the House of Representatives) have roughly equal powers. The United Kingdom's upper house (the House of Lords) until very recently was a bastion of the aristocratic class. But as a rule of thumb, when you hear "lower house," think "more representative" and "more powerful."

head of government (often referred to as a prime minister) who is usually elected from within the legislature. The prime minister is usually the leader of the largest political party in the legislature. The prime minister and the **cabinet** (the body of chief ministers or officials in government in charge of such policy areas as defense, agriculture, and so on) are charged with formulating and executing policy. The head of state in such systems has largely ceremonial duties and is usually either an indirectly elected president or a hereditary monarch.

The **presidential system**, used by Brazil, Mexico, and the United States, combines the roles of head of state and head of government in the office of the president. These systems feature a directly elected president who holds most of the government's executive powers. Presidential systems have directly elected legislatures that to varying degrees serve as a check on presidential authority.

Scholars debate the advantages and disadvantages of these legislative-executive models.[6] Parliamentary systems are often praised for reducing conflict between the legislature and the executive (since the executive is approved by the legislature), thus producing more efficient government. In addition, when parliamentary legislatures lack a majority, political parties must compromise to create a government supported by a majority of the legislature. Parliamentary systems are also more flexible than presidential systems because when prime ministers lose the support of the legislature, they can be swiftly removed through a legislative **vote of no confidence**. Coalition governments are often formed as a result of negotiations and compromise between political parties The appointment of a new prime minister, or the convocation of new elections, can often resolve political deadlocks.

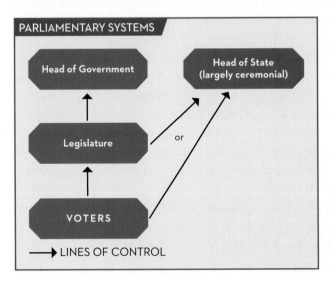

But critics point out that parliamentary systems with a strong majority in the legislature can produce a very dominant, virtually unchecked government. Moreover, in fractious legislatures, it can be difficult to cobble together a stable majority government; and coalitions, when they result, can be unstable.

Presidential systems are often portrayed as more stable than parliamentary systems. There are fixed terms of office for the president and the legislature, which is not the case in most parliamentary systems. Moreover, presidents are directly elected by the public and can be removed only by the legislature and only in cases of criminal misconduct. Nonetheless, presidential systems have been criticized for producing divisive

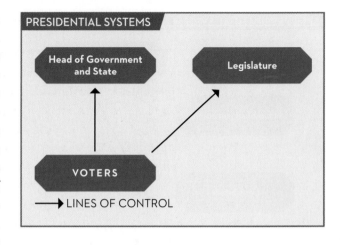

winner-take-all outcomes, lacking the flexibility needed to confront crises, and leading to overly powerful executives in the face of weak and divided legislatures.[7] Also, presidential systems can experience gridlock when the presidency and legislature are controlled by different parties.

In an attempt to avoid the weaknesses of parliamentary and presidential systems, some newer democratic regimes, such as those of France and Russia, have adopted a third model of legislative-executive relations, called the **semi-presidential system**. This system includes both a prime minister approved by the legislature and a directly elected president, with the two sharing executive power. In practice, semi-presidential systems tend to produce strong presidents akin to those in pure presidential systems, but the exact balance between the executives varies from case to case.

Another influential political institution is the **electoral system**, which determines how votes are cast and counted. Most democratic regimes use one of two models. The most commonly employed is **proportional representation (PR)**. Among our 13 cases, Brazil, Russia, and South Africa employ this system. PR relies upon **multimember districts (MMDs)**, in which more than one legislative seat is contested in each electoral district. Voters cast their ballots for a list of party candidates rather than for a single representative, and the percentage of votes a party receives in a district determines how many of that district's seats the party will win. Thus, the percentage of votes each party wins in each district should closely correspond to the percentage of seats allocated to each party. PR systems produce legislatures that often closely reflect the percentage of votes won nationwide by each political party. As a result, they tend to foster multiple political parties, including small ones.

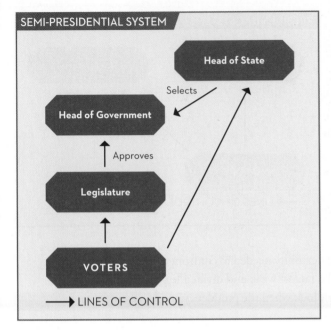

SEMI-PRESIDENTIAL SYSTEM

Head of State

Head of Government

Selects

Approves

Legislature

VOTERS

→ LINES OF CONTROL

A minority of the world's democracies (mainly France, the United Kingdom, and the former British colonies, such as India, Nigeria and the United States, among the cases in this volume) rely upon **single-member districts (SMDs)**. In these systems, there is only one representative for each constituency, and in each district the candidate with the greatest number of votes (not necessarily a majority) wins the seat. As opposed to PR systems, SMD votes cast for all but the one winning candidate are, in effect, wasted: that is, they do not count toward any representation in the legislature. SMD systems tend to discriminate against small parties, especially those with a national following rather than a geographically concentrated following.

As with the legislative-executive models, there is vigorous debate about which electoral system is most desirable.[8] PR systems are considered more democratic, since they waste fewer votes and encourage the expression of a wider range of political interests. The PR model increases the number of parties able to win seats in a legislature and allows parties concerned with narrow or minority interests to gain representation. SMD systems are often endorsed because they allow voters in each district to connect directly with their elected representatives instead of their party, making the representatives more accountable to the electorate. Supporters of SMD argue that it is beneficial for eliminating narrowly-based or extremist parties from the legislature. They view SMD systems as more likely to produce stable, centrist legislative majorities.

Some democracies, including Germany, Japan, and Mexico, have combined SMD and PR voting systems in what is known as a **mixed electoral system**. Voters are given two votes: one for a candidate and the other for a party. Candidates in the SMDs are elected on the basis of a plurality; other seats are elected from MMDs and are allocated using PR.

Much of the diversity of comparative politics is the result of different combinations of the political institutions just described. Even among the ten democratic regimes studied in this volume, different combinations of political institutions

HOW LEGISLATIVE-EXECUTIVE AND ELECTORAL SYSTEMS CAN INTERACT

In some parliamentary systems (for example, in the United Kingdom and, until recently, India), elections regularly produce a majority of seats in the legislature for one party. Such systems tend to use single-member district electoral systems, which usually favor the largest parties at the expense of smaller ones. In other parliamentary systems (for example, in Germany), elections rarely produce a parliamentary majority for any party. As a result, political parties often form coalition governments by dividing cabinet seats among coalition members. Those parliamentary systems tend to employ proportional representation electoral systems, which more often allow smaller parties to gain representation in the legislature.

result in considerable diversity (see "Combinations of Political Institutions," p. 16). For example, Germany and the United States are federal states, but the United States has a presidential legislative-executive system while Germany uses a parliamentary system. Germany and the United Kingdom both use parliamentary legislative-executive systems, but their electoral systems differ.

COMPARING NONDEMOCRATIC REGIMES

Many nondemocratic regimes have institutions that on paper appear quite similar to those in democratic regimes. In most authoritarian regimes, however, a study of the legislature, the judiciary, and the electoral system may not reveal much about the exercise of political power.

Nondemocratic regimes differ from one another in a number of important ways. Common forms of nondemocratic regimes include personal dictatorships, monarchies, military regimes, one-party regimes, theocracies, and illiberal regimes. A **personal dictatorship**, such as that of Porfirio Díaz in Mexico (1876–1910), is based on the power of a single strong leader who usually relies on charismatic or traditional authority to maintain power. In a **military regime** (such as Brazil from 1964 to 1985 or Nigeria from 1966 to 1979), the institution of the military dominates politics. A **one-party regime** (such as that in Mexico

Combinations of Political Institutions

COUNTRY	TYPE OF REGIME	TYPE OF STATE	LEGISLATIVE-EXECUTIVE SYSTEM	ELECTORAL SYSTEM
Brazil	Democratic	Federal	Presidential	PR
China	Authoritarian	Unitary	NA	NA
France	Democratic	Unitary	Semi-presidential	SMD
Germany	Democratic	Federal	Parliamentary	Mixed
India	Democratic	Federal	Parliamentary	SMD
Iran	Authoritarian	Unitary	NA	SMD
Japan	Democratic	Unitary	Parliamentary	Mixed
Mexico	Democratic	Federal	Presidential	Mixed
Nigeria	Democratic	Federal	Presidential	SMD
Russia	Authoritarian	Federal	Semi-presidential	PR
South Africa	Democratic	Unitary	Parliamentary	PR
United Kingdom	Democratic	Unitary	Parliamentary	SMD
United States	Democratic	Federal	Presidential	SMD

from 1917 to 2000) is dominated by a strong political party that relies upon a broad membership as a source of political control. In a **theocracy**, a rare form of government (though one that best characterizes present-day Iran), a leader claims to rule on behalf of God. An **illiberal regime** (as in present-day Russia) retains the basic structures of a democracy but does not protect civil liberties. In the real world, many nondemocratic regimes combine various aspects of these forms. The apartheid regime in South Africa (1948–1994) had largely democratic political institutions but excluded the vast majority of its black population.

Communist regimes are one-party regimes in which a Communist party controls most aspects of a country's political and economic system. Specific Communist regimes (such as China under Mao Zedong or the Soviet Union under Joseph Stalin) have sometimes been described as **totalitarian**. Totalitarian regimes feature a strong official ideology that seeks to transform fundamental aspects of the state, society, and economy, using a wide array of organizations and the application of force. As the case of Nazi Germany illustrates, totalitarian regimes need not be Communist.

Nondemocratic regimes use various tools to enforce their political domination. The most obvious mechanisms are state violence and surveillance. The enforcement ranges from systematic and widespread repression (for example, the mass purges in the Soviet Union or contemporary Iran) to sporadic and selective repression of the regime's opponents (as in Brazil during the 1960s). Another important tool of nondemocratic regimes is **co-optation**, whereby members of the public are brought into a beneficial relationship with the state and the government. Co-optation takes many forms, including **corporatism**, in which citizen participation is channeled into state-sanctioned groups; **clientelism**, in which the state provides benefits to groups of its political supporters; and **rent seeking**, in which the government allows its supporters to occupy positions of power in order to monopolize state benefits. The nondemocratic regime that dominated Mexico for much of the twentieth century skillfully employed all these forms of co-optation to garner public support for the governing party, minimizing its need to rely upon coercion. Finally, the mechanism of control that is most often employed in totalitarian regimes is the **personality cult**, or the state-sponsored exaltation of a leader. The personality cult of Stalin in the Soviet Union and that of Mao in China are prime examples, as is the cult of personality that developed around Ayatollah Ruhollah Khomeini, the leader of the 1979 Iranian Revolution.

Comparing Political Conflict and Competition

Political scientists can compare and contrast patterns of political conflict and competition in both democratic and authoritarian regimes. In democratic regimes, for example, it is common to compare the nature of elections and other forms of competition among political parties (often referred to as the **party system**).

On the most basic level, political scientists can compare the nature of **suffrage**, or the right to vote. In democratic regimes and even in many nondemocratic ones, such as China and Iran, that right is often guaranteed to most adult citizens.[9] Another important feature of elections is the degree to which citizens actually participate by voting and by engaging in campaign activities (see "In Comparison: Average Voter Turnout, 1945–98," below). Party systems also can be compared on the basis of the number of parties, the size of their membership, their organizational strength, their ideological orientation, and their electoral strategies.

A comparative analysis of political conflict and competition cannot focus solely on elections, though. In most political systems, much political conflict and competition takes place in **civil society**, which comprises the organizations

IN COMPARISON	Average Voter Turnout, 1945–98
COUNTRY (NUMBER OF ELECTIONS)	ELIGIBLE VOTERS VOTING (%)
South Africa (1)	85.5
Germany (13)	80.6
United Kingdom (15)	74.9
Japan (21)	69.0
Iran (2)	67.6
France (15)	67.3
India (12)	60.7
Russia (2)	55.0
United States (26)	48.3
Mexico (18)	48.1
Brazil (13)	47.9
Nigeria (3)	47.6
China	N/A

Source: "Turnout in the World: Country by Country Performance," International Institute for Democracy and Electoral Assistance, www.idea.int/vt/survey/voter_turnout_pop2.cfm (accessed 9/8/11).

outside the state that help people define and advance their own interests. In addition to political parties, the organizations that make up a country's civil society often include a host of groups as diverse as gun clubs and labor unions. Many scholars believe that these autonomous societal groups are vital to the health of democratic regimes.[10]

Comparing Societies

The state and the regime exist in the context of their society, and societies differ from one another in ways that can strongly influence politics. For example, ethnic divisions exist within many states. **Ethnicity** refers to the specific attributes that make one group of people culturally different from others: for example, customs, language, religion, geographical region, and history. Some states, such as China, Germany, Japan, and Russia, are relatively homogeneous: one ethnic group makes up a large portion of the society. At the other extreme, countries such as India, Iran, Mexico, Nigeria, and South Africa have a great deal of ethnic diversity. Ethnic diversity can often be a source of political conflict, and even in relatively homogeneous societies the presence of ethnic minorities can pose political challenges (see "In Comparison: Ethnic and Religious Diversity," p. 20).[11]

ETHNICITY AS THE BASIS FOR AUTONOMY OR SECESSION MOVEMENTS

In many of our cases (including China, India, Iran, Nigeria, Russia, and the United Kingdom), regions with a distinct ethnic identity have often sought either greater autonomy from the central state or outright independence. Sometimes states are able to weaken secession movements by granting greater political autonomy to regional ethnic groups.

In other cases, such as in Scotland and the United Kingdom, increased autonomy has only fueled a desire for independence. Some regimes, including authoritarian ones such as China and Iran and illiberal democracies such as Russia, have viewed regionally-based ethnic groups as a threat and have harshly repressed them.

Societies also differ in terms of their political cultures. **Political culture** can be defined as the patterns of basic norms relating to politics. Political scientists have learned a great deal about how political cultures differ in a variety of areas, including citizens' trust in government, respect for political authority, knowledge about politics, and assessment of their political efficacy (the ability to influence political outcomes).[12]

Political scientists also consider **national identity**, or the extent to which citizens of a country are bound together by a common set of political aspirations (most

---

IN COMPARISON — Ethnic and Religious Diversity

COUNTRY	LARGEST ETHNIC GROUP (%)	SECOND-LARGEST ETHNIC GROUP (%)	LARGEST RELIGIOUS GROUP (%)	SECOND-LARGEST RELIGIOUS GROUP (%)
Brazil	55.0	38.0	80.0	20.0
China	92.0	8.0	94–96.0	3–4.0
France*	N/A	N/A	83–88.0	5–10.0
Germany	91.5	2.4	34[†]	34[†]
India	72.0	25.5	81.0	12.0
Iran	51.0	24.0	89.0	9.0
Japan	99.0	1.0	84.0	16.0[‡]
Mexico	60.0	30.0	89.0	6.0
Nigeria	29.0	21.0	50.0	40.0
Russia	81.5	3.8	54.0	19.0
South Africa	75.0	13.0	78.7	19.8
United Kingdom	81.5	9.6	71.6	2.7
United States	67.0**	14.0[††]	52.0	24.0

*The French census does not collect data on ethnicity.
[†]Protestants and Catholics have the same percentage of members in Germany.
[‡]All other religious groups combined.
**Based on the U.S. Census Bureau's 2003 estimate that about 14 percent of citizens are Hispanic.
[††]All other ethnic groups combined.

often self-government and sovereignty). Countries with a long history as consolidated states often have higher levels of national identity than do states with a shorter history. Political scientists use the term **nationalism** to refer to pride in one's people and the belief that they share a common political identity. Individuals who believe they have a common political destiny, or **nationalists**, often seek the creation of a new state for individuals sharing that identity. Scottish nationalists, who seek an independent Scottish state, or Tibetan nationalists, who want Tibet to be independent from China, are excellent examples of nationalism in contemporary politics.

One interesting difference among societies is in the importance they place on religion. In most societies, religiosity has declined with economic prosperity and with the growth of secular (nonreligious) values. France, Japan, Russia, and the United Kingdom are relatively secular societies in which most people do not view religion as very important; the United States continues to be an interesting exception in this regard. In Nigeria and Iran, religion is viewed as important by nearly all citizens.

Individuals and groups within a society can also be distinguished according to their political attitudes and ideologies. **Political attitudes** describe views

Catalan nationalists in Spain seek independence from the Spanish state. The banner states "We are a Nation. We Decide."

regarding the status quo in a society, specifically, the desired pace and methods of political change. **Radical attitudes** support rapid, extensive, and often revolutionary change. **Liberal attitudes** promote evolutionary change within the system. **Conservative attitudes** support the status quo and view change as risky. **Reactionary attitudes** promote rapid change to restore political, social, and economic institutions that once existed. Since political attitudes are views of the status quo, radicals, liberals, conservatives, and reactionaries differ according to their setting. A reactionary in the United Kingdom, for example, might support the creation of an absolute monarchy, a reactionary in Germany might desire a return to Nazism, and a reactionary in China might call for a return to Maoist communism.

Whereas political attitudes are particular and context-specific, **political ideologies** are universal sets of political values regarding the fundamental goals of politics.[13] A political ideology prescribes an ideal balance between freedom and equality. The ideology of **liberalism** (as opposed to a liberal political attitude) places a high priority on individual political and economic freedoms, favoring them over any attempts to create economic equality. Private **property**, capitalism, and protections for the individual against the state are central to liberal ideology. In the United States such views tend to be called "libertarian." **Communism**, in contrast, emphasizes economic equality rather than individual political and economic freedoms. Collective property (state ownership) and a dominant state are cornerstones of communism. **Social democracy** (often referred to as democratic socialism) is in some ways a hybrid of liberalism and communism in that it places considerable value on equality but attempts to protect some individual freedoms. Social democrats advocate a mixed welfare state in which an active state exists alongside a largely private economy.[14] **Fascism**, like communism, is hostile to the idea of individual freedom but rejects the notion of equality. **Anarchism**, like

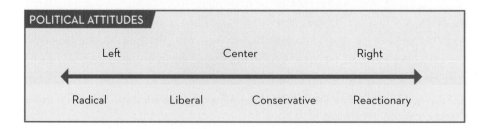

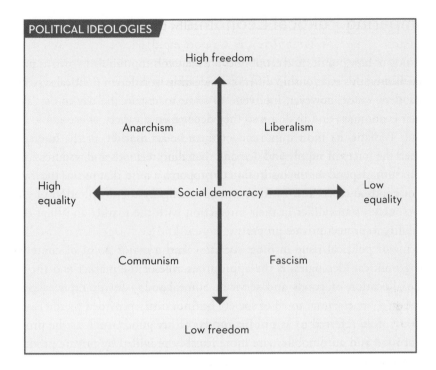

POLITICAL IDEOLOGIES

High freedom

Anarchism   Liberalism

High   Social democracy   Low
equality   ◄────────────────►   equality

Communism   Fascism

Low freedom

communism, is based on the belief that private property and capitalism create inequality, but like liberalism, it places a high value on individual political freedom.

In recent decades **fundamentalism** has emerged as an important ideology. It differs from the five ideologies just mentioned in that it seeks to unite religion with the state, and to make faith the sovereign authority. Fundamentalists thus view some form of theocracy (or rule by clerics) as the way to implement their ideology. Among the cases studied in this text, Iran's political regime is most inspired by fundamentalist ideology.

The strength of each ideology differs across political systems. For example, opinion research demonstrates that citizens in the United States and, to a lesser extent, the United Kingdom have an unusually strong commitment to liberal ideology; large numbers of them support individualism and manifest a notable distrust of state activism. French and Japanese citizens tend to be less individualistic and are more supportive of an active role for the state in the economy. In China, the rise of capitalist economics has eroded popular support for Communist ideology.

Comparing Political Economies

The study of how politics and economics are related is commonly known as **political economy**; this relationship differs considerably in different political systems.[15] All modern states, however, intervene to some extent in the day-to-day affairs of their economies, and in doing so they depend on a variety of economic institutions. Perhaps the most important of these is the **market**, or the interaction between the forces of supply and demand that allocate goods and resources. Markets, in turn, depend on the institution of property, a term that means the ownership of goods and services. In their attempt to ensure the distribution of goods and resources, states differ in their interaction with the market and their desire and ability to protect private property.

A major political issue in most societies, and a major point of contention among political ideologies, is the appropriate role of the market and the state in the allocation of goods and services. Some goods—for example, clean air and water—are essential to all of society but not easily provided by the market; these are often referred to as **public goods**. Other goods, such as the production of food and automobiles, are more feasibly provided by private producers using the market. In between those extremes is a large gray area. States differ in the degree to which they define a wide array of goods and services as public goods. As a result, government **social expenditures** (state provision of public benefits, such as education, health care, and transportation) vary widely among countries.

In the political economic systems of countries such as the United States and the United Kingdom, where liberal ideology is dominant, the state plays a significant but relatively small role. In France, Germany, and Japan, however, the state has played a much larger role in the economy through state ownership (especially in France) and state planning (especially in Japan). Authoritarian regimes have typically had a heavy hand in economic matters, as has certainly been the case in China and Iran. Whereas China's Communist regime has gradually allowed growth in the private sector, the Iranian Revolution of 1979 led to an increase in that state's involvement in the economy.

Economies also differ markedly in their size, affluence, rates of growth, and levels of equality. The most commonly used tool for comparing the size of economies is the **gross domestic product (GDP)**, the total market value of goods and services produced in a country in one year. GDP is often measured in U.S. dollars at **purchasing power parity (PPP)**, a mechanism that attempts to

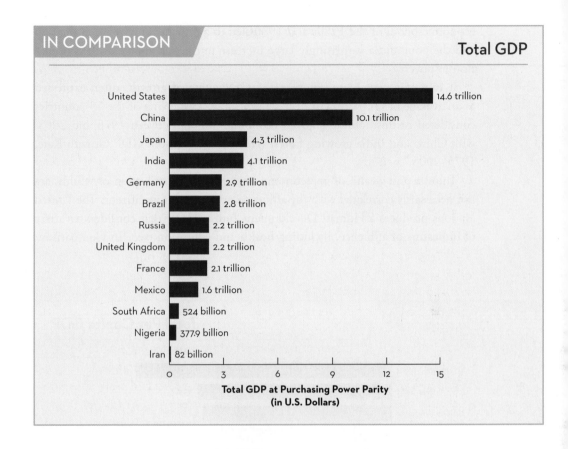

United States	14.6 trillion
China	10.1 trillion
Japan	4.3 trillion
India	4.1 trillion
Germany	2.9 trillion
Brazil	2.8 trillion
Russia	2.2 trillion
United Kingdom	2.2 trillion
France	2.1 trillion
Mexico	1.6 trillion
South Africa	524 billion
Nigeria	377.9 billion
Iran	82 billion

**Total GDP at Purchasing Power Parity
(in U.S. Dollars)**

estimate the real buying power of income in each country using prices in the United States as a benchmark (see "In Comparison: Total GDP at Purchasing Power Parity," above). In terms of the overall size of the 13 economies considered in this volume, China, India, Japan, and the United States, dwarf the other cases. It is sometimes more useful, however, to look at **GDP per capita**, which divides the GDP by total population (see "In Comparison: Total Per Capita GDP at Purchasing Power Parity," p. 26). Because GDP is rarely distributed evenly among the population, the **Gini index** is the most commonly used measure of economic inequality, in which perfect equality is scored as 0, and perfect inequality is scored as 100. Endemic inequality has long been a characteristic of developing countries, such as Brazil, India, Mexico, and South Africa, though some developing countries (like Brazil and India) have made progress in reducing inequality in recent years. In wealthy countries such as the United States, the economic boom of the 1980s and 1990s led to a growing gap between the rich and the poor and a surprisingly large increase in the percentage of the population in poverty.

It is also important to compare the GDP's rate of growth, often expressed as an average of GDP growth over a number of years. Nine of the 13 countries considered in this volume enjoyed economic growth between 1975 and 2005, with China and India growing fastest (see "In Comparison: GDP Growth Rate, 1975–2005," p. 27).

The size and wealth of an economy, and even the distribution of wealth, are not necessarily correlated with the affluence or poverty of its citizens. The United Nations produces a Human Development Index (HDI) that considers a variety of indicators of affluence, including health and education (see "In Comparison:

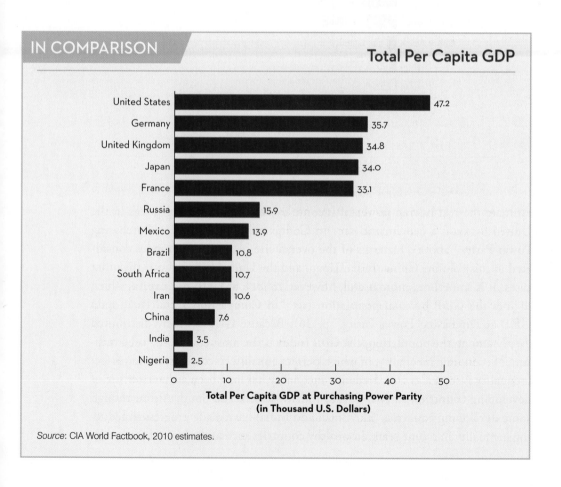

IN COMPARISON

Total Per Capita GDP

Country	Value
United States	47.2
Germany	35.7
United Kingdom	34.8
Japan	34.0
France	33.1
Russia	15.9
Mexico	13.9
Brazil	10.8
South Africa	10.7
Iran	10.6
China	7.6
India	3.5
Nigeria	2.5

**Total Per Capita GDP at Purchasing Power Parity
(in Thousand U.S. Dollars)**

Source: CIA World Factbook, 2010 estimates.

GDP Growth Rate, 1975–2005

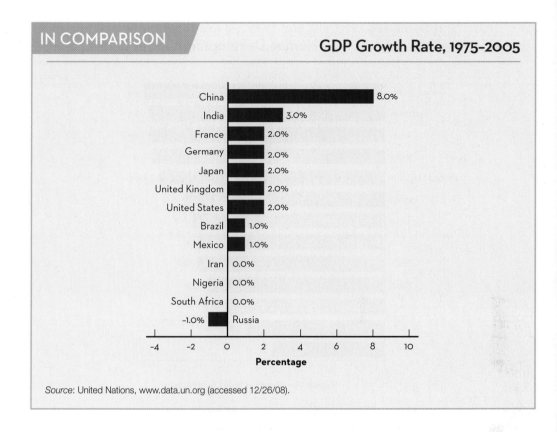

Source: United Nations, www.data.un.org (accessed 12/26/08).

Human Development Index Scores, 2011," p. 28). When considering GDP per capita and the HDI, one sees that the United States, the United Kingdom, Japan, Germany, and France are clearly the most affluent of the countries discussed in this volume. However, since 1980 the developing nations have made the most dramatic improvements in their HDI, with China, Iran, and India leading the way. In the last decade India and China have seen impressive growth in their HDI (see "In Comparison: Average Annual HDI Growth Rates, 1980-2011, and 2000–2011," p. 29).

Governments often struggle with myriad challenges within their economic systems. One concern is the danger of **inflation**, a situation characterized by sustained rising prices. Extremely high levels of inflation (**hyperinflation**) can endanger economic growth and impoverish citizens who live on a fixed income. Governments also fear the consequences of high levels of unemployment, which can place a large burden on public expenditures and reduce the tax base.

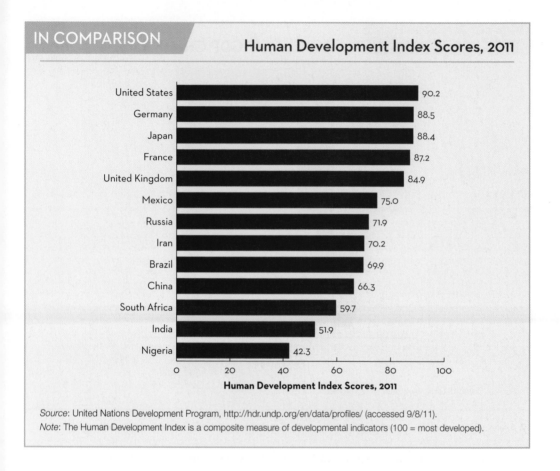

Human Development Index Scores, 2011

United States	90.2
Germany	88.5
Japan	88.4
France	87.2
United Kingdom	84.9
Mexico	75.0
Russia	71.9
Iran	70.2
Brazil	69.9
China	66.3
South Africa	59.7
India	51.9
Nigeria	42.3

Human Development Index Scores, 2011

Source: United Nations Development Program, http://hdr.undp.org/en/data/profiles/ (accessed 9/8/11).
Note: The Human Development Index is a composite measure of developmental indicators (100 = most developed).

The Global Context

A country's politics is not determined solely by domestic factors. Increasingly, international forces shape politics in the context of a rapidly expanding and intensifying set of links among states, societies, and economies. This phenomenon, known as **globalization**, has created new opportunities while posing important challenges to states. Crossborder interactions have long existed, but the trend toward globalization has created a far more extensive and intensive web of relationships among many people across vast distances. People are increasingly interacting regularly and directly through sophisticated international networks involving travel, communication, business, and education.

Average Annual HDI Growth Rates, 1980–2011, and 2000–2011

COUNTRY	AVERAGE ANNUAL HDI GROWTH, 1980–2011	AVERAGE ANNUAL HDI GROWTH, 2000–2011
Japan	.47	.33
United States	.27	.13
Germany	.69	.43
France	.66	.40
United Kingdom	.48	.33
Mexico	.85	.64
Brazil	.87	.69
Iran	1.57	.97
Nigeria	NA	NA
South Africa	.30	.05
India	1.51	1.56
China	1.73	1.43
Russia	NA	.81

Source: United Nations Development Program, http://hdr.undp.org/en/media/HDR_2011_EN_Table2.pdf (accessed 12/12/11).

It is too early to predict the consequences of globalization for governments and citizens of states. Some observers have argued that globalization may eclipse the state, resulting in global political institutions, whereas others contend that states will continue to play an important, albeit changed, role.[16] Governments are increasingly restricted by the international system, both because of international trade agreements (such as those promoted by the World Trade Organization) and because of the need to remain competitive in the international marketplace.

As a result of globalization, a host of international organizations regularly affects domestic politics, economics, and society. **Multinational corporations (MNCs)**, firms that produce, distribute, and market goods or services in more than one country, are increasingly powerful. They are an important source of

social democracy An ideology that places considerable value on equality, but also attempts to protect some individual freedoms

social expenditures State provision of public benefits, such as education, health care, and transportation

states Organizations that maintain a monopoly of violence over a territory

strong states States that perform the basic tasks of defending their borders from outside attacks and defending their authority from internal nonstate rivals

suffrage The right to vote

theocracy An authoritarian regime that has leaders who claim to rule on behalf of God

totalitarian Characterized by a strong, official ideology that seeks to transform fundamental aspects of the state, society, and the economy using a wide array of organizations and the application of force

traditional legitimacy Legitimacy in which the state is obeyed because it has a long tradition of being obeyed

unicameral legislatures Legislatures with a single chamber

unitary states States that concentrate most political power in the national capital, allocating very little decision-making power to regions or localities

upper house The legislative house that often represents geographic subunits

vote of no confidence Legislative check on government whereby a government deems a measure to be of high importance, and if that measure fails to pass the legislature, either the government must resign in favor of another leader or new parliamentary elections must be called

weak states States that have trouble carrying out the basic tasks of defending themselves against external and internal rivals, and often suffer from endemic violence, poor infrastructure, weak rule of law, and an inability to collect taxes

WEB LINKS

CIA World Factbook (www.cia.gov/cia/publications/factbook)
Comparative Politics (http://web.gc.cuny.edu/jcp)
Freedom House (www.freedomhouse.org)
Inter-Parliamentary Union (www.ipu.org/english/home.htm)
Journal of Democracy (www.journalofdemocracy.org)
Political Science Resource Pages (www.psr.keele.ac.uk/area.htm)
World Bank (www.worldbank.org)
The WWW Virtual Library: International Affairs Resources (www2.etown.edu/vl)

Visit StudySpace for quizzes and other review material.
www.norton.com/studyspace

- Vocabulary Flashcards of All Key Terms
- Country Review Quizzes
- Interactive Map Tours

HEAD OF STATE:
Queen Elizabeth II
(since February 6,
1952)

HEAD OF GOVERNMENT:
Prime Minister David Cameron
(since May 11, 2010)

CAPITAL:
London

TOTAL LAND SIZE:
244,820 sq km (80th)

POPULATION:
63 million (22nd)

GDP AT PPP:
$2.2 trillion (9th)

**GDP PER CAPITA
AT PPP:**
$34,800 (33rd)

**HUMAN
DEVELOPMENT
INDEX RANKING:**
28th

UNITED KINGDOM

Introduction

Why Study This Case?

For many reasons, most introductory works about comparative politics begin with a study of the United Kingdom. As the primogenitor of modern democracy, the UK political system is at once strikingly unique and a model for many other liberal democracies. The United Kingdom is the world's oldest democracy. Its transition to democracy was gradual, beginning with thirteenth-century limitations on absolute monarchs and continuing incrementally to the establishment of the rule of law in the seventeenth century and the extension of suffrage to women in the twentieth century. The democratization process persists today, with reforms of the anachronistic upper house of the legislature, decentralization of power, and ongoing discussions about electoral reform. Unlike many other democracies, the United Kingdom cannot attach a specific date or event to the advent of its democracy. It is also unusual in that the main political rules of the game in that country have not been seriously interrupted or radically altered since the mid-seventeenth century.

The United Kingdom is one of only a handful of democracies without a written constitution. The longevity and stability of its democracy have thus depended to a large extent on both traditional legitimacy and a unique political culture of accommodation and moderation. Although its constitution is unwritten, many aspects of its democracy have been adopted by a number of the world's other democracies, especially in areas of the globe that were once part of the far-flung British Empire.

Finally, the United Kingdom deserves careful study because it is the birthplace of the Industrial Revolution, which fueled British economic and political dominance during the nineteenth century. Some have attributed the United Kingdom's early industrialization to the emergence of liberal ideology. The United Kingdom was also the first major industrialized country to experience an extended economic decline after World War II, the reasons for which have been much debated.

The United Kingdom remains a fascinating case. In 1979, **Margaret Thatcher** of the Conservative Party was the first leader of an industrial democracy to experiment with neoliberal economic policies in an attempt to stem economic decline. The policies were very controversial within the United Kingdom but widely emulated in other democracies, including the United States. Even with Thatcher's resignation in 1990, the **Conservatives (Tories)** remained in power until the 1997 election, when they were ousted by the **Labour Party**. Under the leadership of **Tony Blair** and his successor, Gordon Brown, the Labour Party sought to soften some of the harder edges of Thatcher's neoliberalism while still embracing many of the policies executed by her and her Conservative successors. These policies have become known as the **Third Way**, a political compromise between the right and the left that has continued to inform the improbable coalition government of current Conservative prime minister **David Cameron**.

Major Geographic and Demographic Features

Since 1801 the **United Kingdom of Great Britain and Northern Ireland** has been the formal name of the United Kingdom. Separated from France by the English Channel, Great Britain itself consists of three nations (England, Scotland, and Wales). These three nations plus the northeastern part of the island of Ireland constitute the United Kingdom. The remainder of Ireland is called the Republic of Ireland. Although it is confusing, citizens of the United Kingdom are often referred to as British or Britons even if they live in Northern Ireland. Most Welsh, Scots, and Northern Irish consider themselves British, but it would be unwise (and inaccurate) to call a resident of Edinburgh (in Scotland) or Cardiff (in Wales) English.

The United Kingdom is roughly the size of Oregon and about two-thirds the size of Japan. It has approximately 63 million residents, nearly twice the population of California and about half that of Japan. Its population is not equally distributed among England, Scotland, Wales, and Northern Ireland. Five of six Britons live in England. The United Kingdom can be considered a multiethnic state because it contains Scottish, Welsh, and English citizens, who have distinct cultures and languages. Racially, however, it is relatively homogeneous; its nonwhite population, composed mainly of immigrants from the United Kingdom's former colonies, is only about 5 percent of the total. The majority of those immigrants comes from the Indian subcontinent, and about a third are from the Caribbean.

The United Kingdom's physical separation from the European mainland ended in 1994 with the inauguration of the Channel Tunnel, which links Britain and France. For much of British history, the country's isolation provided some protection from the conflicts and turmoil that afflicted the rest of Europe. A diminished fear of invasion may help explain the historically small size and minimal political importance of the United Kingdom's standing army (and the relative importance and strength of its navy). In addition, it may help explain its late adherence to the European Union, its unwillingness to replace the British pound with the euro (the single European currency), and its continued skepticism about European unification.

Historical Development of the State

British citizens owe their allegiance to the Crown, the enduring symbol of the United Kingdom's state, rather than to a written constitution. The Crown symbolizes far more than just the monarchy or even Her Majesty's government. It represents the ceremonial and symbolic trappings of the British state. In addition, it represents the rules governing British political life (the regime) and the unhindered capacity (the sovereignty) to enforce and administer these rules and to secure the country's borders.

The evolutionary changes of the state over the past eight centuries have been thoroughgoing and not without violence. But in comparison with political change elsewhere in the world, the development of the modern British state has been gradual, piecemeal, and peaceful.

EARLY DEVELOPMENT

Although we commonly think of the United Kingdom as a stable and unified nation-state, the country experienced repeated invasions over a period of about 1,500 years. Celts, Romans, Angles, Saxons, Danes, and finally Normans invaded the British Isles, each leaving important legacies. For example, the Germanic Angles and Saxons left their language—except in Wales, Scotland, and other

TIMELINE OF POLITICAL DEVELOPMENT

YEAR	EVENT
1215	King John I forced to sign Magna Carta, thereby agreeing to a statement of the rights of English Barons
1295	Model Parliament of Edward I is convened, the first representative parliament
1529	Reformation Parliament is summoned by Henry VIII, beginning process of cutting ties to the Roman Catholic church
1628	Charles I is forced to accept Petition of Right, Parliament's statement of civil rights in return for funds
1642–48	English Civil War is fought between Royalists and Parliamentarians
1649	Charles I is tried and executed
1689	Bill of Rights is issued by Parliament, establishing a constitutional monarchy in Britain
1707	Act of Union is put into effect, uniting kingdoms of England and Scotland
1721	Sir Robert Walpole is effectively made Britain's first prime minister
1832–67	Reform Act is passed, extending right to vote to virtually all urban males and some in the countryside
1916–22	Anglo-Irish War is fought, culminating in establishment of independent Republic of Ireland, with Northern Ireland remaining part of the United Kingdom
1973	United Kingdom is made a member of the European Economic Community (now the European Union)
1979–90	Margaret Thatcher serves as prime minister
1982	Falklands War is fought with Argentina
1997–2007	Tony Blair serves as prime minister
2007–10	Gordon Brown serves as prime minister
2010	David Cameron becomes prime minister, leading a Conservative–Liberal Democrat coalition government

areas they could not conquer. Local languages remained dominant there until the eighteenth and nineteenth centuries. Today, we still refer to those areas as the United Kingdom's **Celtic fringe**.

In terms of the United Kingdom's political development, another important legacy was the emergence of **common law**, a system based on local customs and precedent rather than formal legal codes. That system forms the basis of the contemporary legal systems of the United Kingdom (with the exception of Scotland), the United States, and many former British colonies.[1]

The last wave of invasions, by the Normans, occurred in 1066. The Normans were Danish Vikings who occupied northern France. In Britain they replaced the Germanic ruling class and imposed central rule. Politically, their most important legacy was the institution of feudalism, which they brought from the European continent. Under feudalism, lords provided vassals with military protection and economic support in exchange for labor and military service. Though hardly a democratic institution, feudalism did create a system of mutual obligation between lord and peasant on one level, and between monarch and lord on another level. Indeed, some scholars have seen in these obligations the foundation for the eventual limits on royal power. The most important initial document in this regard is the **Magna Carta**, which British nobles obliged King John to sign in 1215 and which became a royal promise to uphold feudal customs and rights. The Magna Carta set an important precedent by limiting the power of British monarchs and subjecting them to the law. As a result, the United Kingdom never experienced the type of royal absolutism that was common in other countries (for example, in Russia), and this in turn helped pave the way for public control over government and the state.

The United Kingdom was fortunate to resolve relatively early in its historical development certain conflicts that other states would experience later in the modern era. A prime example is the religious divide. During the reign of Henry VIII (1509–47), a major dispute between the British monarch and the Vatican (the center of the Roman Catholic church) had unintended consequences. When the Catholic church failed to grant Henry a divorce, he used **Parliament** to pass laws that effectively took England out of the Catholic church and replaced Catholicism with a Protestant church that could be controlled by the English state instead of by Rome.

The creation of a state-controlled Anglican Church led to a religious institution that was weaker and less autonomous than its counterparts in other European countries. Supporters of Catholicism fought unsuccessfully to regain power, and religion never plagued the United Kingdom as a polarizing force the way it did in so many other countries. Northern Ireland, where the split between Protestants and Catholics continues to create political division, is the bloody exception to the rule. A second unintended consequence of the creation of the Anglican Church was that Henry VIII's use of Parliament to sanction the changes strengthened and legitimized Parliament's power. As with the Magna Carta, piecemeal institutional changes helped pave the way for democratic control—even if that result was not foreseen at the time.

THE EMERGENCE OF THE MODERN BRITISH STATE

Compared with its European neighbors, the United Kingdom had a more constrained monarchy. This is not to say that British rulers were weak, but in addition to the early checks on monarchic rule, three major developments in the seventeenth and eighteenth centuries decisively undermined the power of British sovereigns and are crucial for our understanding why the United Kingdom was one of the first nations to develop democratic control.

First, the crowning of James I (a Scot) in 1603 united Scotland and England but created a political crisis. James was an absolutist at heart and resisted limits on his power imposed by Parliament. He sought to raise taxes without first asking Parliament, and his son Charles I, whose reign began in 1625, continued this flaunting of royal power, eventually precipitating civil war. The **English Civil War** (1640–49) pitted the defenders of Charles against the supporters of Parliament, who won the bitter struggle and executed Charles I in 1649.

For eleven years (1649–60) England had no monarch and functioned as a republic led by Oliver Cromwell, whose rule soon became a military dictatorship. Parliament restored the monarchy in 1660 with the ascension of Charles II, but its power was forever weakened.

Second, when James II, a brother of Charles II, inherited the throne in 1685, the monarchy and Parliament again faced off. James was openly Catholic, and Parliament feared a return to Catholicism and absolute rule. In 1688 it removed James II and sent him into exile. In his place, it installed James's Protestant daughter Mary and her Dutch husband, William. A year later, Parliament enacted the Bill of Rights, institutionalizing its political supremacy. Since that time, monarchs have owed their position to Parliament. This so-called Glorious Revolution was a key turning point in the creation of the constitutional monarchy.

Third, in 1714, Parliament installed the current dynastic family by crowning George I (of German royalty). The monarch, who spoke little English, was forced to rely heavily on his **cabinet** (his top advisers, or ministers) and, specifically, his **prime minister**, who coordinated the work of the other ministers. From 1721 to 1742, Sir Robert Walpole fashioned the position of prime minister into much of what the office is today. By the late eighteenth century, in large part in reaction to the loss of the colonies in America, prime ministers and their cabinets were no longer selected by monarchs but were instead appointed by Parliament. Monarchs never again had the power to select members of the government.[2]

THE BRITISH EMPIRE

The United Kingdom began its overseas expansion in the sixteenth century, and by the early nineteenth century it had vanquished its main European rivals to become the world's dominant military, commercial, and cultural power. Its navy helped open new overseas markets for its burgeoning domestic industry, and by the empire's zenith in 1870, the United Kingdom controlled about a quarter of all world trade and probably had the globe's wealthiest economy. The dimensions of the British Empire were truly exceptional. In the nineteenth century, it governed one quarter of the world's population, directly ruled almost 50 countries, and dominated many more with its commercial muscle.

Paralleling the gradual process of democratization in the United Kingdom, the erosion of the British Empire was also slow and incremental. It began with the loss of the American colonies in the late eighteenth century, though subsequently the empire continued to expand in Asia and Africa. By the early twentieth century, however, it had begun to shrink. Following World War I, the United Kingdom granted independence to a few of its former colonies, including Egypt and most of Ireland. With the conclusion of World War II, the tide turned even more strongly against the empire. Local resistance in many colonies, international sentiment favoring self-determination for subject peoples, the cumulative costs of two world wars, and the burden of maintaining far-flung colonies helped spell the end of the British Empire. Independence was willingly granted to most of the remaining colonial possessions throughout Southeast Asia, Africa, and the Caribbean.

The United Kingdom managed to retain control of a few small colonies, and in 1982 it fought a brief war with Argentina to retain possession of the remote Falkland Islands. One of the United Kingdom's last colonial possessions, Hong Kong, was returned to China in 1997. Today, the **Commonwealth** includes the United Kingdom and 54 of its former colonies and serves to maintain the economic and cultural ties established during its long imperial rule.

THE INDUSTRIAL REVOLUTION

The United Kingdom lays claim to being the first industrial nation, and industrialization helped support the expansion of its empire. The country's early industrialization, which began in the late eighteenth century and developed slowly, was based on its dominance in textiles, machinery, and iron production. By the mid-nineteenth century, most of the United Kingdom's workforce had moved away from the countryside to live in urban areas. While industrialization dramatically changed British politics and society, the process did not create the kind of political upheaval and instability that was seen in many late-developing nations, where it occurred more rapidly. Because the British were the first to industrialize, the United Kingdom faced little initial competition and therefore amassed tremendous wealth. Moreover, the rise of a prosperous and propertied middle class demanding a stronger political voice also facilitated the country's first steps toward democracy.[3]

But the benefits of early industrialization may also have been factors in its economic decline. As a world leader, the United Kingdom spent lavishly on its empire and led the Allied forces in World Wars I and II. Although the Allies won both wars, the United Kingdom was drained economically. The end of World War II also signaled the end of colonial rule, and the United Kingdom began to relinquish its empire. Finally, as the first industrialized country, it would also be one of the first nations to experience economic challenges inherent in industrialization. When British industries faced new competition and obsolescence after World War II, the country found it increasingly difficult to reform its economy, which began to decline.

GRADUAL DEMOCRATIZATION

We have seen how Parliament weakened the power of the British monarchs, but at the same time we should note that Parliament itself originally represented the interests of the British elite: only the wealthy could vote. The United Kingdom had an "upper" **House of Lords**, which represented the aristocracy, and a "lower" **House of Commons**, which represented the interests of the lower aristocracy and the merchant class. In addition, by the time Parliament was established, British monarchs were no longer absolute rulers, although they continued to wield considerable political power. Two factors gradually democratized Parliament and further weakened monarchical power.

The first was the rise of political parties, which emerged in the eighteenth century as cliques of nobles but eventually reached out to broader sectors of society for support. The two largest cliques became the United Kingdom's first parties:

the Conservatives (Tories) supported the monarch, and the **Liberals (Whigs)** opposed the policies of the monarch. The Whigs were the first to cultivate support among members of the United Kingdom's burgeoning commercial class, many of whom were still excluded from the political system.

The second factor was the expansion of suffrage. In 1832, the Whigs were able to push through a Reform Act that doubled the size of the British electorate, though it still excluded more than 90 percent of British adults. Over the next century, both parties gradually supported measures to expand suffrage, hoping in part to gain a political windfall. The process culminated in 1928, when women over the age of 21 were granted the right to vote.

The gradual expansion of the vote to include all adult citizens forced the political parties to respond to demands for additional services. The new voters wanted the expansion of such public goods as health care, education, and housing, and they looked to the state to provide them. The Labour Party, formed in 1900 as an outgrowth of the trade union movement, had become by the end of World War I the main representative of the working class and the primary beneficiary of expanded suffrage. By the 1920s, Labour became the United Kingdom's largest center-left party and pushed for policies that would develop basic social services for all citizens, or what we commonly call the welfare state. The British workers who defended the United Kingdom so heroically during World War II returned from that conflict with a new sense of entitlement, electing Labour to power in 1945. Armed with a parliamentary majority, the Labour government quickly moved to implement a welfare state. This was accompanied by the nationalization of a number of sectors of industry, such as coal, utilities, rail, and health care.

POSTWAR POLITICS, DEBATE ON THE STATE, AND A "HUNG PARLIAMENT"

The Labour Party initiated the welfare state, but British Conservatives generally supported it during much of the postwar period in what has been called the postwar **collectivist consensus**. By the 1970s, however, the British economy was in crisis, and a new breed of Tories (dubbed neoliberals because of their embrace of classical liberal values of limited state intervention) began to blame the United Kingdom's economic decline on the excesses of the welfare state. When Margaret Thatcher became prime minister in 1979, she broke with traditional Tory support for what she derided as the United Kingdom's "nanny" state and pledged to diminish government's role in the economy. She sought to lower taxes and cut state spending on costly social services, and she replaced some state services (in areas as diverse as housing and mass transit) with private enterprise. Her government thus marked the end of the postwar collectivist consensus.

Yet in some ways, a new consensus emerged around Thatcher's reforms.[4] Although the Labour Party's landslide victory over the Tories in 1997 can be seen as a rejection of some aspects of Thatcher's rollback of the state, the Labour Party returned to office that year under the banner of "New Labour." By adopting this new name, Prime Minister Tony Blair sought to

Political cartoon depicting party leaders Cameron (Conservatives), Clegg (Liberal Democrats), and Brown (Labour), none of whose parties earned a majority in the 2010 elections. The resultant "hung parliament" led to the UK's first full coalition government in 70 years.

rebrand the party and distinguish his government's "Third Way" centrist program from both Thatcher's hard-edged laissez-faire policies and Labour's more traditional platform as staunch defender of an elaborate welfare state. New Labour held government for 13 years, balancing popular progressive social reforms with policies of devolution and continued limits on social expenditures. The 2010 parliamentary election resulted in a **"hung parliament"** in which no party obtained a majority of seats. In what can be seen as a nod to both Thatcher and Blair, Prime Minister David Cameron and the Conservatives formed a coalition government with the Liberal Democrats, calling for a return to "big society" in which more government authority and responsibility is devolved to communities, families, and individuals.

Political Regime

The political regime of the United Kingdom is notable among the world's democracies because of its highly **majoritarian** features. Under the rules of British politics, the majority in Parliament has virtually unchecked power. Unlike political parties in other democracies, even parliamentary democracies, the majority party in the United Kingdom can enact policies with few checks from other branches of government. Also unlike other democracies, there are no formal constitutional limits on the central government, few judicial restraints, and no constitutionally sanctioned local authorities to dilute the power of the government in London.

Only the historical traditions of democratic political culture and, increasingly, restrictions imposed by the European Union keep the British government from abusing its power.

Political Institutions

THE CONSTITUTION

The United Kingdom has no single document that defines the rules of politics, but the constitution is generally understood to include a number of written documents and unwritten rules that most British citizens view as inviolable.[5] In 1215 the Magna Carta set a precedent for limits on monarchical power. Other documents include the 1689 Bill of Rights and the 1707 Act of Union, which united Scotland and England. What makes the United Kingdom's constitution particularly unusual is that it also consists of various acts of Parliament, judicial decisions, customs, and traditions. Since Parliament is viewed as sovereign, the democratically elected lower house of the legislature can amend any aspect of the constitution by a simple majority vote. This power extends to the very existence of the monarchy, the powers of regions or local governments, and the powers of the houses of Parliament. Therefore, unlike most other democratic regimes, the United Kingdom has no constitutional court, because any law passed by Parliament is by definition constitutional.

The absence of written constitutional guarantees has consistently alarmed human rights advocates and has given rise to demands for a more formal constitution or, at the very least, *written* constitutional protections of basic rights. Since

ESSENTIAL POLITICAL FEATURES

- **Legislative-executive system:** Parliamentary
- **Legislature:** Parliament
- **Lower house:** House of Commons
- **Upper house:** House of Lords
- **Unitary or federal division of power:** Unitary
- **Main geographic subunits:** England, Scotland, Wales, Northern Ireland
- **Electoral system for lower house:** Plurality
- **Chief judicial body:** House of Lords

TWO DOMINANT PRIME MINISTERS: THATCHER AND BLAIR

Margaret Thatcher and Tony Blair are arguably the United Kingdom's most important and controversial prime ministers since the end of World War II. Despite the fact that Thatcher, who served from 1979 to 1990, was a Conservative and Blair, who served from 1997 to 2007, a Labourite, they share some remarkable similarities. Defying the Conservative Party's traditional ties to the aristocracy, Thatcher was a grocer's daughter who came to political power through sheer force of will. She steered the Tories away from the party's traditional social paternalism and toward a more free-market economy. Blair reoriented the Labour Party away from its traditional hostility toward the free market and sought to make the party less dependent on its trade union supporters. Both of these leaders are credited with reinvigorating political parties that were in crisis after having suffered from long periods of being out of government.

Once in office and armed with large majorities in the House of Commons, both leaders implemented important domestic reforms that were radical departures from the past. The Iron Lady, as Thatcher was dubbed, undertook a series of dramatic steps to reverse Britain's economic stagnation and to repeal the social-democratic policies that had been created under the collectivist consensus. Her government privatized many state-owned businesses and allowed numerous ailing firms to go bankrupt. Thatcher also confronted and eventually defeated powerful trade unions during widespread strikes by unions opposed to her policies. One particularly controversial but popular policy was her decision to sell millions of public housing units to their occupants in order to create more private homeowners in the United Kingdom. Her boldest policy was the ill-advised introduction of the so-called poll tax, designed to move local governments' tax burden from property owners to all citizens. This legislation generated widespread resentment and even rioting.

Blair's domestic reforms were no less dramatic, although they were less controversial. Although he continued most of Thatcher's economic policies, he implemented an ambitious set of constitutional reforms. He devolved power to regional and local governments (some of which had lost power under Thatcher), creating new legislatures in Scotland and Wales. He began to reform the archaic House of Lords, established a Supreme Court, and made the central bank (the Bank of Britain) independent of the government.

In their foreign policies, both leaders favored an extremely close relationship with the United States, often at the expense of relations with the United Kingdom's European allies. Thatcher and Blair also took the country into controversial wars. Thatcher launched a costly war against Argentina in 1982 to retake the distant Falkland Islands, and the United Kingdom's victory in that war temporarily buoyed her political success. In 2003, Blair joined the United States in the Iraq War, a move that was bitterly opposed by many within his own party and by a large majority of the UK public. As the war bogged down, Blair's popularity plummeted.

Thatcher and Blair were exceptional communicators, with charismatic personalities that charmed the public. Thatcher was known for her tough, often blunt public statements and her fierce debating skills. Blair had wit and charm that captivated Britons for over a decade. However, both were unpopular by the end of their time in office. Thatcher was viewed by many as insensitive and out of touch, and Blair increasingly as a spinmaster who often skirted the truth. Both of them stubbornly refused to budge from policies that were bitterly opposed by the British public (such as Thatcher's poll tax and Blair's stance on the Iraq War).

After over a decade in power, Thatcher and Blair each resigned their positions without ever having lost an election. Thatcher quit when she faced growing opposition and a challenge to her leadership within the Conservative Party. After Labour won its third consecutive majority in the Commons, the increasingly beleaguered Blair agreed to step down and hand power to his longtime Chancellor of the Exchequer, Gordon Brown. One final similarity is worth noting: Thatcher and Blair both handed power to competent but less charismatic party leaders who proved less controversial and less successful.*

*"Captain Malaprop," *The Economist*, June 26, 2008.

1973, when the United Kingdom became a member of the European Union, British citizens have increasingly appealed to European laws to protect their rights. In response to such concerns, in 1998 the government incorporated into law the European Convention on Human Rights, a document that now serves as a basic set of constitutional liberties.

Although it is a source of concern to some political analysts, others have lauded the United Kingdom's constitution for its unparalleled flexibility and responsiveness to the majority. Changing the constitution in most democracies is a cumbersome and often politically charged process. In the United Kingdom, however, changes can be implemented more quickly and without lengthy political battles. Blair's Labour government (1997–2007) carried out piecemeal constitutional reforms that have proven so significant in their effects as to be compared to the Great Reform Act of 1832.[6] Admirers of the British constitution argue that it has delivered both political stability and flexibility since the late seventeenth century; in their view, a formal document does not necessarily make for a more democratic government.

THE CROWN

We can think of the **Crown**, the legislature, the judiciary, the prime minister, and the cabinet as the main branches of government in the United Kingdom. In most respects, we can think of the British Crown as the head of state. The Crown, embodied by the monarch, is the symbolic representative of the continuity of the British state. The monarch (currently Queen Elizabeth II) thus acts as a purely ceremonial figure, and on matters of importance, she must act at the behest of the cabinet even though the cabinet is referred to collectively as Her Majesty's government. The British monarchy is a continual source of popular fascination, in part because the institution and all its pomp and circumstance appear to be a relic in the twenty-first century. The reality, however, is less glamorous. The British monarch today is essentially a paid civil servant: the government allocates a budget to cover the royal family's expenses, and the queen spends much of her time signing papers, dedicating public works, and performing diplomatic functions.

The UK monarchy has survived for centuries precisely because it has agreed to act constitutionally. Since the nineteenth century, this has meant that it must always follow the orders of elected representatives. For example, although the monarch always selects the head of government, the choice must always be the leader of the majority party in the lower house of Parliament. Only in the unlikely event that the legislature found itself deadlocked and unable to form a government could a monarch have any real influence on politics, and even in that case her choice would be severely constrained. Likewise, the monarch is officially the commander of the British armed forces, but it is the prime minister who has the power to declare wars and sign treaties.

The British monarchy is a hereditary institution, which until recently followed the rule of primogeniture—that is, the oldest son (or oldest daughter if there were no sons) inherited the throne. In an effort to modernize this most traditional of institutions, however, the Cameron government secured passage of a bill in 2011 abolishing male precedence in royal succession. Approved by the 16 other countries in the British Commonwealth that recognize the British monarch as their head of state, this reform means that the eldest born of each generation, regardless of gender, is entitled to inherit the throne. However, the cardinal constitutional principle of parliamentary supremacy means that Parliament itself may actually choose the monarch. In 1701, for example, Parliament imposed a new dynastic family (the Hanovers) to replace the reigning Stuarts. Since that time, only Protestants have been allowed to succeed to the throne. Since 1952, Elizabeth II has been queen, succeeding her father, George VI.

Despite the series of high-profile scandals that have rocked the monarchy during her reign, polls consistently show that the institution remains highly popular, as evidenced by the public celebrations of the queen's diamond jubilee (60 years on the throne) in 2012 and the great national interest in the 2011 wedding of Prince William (the queen's eldest grandson) and Kate Middleton. There have been occasional movements in the United Kingdom to eliminate the monarchy, but these have failed to garner much support. In spite of scandals and the costs of royalty, public support for the institution remains strong. A 2007 poll, for example, showed nearly 70 percent of the public in favor of retaining the institution.[7]

The Branches of Government

THE PRIME MINISTER

Parliament is supreme in the United Kingdom's political system, but real power is concentrated in the prime minister and the cabinet, which together constitute the government. The prime minister is the head of government and, as in all parliamentary systems, must be an elected member of the legislature. He or she is the head of the largest party in the lower house, the House of Commons (with selection as party leader handled in a party convention prior to a general election). Once named prime minister by the monarch (a mere formality), he or she selects the cabinet.

British prime ministers are probably the most powerful heads of government of any contemporary democracy. Because they can expect their parliamentary majority to approve all legislation, because party discipline in the United Kingdom is very strong, and because there are few checks on the power of the central government, prime ministers usually get their way. They wield less power, though, when their parties hold a slim majority (as was the case with John Major from 1990 to 1997) or when they are forced to depend on a coalition of parties (as is currently the case with the Conservative-Liberal Democrat coalition). Like any **member of Parliament (MP)**, prime ministers in the United Kingdom are elected to a maximum term of five years, but they alone can decide to call elections at any time before that term has expired. Prime ministers commonly call early elections to take advantage of favorable political conditions. After the United Kingdom's victory in the 1982 Falklands War, for example, Margaret Thatcher called an election despite the fact that she had two years remaining on her mandate.

Prime ministers are subject to a legislative **vote of no confidence**. This would occur if a government deemed a measure to be of high importance but the legislature rejected that measure. In such situations, either the entire cabinet must resign (and be replaced by a new one) or new elections must be called. Although such a check on the government exists, it is rarely used; over the past century, only two governments have been toppled by a legislative vote of no confidence. In fact, the prime minister can use the threat of a no-confidence vote as a way to rally support. In 2003, Tony Blair submitted a motion to the House of Commons to support the use of force against Iraq even though a prime minister may take the country to war without parliamentary approval.

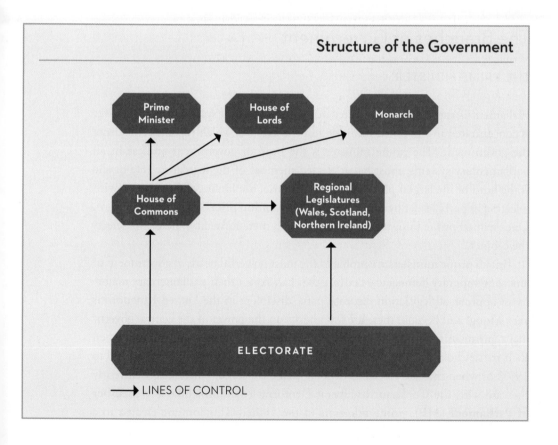

Structure of the Government

LINES OF CONTROL

Yet he chose to submit his decision to the House of Commons, threatening to resign if he failed to win support. The tactic worked: despite widespread opposition to the war among Labour Party backbenchers, a large majority in Parliament supported the war.

Prime ministers play a number of roles. As leaders of their party, they must maintain the support of their fellow MPs, a condition that has plagued every prime minister since Thatcher. They must appear in the legislature weekly for a televised question period, during which they must defend government policies and answer questions from MPs—and in so doing, display strong oratorical skills.[8] As head of government, the prime minister must direct the activity of the cabinet and smooth over differences among cabinet members. As a politician, he is expected to guide his party to victory in general elections and, in the case of the current Cameron government, manage to hold together a sometimes fractious coalition. Even though the monarch is head of state and the nation, the prime minister is expected to provide national leadership. British prime ministers are also diplomats and world leaders, roles that Tony Blair, for example, especially relished, despite the objections of many of his own party members, particularly regarding the war in Iraq.

Prime ministers are always seasoned political veterans with, on average, more than two decades of experience in the House of Commons. As a result, British prime ministers are usually outstanding debaters, effective communicators, and skilled negotiators. In the British system, a political outsider has virtually no chance of becoming prime minister; one must move up the ranks of the party before gaining the highest office.

THE CABINET

Cabinets evolved out of the group of experts who originally advised Britain's monarchs. Contemporary British cabinets have about 20 members (called ministers), all of whom must be Members of Parliament. They are usually from the lower house but occasionally are MPs from the upper house, the House of Lords. The prime minister generally appoints leading party officials to the top cabinet positions. Although the prime minister and the cabinet emerge from the Parliament, they stand apart from the legislature as a separate executive, with few checks on their powers.

As in most democracies, cabinet ministers in the United Kingdom preside over their individual government departments and are responsible for answering to Parliament (during question time) about actions of the bureaucracies they oversee.

Currently, there is considerable debate in the United Kingdom about the future of the upper house and whether it should be directly elected and given greater powers. Over the past decade, various commissions and cross-party parliamentary groups have recommended reforms designed to increase the upper chamber's authority and relevance. Advisory votes held in the House of Commons have been inconclusive, but clearly seem to favor a directly elected upper house, perhaps with fixed terms of 12 to 15 years. Not surprisingly, the House of Lords has rejected any such reform, voting instead for a fully appointed chamber. Equally unsurprising may be the hesitance of the House of Commons to enact any actual reforms that would strengthen the legislative power of a second chamber at the expense of its own.[9]

THE JUDICIARY

Compared with the United States and even with other parliamentary democracies, the judiciary in the United Kingdom has a relatively minor role. Until recently there was no tradition of judicial review (the right of courts to strike down legislation that contradicts the constitution), because the British parliament was always supreme: any law passed by the legislature was, by definition, constitutional. Thus the role of the courts in the United Kingdom has been mainly to ensure that parliamentary statutes have been followed. Formerly the responsibility of law lords in the House of Lords, since 2009 a separate Supreme Court of the United Kingdom has served as the highest court of appeal on most legal matters. Reflecting their former jurisdiction, all current Supreme Court justices are also law lords from the House of Lords, selected from among distinguished jurists by the lord chancellor (the minister who heads the judiciary) and serving until retirement. Their replacements, however, will no longer be members of the House of Lords, but will be appointed by a commission. To the extent that the vast majority of judges come from relatively wealthy families and are educated at elite universities, it could be assumed that the judiciary has a conservative bias.

Though politically weak, over the past couple of decades a slow move toward greater political involvement of the courts has occurred. In part, this is because British governments have sought legal interpretations that would support their actions. A second factor in this development has been the embrace of international laws, such as the adoption of the European Convention on Human Rights in 1998, which codified for the first time in the United Kingdom a set of basic civil rights. These laws have given the courts new authority to strike down legislation as unconstitutional, though these powers have so far been used sparingly. Still, the days when we could speak of the United Kingdom as lacking judicial review may be slowly coming to an end.

The broader legal system, based on common law and developed in the twelfth century, stands in stark contrast to the stricter code law practiced in the rest of Europe, which is less focused on precedent and interpretation. Like most democracies, the United Kingdom has an elaborate hierarchy of civil and criminal courts, and a complex system of appeals.

The Electoral System

Like the United States, the United Kingdom uses the single-member district (SMD) system based on plurality, or what is often known as "first past the post" (FPTP). Each of the 650 constituencies elects one MP, and that member needs to win only a plurality of votes (that is, more than any other candidate), not a majority. Electoral constituencies are based mostly on population, and they average about 68,000 voters. Constituencies are revised every five to seven years by a government commission.

The implications of the plurality SMD system are fairly clear. First, as shown in the table "Consequences of the British Electoral System, 1987–2010," p. 60, the system favors and helps maintain the dominance of the two main political parties, Labour and Conservative. Second, and related, it consistently penalizes smaller parties. The Liberal Democrats, whose support is spread evenly across the country, regularly garner between one-fifth and one-quarter of votes in many districts, but can rarely muster enough votes to edge out the larger parties. In 2010, the Liberal Democrats won 23 percent of the vote but only 57 seats (about 9 percent of the total). With only 7 percent more of the national vote (29 percent), Labour won more than four times as many seats (258). The Conservatives won the most seats (nearly half the total), but did so by capturing only 36 percent of the votes. Small parties that are regionally concentrated, such as the Scottish Nationalist Party, do somewhat better, but even they are underrepresented.

Third, the British electoral system has almost always produced clear majorities in the House of Commons, even when there was no clear majority in the electorate. Indeed, in the elections of 1951 and 1974, the party with the smaller percentage of the vote won the most seats because of the nature of the electoral system. Even in 1997, Labour won a huge (179-seat) majority in the Commons

Consequences of the British Electoral System, 1987–2010

ELECTION YEARS	% OF VOTES	SEATS WON	% OF SEATS
Labour			
1987	31	229	35
1992	34	271	42
1997	43	419	64
2001	41	412	63
2005	35	355	55
2010	29	258	40
Conservative			
1987	42	375	58
1992	42	336	52
1997	31	165	25
2001	32	166	25
2005	32	197	30
2010	36	306	47
Liberal Democrat			
1987	23	22	3
1992	18	20	3
1997	17	46	7
2001	18	52	8
2005	22	62	10
2010	23	57	9
Others			
1987	4	24	4
1992	6	24	4
1997	9	29	4
2001	9	29	4
2005	10	32	5
2010	10	27	4

Note: Due to rounding, percentages do not always equal 100.

with only 43 percent of the vote. These distortions occur when more than two parties contest a seat, so that a majority of votes is wasted—that is, the votes are not counted toward the winning party. Since World War II, more than 60 percent of all seats have been won with a minority of votes.

In a system that gives virtually unchecked power to the party with the majority of seats, an electoral process artificially producing majorities could be considered a serious distortion of democratic rule. It is no wonder that the parties most hurt by the electoral system, especially the Liberal Democrats, have long called for electoral reform. The Labour government elected in 1997 appointed an independent commission to consider a more proportional electoral system, but as the party in government and the chief beneficiary of the current system, Labour had little incentive to act on the recommendations.

The 2010 election, which departed from the outcome predicted by political scientists and confirmed by most UK general elections, afforded the Liberal Democrats the opportunity to press their demand for electoral reform. For the first time since 1974, no party managed to obtain a majority of seats in the election, resulting in a "hung parliament." Among other consequences (examined later in this chapter), the successful effort by the Conservatives to draw the Liberal Democrats into a majority coalition included the promise to hold a referendum on electoral reform. In 2011, the referendum was held, allowing voters to choose between retaining the existing plurality SMD system and instituting a majority SMD system known as "alternative vote" (AV). Whereas in the current arrangement the candidate with a plurality of votes is elected, the proposed AV system would have allowed voters to rank candidates by preference. If no candidate obtained an outright majority based on first preferences, then the candidate with the fewest first choice votes would be eliminated and the second-choice candidate on those ballots awarded those votes. This process of elimination and reallocation would be repeated until a top candidate obtained a majority of votes.

Ultimately, the 2011 referendum failed resoundingly, with over two-thirds of voters rejecting the AV system. Despite agreeing to bring the referendum forward, the Conservatives were clear in their preferences to retain the existing plurality system. Labour took no position on the referendum, and even the Liberal Democrats would not have been fully satisfied with a yes vote, far preferring a more radical reform to a proportional representation (PR) system.

Devolution has led to more electoral experimentation in regional legislatures. Scotland and Wales have adopted a mixed PR-SMD electoral system and Northern Ireland uses a system known as single-transferable vote, similar to the

AV system discussed above. Ironically, the governing Labour Party that authorized these regional parliaments in the 1990s, and which benefited greatly from plurality SMD, favored a mixed system for the regional legislatures, fearing that plurality SMD would produce large majorities for the local nationalist parties.

Local Government

Unlike the United States, the United Kingdom has traditionally been a unitary state: no formal powers are reserved for regional or local government. Indeed, during the Conservative governments of Margaret Thatcher the autonomy of municipal governments was sharply curtailed. The Labour government elected in 1997 took bold steps to restore some political power to the distinct nations that compose the United Kingdom and to local governments. The Conservative–Liberal Democrat coalition that came to government in 2010 has pledged to continue these efforts of handing more authority to local governments and communities.

Although there has never been a constitutional provision for local autonomy, British localities have enjoyed a long tradition of powerful local government. Concerned that local governments (or "councils" as they are known in the United Kingdom), especially left-leaning ones in large urban areas, were taxing and spending beyond their means, Thatcher's Conservative government passed a law sharply limiting the ability of these councils to raise revenue. The struggle between the central government and the councils came to a head in 1986, when Thatcher abolished the Labour-dominated Greater London Council and several other urban governments, a move deeply resented by urban British citizens. London was left with councils in each of its 32 boroughs, but it had no single city government or mayor. In 1989, Thatcher further threatened local governments by replacing the local property tax with a poll tax—that is, a flat tax levied on every urban citizen. The new policy shifted the tax burden from business and property owners to individuals (rich and poor alike) and was among the most unpopular policies of Thatcher's 11 years in power. In response, rioting broke out in London.

Thatcher's successor, John Major, abandoned the poll tax but continued to limit the financial autonomy of local governments. After 1997, Tony Blair restored considerable autonomy to municipal government, enacting reforms that allowed Londoners to directly elect a mayor with significant powers and to choose representatives to a Greater London Assembly. Ironically, in the first

GOVERNING LONDON: "RED KEN" AND BORIS

As prime minister, Tony Blair reinvigorated the United Kingdom's system of local government, which had been weakened under Conservative governments, restoring the post of mayor of London that Thatcher had eliminated. The first occupant of that new office was Ken Livingstone, nicknamed "Red Ken" because of his identification with the radical left of the Labour Party. During his two terms in office, Livingstone was a controversial, enigmatic mayor, and he became one of the United Kingdom's most visible politicians. In order to reduce London's sclerotic traffic, he charged drivers a fee when they brought their vehicles into the city. In order to improve service and investment, he privatized much of the city's mass transit system. He was widely applauded not only for his response to the 2005 London terrorist bombings but also for his ability to lure the 2012 Olympic Games to the city. He was criticized, however, for a steady stream of imprudent and often incendiary political statements. Livingstone was narrowly defeated in 2008 by an equally controversial and flamboyant Conservative, Boris Johnson. Livingstone's defeat was viewed by many political analysts as both a referendum on the increasingly unpopular Brown government and a backlash against some of Livingstone's more controversial policies. During his four-year tenure, the charismatic Mr. Johnson further reduced crime and managed to wrest a bit more authority from the national government. The arrival of the Olympics in 2012 brought another sort of competition to London: a rematch election between Labour's "Red Ken" and Boris, the Conservative incumbent. Johnson won re-election on May 3, 2012.

such election, in 2000, a left-wing Labour opponent of the prime minister was elected (see "Governing London: 'Red Ken' and Boris," above). Nevertheless, Blair maintained the financial limitations on local government that were imposed during Thatcher's tenure. Under the promise of creating a "big society," the current Conservative-led ruling coalition has sought to continue this process of devolution, requiring greater transparency in local government and giving local citizens more decision-making power regarding local taxation and public services. In 2012, the coalition also authorized mayoral elections in an additional 11 major cities.

Representation at the regional level has historically been very limited. Of the four nations that constitute the United Kingdom (England, Scotland, Wales, and Northern Ireland), only Northern Ireland had its own legislature, until political violence there caused the central government to disband it in 1972. Each of the four nations has a cabinet minister in the central government, called a secretary of state, who is responsible for setting policies in each region.

As it did with local government, the Labour Party promoted devolution, or the decentralization of power, to the United Kingdom's regions. In 1997, Scotland and Wales voted in referenda to create their own legislatures to address local issues, though their powers are not uniform: Scotland's Parliament is substantially more powerful and autonomous than Wales's Assembly, a reflection of the much stronger nationalist tendencies in Scotland. Meanwhile, the 1998 **Good Friday Agreement** between Catholics and Protestants in Northern Ireland has allowed for the reestablishment of the Northern Ireland Assembly. Some observers view the development of these bodies as the first step toward a federal United Kingdom.[10]

Presently, England remains the only nation within the United Kingdom without devolved representation. Despite devolution measures and talk of a "big society," the United Kingdom remains a centralized, unitary state. Regional and local authorities clearly enjoy greater legitimacy and far more powers than in the past—a trend that is likely to continue—but the central government still controls defense policy, most taxation power, and national economic policy, among other aspects of government. The central government also retains the power to limit (or even eliminate) local government if it so chooses.

Political Conflict and Competition

The Party System

In the United Kingdom's majoritarian parliamentary system, political parties are extremely important. The majority party controls government and can generally implement its policy goals, which are spelled out in the party manifesto.

From the end of World War II to 1970, the United Kingdom had a two-party system. The Conservative Party and the Labour Party together garnered more than 90 percent of the popular vote. The two large parties were equally successful during that period, with each winning four elections. After 1974, a multiparty system emerged, which included the birth of a stronger centrist Liberal Democratic Party and a surge of support for nationalist parties in Scotland, Wales, and Northern Ireland. But since the Conservatives and Labour continue to prevail, the current system is often called a two-and-a-half-party system, with the Liberal Democratic Party trailing far behind the other two parties.

The United Kingdom's party system differs regionally, even for national elections. In England the three major parties (Labour, Conservative, and Liberal Democrat) compete with one another. In Scotland, Wales, and Northern Ireland, important regional parties compete with the three national political parties. In the 2001 elections the two leading parties together won about 68 percent of the vote, while the remaining votes were divided among a variety of parties. In total, 10 parties won seats in the House of Commons.

The two main parties may be losing votes as a result of the growth of smaller parties.[11] The percentage of the vote cast for parties other than the three major parties has steadily increased over recent elections, and no party since 1935 has won an outright majority of the vote. Moreover, the hung parliament resulting from the 2010 election also underlines the challenges facing the two leading parties and demonstrates the unlikely prospects for a third party to have significant influence in this majoritarian parliamentary system (see "2010 Election: Expenses Scandal, Campaign Debates, and Coalition Government," p. 66).

THE LABOUR PARTY

We have discussed the democratization of the United Kingdom as a gradual process that incorporated previously excluded groups into the political system. The Labour Party is a clear example of this, as it was formed in 1900 as an outgrowth of the trade union movement. Initially, it sought to give the British working class a voice in Parliament. Only after the mobilizing effect of World War I and the expansion of suffrage in 1918 was the Labour Party able to make significant progress at the polls. By 1918, it had garnered almost one-quarter of the vote. Labour's turning point and its emergence as one of the United Kingdom's two dominant parties came with its landslide victory in 1945, just after the end of World War II.

Like virtually all working-class parties of the world, the British Labour Party considered socialism its dominant ideological characteristic. British socialists, however, were influenced by Fabianism, a moderate ideology that advocated working within the parliamentary order to bring about social-democratic change. While Labour championed a strong welfare state and some state ownership of industry, the party's moderate politics never threatened to replace capitalism.

For most of its history, the Labour Party depended heavily on working-class votes, winning the support of about two-thirds of the United Kingdom's manual

2010 ELECTION: EXPENSES SCANDAL, CAMPAIGN DEBATES, AND COALITION GOVERNMENT

If British politics are supposed to be about staid traditions and predictable continuity, the 2010 general election stood much of that on its head.* Until 2010, every government since 1945 was run by either the Conservatives (Tories) or Labour, and only once (1974-79) did either party fail to have a majority in the House of Commons. Until 2010, it had been nearly 70 years since the United Kingdom was governed by a peacetime coalition. (Britain was led during both world wars by coalition governments.) And prior to 2010, UK political candidates had also carefully avoided televised debates, considering them both unhelpful and un-British.

The initial impetus for all of this change was a British press exposé in 2009 that revealed a parliamentary expenses scandal. British MPs receive relatively meager salaries for their services and over time had supplemented their income with a very generous and largely unmonitored system of allowances for staff, second homes, and other expenses. The revealed details of unethical and in some cases illegal payments and reimbursements implicated a number of Labour and Tory MPs, tarnishing both parties and angering the electorate. This scandal meant that neither party went into the 2010 general election with a comfortable prospect of obtaining a majority of parliamentary seats, and therefore both parties were more willing to consider an American-style "presidential" debate, hoping to boost their party's prospects. The Liberal Democrats seemed to gain most from the national exposure, as their leader, Nick Clegg, outshone both Labour's Gordon Brown and the Conservative's David Cameron, particularly in the first of three televised debates. Following the debates, there was talk of a dramatic upset that might even give the most votes (if not seats) to the Liberal Democrat underdogs, allowing the party to form a government or at least demand a change in the electoral system that had long hampered its prospects.

In the election itself, however, all three of the parties failed to impress. Predictably, as the incumbent government, Labour lost both votes and seats. The Conservatives gained seats and votes, but fell short of obtaining an outright majority in the House of Commons. Liberal Democrats gained votes, but lost seats, confirming their resolve in a "hung parliament" to demand reform of the electoral system as a condition for their participation in a coalition government. After several days of horse trading, the Tories and Liberal Democrats announced a deal allowing the formation of a coalition with David Cameron as prime minister and Nick Clegg as deputy prime minister, and the promise to call a national referendum on electoral reform. Although the 2011 referendum proved inconsequential, failing to garner much support for even a much milder reform than that hoped for by the Liberal Democrats, the election did produce a government with a sufficient mandate to tackle many of the difficult challenges facing the United Kingdom.

*For an engaging discussion of the expenses scandal and the 2010 election, see John Lanchester, "Party Games," *The New Yorker*, June 7, 2010.

laborers. Starting in the 1970s, however, the composition of the class structure began to change, with fewer Britons engaging in blue-collar jobs. At that point, the solid identification of workers with Labour began to erode, creating a serious challenge for the party.

By the mid-1970s, the Labour Party was badly divided between radical socialists who wanted the party to move to the left to shore up its working-class credentials and moderates who wanted it to move toward the political center. These divisions involved the party's relationship to the trade unions and its stand on economic and foreign policy. This internal division caused the party's more conservative elements to bolt in 1981. Most serious, the internal bickering led to the defeat of Labour in every election from 1979 to 1997.

In the 1980s and 1990s the Labour Party began a process of ideological and organizational moderation. The party's constitution was rewritten to weaken severely the ability of trade unions to control party policy. Labour also abandoned its commitment to socialism and advocated a cross-class appeal. Tony Blair, who became party leader in 1994, consolidated these changes and advocated moderate free-market policies with ambitious constitutional reform, policies that were eventually known as the Third Way.[12] Blair's landslide victory in the 1997 elections marked the beginning of a period of party unity and electoral success that has been termed New Labour, and the election results of 2001 and 2005 confirmed this success. Labour's victory in the 2005 elections marked the first time in history that the party had been elected to office three consecutive times. However, those elections reduced Labour's majority by 47 seats, and two years later Blair handed power over to his chancellor of the exchequer, Gordon Brown. Brown's Labour government fared even worse in the 2010 elections, dropping 91 additional seats and losing its majority in Parliament. Brown stepped down as both prime minister and leader of his party, and later that year **Ed Miliband**, running with strong backing from trade unions, defeated his older brother in

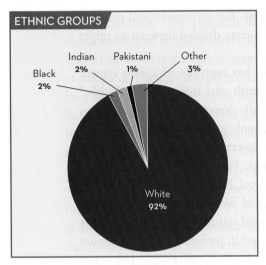

ETHNIC GROUPS

Indian 2%
Pakistani 1%
Other 3%
Black 2%
White 92%

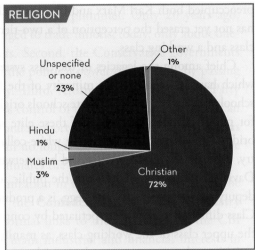

RELIGION

Other 1%
Unspecified or none 23%
Hindu 1%
Muslim 3%
Christian 72%

by both national and class differences, with Catholics discriminated against in employment and education. Starting in the 1960s, members of the Irish Republican Army (IRA) turned to violence against British targets in the hope of unifying the region with the Republic of Ireland, and the British army and illegal Protestant paramilitary organizations fought back. Nearly 4,000 individuals on both sides, many of them civilians, died in the conflict. In the 1990s, the British government and the IRA began talks with the aim of establishing peace, which resulted in the 1998 Good Friday Agreement (see "Giving Peace a Chance in Northern Ireland," p. 76), which bound the IRA to renounce its armed struggle in return for political reforms that would give the Catholic population greater say in local government. Since 1998, the region has been relatively peaceful for the first time in decades, although several killings in 2009 rekindled fear about a return to political violence.

Elsewhere, however, new divisions are emerging. Since the 1960s, former colonial subjects (primarily from Africa, the West Indies, India, and Pakistan) have immigrated to the United Kingdom in increasing numbers, giving British society a degree of racial diversity. For the most part, British society has not coped particularly well with this influx. Racial tension between the overwhelming majority of whites and the non-European minority (totaling less than 5 percent of the population) has sparked conflict and anti-immigrant sentiment, both of which nonetheless remain moderate by American and continental standards.

Lacking proportional representation, the British electoral system has limited the impact of both the nonwhite and the far-right vote in most elections. Parliament has also sought to limit the nonwhite population by imposing quotas that restrict the entrance of nonwhite dependents of persons already residing in the United Kingdom. In spite of this, the country continues to face growing rates of immigration, with some predicting that another 2 million immigrants will enter the United Kingdom over the next decade. This will undoubtedly change the social dynamics and may increase xenophobic sentiment, strengthening parties such as the British National Party. As discussed in the "Current Issues" section, the integration (or lack thereof) of the United Kingdom's Muslim population has been a growing concern since the 2005 terrorist attacks on London's transit system.

In addition to ethnic groups, the United Kingdom also comprises a number of national groups, a fact outsiders tend to overlook. The United Kingdom of Britain and Northern Ireland is made up of four nations—England, Scotland, Wales, and Northern Ireland—with substantial cultural and political differences among them. Most UK citizens first identify themselves not as British but as belonging to one of these four nationalities.[16] (The U.S. equivalent to this would be a resident of Los Angeles identifying herself first as a Californian, not as an American.)

Long-standing yearning for greater national autonomy has gained increasing political significance since the 1960s. Local nationalist parties—including the **Scottish Nationalist Party (SNP)** and the Welsh Plaid Cymru—with the support of the Labour Party, have advocated devolution: that is, turning over some central-governmental powers to the regions. Tony Blair's Labour government delivered on its campaign promise of devolution in 1999 with the establishment of local legislatures for Northern Ireland, Scotland, and Wales. Some feared that rather than pacify nationalist tendencies, devolution would contribute to the eventual breakup of the country, most notably with an independent Scotland (see the discussion "The Future of Scotland" in the "Current Issues" section, pp. 85–87).

While persistent regional loyalties and the localization of government have challenged the British national identity, so, too, has the United Kingdom's growing dependence on the European Union. As the twenty-first century progresses, British identity (and perhaps even Scottish and Welsh identity) may be eclipsed or at least diluted by an increasing allegiance to Europe. Despite this diffuse loyalty, Britons remain generally very loyal to the Crown and to the notion of a sovereign British people.

GIVING PEACE A CHANCE IN NORTHERN IRELAND

After years of negotiation, Northern Ireland's status seemed finally resolved by the 1998 Good Friday Agreement. Both the British and the Irish governments supported the decision, as did important Northern Irish political groups, including Catholic republicans, who favor Northern Ireland's unification with the Republic of Ireland, and Protestant unionists, who favor maintaining Northern Ireland's inclusion in the United Kingdom. Among other provisions, the Good Friday Agreement allows for the institution of a Northern Irish legislature and a voting system that ensures proportional representation. ("First past the post" had effectively marginalized the Catholic minority.)

With this agreement, violence by both republican and unionist paramilitary organizations virtually came to an end. However, one major sticking point remained: as part of the Good Friday Agreement, all paramilitary forces were expected to destroy their weapons. This stipulation was directed primarily toward the republican party (known as Sinn Féin) and its military wing, the Irish Republican Army, which retained a formidable arsenal. Even as the benefits of the peace became widespread and Sinn Féin assumed a role in local government, the party continued to resist the decommissioning of its military presence. Critics accused Sinn Féin of maintaining a ballots-and-bullets strategy: ready to take up arms if the democratic process did not go its way. Given the long and violent campaign waged by the IRA, immediate disarmament was not an easily achieved goal. Indeed, in the aftermath of the Good Friday Agreement, a car bombing by an IRA splinter group killed 29 civilians in the town of Omagh in 1998.

As a result of Sinn Féin's failures to decommission its military, the British government suspended Northern Ireland's legislature in October 2002. Yet the IRA has not resumed a violent campaign, and in 2003, it announced some limited destruction of weapons. For this it was rewarded with new elections to the reinstated regional legislature. In 2005, the IRA finally renounced the use of armed conflict altogether, a move widely regarded as crucial to the achievement of lasting peace in Northern Ireland. Perhaps the most visible sign of the success of the Good Friday Agreement was that the United Kingdom restored self-rule to Ulster in 2007. The first leader of the restored Northern Ireland government was the Protestant minister Ian Paisley, leader of the only mainstream Ulster party to oppose the agreement. His deputy leader was the former IRA terrorist Martin McGuinness.* The murder of two British soldiers and a police officer claimed by Republican dissidents in 2009 were denounced by both sides and have not derailed efforts to maintain the peace, though the political future of the region still remains uncertain.

* For an excellent overview of the success of and challenges facing the Good Friday Agreement, see "The Hand of History Revealed," *The Economist*, April 3, 2008.

Ideology and Political Culture

In terms of the goals of politics, British political values have been strongly influenced by the development of classical liberalism and the conviction that government's influence over individuals ought to be limited. However, the postwar goals of an expanded franchise of full employment and the creation of a welfare state led to a new consensus as many Britons embraced the social-democratic values of increased state intervention and less individual freedom in exchange for increased social equality. Economic decline during the 1970s shifted the pendulum back toward personal freedom, which spurned consensus politics, rejected socialist redistributive policies, and advocated privatization.

The electoral success of the Labour Party in 1997 came on the heels of its new policy to reconcile social-democratic and liberal ideologies, the so-called Third Way. While this may indicate that British voters did not fully embrace the stark individualism of the Thatcher revolution, much of Labour's subsequent success came from embracing a kinder, gentler version of her neoliberal program. Cameron's and the Conservative–Liberal Democrat coalition's calls for a "big society" can also be seen in this light—a shift of governance and stewardship from national to local, public to private. That said, most British—like their continental neighbors—tend to be more socially and morally liberal than citizens of the United States. The United Kingdom outlawed capital punishment and legalized abortion and homosexuality, all in the mid-1960s. Handguns were banned outright in 1998. Also, there is far less emphasis on religion and traditional family values.

British political culture is typically described as pragmatic and tolerant. Compared with other societies, British society is thought to be less concerned with adhering to overarching ideological principles and more willing to tinker gradually with a particular political problem. Scholars often account for this pragmatism by pointing to the incremental and ad hoc historical development of British political institutions, noting that there was no defining political moment in British history when founders or revolutionaries sat down and envisioned or established a political system or a set of rules based on abstract ideals or theoretical principles. Political radicalism, on either the left or the right, is rare in the United Kingdom, with virtually all political actors embracing a willingness to seek evolutionary, not revolutionary, change. This pragmatism is bolstered by a classical liberal tolerance for opposing viewpoints, a strong sense of fair play, and a generally high level of consensus on the political rules of the game.

Although such general characterizations have some utility in accounting for British politics, British political culture in reality comprises multiple subcultures, as is the case in any complex modern or postmodern society. One can certainly still see evidence of an aristocratic culture among the political elite, who share a sense of superiority and noblesse oblige toward those they deem less able to rule, and a mass or working-class culture of deference to those in authority. But in addition, policies of devolution, immigration, and multiculturalism combined with the blurring of class lines have challenged and complicated these dominant subcultures. And with the onset of economic recession, growing social inequality and the imposition of austerity measures, simmering tensions within some of these groups have boiled over. Several days of violent and destructive riots in the summer of 2011 in London and other cities across England pitted angry inner-city youth against the police and served as a sober reminder that elements among these subcultures were fully prepared to reject deference toward authority (see "England's 2011 Summer Riots" in the "Current Issues" section, pp. 88–89). In that same year, labor unions and university students launched widespread anti-austerity demonstrations against deep public sector spending cuts, protests that also spoke to significant political divisions within the political culture.

Political Economy

The United Kingdom is noteworthy for its contribution to the liberal economic model. Indeed, most political analysts would trace classical liberalism itself to the United Kingdom, where philosophers such as John Locke spoke of the inalienable rights of "life, liberty and estate," setting the stage for such political innovations as the U.S. Declaration of Independence.[17] Yet liberalism in the United Kingdom has undergone a number of shifts over the past decades, from a greater emphasis on social-democratic values after World War II to the neoliberal-

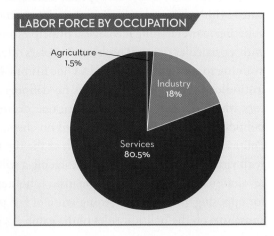

LABOR FORCE BY OCCUPATION

Agriculture 1.5%

Industry 18%

Services 80.5%

ism under Margaret Thatcher, which has been softened but largely continued in subsequent governments.

If there is a common theme in the UK economy in the four decades since the end of World War II, it is decline. As we recall, during the Industrial Revolution, the United Kingdom was "the workshop to the world" and the richest country on the planet. Yet over time, this position of dominance deteriorated. As of 2011, the country's per capita GDP at purchasing-power parity ranked 33rd in the world, behind once far-poorer colonies such as Ireland and Australia (though the UK economy remains one of the 10 largest in the world).

Why the decline? There is no single explanation, but one of the basic causes is the downside of early industrialization, which made the country the world's first industrial power, but also allowed it to be the first country to face the obsolescence of its technology and the difficulty of shifting to a new economic environment. A second factor is the burden of empire. Although industrialization helped fuel imperialism (and vice versa), the British Empire soon became a financial drain on the country rather than a benefit to it. Related to this is the argument that the United Kingdom's orientation toward its empire meant that it was slow to pursue economic opportunities with the rest of Europe when the continent moved toward greater integration after World War II. Finally, many political analysts have argued that the collectivist consensus not only blocked meaningful economic reform in the United Kingdom for much of the postwar era, but also focused the country on social expenditures while causing it to ignore the simultaneous need to modernize its economy.

Where does this leave the UK economy in the new century? Like other advanced democracies, the United Kingdom is a postindustrial economy. Although such industries as steel, oil, and gas still play an important role, nearly three-quarters of the country's wealth is generated by the service sector, in particular financial services and tourism. Privatization has significantly shrunk the role of the state in the economy, including the sale of a range of assets, among them public utilities and housing, British Airways, Rolls-Royce, and Jaguar. Recent governments have sought to extend privatization to railroads, health care, and even the Underground (London's famous subway system). There have also been substantial changes in the welfare state, moving it from a system that provided direct benefits to the unemployed to one that sponsors "welfare-to-work" programs emphasizing training in order to find employment. Even though Labour governments have tended to spend more on social welfare than do their Tory counterparts, even Labour has ended its traditional call for a greater role for the state in the economy—nationalization of industry was enshrined in the Labour

Party constitution until 1995—and has distanced itself from its once-close ties with organized labor.

To some observers, the Thatcher revolution, and its preservation under subsequent governments, helped the United Kingdom finally turn a corner. Until the global recession hit in 2008, the country enjoyed a decade of strong economic growth. Prior to the global economic downturn, the UK economy performed much better than the economy of France, Germany, or Japan. However, as in many other countries, neoliberal economic policies have increased financial inequality throughout the United Kingdom, which has one of the highest levels of inequality in Europe. This inequality also has a regional element, with the country's south growing much faster than the north, which is the traditional home of heavy industry. Whether this gap is widening or shrinking is hotly debated. It has also been argued that welfare reform is a costly program that has done little to ease unemployment.

Moreover, public spending has exacerbated the United Kingdom's growing gap between government revenues and government spending, a malady that Britain shares with the United States and most other industrialized countries. Britain's budget deficit became acute following the 2008 global financial crisis and was exacerbated by an inflated housing bubble and an economy largely dependent on financial services—the industry hardest hit by the financial crisis. In response, the Labour government partially nationalized a number of private banks, increased income taxes for the wealthy, and stepped up both public borrowing and public spending in an effort to stimulate the economy. After coming to office in 2010, the Conservative–Liberal Democrat coalition government shifted to a more liberal tack, cutting public spending and pursuing deregulation in an effort to reduce the government's growing deficit. The government has faced great resistance from public-sector unions, university students, and others as it has pursued these tough austerity measures.

Finally, there is the issue of the United Kingdom's economic relationship with the outside world. Historic ties notwithstanding, over the past half century the country has become closely tied to the rest of Europe, with half of its trade going to other EU member states. However, the United Kingdom has still not accepted the euro, which is the common currency of the European Union and was fully introduced in most member states in 2002. British leaders and the public have been cool toward the idea of giving up the pound; they fear the change will undermine the country's sovereignty, placing important economic decisions (such as interest rates) in the hands of other EU member countries and EU bureaucrats. Opponents also argue that the British economy is significantly different from the

British workers and students protest austerity measures imposed by the Conservative-Liberal Democratic Coalition.

economies on the continent, and that a single currency would reduce the United Kingdom's flexibility in responding to the different economic challenges it faces. Recent financial struggles within the euro zone have only strengthened the resolve of the Euroskeptics to keep the United Kingdom apart.

Supporters of the euro argue that if the United Kingdom were to make the change, the country would avoid the current fluctuations in the exchange rate between the euro and the pound. Adopting the euro, they contend, would help trade (because there would no longer be the threat of a rising pound, making British goods too expensive for other Europeans) and promote investment (because investors would not worry about how exchange-rate volatility might affect their exports to the rest of Europe). Although the Liberal Democrats have long been supporters of joining the single currency, adoption of the euro does not seem to be an option at this time, given the currency's recent existential challenges. In the end, these issues tie into a much broader question: What is the UK's place in the contemporary international system?

Foreign Relations and the World

The United Kingdom's political future does not rest on domestic politics alone. Although the country is no longer a superpower, it retains a relatively large army, has its own nuclear weapons, and boasts one of the largest economies in the world. It remains a major player in world affairs, but struggles to define its place and role in a post-imperial and post–Cold War world. The central difficulty lies in the United Kingdom's self-identity. As citizens of an island nation and a former imperial power, the British have long seen themselves as separate from continental Europe, which was slower to adopt democracy and remains much more skeptical of the liberal values that first emerged in the United Kingdom. Rather than identifying itself with the continent, the United Kingdom built its identity around its empire, orienting itself toward the Atlantic. When the empire eventually declined, the emergence of the United States gave the United Kingdom the sense that its power had in a way been resurrected in a former colony, whose citizens were imbued with the same liberal values and spoke a common language. Since the end of World War II, the United States has counted on the United Kingdom as its most dependable ally.[18]

The United Kingdom also remains willing to defend its interests militarily. In 1982, the Falkland Islands—a remote British territory of about 2,000 residents some 300 miles off the coast of Argentina—were seized by Argentina after a long-running dispute over ownership of the islands. The United Kingdom dispatched its military to retake the colony and succeeded in driving out the Argentine forces. In the process, more than 200 British soldiers and more than 600 Argentine soldiers were killed. Many observers may find the deaths of so many soldiers over two small, sparsely populated islands illogical, but the conflict reflects the United Kingdom's post-imperial identity and its desire not to surrender its international power. More recently, both Labour- and Tory-led governments have strongly supported the U.S.-led wars in Afghanistan and Iraq, and the United Kingdom was the only other country to contribute a significant military force to the Iraq conflict.

But despite the government's support of U.S. foreign policies, the United Kingdom's Atlantic orientation is uncertain. Since 1989, most European countries have engaged in a new effort to expand and strengthen the European Union, which has forged ever-closer political, economic, and social ties among its members. As noted earlier, the United Kingdom was late in warming to the idea of the European Union, initially skeptical of membership and then later kept out by the French (who saw British membership as a Trojan horse through which the United States could influence Europe). The United Kingdom has continued to be less than enthusiastic about the EU, especially with respect to the latter's ambitions for taking on more power and responsibilities, such as effecting monetary union or promulgating unified foreign policy. During the 1970s and 1980s, this attitude was less of a problem, because the European Union had entered a period of relative stagnation. Since the 1990s, however, many European leaders have moved forward to strengthen the European Union, enabling it to ensure regional stability and act as a counterweight to the "hyperpower" of the United States.

To many Britons, the notion of a stronger European Union is unacceptable, because they fear it will become an unwieldy superstate, undermining national sovereignty, draining the domestic budget, and imposing continental values.[19] The fact that half of the European Union's budget is spent on agricultural subsidies, of which the United Kingdom gets relatively little, only underscores this suspicion. According to a 2008 poll, only 30 percent of those surveyed in the United Kingdom thought that membership in the European Union was a good thing, one of the lowest levels of support of any member state (see "In Comparison: European Union," p. 84). The United Kingdom's reluctance to adopt the euro is further evidence of this skepticism, a skepticism shared by an increasing number of Britons in the wake of the 2011 euro crisis. Others worry that if the United Kingdom continues to resist European integration, it will lose even more economic and diplomatic power, and may marginalize itself, becoming a peripheral player in the creation of a single European power.

In short, Britain's position vis-à-vis Europe remains ambiguous. Blair and his Labour government had promised a referendum on adoption of the euro, but never followed through on the pledge, and Labour also backed away from its initial commitment to the euro. Conservatives and Liberal Democrats agreed at the formation of the coalition that their government would not join the euro while the coalition was in effect, but would remain a positive force in the European Union. In 2011, the coalition government codified the compromise, passing a law requiring that a national referendum be held in order to amend the treaties now in place linking the United Kingdom to the European Union. Even the Liberal Democrats, the most pro-EU party, has given its European policies a low profile in recognition that its position on Europe may be an electoral liability in an era of euro crisis. The growing popularity of a fringe party, the United Kingdom Independence Party, which advocates a complete withdrawal from the European Union, has benefited from widespread Euroskepticism in the United Kingdom. In the 2010 general election, the party garnered nearly a million votes and fielded candidates in nearly all 650 electoral districts.

While the United Kingdom continues to resist European integration, its relationship with the United States remains a powerful, if problematic, alternative. As we noted, the United Kingdom shares a strong historical affinity with this former colony and current superpower across the Atlantic. Even though the disparity in power between the two countries is enormous, British supporters of the Atlantic alliance argue that limited influence over the only superpower is superior to a more equal standing in a body such as the European Union, whose international authority remains rather limited.

European Union

Do you think our membership in the European Union is a good thing?
Percentage saying yes:

COUNTRY	PERCENTAGE
Germany	50
France	44
United Kingdom	29

Do you trust the European Union? Percentage saying yes:

COUNTRY	PERCENTAGE
France	39
Germany	37
United Kingdom	20

Source: Eurobarometer 73, 2010.

But particularly in the aftermath of September 11 and the Iraq War, many Britons have come to the disappointing conclusion that the United States sees the United Kingdom not as a critical ally but rather as a junior partner duly expected to follow U.S. foreign policy and provide a veneer of multilateralism no matter what the United States wants to do. This perception has fueled British anti-Americanism much like that seen elsewhere in Europe today. As of 2003, one poll showed that fewer than half of Britons had a favorable view of the United States, down from more than 80 percent in 2000. Nearly half of those surveyed also believed that the United Kingdom should act more independently of the United States. Following the election of President Obama, the same research center found that British attitudes toward the United States had improved, with 69 percent of those polled in 2009 indicating a favorable attitude toward America.[20] The United Kingdom also finds itself in greater agreement with its European partners on the centrality of resolving the Palestinian-Israeli conflict in order to effect a lasting Middle East peace. This conflict between European and U.S. foreign policies has left the United Kingdom in the middle, with diffuse and uneasy ties to both centers of power. In 2011, Britain joined France in leading a military intervention in Libya that involved a coalition of 19 countries, including the United States. Although leadership of the limited intervention ultimately shifted to NATO, some observers have pointed to this example of French and British cooperative leadership and American followership as an indication both of declining American hegemony and of growing British security collaboration with at least some of its European neighbors.[21]

The United Kingdom, then, remains unique, as it was centuries ago. Its economic and political systems gave rise to liberalism but remain shaped by centuries-old institutions that have never been fully swept away. Its industrial strength once propelled it to empire status, though now it is overshadowed by its former colony across the Atlantic and an ever-converging Europe. In recent years, the United Kingdom has grappled with these issues, hoping to modernize old institutions yet retain its distinct identity, and hoping, too, to retain its international stature while reevaluating its relationship to the United States and the rest of Europe. Will the United Kingdom break from its past, creating a new identity to meet its domestic and international challenges? This will be a critical issue in its immediate future.

CURRENT ISSUES IN THE UNITED KINGDOM

The Future of Scotland

Northern Ireland is not the only region where a sector of the population has sought to leave the United Kingdom. Scotland was an independent state until the 1707 Act of Union—passed by the Scottish legislature despite widespread popular protest—fused it with England to form Great Britain. Scotland preserved its own legal system, its own church, and many of its own traditions. The Scottish Nationalist Party, formed in the 1930s, advocated Scottish independence but was relatively unsuccessful until fairly recently. In 1974, the SNP won about a third of all votes in Scotland and sent a record 11 representatives to the House of Commons in London. Both the discovery of oil in the North Sea in the 1960s and the opposition to Thatcher's economic policies in the 1980s helped reinforce the independence movement.

As a result of Labour's push for devolution in 1998, Scotland received its own legislature and government, as well as broad powers over regional issues. It has long had its own legal system, but it increasingly differs from the rest of the

United Kingdom on a variety of policies. For example, citizens of Scotland pay no tuition to attend university, unlike other UK citizens, and Scots pay less for health care and prescription drugs than do other UK citizens. Scotland's football federation rejected plans by the British Olympic Association to field all-Britain men's and women's soccer teams for the 2012 London Olympic Games, preferring, like Wales and Northern Ireland, to field its own Scottish national team.[22]

The Labour Party, in coalition with the Liberal Democrats, controlled the Scottish government from 1998 until 2007. The SNP capitalized on an economic revival in Scotland and widespread Scottish opposition to Blair's Iraq War policy to win the 2007 regional elections. Alex Salmond, the SNP leader, became first minister (leader) of an SNP minority government, pledging to hold a referendum on independence from the United Kingdom in the future. Four years later, the 2011 general elections returned Salmond and the SNP to government, giving the Scottish Nationalist Party its first-ever majority government. The SNP's capturing of an absolute majority is even more remarkable because of the mixed PR-SMD electoral system in place in Scotland, established in part to prevent the dominance of a single party. With majority control of the Scottish parliament, Salmond and the SNP have renewed their pledge to hold a referendum on "home rule," announcing in 2012 that the vote will be held in 2014.[23]

The announcement marked another round in the subtle bargaining between Salmond's devolved SNP government and the government of the United Kingdom. Following Salmond's announcement, Prime Minister Cameron reminded the SNP government that a referendum on independence held without the authorization of the British parliament would be unlawful. Cameron further pledged to do all within the power of his government to defend the union, but conceded that the referendum could take place if it were on Westminster's terms. These terms include the demand that the referendum consist of a straight up-or-down vote for independence rather than a three-option plan put forward by the SNP featuring a middle ground option of even greater devolution of authority to the Scottish parliament. Pro-union parties are confident there is insufficient support among the citizens of Scotland to embrace full independence and see no need to risk ceding additional political power. First Minister Salmond responded with a call to allow 16- and 17-year old Scots (who strongly favor independence) to participate in the referendum, a measure resisted by London.[24]

At this point, all such bargaining still begs the question as to whether or not Scotland could viably function as an independent state. First, it is not fully clear whether the United Kingdom would allow Scotland to declare independence. The United Kingdom is a unitary state in which all power emanates from London, and the Scottish government was created (and could be revoked) by an act of Parliament. Scotland also lacks a military with which to defend its sovereignty. Second, it is integrally linked to the United Kingdom. Because countless Scots live and work in the rest of the United Kingdom and vice versa, creating distinct citizenship would be extremely complex. Scotland would lose its economic support from London and its military protection. It sends 59 members to the House of Commons in London; moreover, many prominent UK politicians, including former Labour prime ministers Tony Blair and Gordon Brown, are Scots. Finally, it is not at all clear that a majority of Scots would support independence, even by 2014. Despite the SNP's resounding victory at the polls, a 2011 survey of Scottish adults found only 29 percent in favor of outright independence, 58 percent opposed, and 13 percent undecided.[25]

Terrorist Attacks, Religious Minorities, and "Britishness"

Like the events of September 11, 2001, in the United States, the July 2005 bombings in London—in which Islamic extremists targeted the London transport system, killing 52 and injuring hundreds of commuters—focused the entire political system on preventing future attacks. The bombings and evidence of what some have identified as growing ethnic segregation in British society have prompted debate over issues of multiculturalism and national identity.

Much public scrutiny was directed toward the United Kingdom's Muslim community. The United Kingdom is a relatively homogeneous country in terms of ethnicity and religion, especially when compared with many of the other cases studied in this volume. Islam is currently the second-largest religion there, after Christianity, but less than 3 percent of the population is Muslim. The vast majority of this population has ties to former UK colonies in South Asia. Muslims in the United Kingdom are heavily concentrated in urban areas, especially London, where they make up about 9 percent of the population. After the terrorist attacks, the UK press began to highlight the presence of extremists within the Muslim community. Leaders of that community complained about the wave of anti-Muslim violence that resulted from the 2005 attacks. In this context, the archbishop of Canterbury, the United Kingdom's most important religious official, raised a furor when he observed that many British Muslims did not "relate to the UK legal system" and suggested that adopting parts of Sharia (Islamic religious law) could help "maintain social cohesion."[26]

Others, including Prime Minister David Cameron, have been highly critical of Britain's decades-long policy of multiculturalism, a policy that critics contend has encouraged segregated communities where Islamic extremists can thrive and where local communities live "parallel lives" devoid of a sense of common national identity. These critics also believe that social cohesion and public safety require promoting a British civic identity centered on values of human rights, democracy, social integration, and equality before the law.[27]

Another consequence of the terrorist attacks has been a series of attempts to improve the United Kingdom's law enforcement system. Despite fierce protests from the Liberal Democrats and many within the Labour and Conservative parties, in 2008 the Labour government narrowly passed a law that doubled to 42 days the time that terrorist suspects could be held without being charged with a crime. The government also passed laws that criminalize the glorification of terrorism and the incitement of religious hatred. In an attempt to detect terrorist threats and reduce crime, the United Kingdom has employed the use of millions of surveillance cameras, and it is estimated that there is one surveillance camera for every 14 citizens, making the United Kingdom the most electronically monitored society in the world.[28] These and other measures have given rise to concerns that not just civic identity but also civil liberties in the United Kingdom are in serious jeopardy.

England's 2011 Summer Riots

Although not as deadly as the 2005 London terrorist bombings, riots that broke out in over a dozen cities across England in August of 2011 have also raised questions and stirred debate about civility, inequality and state–society relations in Britain. The riots were sparked by the fatal police shooting of a London resident during an attempted arrest. A peaceful protest in the neighborhood of the shooting turned violent, igniting rioting, looting, and the widespread destruction of property, first across London and then in other cities throughout England over the next few days. Five people were killed and hundreds were injured, including nearly 200 police officers. In all, over 3,000 rioters were arrested and over 1,000 were charged with crimes of theft, arson, assault, and inciting riots.

Images of raw violence, looted storefronts, and burned-out vehicles filled British television screens and prompted a great deal of discussion and introspection among Britons. What were the causes of the riots? David Cameron, speaking from a decidedly Tory position, pointed to moral failings in contemporary British society and blamed the violence largely on criminals and opportunists. Ed

Scene from the aftermath of urban rioting, looting, and destruction during England's 2011 summer riots.

Miliband and others on the political left pointed to the government's austerity measures, growing income inequality, and the absence of opportunities for British urban youth. A study commissioned to investigate the causes of the riots conducted by researchers from the London School of Economics and the *Guardian* newspaper identified a number of contributing factors.[29] The study concluded that criminal opportunism, rising unemployment, shrinking social programs, and growing inequality likely all played a role in igniting and propelling the riots. Some interviewed rioters admitted they participated in the hopes of "getting free stuff." Income inequality in Britain today is at its highest level since the 1930s. A European Union study found that Britain has 600,000 young adults under the age of 25 who have never worked a day in their lives. Government youth service budgets providing social opportunities for the young have in some cities been cut by as much as 75 percent. But beyond these factors, the study determined that the primary cause may have been poor policing. Nearly three-fourths of the rioters interviewed said they had been stopped and searched by the police in the last year, in many cases unfairly. Whatever the causes, the unrest has reminded British politicians and citizens alike that a nation's social fabric is important and must be managed properly and with care. As one British columnist concluded, quoting Martin Luther King, Jr., "a riot is the language of the unheard."[30]

NOTES

1. R. C. van Caenegem, *The Birth of the English Common Law* (Cambridge, UK: Cambridge University Press, 1989).
2. Jeremy Black, *Walpole in Power* (Stroud, UK: Sutton, 2001).
3. For a discussion of the link between economic and democratic development, see Barrington Moore Jr., *Social Origins of Dictatorship and Democracy* (Boston: Beacon Press, 1966).
4. For a discussion of Thatcherism and its effects, see Earl Reitan, *The Thatcher Revolution: Margaret Thatcher, John Major, and Tony Blair, 1979–2001* (Lanham, MD: Rowman and Littlefield, 2003); for her own perspective, see Margaret Thatcher, *The Downing Street Years* (New York: HarperCollins, 1993).
5. For a discussion of the constitution in practice, see Peter Hennessy, *The Hidden Wiring: Unearthing the British Constitution* (London: Victor Gollancz, 1995).
6. Vernon Bogdanor, "An Era of Constitutional Reform," *The Political Quarterly* (September 2011): S53–S64.
7. Monarchy Poll, MORI, June 24, 2007, www.ipsos-mori.com/content/polls-06/monarchy-poll.ashx (accessed 12/29/08). For an interesting discussion of the value of the British monarchy to political life, see Vernon Bogdanor, *The Monarchy and the Constitution* (Oxford, UK: Clarendon Press, 1996).
8. British question time can be seen regularly on the public affairs channel C-SPAN and can be accessed online at www.cspan.org.
9. Meg Russell, "Is the House of Lords Already Reformed?" *Political Quarterly* 74 (July 2003): 311–18.
10. "Breaking the Old Place Up," *The Economist*, November 4, 1999.
11. Philip Lynch and Robert Garner, "The Changing Party System," *Parliamentary Affairs* 58, no. 3 (June 2005): 533–54.
12. Anthony Giddens, *The Third Way: The Renewal of Social Democracy* (Malden, MA: Blackwell, 1998).
13. Mark Garnett and Philip Lynch, *The Conservatives in Crisis* (Manchester, UK: Manchester University Press, 2003).
14. An interesting discussion of the changing nature of class and civil society in Britain can be found in Peter A. Hall, "Great Britain: The Role of Government and the Distribution of Social Capital," in Robert D. Putnam, ed., *Democracies in Flux: The Evolution of Social Change in Contemporary Society* (New York: Oxford University Press, 2002), pp. 21–57.
15. Martin Durham, "Abortion, Gay Rights, and Politics in Britain and America," *Parliamentary Affairs* 58, no. 1 (January 2005): 89–103.
16. For further discussion, see the MORI/*Economist* poll results at www.mori.com/polls/2002/cre.shtml (accessed 8/5/05).
17. John Locke, *Two Treatises on Government: Of Civil Government Book II*, ch. 7, (1689; Electronic Text Center, University of Virginia, 2002), http://religionanddemocracy.lib.virginia.edu/library/tocs/LocTre2.html (accessed 8/5/05).
18. Lawrence D. Freedman, "The Special Relationship: Then and Now," *Foreign Affairs* 85, no. 3 (May/June 2006).
19. David Baker and Philippa Sherrington, "Britain and Europe: The Dog That Didn't Bark," *Parliamentary Affairs* 58, no. 2 (April 2005): 303–17.
20. Pew Research Center for the People and the Press, http://people-press.org/reports/display.php3?ReportID5175 (accessed 8/5/09).

21. "NATO Libya Coalition Shows Cracks," *Washington Post*, April 14, 2011.

22. Jeré Longman and Sarah Lyall, "A British Soccer Team? What's That? Say Scots, Welsh and Irish," *New York Times*, September 19, 2011.

23. W. Elliot Bulmer, "An Analysis of the Scottish National Party's Draft Constitution for Scotland," *Parliamentary Affairs* 64, no. 4 (October 2011): 674–93.

24. See "Scotland's Referendum: If at first you don't succeed," *The Economist*, January 14, 2012. For a fascinating comparison of independence movements in Scotland and Quebec, see Peter Lynch, "Scottish Independence, the Quebec Model of Seccession, and the Future of the Scottish National Party," *Nationalism and Ethnic Politics* 11 (2005): 503–31.

25. For a good summary of the polling on Scottish independence, see http://ukpollingreport.co.uk/blog/archives/3570 (accessed 11/27/11).

26. http://news.bbc.co.uk/1/hi/uk/7232661.stm (accessed 6/30/08).

27. See John F. Burns, "Cameron Criticizes 'Multiculturalism' in Britain," *New York Times*, February 5, 2011, and Dominic Casciani, "Segregated Britain?" at http://news.bbc.co.uk/2/hi/uk_news/4270010.stm (accessed 11/28/11).

28. http://news.bbc.co.uk/1/hi/uk/6108496.stm (accessed 6/15/08).

29. "Reading the Riots: Investigating England's Summer of Disorder" www.guardian.co.uk/uk/series/reading-the-riots (accessed 2/6/12).

30. Gary Younge, "Indifferent elites, poverty and police brutality—all reasons to riot in the UK," *The Guardian*, December 4, 2011.

KEY TERMS

Blair, Tony Labour prime minister from 1997 to 2007

cabinet Top members of the UK government who assist the prime minister and run the major ministries

Cameron, David Leader of the Conservatives; the prime minister and head of the ruling coalition government since 2010

Celtic fringe Refers to Scotland and Wales, which were not conquered by the Angles and Saxons

Clegg, Nick Leader of the Liberal Democrats, the third-largest political party, and deputy prime minister in the coalition government since 2010

collective responsibility Tradition that requires all members of the cabinet either to support government policy or to resign

collectivist consensus Postwar consensus between the United Kingdom's major parties to build and sustain a welfare state

common law Legal system based on custom and precedent rather than formal legal codes

Commonwealth Organization that includes the United Kingdom and most of its former colonies

Confederation of British Industry (CBI) The United Kingdom's most important group representing the private sector

Conservatives (Tories) One of the United Kingdom's two largest parties, since 2010 it has led a coalition government with the the Liberal Democratic Party

Crown Refers to the British monarchy and sometimes to the British state

English Civil War Seventeenth-century conflict between Parliament and the monarch that temporarily eliminated and Permanently weakened the monarchy

Good Friday Agreement Historic 1998 accord between Protestants and Catholics in Northern Ireland that ended decades of violence

hereditary peers Seats in the House of Lords that were granted to aristocratic families in perpetuity but were largely eliminated by recent legislation

House of Commons Lower house of the UK legislature

House of Lords Upper house of the UK legislature, whose reform is currently being debated

"hung parliament" An election result in which no party wins a majority of parliamentary seats, such as the 2010 House of Commons general election

Labour Party One of the United Kingdom's two largest parties, since 2010 it has been the party in opposition

Liberals (Whigs) The United Kingdom's historic first opposition party, and one of its two major political parties until the early twentieth century

life peers Distinguished members of society who are given lifetime appointments to the House of Lords

Magna Carta The 1215 document signed by King John that set the precedent for limited monarchical powers

majoritarian Term describing the virtually unchecked power of a parliamentary majority in the UK political system

member of Parliament (MP) An individual legislator in the House of Commons

Miliband, Ed Leader of the opposition Labour Party since 2010

Northern Ireland Northeastern portion of Ireland that is part of the United Kingdom, also known as Ulster

Parliament Name of the UK legislature

prime minister Head of government

quangos Quasi-autonomous nongovernmental organizations that assist the government in making policy

Scottish Nationalist Party (SNP) The party seeking Scottish independence, and currently in control of the Scottish regional government

Thatcher, Margaret Conservative prime minister from 1979 to 1990

Third Way Term describing recent policies of the Labour Party that embrace the free market

Trades Union Congress (TUC) The United Kingdom's largest trade union confederation

United Kingdom of Great Britain and Northern Ireland Official name of the British state

vote of no confidence Legislative check on government whereby a government deems a measure to be of high importance, and if that measure fails to pass the legislature, either the government must resign in favor of another leader or new parliamentary elections must be called

WEB LINKS

BritainUSA, web site of the British government in the United States (www.britain-info.org)

British Broadcasting Corporation (www.news.bbc.co.uk)

British Politics Group (www.uc.edu/bpg)

British Prime Minister (www.pm.gov.uk)

Conflict Archive on the Internet, on conflict and politics in Northern Ireland, 1968 to the present (www.cain.ulst.ac.uk)

Foreign and Commonwealth Office (www.fco.gov.uk)

London University, on constitutional reform (www.ucl.ac.uk/constitution-unit)

Parliament (www.parliament.uk)

Scottish Parliament (www.scottish.parliament.uk)

Welsh Assembly (www.wales.gov.uk)

 Visit StudySpace for quizzes and other review material.
www.norton.com/studyspace

- **Vocabulary Flashcards of All Key Terms**
- **Country Review Quizzes**
- **Interactive Map Tours**

3

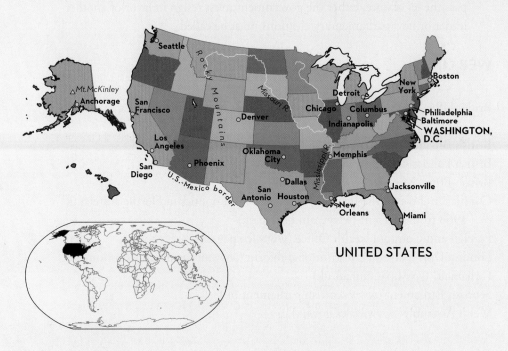

UNITED STATES

**HEAD OF STATE
AND GOVERNMENT:**
President Barack Obama (since
January 20, 2009)

CAPITAL:
Washington, District of Columbia

TOTAL LAND SIZE:
9,161,966 sq km (3rd)

POPULATION:
314 million (3rd)

TOTAL GDP AT PPP:
$14.66 trillion (1st)

GDP PER CAPITA AT PPP:
$47,200 (11th)

**HUMAN DEVELOPMENT
INDEX RANKING:**
4th

UNITED STATES

Introduction

Why Study This Case?

Some readers may believe that the United States is the standard against which to measure advanced industrial democracies. After all, the United States is governed by the oldest written constitution still in effect and it is the world's greatest military and economic power. Nevertheless, compared with other advanced capitalist democracies, the United States is best viewed as an anomaly full of paradoxes. It is a large and wealthy nation with a relatively weak state. The United States has a highly legitimate political regime and enjoys widespread adherence to the rule of law despite having a political system deliberately designed to prevent decisive and coherent policy making. U.S. citizens are deeply proud of their state but distrust it and its bureaucracy in far greater numbers than the citizens of other industrialized democracies distrust theirs. Its political system has long been dominated by two political parties, but those parties are themselves relatively weak, and at times undisciplined. It has a vibrant civil society but very low voter turnout. The United States is a secular democracy in which religion continues to play a comparatively large role in politics and society. It began as a society of immigrants, and national and regional identities are still in flux because of migration and geographic mobility. The United States has more wealth and more social mobility than any other democracy, but is plagued by persistent inequality and the presence of an impoverished underclass more characteristic of developing countries. The United States leads the world in medical technology, but has more citizens without medical insurance than any other advanced democracy. The United States, blessed with peaceful borders and isolation from major world conflicts, initially favored an isolationist foreign policy, but has in recent decades intervened militarily in numerous global conflicts.

It is especially vital to understand the unusual workings of the U.S. political system given the country's tremendous power in today's world. The importance of U.S. technology, culture, military power, and economic might is undeniable, and the projection of those strengths is often a source of both admiration and resentment by citizens of other countries.

The twenty-first century has posed new challenges and new questions to the U.S. political system. A bitter dispute over a closely contested presidential election in 2000 raised serious doubts about the integrity of the electoral system and the fairness of the political system. A nation that had become assured of its military might and sovereignty suddenly felt vulnerable after the terrorist attacks of September 11, 2001. The U.S.-led invasion of Iraq in 2003 deeply polarized politics in the United States, and ongoing conflict in Afghanistan has been costly in both lives and wealth. Economic and international concerns have led many Americans to believe that their country's political and economic systems must undergo major changes in order to respond to the challenges of the future, which was reflected in the 2008 election of Barack Obama. Once in office, and especially after the victory of conservative Republicans in the 2010 midterm elections, Obama saw much of his reform agenda fall victim to a deeply polarized legislature and a major economic recession. A central question for this case is: Can the oldest constitutional democracy in the world, designed to prevent rapid change, deliver the necessary reforms to meet the challenges of the present and future?

Major Geographic and Demographic Features

By 2012, the population of the United States exceeded 310 million, third in the world after China and India. In terms of land size, the United States also ranks third in the world; it is slightly larger than Brazil and China but about half the size of Russia and slightly smaller than Canada. The United States occupies the central portion of the North American continent, sandwiched between Canada and Mexico, spanning from the Pacific to the Atlantic Ocean. It comprises 48 contiguous states (and the District of Columbia), Alaska (at the extreme northwest of the continent), and the island state of Hawaii, located about 2,100 miles west of the California coast. In addition, it possesses numerous overseas territories in the Caribbean and the Pacific. U.S. states are extremely diverse in area, population, geography, climate, and culture.

The United States is blessed with stunning geographic and climatic diversity. Almost half its territory is made up of agriculturally rich lowlands that have become the world's breadbasket. Its climatic diversity allows for the production of food year-round. Several major mountain ranges divide the continental United States, but its extensive coastline and navigable river systems facilitate trade and commerce. The United States is richly endowed with natural resources, including minerals, gas, and oil.

For an industrial democracy, its population is unusual in some ways. Continually replenished by immigration, the population has continued to grow more than that of other industrialized democracies, and the United States currently has a birth rate higher than both China's and Brazil's. As a result, unlike Japan and some European countries, the United States does not face a labor shortage in the foreseeable future.

The U.S. population is also more geographically mobile than is common in most industrialized democracies. Despite a very high level of home ownership, approximately one in seven Americans moves from one house to another in a given year. In recent decades, this mobility has hurt the old industrial core of the Northeast and the Midwest, whose cities have lost population and wealth, and has favored the Southwest and the West.

Historical Development of the State

AMERICA AND THE ARRIVAL OF THE EUROPEAN COLONIZERS

The origins of the U.S. state can be found in the geographic expansion of European states in the early sixteenth century. A number of European countries began to explore and establish trading missions in the eastern part of the future United States. The French, the Dutch, the Spanish, and the English all attempted to form permanent settlements there.

English citizens migrated to America in search of land, which was becoming scarce in England, and religious freedom. **Puritans**, radical Protestants, constituted a large portion of the early English settlers in North America. English colonists began to establish permanent settlements in the early seventeenth century in present-day Virginia and Massachusetts. The Virginia colony began as a business venture and developed into a slave-based plantation society geared toward the production of tobacco and dominated by white landowners. The Massachusetts colonies were settled largely by Puritans and developed into a society of small family farmers. Although Massachusetts was established by settlers who had been persecuted for their religious beliefs in

England, the colonies themselves were characterized by religious intolerance and repression.

By 1640, England had established six of the 13 colonies that would later form the United States. By the 1680s the English had established six additional colonies, including New York, which was taken from the Dutch, and Pennsylvania. The early colonists faced numerous challenges, including food shortages, disease, isolation from England, and understandable resistance by Native Americans.

TIMELINE OF POLITICAL DEVELOPMENT

YEAR	EVENT
1607	First permanent English settlement in America
1754–63	French and Indian War ends the French Empire in America
1775–83	American Revolution is fought
1776	Declaration of Independence is signed
1781	Articles of Confederation ratified
1788	U.S. Constitution ratified
1803	Louisiana Purchase expands the U.S. frontier westward
1846–48	Mexican War is fought, further expanding U.S. territory
1861–65	Civil War takes place
1865	Thirteenth Amendment to the Constitution, abolishing slavery, is ratified
1903–20	Progressive era
1933–38	Era of the New Deal
1955–65	Civil rights movement takes place
2001–	War on terrorism
2008	Barack Obama elected president

NATIVE AMERICANS: "ETHNIC CLEANSING" AS THE BASIS FOR WESTERN EXPANSION

Though it is convenient to begin our discussion of the origins of the American political system with the establishment of the English colonies in the seventeenth century, more than 100 indigenous tribes inhabited what is now the United States, and they had their own political regimes. With the arrival of Europeans, many Native American societies collaborated with or tolerated the colonists, while others violently resisted.

The chief cause of the declining indigenous population after the arrival of Europeans was disease, against which Native Americans lacked resistance. But Native American societies were also subject to military repression, murder, and forced relocation. One infamous example was the 1830 Indian Removal Act, initiated by President Andrew Jackson, which evicted the Cherokee and other tribes from their homelands in the southeastern United States and forced them to relocate to reservations in distant Oklahoma. The forced removal resulted in the deaths of thousands of Native Americans. The eviction of indigenous peoples by European colonizers in the United States bears numerous similarities to the Afrikaner treatment of blacks in South Africa.

By the late seventeenth century, the British had begun to assert more control over their remote North American colonies. The British government, with the Navigation Act of 1651, sought to force the colonies to conduct their trade using only English ships, thereby creating colonial dependency. By the early eighteenth century the British government had allowed elected legislatures to be established in the colonies, transplanting its own embryonic democratic institutions, and had imposed royally appointed colonial governors.

The colonies grew very rapidly, fueled by a high birth rate, the importation of enslaved Africans, mostly to the southern colonies, and continued emigration from England and other European countries. For Europeans, the lure of a seemingly endless supply of land was irresistible. Indeed, since colonial days, America has been viewed by immigrants worldwide as a land of opportunity and promise.

Between the 1680s and the 1760s the English colonists faced numerous foes. They fought indigenous tribes whose land they had taken. They also fought with the growing Spanish and French empires in America, who often allied themselves with Native American tribes and threatened to limit the English settlers' prospects for colonial expansion. In the French and Indian War (1754–63), the

British effectively defeated the French Empire in North America and weakened the Spanish Empire (with Spain giving up claims to Florida in 1763). At the end of the French and Indian War, Britain inherited a vast empire in America that would prove both costly and difficult to control.

THE REVOLUTION AND THE BIRTH OF A NEW STATE

The United States was the first major colony to rebel successfully against European colonial rule, leading one scholar to call it "the first new nation."[1] At its core, the American Revolution was caused by a conflict between two sovereignties: the sovereignty of the English king and Parliament, and the sovereignty of the colonial legislatures that had been established in America. Both believed that they had the exclusive right to raise the taxes paid by colonists. In the 1760s, the British Parliament had unilaterally passed a number of taxes on colonists that sparked a spiral of colonial petitions, protests, boycotts, and acts of civil disobedience. The British responded by disbanding the colonial legislatures and repressing protest with military force. In the Boston Massacre (1770), British soldiers attacked a mob of colonists, further fueling the colonists' opposition to British intervention in colonial affairs. Colonial militias clashed with British military forces, a precursor to the impending revolution.

In 1774, in response to British repression, anti-British colonial elites convened a Continental Congress in Philadelphia, comprised of delegates from each of the 13 colonies. It asserted the exclusive right of the colonial legislatures to raise taxes. The Second Continental Congress, meeting in 1775, created a Continental Army, with **George Washington** at its command. In 1776, the Congress appointed a committee to draft a constitution and approve the **Declaration of Independence**.

The declaration of a new state and a new regime evoked an attack by a large and powerful British army. In the **American Revolution** (1775–83), the colonists were greatly outnumbered but were aided by their knowledge of the terrain and an alliance with France, an enemy of England. With the defeat of the British at Yorktown, Virginia, in 1783, Britain granted independence to the 13 rebellious American colonies.

THE CONSOLIDATION OF A DEMOCRATIC REPUBLIC AND THE DEBATE OVER THE ROLE OF THE STATE

A unique theme of the American Revolution was its opposition to a British state perceived as overbearing. Distrust of a strong state is still a feature of U.S. politics, but it presented special challenges during the Revolution. Fighting a war against the British required a central authority transcending the 13 colonial governments, each of which had begun functioning under new constitutions. The **Articles of Confederation**, approved in 1781, created a loose alliance of sovereign states. It featured a unicameral legislature with a single vote for each state. The Confederation Congress assumed important powers regarding conflicts between states and the regulation of settlement to the west, but it required unanimity for the passage of all legislation, lacked a national executive, and did not have the ability to raise taxes or create a national currency. This weak central state made it difficult for the country to conduct foreign relations, control inflation, or carry out international trade.

In response to those problems, a Constitutional Convention of state delegates was held in 1787 to consider a stronger national state. The resulting constitutional document was a compromise between advocates of a strong federal state and supporters of sovereignty for the individual states. After a series of compromises, the states ratified the new constitution in 1788, effectively creating a new national state and a new political regime.

The first U.S. Congress met in 1789. It passed legislation that strengthened the state, built a federal judiciary, and imposed a tariff on imports to fund federal expenditures. It also attempted to address the concerns of those who feared the power of a strong central state, by passing 12 amendments to the Constitution, ten of which were ratified by the states and became known collectively as the **Bill of Rights**. The ten constitutional amendments that constitute the Bill of Rights aim in large part to protect the rights of individuals against the federal government.

A major political division in the young American republic was between **Federalists**, led by President Washington's secretary of the treasury, Alexander Hamilton, and **Democratic-Republicans**, led by the future president Thomas Jefferson. Hamilton, who advocated a strong central state, was responsible for consolidating the Revolutionary War debt incurred by the states, imposing a federal excise tax, and creating a federal bank to print and regulate currency. When Jefferson became president in 1801, he moved to reduce the power of the U.S. federal government by paying off the national debt, repealing the excise tax, and reducing the size of the federal bureaucracy and the military. At the same time, Jefferson was responsible for a massive increase in the territory of the United States when he acquired much of France's remaining North American territory in the **Louisiana Purchase** (1803). The Louisiana Territory extended America's westward borders to the Rocky Mountains and expedited future westward migration.

THE MOVE WEST AND EXPANSION OF THE STATE

With the Louisiana Purchase in 1803, acquisition of Florida from Spain in 1819, and end of the War of 1812 with Britain in 1815, Americans were free to move westward. This movement, like the original European settlements, came at the expense of Native Americans. As Americans moved westward in search of land to be used for agriculture, the United States used legislation and military force to contain, relocate, or exterminate Native American populations. The westward expansion continued with the 1845 annexation of Texas, a Mexican territory prior to a successful separatist movement led by non-Hispanic Americans. The United States declared war on Mexico in 1846 (the Mexican War, also known as the **Mexican-American War**) to protect its acquisition of Texas and to lay claim to vast Mexican territories in present-day Arizona, California, Colorado, Nevada, New Mexico, Utah, and Wyoming. In all, the rapidly expanding United States gained one-third of Mexico's territory through military conquest, further encouraging the flood of migrants westward.

CIVIL WAR AND THE THREAT TO UNITY

The American Revolution had temporarily united the English colonies, and under George Washington's leadership and the work of Federalist leaders, the foundations of a strong central state were constructed. But the Federalist project was always controversial, and the creation of a unified United States could not eliminate simmering regional differences that threatened to destroy the Union. These differences culminated in the **Civil War** (1861–65). At its roots were the divergent paths of socioeconomic development in the southern and northern regions of the country. While the North experienced an industrial boom based on its prosperous cities, southern agriculture was still based on slave labor and export-oriented plantations.

In order to gain agreement on a federal constitution, the founders of the Republic had largely sidestepped the issue of slavery. Slavery had been abolished in the North after the Revolution, but the Constitution tolerated it. A number of factors brought the issue of slavery to center stage by the mid-nineteenth century. First, the westward expansion of the United States raised the contentious issue of whether new territories would be "slave" states or "free" states. Then, in the first half of the nineteenth century, slavery was banned by England and most of Latin America, and the northern states increasingly viewed the South as an anachronistic threat to free-market capitalism based on individual liberty and a free labor market. Finally, the early nineteenth century saw the emergence of a rapidly growing abolition movement, largely in the North, which viewed slavery as both undemocratic and anathema to Christian values.

The 1860 election of Abraham Lincoln and the rise to power of the new anti-slavery Republican Party provoked the secession of 11 southern states and the commencement of the Civil War. The southern states formed a rebel state, called the Confederate States of America, and enacted their own constitution, which guaranteed the institution of slavery.

During the war, the North held important advantages over the South in terms of population (it was more than twice as large), wealth, and industry. Nevertheless, the South had the advantage of playing defense on difficult terrain, and it hoped to prolong the war long enough to wear down the northern invaders. The long and bloody conflict cost an estimated three-quarters of a million lives before the South was defeated in 1865 and the Union was preserved. In the same year, the **Thirteenth Amendment** to the Constitution, abolishing slavery, was ratified.

The importance of the Civil War in the development of the U.S. state was immense. The federal government had increased spending and built a huge army in order to subdue the South. It also gained enormous power through its role in reforming the South and reintegrating the southern states into the Union. This use of state power to end race-based slavery and promote democratic values established an important precedent.

THE PROGRESSIVE ERA AND THE GROWTH OF STATE POWER

The U.S. state used its newfound clout to promote democratic reform during the **Progressive era** (1903–20). Progressives sought to use the federal state to restrict the power of big business, attack corruption, and address inequality. Under President Theodore Roosevelt (1901–09) the federal government attacked monopolistic businesses and enhanced the ability of the Interstate Commerce Commission to regulate trade among the states. In order to protect public land from private development, Roosevelt created a vast system of national parks. Under President Woodrow Wilson (1913–21), laws were passed to curb further the power of large monopolies and to establish the centralized Federal Reserve System as a national lender of last resort. Perhaps the single greatest impetus for the growth of a centralized state was the adoption of the Sixteenth Amendment in 1913, which gave Congress authority to levy a national income tax. In addition, Wilson took the United States into World War I, despite considerable popular opposition, an act that dramatically increased the size and power of the state.

THE GREAT DEPRESSION AND THE NEW DEAL

The stock market crash of 1929 and the ensuing Great Depression devastated the U.S. economy. One-quarter of the workforce lost jobs, the gross domestic product (GDP) dropped by about one-third, and there were massive bankruptcies and bank failures. The economic crisis was a pivotal factor in the 1932 election of the Democratic Party candidate Franklin D. Roosevelt and the implementation of a set of social democratic welfare policies known collectively as the **New Deal**.

The New Deal policies were aimed at ameliorating the economic crisis, but their long-term impact was to increase dramatically the power of the U.S. state. Despite opposition from conservatives and the Supreme Court, Roosevelt, with a Democratic majority in both houses of Congress, passed a series of unprecedented measures. Some of the most controversial pieces of legislation guaranteed workers the right to bargain collectively with employers, created state agencies to generate electric power, provided state subsidies to farmers who agreed to limit production, and heavily regulated the stock market. In order to carry out these policies, a massive extension of the state bureaucracy and the creation of numerous state agencies, such as the Securities and Exchange Commission and the National Labor Relations Board, were needed. Many of those agencies still exist today. The Social Security Act (1935) established the foundation for the U.S. welfare state (though much later and much less comprehensively than in many northern European countries), creating unemployment insurance, retiree pensions, and other social welfare measures.

Although these New Deal policies increased the role of the state, the entry of the United States into World War II enhanced state power even further. The military grew rapidly, the state set wages and prices, and it directly intervened in private enterprise to serve the war effort. In wartime, the state trampled on civil liberties, censoring the press and sending thousands of citizens of Japanese ancestry to prison camps. The United States emerged from World War II a global power, and the state apparatus expanded to meet the perceived needs and demands of this rising hegemon. In the context of the Cold War with the Soviet Union, the state took domestic measures to persecute suspected Communists, firing them from government positions. Internationally, the United States maintained a large standing army in peacetime, extended its international commitments, and intervened in the domestic affairs of other states.

STRUGGLING FOR DEMOCRATIC RIGHTS: THE CIVIL RIGHTS MOVEMENT AND THE WAR ON POVERTY

Despite constitutional protections and the defeat of the South in the Civil War, U.S. democracy suffered from the legacy of slavery. Widespread discrimination against African Americans continued, most notably in the South but also in the North. After World War II (in which African Americans served and made valuable contributions), a growing **civil rights movement**, often backed by the federal government and the federal judiciary, advocated an end to all forms of racial discrimination.

The struggle for civil rights was only one of the popular reform movements that crystallized in the 1960s. During that decade, many U.S. citizens began to view economic inequality, gender discrimination, and environmental degradation by private business as impediments to democracy. In the mid-1960s, popular movements focused on those concerns combined with growing popular opposition to the **Vietnam War**, contributing to an atmosphere of unrest and rebellion.

Partly in response to popular pressure, the U.S. government attempted to address a number of socioeconomic problems. Under President John F. Kennedy (1961–63), the federal government played a crucial role in imposing civil rights legislation on recalcitrant southern states. President Lyndon Johnson (1963–69) announced a **War on Poverty**, with a dramatic increase in federal spending to combat economic inequality. Johnson launched new programs and founded new state institutions to protect the environment, build low-income housing, fund the arts, and redress racial discrimination. The growing state role in the economy and society continued under the Republican president Richard Nixon (1969–74), who imposed wage and price controls to stem inflation and signed into law a measure that provided food stamps to the poorest Americans.

Like Margaret Thatcher, his neoliberal counterpart in Britain, President Ronald Reagan (1981–89) was elected on a platform of reversing the trend toward increased state involvement in the economy. Reagan viewed government as "the problem, not the solution," and rode to power on a wave of conservatism critical of the preceding decades of state-led social activism. Reagan cut social spending and reduced taxes while dramatically increasing defense spending. The reform of a welfare state widely viewed as bloated and inefficient continued under the Democratic president Bill Clinton (1993–2001) and the Republican president **George W. Bush** (2001–08). However, these Bush presidency reforms occurred alongside massive increases in spending on both defense and domestic policies. The 2008 election of **Barack Obama**, the first African American president, took place amid a major economic crisis. Obama campaigned on a platform that included health care reform and the gradual withdrawal of U.S. troops from Iraq.

In retrospect, it is clear that the United States was fortunate to build and consolidate its state under extremely favorable conditions. It did not have to contend with hostile neighbors and, after its founding, faced no appreciable external threats to its sovereignty. The development of the U.S. state during its first two centuries also coincided with the generally steady success of the economy and the steady expansion of U.S. power abroad.

Political Regime

Because of their fresh experience with, and deep distrust of, authoritarian colonial rule, the Founders of the United States established a democratic regime governed by the **rule of law**. This means that government can act and citizens can be punished only as authorized by legal statute, all citizens are equal before the law, and no one is above the law, not even political leaders. Those concepts were framed in a written constitution establishing a democratic regime grounded in rational-legal legitimacy.

But the rule of law by itself was judged insufficient. The power of legitimate government in the hands of a misguided minority or even a well-intentioned majority could still lead to tyranny. Wariness about this possibility led the Founders to establish a liberal democratic political system with institutions intentionally designed to weaken the power and authority of the state. Those institutions included federalism, the separation of powers, and the Bill of Rights. In a sense, the legitimacy of the state was based on its inherent weakness. But this raised a dilemma: How could a state and its elected government manage from a position of weakness the tasks of leading a new and growing nation facing a host of increasingly complex challenges?

The ongoing effort to resolve that dilemma required two regimes in the eighteenth century, a civil war in the nineteenth century, and a dramatic strengthening of central government authority in the twentieth century. In 1777, the Continental Congress established the new nation's first regime under the Articles of Confederation and Perpetual Union. The Articles called for a decentralized confederation of highly autonomous states that vested most authority in the individual states. The ineffectiveness and insufficiency of this confederal regime grew increasingly apparent as the new republic faced potential threats of internal rebellion and costly foreign trade disputes. By 1787, the Articles of Confederation had been jettisoned, replaced by an entirely new constitution, which became the codified embodiment of U.S. rule of law. Inaugurated in 1789, the Constitution established a representative democratic regime governed by a presidential system. The following section examines the institutional components of this regime, including its guiding principles of federalism and separation of powers.

Political Institutions

THE CONSTITUTION

In a nation governed by the rule of law, this 1789 document constituting the regime became all-important. The Constitution of the United States of America was passed in large part as a compromise: between less and more populous states, between northern merchants and southern planters, between slaveholders and those not holding slaves, and between Federalists (who supported a strong central government) and Antifederalists (who advocated states' rights and preferred the decentralized confederal status quo). But the Constitution's framers and citizens on both sides of the debate shared two characteristics: a fear of too much government in the form of an overbearing central authority, and the recognition that the Articles of Confederation had provided too little government. The constitutional compromise was one of strengthened but nonetheless limited government checked by **federalism**, which divides governing authority between the national and state governments; the **separation of powers**, which prevents any one branch or office of government from dominating; and the Bill of Rights, which protects the freedoms of individual citizens. In an unprecedented way, the U.S. Constitution created, tempered, and buffered three sovereign spheres—national, state, and individual—within a single political system.

The U.S. Constitution also stands out as the oldest written constitution still in force. Although it has been regularly interpreted by judicial action and occasionally amended (27 times in total), it has been remarkably durable—indeed, it has proven difficult even to amend. Most of it remains fully in effect after more than two centuries, guiding U.S. politics and policy making under circumstances that could hardly have been imagined by its framers. For better or worse, it has served as the model for constituting the regimes of many newly established countries, and its guiding principles of federalism and separation of powers have become standards for numerous democracies.

The Branches of Government

At the national level, the power of government is shared by three institutions: a president; a bicameral legislature (Congress); and a judiciary, led by the Supreme Court, which has the power to interpret the Constitution. The framers put in place several institutions designed to check and balance the powers of each respective branch of government. For example, the upper chamber of the legislature (the **Senate**) is given the authority to approve or disapprove executive appointments and to ratify or not ratify treaties. Both the Senate and the **House of Representatives** (the House) can refuse to pass legislation. The House can impeach, and the Senate can convict and remove from office, a president or a federal judge (for grievous offenses). The executive (the president) can veto legislation passed by the legislature and appoint judges to the judiciary. The judges, once appointed, have lifetime tenure and serve without political oversight. Most significantly, they have the power of concrete judicial review, meaning they can interpret the Constitution and void any act of the other two branches that they deem unconstitutional, if that act is brought before them in a court case. Ultimately, the framers sought to give Congress the upper hand, allowing it to override a presidential veto of legislation (with a two-thirds majority) and to overturn a constitutional decision of the Supreme Court by amending the Constitution (statutory interpretations can be overturned by a simple majority).

The Constitution's framers also intentionally gave each branch sources of legitimacy. Unlike a parliamentary system, in which executive authority and legislative authority are fused, and only members of parliament are directly accountable to voters, the U.S. system seats its president and members of the legislative chambers in separate elections. Separate branches and separate elections can also allow a third possible check on power: divided government, in which different parties

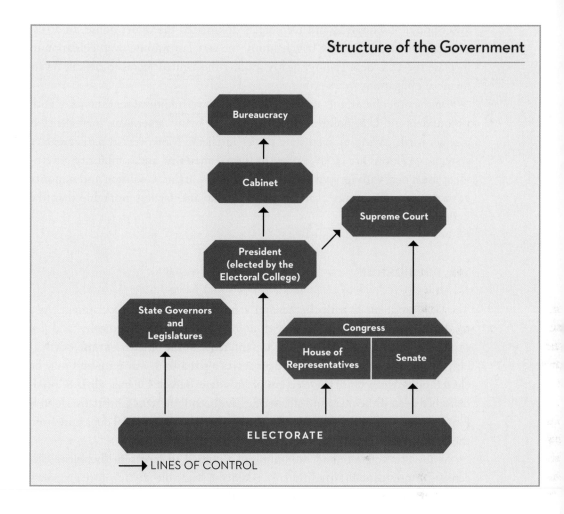

Structure of the Government

- Bureaucracy
- Cabinet
- Supreme Court
- President (elected by the Electoral College)
- State Governors and Legislatures
- Congress
  - House of Representatives
  - Senate
- ELECTORATE

→ LINES OF CONTROL

control the executive and legislative branches. Although a single party has often dominated both, the United States has experienced divided government over 40 percent of the time since 1830 and nearly 60 percent of the time since the end of World War II. Thus, what politicians and analysts often criticize as the tendency for American policy-making "gridlock" is an intended consequence of the system of checks and balances. It fosters a state with weak autonomy and a relatively fragmented policy-making process. This formula has led some observers to argue that the United States would be better served by a parliamentary system, which can respond more decisively to threats or needs and can change the executive quickly when it has lost the support of the legislature. The propensity toward gridlock was in evidence after the 2010 midterm elections, when Republicans controlled the lower house of Congress, and Democrats dominated the upper house. In 2011, a bitterly divided legislature haggled until the very last minute over legislation to increase the U.S. debt ceiling, nearly leading the United States to default on its financial obligations.

On the other hand, this system reflects the powerful liberal sentiments of both its founders and U.S. political culture today. For many Americans, inefficiency is a price worth paying to keep state power in check. Moreover, in parliamentary systems, coalitions are often needed to form a majority, and a minority government must deal with its own sort of divided government. Coalition and minority governments, it is argued, can be far less stable and far less workable than the U.S. system.

THE PRESIDENCY

The U.S. president is both the head of state and the head of government. As a result, the presidency is invested with a great deal of formal authority, and key presidents have expanded the power and influence of the office over time, particularly in the past century. The president serves a fixed four-year term and may be elected only twice. Until the election of President Barack Obama, all U.S. presidents had been white men, and all but one have been Protestant Christians. (John F. Kennedy was Catholic.) Obama's election was clearly a substantial departure from the norm in this regard.

As the head of state and the only leader elected to represent the entire citizenry, the president has traditionally taken the lead role in U.S. foreign policy (although treaties are subject to approval of the Senate). The president is also commander in chief of the military. As head of government, the president—similar to a prime minister—is also responsible for managing the day-to-day affairs of the government and makes senior appointments to the executive and judicial branches (again, with approval of the Senate). Moreover, the president can initiate proposals for legislative action and veto legislative bills.

The president also manages an enormous bureaucracy, which has mushroomed over the years so that the civilian workforce now approaches 3 million employees, with the assistance of a **cabinet** composed mostly of the heads of key departments, offices, and agencies. Unlike its parliamentary counterparts, for which the cabinet is the government, the U.S. Cabinet has no legal authority or standing; the influence of its officers and the institution, moreover, has varied from president to president. Some presidents come to rely upon a smaller inner cabinet (including, for example, the chief adviser of the National Security Council, a group of officials in the Executive Office of the President) or an informal "kitchen" cabinet of trusted advisers who may not be department heads. The U.S. bureaucracy is technically responsible to the executive branch and is further constrained by the legislature's control of its many budgets. In some respects, U.S. bureaucrats lack both the autonomy and the respect historically accorded to their counterparts in countries such as France, Germany, and Japan. (*Bureaucrat* and *bureaucracy* remain derogatory terms to many Americans.)

With a few exceptions (such as Andrew Jackson in the 1830s and Abraham Lincoln in the 1860s), presidents prior to the twentieth century were relatively weak leaders who exerted little political influence. The White House and the Executive Office of the President strengthened considerably over the course of the twentieth century, something seen in executive institutions in other advanced democracies. In recent years the public has expected, and presidents have sought to deliver, a strong executive offering genuine if not dominant leadership. Predictably, both the legislative and the judicial branches have sought to challenge and check this growing influence.

THE LEGISLATURE

The framers of the Constitution intended Congress to be the dominant branch of the U.S. government. In many ways, despite the growing influence of the presidency and the substantial clout of the Supreme Court, this remains the case. Scholars have argued that the U.S. Congress is "the only national representative assembly that can actually be said to govern."[2] They note that although most countries today have some form of national legislature, the legislatures in authoritarian systems do little more than affirm and legitimate the decisions of the political leadership. And although the parliamentary democracies of western Europe and Japan possess the authority to say no to the executive (at the risk, in many cases, of having the parliament dissolved), those assemblies have less power to modify or initiate legislation. Amongst the world's legislatures, only the U.S. Congress has the degree authority that it has.

The Constitution reserves the supreme power—the power to legislate—for Congress. It also gives Congress the power of the purse: that is, sole authority to appropriate funds, and thus to control the way in which its laws are implemented. Whereas the U.S. Congress never accepts the president's annual budget without making its own significant adjustments, governments in Britain and Japan can anticipate their parliaments' acceptance of their budgets without changes.

Another indication of the framers' appreciation for congressional power was their decision to divide the legislature against itself by making it bicameral. The House of Representatives consists of 435 members (a number unchanged since 1910), who are elected to two-year terms in single-member plurality districts. The number of seats and districts allotted to each state is determined by and distributed according to each state's population. For example, following the 2010 national census, Texas saw an increase in its allotment of House seats from 34 to 38, and New York's seat allotment dropped from 29 to 27 based on changes in population; Wyoming retained its single seat. In 1789, there was an average of 1 representative for every 30,000 people; in 1910, the average was more than 200,000; since 2010, each member of Congress has represented more than 700,000 citizens on average.

There are 100 members of the Senate, each serving staggered terms of six years, with one-third of the body elected every two years. Since 1913, senators have also been elected in single-member plurality districts; prior to that, they were elected indirectly by the state legislatures. Each state is allotted two seats regardless of its population, making most senate districts far larger than those in the House. In

DIFFERENT CHAMBERS, DIFFERENT ROLES

Given the differences in size, tenure, and assigned responsibilities, it is not surprising that the two chambers of Congress play different roles. The Senate is authorized to ratify treaties and approve presidential appointments, whereas the House is given exclusive power to originate tax and revenue bills. The Senate tends to be more deliberative, providing a forum for wide-ranging opinions and topics, whereas the House is more centralized and places strict limits on debate. Because they serve a larger and more diverse constituency, senators tend to be less specialized, less partisan, and more hesitant to take a position that might offend any major portion of their broad base of voters. House representatives, in contrast, stand for election every two years and are by necessity more attuned to the needs and interests of their more narrowly defined constituencies. House members tend to be more specialized in their expertise and less reliant on a staff. The House is generally more politicized and partisan. Whereas senators are more likely to cross the aisle to form an alliance or vote with members of the opposing party on an important issue, representatives are generally more likely to vote along partisan lines.

California, for example, each senator represents approximately 18 million constituents, whereas each of North Dakota's senators represents just over 300,000 constituents.

THE JUDICIARY

The third branch of the U.S. government, the judiciary, was the least defined by the Constitution and initially was quite weak. But given the trust and legitimacy vested in the Constitution and the rule of law, it should not surprise us that the U.S. judiciary has come to play a prominent role in the American political system. Over time, the federal court system devised new tools of judicial authority and significantly broadened the scope of its jurisdiction. In 1789, Congress created the federal court system authorized by the Constitution, endowing it with the power to resolve conflicts between state and federal laws and between citizens of different states.

In the landmark decision of *Marbury v. Madison*, the Supreme Court in 1803 established its right of judicial review: the authority to judge unconstitutional or invalid an act of the legislative or executive branch or of a state court or legislature. Although this power of judicial review can be exercised by federal and state courts, the Supreme Court is the court of last resort, with the final word on the interpretation of the U.S. Constitution. This kind of concrete judicial review is uncommon but not exclusive to the United States; Australian and Canadian courts also have such authority.

Federal judges are given lifetime appointments, which afford them substantial autonomy from both partisan politics and the executive and legislative branches of government. But the Court's power is checked by its reliance upon presidential nomination and Senate approval of nominees to the federal bench, and by legislative or executive enforcement of its decisions. Nonetheless, the federal courts have played an increasingly influential role, particularly since the second half of the twentieth century, determining important policy outcomes in such areas as school desegregation and abortion, and even determining the winner of the 2000 presidential election. In that case, the Court overturned a decision of a state supreme court (Florida's), and in so doing invalidated a partial recount of ballots in that hotly contested election. It is little wonder that appointments to the Supreme Court have become bitter political struggles as partisan forces seek to project their influence on this now-prominent third branch of the U.S. government.

The Electoral System

Nearly all elections in the United States are conducted according to a single-member district plurality system, in which there is one representative per district, and in which the seat is awarded to the candidate with the most votes (but not necessarily with a majority). This system has favored the emergence of two broadly defined parties and has effectively discouraged the survival of smaller and single-issue parties. Unlike a system of proportional representation, the plurality system in effect wastes votes for all but the dominant candidate, forcing coalitions to emerge to compete in the winner-take-all contests.

One way in which parties have sought to enhance their prospects for electoral success has been through the process of drawing up electoral districts, which are used to determine constituencies for the House of Representatives and many state and local offices. State legislatures are required to adjust voting districts every ten years to reflect changes in population, and the dominant party in the legislature is often able to control the process. Parties seek to influence electoral outcomes by redrawing the districts in ways that will favor their candidates and voting blocs. Political architects often employ **gerrymandering**, the manipulation of district boundaries by one political party to favor the candidates of that party (nowadays achieved with the aid of sophisticated computer analyses of demographic data).

Although members of both chambers of Congress are elected directly by a popular vote, the president and the vice president are elected indirectly by the electoral college. The Founders established the electoral college as a means of tempering the particular interests (and feared ignorance) of voters. In this system, voters technically do not vote for a presidential candidate but choose instead a slate of electors from their state, with the electors chosen or appointed by each party from each state. Each state receives a total of electoral votes equal to its combined number of senators and representatives. In addition, the federal District of Columbia has 3 votes, for a sum of 538 electoral votes (100 plus 435 plus 3). But unlike in a plurality system, with the electoral college, a candidate requires a majority of votes (270) to claim victory. If no candidate obtains a majority, the contest is determined by the House of Representatives (as was the case twice in the early nineteenth century).

Because all but two states use a winner-take-all formula for awarding electoral votes, winning a plurality of the popular vote in a state earns a candidate all of the state's electoral votes. Thus, winning many states by large margins but losing key electoral-rich battleground states by narrow margins can lead to a popular victory

National Election Results, 1992–2010

LEGISLATIVE ELECTIONS

YEAR OF ELECTION	HOUSE OF REPRESENTATIVES* TOTAL SEATS: 435†		SENATE* TOTAL SEATS: 100†		PRESIDENTIAL ELECTIONS* (PARTY)
	DEMOCRATS	REPUBLICANS	DEMOCRATS	REPUBLICANS	
1992	258	176	57	43	Clinton (Democrat)
1994	204	230	48	52	–
1996	206	228	45	55	Clinton (Democrat)
1998	211	223	45	55	–
2000	212	221	50	50	Bush (Republican)
2002	204	229	51	48	–
2004	202	232	44	55	Bush (Republican)
2006	233	202	49	49	–
2008	257	178	56	41	Obama (Democrat)
2010	193	242	53	47	–

*House terms of office are fixed at two years, with all seats elected every two years. Senate terms are fixed at six years, with one-third of the seats elected every two years. Presidential terms are fixed at four years, with elections held every four years.
†When Democrats and Republicans together comprise less than the total number of seats, the independent representatives account for the difference.

but a loss in the electoral college. This has happened three times in U.S. history, most recently in the controversial 2000 election between George W. Bush and Al Gore.

Even prior to the 2000 election, many observers had called for the elimination of the electoral college, to match the elimination of the similarly indirect election of

IN POOR HEALTH: THE HEALTH CARE CRISIS IN THE UNITED STATES

The United States is unusual among industrialized democracies in its approach to health care.* Like other wealthy democracies, the federal government provides public health care, doing so through two national programs (Medicare and Medicaid), which cover roughly one-third of Americans and account for approximately half of total health care spending in the United States. But unlike most other advanced democracies, these programs do not cover all citizens; until recently, almost 17 percent of Americans (more than 50 million people) lacked health insurance.[†] Most Americans who do have insurance are covered by private insurance, often provided through employers. Overall, the United States spends about twice as much per capita on health care compared with other advanced democracies, but these expenditures deliver no better overall health outcomes than those in other countries.

Although other presidents had failed in their attempt to reform health care (most notably Clinton in the early 1990s), Barack Obama was elected in 2008 on a platform promising health care reform. Obama's Democratic Party held a majority in both houses of Congress, but lacked enough votes in the Senate to guarantee passage for his proposed health care legislation. As a result, the Patient Protection and Affordable Care Act that

Obama confronted myriad groups with significant (and often competing) vested interests in the outcome of the health care reform efforts.

passed in 2010 was a compromise between Democrats and Republicans. It called for the gradual creation of a system of mostly private health insurance that would cover the vast majority of Americans, and that would require most Americans to purchase insurance. The resulting compromise reform act fell short of the hopes of Democrats, and the feature of the law mandating the purchase of insurance led dozens of states and other opposing organizations to file legal actions against the legislation, declaring it an unconstitutional violation of both state and individual rights. In 2012, the Supreme Court ruled that the individual mandate represented a constitutional use of Congress's taxing powers, but struck down other parts of the act.

*An excellent comparative analysis is Steinmo, *Evolution of Modern States*, pp. 156–59.
[†]Richard Wolf, "Number of Uninsured Americans Rises to 50.7 million," in *USA Today*, September 17, 2010, www.usatoday.com/news/nation/2010-09-17-uninsured17_ST_N.htm (accessed 8/22/11).

turnout are on average lower in the United States than in all other advanced democracies considered in this volume. Although voter turnout has actually increased in recent presidential elections—59 percent in 2004 and 62 percent in 2008, the highest level since 1968—only about 40 percent of eligible Americans vote regularly. (The turnout rate was only about 38 percent in the 2010 midterm elections.)

Suffrage in the United States, as in other democracies, has expanded over time. Limited originally to white male landholders, the franchise was extended first to nonpropertied white males; then, by the end of the Civil War, to African American men (though African Americans' full participation was not possible until Congress passed the **Voting Rights Act** in 1965); and to women in 1920. Most recently, in 1971, the voting age was lowered from 21 to 18.

The Party System

Another factor sometimes blamed for declining rates of voter turnout is the weakness of political parties. Formerly bottom-up organizations linking party members tightly together in purposive grassroots campaigns, political parties in the United States have evolved over time into top-down, candidate-driven national organizations with much looser ties to voters and citizens. American political parties today tend to be weaker and more fragmented than their counterparts in most other countries.

But with much talk recently about the ideological and even geographic polarization of American voters into "red" (Republican) states and "blue" (Democratic) states, it is clear that the U.S. two-party system has certainly endured even as it has evolved. The U.S. plurality system has fostered a two-party system in which the Democratic and Republican parties have won virtually all votes and political offices since their rivalry began over 150 years ago.

THE DEMOCRATIC PARTY

The Democratic Party has its roots in the Democratic-Republican Party, which formed in the 1790s with southern agrarian interests as its base. Andrew Jackson led a splinter group to presidential victory in 1828, calling it the Democratic Party and portraying it as the party of the common man. The Democrats dominated the political scene until 1860 and for most of the years between 1932 and 1968.

As a coalition party, like its Republican rival, the Democratic Party is difficult to characterize fully in terms of a set of philosophical principles or even policy preferences. It may be said, however, that the party tends to embrace policies that support minorities, urban dwellers, organized labor, and working women. Although less so than European social democrats, Democrats in the United States generally perceive state intervention designed to temper the market and enhance equality as both legitimate and necessary. As has been the case with social democratic parties in Britain and elsewhere, however, neoliberal trends since the 1980s have weakened the Democratic coalition, causing conflict over traditional New Deal–type social welfare programs providing such benefits as affirmative action. The party has also struggled with divisive social issues such as abortion and gay marriage, which are often opposed by working-class and immigrant communities that would otherwise be drawn to the Democratic Party.

THE REPUBLICAN PARTY

The Republican Party, nicknamed the Grand Old Party (GOP), is in fact not as old as its rival. It first contested elections in 1856 on an antislavery platform that also appealed to northern commercial interests. With Lincoln's presidential victory in 1860, the party dominated national politics until the 1930s, when the Great Depression brought that era of its supremacy to an end. By the late 1960s the GOP had regained the presidency, and by the 1990s it had obtained congressional majorities as well.

The Republican Party currently brings together a coalition that includes both economic and moral conservatives. It draws support disproportionately from rural dwellers, upper-income voters, evangelical Christians, and voters favoring individual freedom over collective equality, such as libertarians and owners of small businesses. Although there are fewer registered Republican voters than Democratic voters, registered Republicans have tended to vote more regularly than their rivals. Americans identify themselves with both parties in roughly equal numbers, with approximately one-third of adults expressing a preference for each of the two parties and most of the remaining one-third identifying themselves as independents. As with Democrats, Republicans are often divided between those who favor greater liberalism in economic and moral issues and those whose cultural or religious preferences call for a greater state role in social issues.

NOT YOUR AVERAGE TEA PARTY

U.S. politics has been profoundly influenced by the emergence of the **Tea Party** movement within the Republican Party. The movement takes its name from the 1773 protest by colonists against the British imposition of taxes on tea. The modern-day movement emerged in 2009 as a reactionary group within the Republican Party. Although members of the movement share a strong opposition to any increase in taxation, they are divided between small-government libertarians (such as Texas representative Ron Paul, a Republican candidate for president in 2008 and 2012) and social conservatives, such as Wisconsin representative Michele Bachmann (an early contender for the Republican nomination in 2012). The movement gained strength in opposition to the perceived increase in federal government power and spending, including federal stimulus spending in response to the recent recession, and to passage of health care legislation in 2010. More than 100 candidates backed by the Tea Party ran for office in the 2010 midterm legislative elections. Although only about a third of them won office, the Tea Party wielded substantial influence, effectively anchoring the Republican Party on

A 2011 rally of the Tea Party, staged on the day Americans' taxes are due.

the far right.* In 2011, the refusal of Tea Party Republicans to accept any tax increases as a means to reduce the budget deficit led to a dangerous stalemate over legislation to increase the U.S. debt ceiling. Republicans associated with the Tea Party performed fairly well in some congressional races in 2010, though in some cases Tea Party members beat out Republican moderates in the primaries only to lose to Democrats in the general election. While candidates in the Republican presidential primaries in 2012 vied for Tea Party support, the movement did not prove decisive in either the Republican nominating race or the general election.

*On the Tea Party movement, see Vanessa Williamson, Theda Skocpol, and John Coggin, "The Tea Party and the Remaking of Republican Conservatism, *Perspectives on Politics* 9 (March 2011): 25-43.

THIRD PARTIES

If fully one-third of Americans do not identify themselves with either party, is there political space for a third party? Certainly single-member plurality systems in other countries, such as the United Kingdom, have yielded more than two parties. But in the U.S., establishing the kind of presence essential for national viability has proved difficult, if not prohibitive, for smaller parties. Moreover, the dominant parties have all the advantages of incumbency, such as the ability to establish and preserve laws discouraging the financing of third-party candidates and including them on the ballot.

That said, third parties have emerged on the U.S. political scene occasionally as protest voices. In that sense, third parties and their candidates can claim to have had an impact on the political process even if few of them have had any prospect of national electoral success. Among the third-party movements, the Populists of the late nineteenth century and the Progressives of the early twentieth have been the most successful. More recently, protest voices have emerged from each side of the political spectrum: Ross Perot's populist United We Stand Party earned nearly 20 percent of the presidential vote in 1992, and Ralph Nader's pro-environment Green Party garnered nearly 3 percent in 2000. In both cases, one can argue that the third-party candidates took crucial votes from the losing candidate. Nader, for example, garnered nearly 100,000 votes in Florida in the 2000 election. If only 1 percent of his supporters had voted for Gore instead, Gore would have won Florida and the national election. This result had the effect of suppressing third-party candidates in subsequent presidential elections, though they are likely to reemerge in the future.

One factor contributing to the lack of third-party success in the United States is that the dominant parties have routinely embraced key elements of the more successful third-party movements, bringing at least some of the disaffected voters back into the two-party fold, even as they weaken the third parties.

Elections

In the United States, in contrast to countries governed by parliamentary systems, terms for all elected offices—and therefore the sequencing of elections—are fixed. Each state determines the conduct of its elections, including the rules for any primary elections: that is, preliminary direct elections that are held in many states and are designed to narrow the field of candidates. Since the 1950s, electioneering in the United States has shifted from campaigning done almost exclusively by party leaders and grassroots party workers to highly centralized and professionalized media campaigns. Election contests today are hugely expensive and marked by media sound bites, talk show interviews, televised debates, and advertising blitzes, all guided by polls and sophisticated demographic studies.

No campaigns are more illustrative of this American-style electioneering than those for the U.S. presidency. As voters have apparently become less loyal to either party, and in many cases less interested in voting or participating at all, the parties and their candidates have redoubled their efforts (and expenditures) to attract support. In total, the 2008 presidential candidates raised over $1.7 billion and spent more than $1.3 billion, far more than that spent on campaigns in any other country. Campaigns begin early, with an extensive season of primaries, and involve an all-out effort both to promote the candidate and to denigrate the opponents, all in an attempt to mobilize new voters and persuade the undecided.

Civil Society

Since nineteenth-century French political philosopher Alexis de Tocqueville, observers have marveled at the vibrancy of U.S. civil society and the willingness of its citizens to become civically engaged. Recently, however, analysts have pointed to an apparent weakening of that civic commitment, noting low voter turnout and other signs of growing political apathy among U.S. citizens as evidence of a broader, generational decline in social capital.[5] Others argue, however, that the participation of individuals and the organized groups that represent their interests has perhaps not declined as much as simply changed: individual citizens associate with one another and seek to influence politics and policy in a variety of new and nontraditional ways.[6]

But precisely because the U.S. policy-making process is so complex and allows so many points of access—including individual officeholders at the national, state, and local level; legislative committees; regulatory agencies; and the initiative process—it has been difficult for individual citizens to influence the political process. As U.S. political parties have grown weaker and less cohesive, various special-interest groups have emerged and expanded their influence. The remarkable proliferation and enormous influence of these groups in the United States set this case apart from that of other democracies.

Republican candidate Senator John McCain and Democratic candidate Senator Barack Obama at a 2008 presidential election debate. Debates are a standard part of what is a long campaign season compared to other countries.

Interest groups are often organized around a single issue or a cluster of issues and therefore typically do not officially affiliate with a particular party or candidate. These organized interests can include a single corporation or business association, public interest groups, and even state or local governments. Perhaps most well known are the political action committees (PACs), political fundraising organizations that allow corporations and trade unions to support individual candidates. Although a 2002 campaign finance law banned so-called "soft money," or unregulated donations to political parties, organized interests were undeterred. Interest groups quickly discovered a loophole in the law in a new type of tax-exempt organization (known as a 527 for the section of the federal tax code governing its behavior) that could raise unlimited campaign funds as long as the funds were spent on voter mobilization and issue advocacy rather than specifically promoting a candidate or party. Then, in 2010, the Supreme Court ruled the 2002 campaign finance law unconstitutional in its restrictions on the ability of companies, unions, and other groups to pay directly for political advertisements during election campaigns. This ruling substantially increased special-interest spending in the 2010 midterm legislative elections and paved the way for "super PACs" in the 2012 presidential election, which were freed from any restrictions on donations, spending, or public disclosure. In the 2012 Republican primary campaign in Iowa, for example, a super PAC supporting Mitt Romney (though not "officially" linked to him) spent more than the candidate himself. The effects of this on American democracy remain in dispute. In addition to financing political campaigns, these interest groups, along with business corporations and wealthy individuals, exercise their influence through various lobbying techniques, both legal and questionable, to promote the interests of their constituencies.

Society

Ethnic and National Identity

The first European colonists in America were largely English-speaking Protestants, but early in the country's history the importation of enslaved Africans and a steady stream of emigration from Europe quickly diversified American society. In the mid-nineteenth century, the California gold rush spurred a wave of Asian immigration, and another major migration from southern and eastern Europe began in the 1880s. In the 1920s, Congress reacted to the new immigrants by imposing a series of restrictive immigration quotas favoring immigrants from northern Europe. With the amended Immigration and Nationality Act of 1965, Congress abandoned those quotas. As a result, immigration surged again, with the bulk of the new immigrants arriving from Latin America and Asia. The influx of non-European immigrants, especially **Hispanics**, has become an important issue in U.S. politics (see "Cultural Diversity and U.S. National Identity" in the "Current Issues" section, p. 138). As of 2011, about 13 percent of U.S. citizens were born abroad. (In Canada, the figure is 20 percent.)

Contrary to the common perception of the United States as a peaceful **melting pot** of cultures, immigrants have always faced resentment and discrimination. The debate about the impact of immigrants on U.S. society has deep roots in American history, with changes to the debate depending on which group of immigrants is predominant at the time (Catholics, Asians, Hispanics). The debate continues today and is centered largely on the rapidly growing presence of immigrants (many of whom reside in the United States illegally) from Latin America.

Contrary to expectations, however, these conflicts were less of an issue in the 2008 presidential elections, as improvements in Iraqi security and economic recession shifted public attention and compelled the Obama administration to abide by promises to draw down forces in both theaters. Some political analysts hope these measures will improve frayed relations with much of the world, which has grown critical of many of the United States' unilateralist policies. However, tense relations with Russia, Iran, North Korea, and, at times, China mean that the United States will continue to face challenges in the international system.

CURRENT ISSUES IN THE UNITED STATES

Cultural Diversity and U.S. National Identity

Despite the United States being from the outset a nation of immigrants, the current wave of immigration has nonetheless once again proven to be a hot political issue. In recent years, several states have passed increasingly stringent anti-immigration laws, increasing penalties for employers who hire illegal immigrants, requiring schools to determine the immigration status of students' parents, forbidding illegal immigrants from working or asking for work, and forbidding anyone from renting apartments or even giving rides to illegal immigrants. Some observers have gone so far as to warn that the very volume of Mexican immigration in particular will undermine the fundamental values of the United States, claiming that this group is so large and distinct that it will resist assimilation.[21] These fears, combined with concerns about crossborder drug trade and violent crime, led to the construction of hundreds of miles of security fences along the U.S.-Mexico border. (Roughly 25 percent of the 2,000-mile boundary is fenced.) Others are more optimistic about prospects for integration, noting that since the founding of the United States, successive waves of immigrants have been viewed as a threat to American political culture but over time have been assimilated. Even those observers who agree that the current flow of immigration differs in many important respects from those of the past generally disagree with the assessment that Mexican immigration poses a threat to U.S. society.[22] Much evidence points to the fact that Hispanic immigrants are speaking English and otherwise assimilating into U.S. culture: more than 90 percent of second-generation Hispanics are either bilingual or mainly English speakers, and many intermarry with non-Hispanic partners. As one scholar has concluded, "Hispanic immigration is part and parcel of broader American patterns of assimilation and integration. Their story, like that of the Irish, Jews, and Italians before them, is an American story."[23]

Similarly, the broader public reflects these same mixed views regarding immigration. After the September 11, 2001, attacks, there was a sharp increase in support for restricting immigration, but this support has steadily declined in recent years.[24] More generally, several scholarly studies indicate that the relatively weak level of social expenditures in the United States has much to do with the country's cultural diversity. In short, while citizens may be willing to support immigration, they also appear much less willing to redistribute wealth to those they feel are not like them.[25] Indeed, the rise of the welfare state in the United States coincides with heavy restrictions on immigration after World Wars I and II; and the rollback of the welfare state, with the rapid increase in immigration starting in the 1980s. The United States continues to be a melting pot of cultures fed by a steady stream of immigrants, but Americans remain ambivalent and deeply divided about this aspect of their society. If economic difficulties persist over the long term, this may increase pressure for restrictions on immigration, as immigrants become the flashpoint for anxieties about economic security. That said, it is projected that by 2042, minorities in the United States will in fact become the majority population.

Boom and Bust in the U.S. Economy

The U.S. and global economies are suffering from a bad hangover. Over the course of the 2000s, there was an enormous boom in the U.S. housing market, facilitated by low interest rates backed by the Federal Reserve and large inflows of foreign funds seeking to profit from the boom. This easy money made cheap loans available to American consumers and fueled a housing construction frenzy and, ultimately, a housing bubble. Unrestrained by government regulators, financial institutions issued increasingly risky loans to increasingly indebted consumers and then bundled these mortgages together into complex securities and sold them to investors at great profit.

For a season, this bubble kept everyone aloft and happy. Americans were living the American dream of home ownership, jobs were plentiful, and banks were extremely profitable. But as the inflated housing bubble popped and housing prices declined, so too did the value of these mortgage-backed securities. The Wall Street financial institutions that had invested heavily in these securities began

4

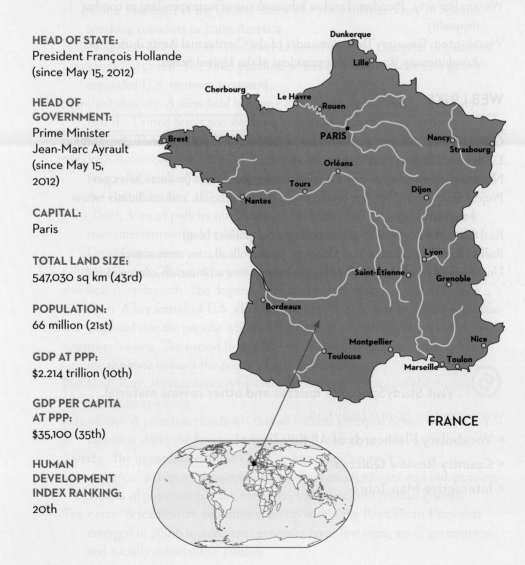

HEAD OF STATE:
President François Hollande
(since May 15, 2012)

**HEAD OF
GOVERNMENT:**
Prime Minister
Jean-Marc Ayrault
(since May 15,
2012)

CAPITAL:
Paris

TOTAL LAND SIZE:
547,030 sq km (43rd)

POPULATION:
66 million (21st)

GDP AT PPP:
$2.214 trillion (10th)

**GDP PER CAPITA
AT PPP:**
$35,100 (35th)

**HUMAN
DEVELOPMENT
INDEX RANKING:**
20th

Dunkerque

Lille

Cherbourg

Le Havre

Rouen

Brest

PARIS

Nancy

Strasbourg

Orléans

Tours

Dijon

Nantes

Lyon

Saint-Étienne

Grenoble

Bordeaux

Montpellier

Nice

Toulouse

Toulon

Marseille

FRANCE

FRANCE

Introduction

Why Study This Case?

In a fundamental sense, comparative politics is the comparative study of political **regimes**. The term *regime*, fittingly, comes from the French word for "rule" or "order" and refers to the norms and rules that govern politics. These norms and rules are institutionalized—often embodied in a constitution—but can and do change as a result of dramatic social events or national crises. Regimes express fundamental ideals about where authority should reside and to what end this authority should be employed.

The French case offers a fascinating study of regimes. In little more than two centuries, France has endured a remarkable range of regimes, including both authoritarian (from absolute monarchy to revolutionary dictatorship) and democratic (such as parliamentary and semi-presidential). During this period, France has been governed by no fewer than three monarchies, two empires, five republics, a fascist regime, and two provisional governments, and has promulgated 15 separate constitutions. A popular nineteenth-century joke had a Parisian bookseller refusing to sell a copy of the French constitution to a would-be customer, claiming he did not sell periodicals.[1] The most dramatic transition was, of course, the **French Revolution** (1789–99), in which French citizens overthrew the **ancien régime** (the European old order of absolute monarchy buttressed by religious authority) and replaced it, albeit briefly, with a democratic republic guided by the Declaration of the Rights of Man and of the Citizen.

France can claim title to the birthplace of modern democracy on the European continent, but democracy has not come easily. The French Revolution embraced a set of universal rights for all people and redefined French subjects as citizens.

149

But French revolutionaries concluded that the state had to be strong enough to destroy the old regime, impose the new, and forge a strong national identity. French republicanism established a short-lived revolutionary dictatorship that was followed by Napoleon Bonaparte's **coup d'état**—a forceful and sudden overthrow of government. Over the next seven decades, French reactionaries battled radicals, and France oscillated between empires, monarchies, and republics, with two more revolutions as well.

Not until the present **Fifth Republic** (established in 1958) has France seemed able to break this alternating cycle of stern authoritarian rule and chaotic, or at least dysfunctional, democracy. Although revolution is no longer politics-as-usual and today's French citizens are more centrist, French political life is far from mundane. French citizens remain skeptical, if not cynical, about politics and politicians and vigorously divided on issues such as immigration, unemployment, European integration, and the proper role of the state. Whereas most established democracies have vested their constitutions with a certain sanctity and have only cautiously amended them, France's willingness to write and rewrite the rules of the political game offers us a fascinating study in comparative politics and gives us insights into French politics and its political culture.[2]

Major Geographic and Demographic Features

France is a large country, roughly the size of Texas. By European standards, it is substantial, twice the area of Great Britain; in Europe, it is third in size only to Russia and Ukraine. France seems even larger than it is because of its span across much of Western Europe; it shares borders with six countries and is at once an Atlantic, continental, and Mediterranean country.

Although this geography has facilitated foreign commerce, it has also exacerbated French feelings of vulnerability. Protected by mountains to the southwest (the Pyrenees) and the southeast (the Alps), France enjoys no such natural barriers on its border with Belgium and Germany, to the north and northeast. Through the centuries, this corridor has been the locus of repeated invasions and confrontations. Abundant mineral resources (in the Saar region) and productive farmland (in Alsace-Lorraine) have raised the stakes and aggravated the conflicts. Vulnerability has also motivated France's preoccupation with establishing a formidable standing army and a strong centralized state (unlike England, which had a strong navy but a weak army). The French solution to its geographic vulnerability after World War I was the construction of the Maginot Line, a series of concrete fortifications along the French-German border designed to prevent the next war. Nazi forces, however, simply skirted these defenses and invaded France through Belgium. The French solution after World War II—integration with its long-standing German nemesis in the form of the European Union (EU)—has proved much more effective.

Within France, there are no significant geographic obstacles to transportation or communication. A number of navigable rivers have, over the centuries, been supplemented by canals and a highly developed rail system. This ease of internal travel and communication, combined with France's natural mountain and ocean boundaries, has given the French a strong sense of national identity and has facilitated France's economic and political integration.

At the hub of this national integration, both literally and organizationally, lies the capital, Paris. For centuries Paris has served as the administrative, commercial, and cultural nucleus of France. Generations of Parisian bureaucrats have imposed taxes, corvée (mandatory labor assessments), and even the Parisian dialect on all regions of the country. In addition to this linguistic homogeneity, more than 80 percent of all French are at least nominally Catholic.

This national unity should not be exaggerated, however. Although metropolitan Paris is home to roughly one-sixth (10 million) of France's 60 million citizens, the cultural ideal of "provincial" life, with its more rustic and relaxed lifestyle, is mythologized by many French people over the hustle and bustle of urban life. One enduring effect of this view is that while the number of farmers has shrunk in France, they have a disproportionate amount of power and have strongly influenced not only domestic politics but also those of the European Union. The preservation of rural life as a symbol of French identity has led to conflicts over agricultural subsidies and globalization, complicating domestic and international politics. Similarly, although French citizens are proud of their national heritage, many are likewise proud of their regional differences. Generally speaking, southern France is more rural, conservative, religious, and agrarian—and relatively less prosperous—than northern France, which is more urban, politically liberal, secular, and industrial.

Historical Development of the State

Whereas French history offers us valuable insights into the study of regimes, this same history is also an essential primer on the rise of the modern nation-state. From Louis XIV's declaration "L'état, c'est moi" (I am the state) to Napoleon's establishment of bureaucratic legal codes and the rule of law, the development of the French state offers an archetype for the emergence of a powerful state. Yet this exists alongside a society that views mass demonstrations against authority as an important tool of political change.

ABSOLUTISM AND THE CONSOLIDATION OF THE MODERN FRENCH STATE

In carving out the Holy Roman Empire in the early ninth century, Charlemagne, leader of a Germanic tribe known as the Franks, established a realm encompassing much of Western Europe. In doing so, he unified the area we know as France earlier than would occur in any of the other European states, including Britain. But with Charlemagne's death, Frankish control was reduced to an assortment of small feudal kingdoms and principalities well within the confines of what is now France. As with feudal kings elsewhere, the Frankish rulers sought to increase their holdings, stature, and security by squeezing wealth from their subjects. In the United Kingdom, struggles among the aristocracy led to a gradual decentralization of power, as signified by the Magna Carta. In France, however, feudalism led to absolute monarchs, who centralized authority and developed bureaucracies capable of taxing the subjects and administering the other affairs of state.

Absolute monarchy—the stage in the evolutionary development of Europe between the more decentralized feudal monarchies of the Middle Ages and the constitutional governments of the modern era—made several important contributions to the modern French state.[3] Though many of the responsibilities we associate with a modern state, such as education, welfare, and transportation, were at that time handled by the family, the church, an odd assortment of local authorities, or simply not at all, three primary duties—making and executing laws, waging war and providing defense, and raising money to defend the state—became the responsibility of the French kings.

In carrying out these responsibilities, the monarchs did not ignore the social classes outside the court. In fact, the Crown initially allied itself with and—as its autonomy grew—ultimately employed each relevant class, or "estate," in carrying out its duties. The Catholic clergy, or First Estate, had primary responsibility for administering the legal system; the landed aristocracy, or Second Estate, prosecuted the king's wars; and financiers from the commoners who made up the commercial class, or Third Estate, gathered the taxes that paid for the military, the luxuries of the court, and the rest of the state apparatus. In order to co-opt these groups

TIMELINE OF POLITICAL DEVELOPMENT

YEAR	EVENT
800 C.E.	"France" first emerges as an independent power under Charlemagne
1661–1715	Absolute monarchy culminates in rule of Louis XIV
1789	French Revolution is launched with storming of the Bastille in Paris
1799	Napoleon Bonaparte seizes power and brings revolution to an end
1848, 1871	Popular uprisings lead to the Second and Third republics
1940	Third Republic is replaced by Vichy (German puppet) regime
1946	The weak Fourth Republic is established
1954	The French leave Vietnam in defeat
1958	Threat of civil war over Algeria returns Charles de Gaulle to office, leading to the ratification of his presidency and the Fifth Republic by referendum
1968	The Events of May rioters in Paris demand social and educational reforms
1969	De Gaulle resigns
1981	François Mitterrand and the Socialists are elected
1986	First period of "cohabitation" between Socialist president Mitterrand and neo-Gaullist prime minister Jacques Chirac takes place
1992	Slim majority of French voters approve Maastricht Treaty, establishing the Economic and Monetary Union (within the European Union) and the euro
2005	In referendum, French voters reject proposed European Union constitution
2007	Nicolas Sarkozy elected president
2012	François Hollande elected president

initially, in the fourteenth century the monarchy established an assembly known as the **Estates General**, with representatives from each of the three estates.

By the fifteenth century, Louis XI had sufficiently centralized his authority such that he could wage expansive wars, doubling the size of his kingdom to roughly France's current borders. He was also able to weaken the influence of the nobility and largely ignore the Estates General. His successors over the next three

the British House of Lords, there have been regular calls for constitutional reform of the upper house, but since de Gaulle's failed attempt in 1969, and unlike in the United Kingdom, there have been few constitutional changes. In perhaps the biggest shift, in 2011 the majority of seats in the Senát were won by candidates on the left, which reflected unhappiness over local government reform that put many council members out of jobs.

THE JUDICIARY

As in most democracies, the French judiciary is divided into several branches, including civil, criminal, and administrative. The French judicial system is based on continental European **code law**, in which laws are derived from detailed legal codes rather than from precedent (as in common law used in the United States, Canada, and the United Kingdom). During Napoleon's rule, French laws were systematically codified, and much of that original code remains in place today. The role of judges is simply to interpret and apply those codes. Consequently, judges in France have less discretion and autonomy than those in the common law systems.

The French court system also operates very differently from that in the United States or Canada. Judges play a much greater role in determining whether charges should be brought, and they assume many of the roles of prosecuting attorneys. In France, judges, not lawyers, question and cross-examine witnesses. Because the 1958 constitution created a semi-presidential system with built-in potential for deadlock of the legislature and the executive, the Fifth Republic also created a **Constitutional Council** to settle constitutional disputes.[12] The Constitutional Council is comprised of nine members, who are appointed for a single nine-year term by the president and heads of the National Assembly and Senate. Former presidents of France also serve as members of the council, for life, once they have left office. The council is empowered to rule on any constitutional matter, so long as there is a request from the government, the president, or at least 60 members of either house of the legislature. In its early years, the Constitutional Council tended to act rarely, and usually backed presidential actions. In recent decades, however, it has shown more independence; in 2008, it rejected legislation that would have allowed for the indefinite imprisonment of dangerous criminals even after their terms had been served. One role that the Constitutional Council does not serve is that of a court of last appeal for cases from lower courts; that function is held by other judicial bodies.

The Electoral System

France's electoral system is majoritarian rather than proportional, thus looking more like the United States, Canada, and the United Kingdom than continental Europe. However, the use of a two-round runoff between candidates distinguishes it from the plurality-based system found in those countries. French presidents are directly elected in two rounds of voting every five years. Unless a candidate gets over 50 percent of the vote in the first round (which has never happened in the Fifth Republic), a second round of balloting two weeks later pits the top two candidates against each other.

France also employs a two-round electoral system for its single-member district (SMD) elections of members of the National Assembly. In each district, candidates with over 12.5 percent of the vote face off in a second round of balloting (again, unless a candidate gains over 50 percent of the votes in the first round). During the Socialist administration of François Mitterrand, France experimented with proportional representation for lower house elections, as it had in the Fourth Republic, but returned to SMDs two years later. Using two rounds of voting does ensure that winning candidates have a majority of the vote in each district, but it still delivers disproportionate outcomes common in SMD elections. In 2012, for example, President Hollande's party won 49 percent of the lower house seats with only 41 percent of the nationwide vote.

By using two rounds of voting for presidential and lower house elections, the French system encourages more parties and candidates than do SMD systems in Canada, the United Kingdom, or the United States. At the same time, the second round of elections still uses a winner-take-all format, and the 12.5 percent threshold for entry into the second round of legislative elections severely limits the number of parties that actually win. The National Front, for example, won nearly 5 percent of the vote in the first round of the 2007 elections, but not a single seat. The complexity of a two-round system can create a rather confusing electoral landscape, as parties and individuals compete for seats with the expectation not necessarily that they can win, but rather that a good showing in the first round can translate into leverage to be used against more powerful parties. Small parties or coalitions or candidates may throw their support behind a stronger rival as part of a political deal. Still, these calculations can backfire, as they did in the 2002 presidential elections, when candidates on the left fragmented their vote—with a disastrous outcome. We shall speak more about this in the "Party System and Elections" section (see p. 172).

Referenda

The constitution of the Fifth Republic allows the president to call national referenda. President de Gaulle held five referenda, staking his reputation and political capital on each one. Referenda were used to approve controversial policies, such as independence for Algeria, and to approve the direct election of the president. When de Gaulle lost a 1969 referendum aimed at reforming the upper house of the legislature, he resigned. Since then, referenda have been used less frequently, though often regarding changes to the European Union. In 1972, President Pompidou used a referendum to approve the enlargement of the European Union, and in 1992, President Mitterrand asked voters to approve the European Union's Maastricht Treaty. More recently, in 2005, President Chirac submitted a proposed European constitution to a referendum. Voters delivered a resounding rejection of the document despite Chirac's support for it. The defeat weakened Chirac, and since that time, the government has not been willing to submit further EU treaty reforms to a national vote (it is not required by the constitution). France has suggested, however, that it might require a public referendum on Turkish membership in the European Union, if it is offered. As such a referendum would surely fail, this has engendered consternation among other EU members as well as Turkey.

Local Government

France is usually considered a prototypical unitary state, with all power concentrated in Paris, the capital and largest city. Furthermore, compared with most of its neighbors, it has experienced relatively little separatism or demands for greater regional autonomy (an independence movement on the island of Corsica is a rare exception). Whereas this is a generally accurate picture, France also has a long history of localism and regionalism that should not be discounted, and three levels of local government—region, department, and commune—that have enjoyed increasing power over time.

There are 27 regions in France, five of which are overseas. The regions' primary responsibilities are regional planning and economic development. The regions are led by a council, elected every six years. At the next level there are 96 departments (and the five overseas territories), with responsibility in such areas as health services and infrastructure. For nearly two centuries, power in the departments resided with a **prefect** appointed by the central government, but a series of reforms in

1982 transferred a great deal of power to a directly elected council. Finally, at the municipal level there are communes, directly elected councils and mayors who handle the main tasks of these communities. Since the 1982 reforms, local governments have been given some control over taxes and revenues, and as a result their powers have slowly grown. However, their share of the budgetary pie remains very small. There have been proposals to streamline and reduce the layers and size of French local government. Local governments have decried this project as an attempt to recentralize the country, while the national government has retorted that the current system is too cumbersome and costly.

Other Institutions: The French Bureaucracy

The development of the French state is associated with the creation of one of the world's earliest and most efficient bureaucracies, the legacy of which can be seen in contemporary French politics. Compared with that of most other democracies, where the notion of bureaucracy conjures up the image of inefficiency and red tape, the civil service in France retains a high profile and considerable prestige, and serves as an important springboard to elected office. One gateway to the bureaucracy is the **École Nationale d'Administration (ENA)**, a state educational institution whose primary mission is to train civil servants. Indeed, the highest category of civil servants is usually recruited through ENA and several other elite state institutions.

This specialized training, combined with few barriers between civil service and politics, means that the links between the bureaucracy and elected office are strong and considered normal. The *enarques*, as graduates of ENA are known, commonly move between the civil service and elected or appointed political office. Former president Chirac graduated from ENA in 1959 and was a civil servant for nearly a decade before running for office; his last prime minister, Dominique de Villepin, also was an *enarque* with a long career within the state—indeed, Villepin had never held any elected office prior to becoming prime minister. This blurry line between state and politics extends to the economy, which has long been subject to state guidance and partial state control. Career bureaucrats often move from the civil service to positions within business: a transition that is known as ***pantouflage***—literally, putting on slippers. The largest private companies in France remain dominated by *enarques*, though this has declined of late. The impact of the civil service on French life thus is hard to overstate. By one estimate, over half the population either works for, or has a parent, child, or spouse who works for, the public sector; of course, such a large state comes with a cost, in the form of wages and benefits, and as the French population ages, supporting the civil service and its retirees will be an increasingly costly proposition.

Political Conflict and Competition

The Party System and Elections

As a political leader de Gaulle was deeply suspicious of political parties, blaming them for much of the political turmoil of the Third and Fourth republics. The SMD system helped narrow the field of parties and often produced stable majority governments. By the 1960s, the badly fragmented party system of the Fourth Republic had been replaced by a less fragmented multiparty system that featured a bipolar alternation of coalitions of the center right and the center left. By the late 1970s, the political bloc of the right, composed mainly of the **Rally for the French Republic (RPR)** and the **Union for a Popular Movement (UMP)**, and the political bloc of the left, composed mainly of the **French Communist Party (PCF)** and the **French Socialist Party (PS)**, each earned about half the vote in French elections. The four major parties together won over 90 percent of the vote. The electoral system helped this dominance of the two major blocs, as the SMD system, with its two rounds of voting, required coalition building in the second round.

Since the 1980s, the **four-party, two-bloc system** has been in transition. One important ideological change has been the spectacular demise of the PCF on the left and the emergence of the **National Front (FN)** on the right, changing the prospects for electoral coalitions. In addition, constitutional changes may have brought cohabitation to an effective end, also transforming the power of political parties to act as a counterweight to the president. The French system may be coalescing into a more standard two-party system, though the two-round electoral system probably means that smaller parties will continue to play a role in French political life. In addition, the institution of the presidency also encourages party formation as a springboard for presidential campaigns, while weakening the internal coherence of the parties themselves. Next we discuss the main ideological groups in the party system.

THE FRENCH LEFT

The Communist Party and the Socialist Party have been the dominant parties of the French left since the end of World War II. The Communist Party played a major role in the French resistance to the Nazi occupation and was rewarded at the polls after the war. The Communists had long been a party staunchly loyal to

Moscow, and supported the Soviet Union's invasion of Czechoslovakia in 1968 (though it drifted away from its allegiance by the 1970s). Historically, the PCF had a very strong base of support among French workers and in France's trade union movement, and for much of the post–World War II period it did well in local and national elections, usually winning about 20 percent of the vote. However, this did not translate into significant national power, even though the PCF participated in government coalitions led by the rival Socialist Party and briefly held cabinet positions in Socialist governments. Rather than giving the PCF credibility, government experience only tarnished its image as a principled party of the opposition; the collapse of the Soviet Union undermined the appeal of its ideology. In 2007, the PCF polled only 4 percent of the votes in the first round of parliamentary elections.

The Socialist Party, formed in 1905, was also long divided into social democratic and Marxist camps. In the 1930s, the Socialists were elected to power and led a brief and ill-fated government. After World War II, the Socialist Party reemerged, though it regularly gained fewer votes than the Communists, and stagnated. Its fortunes began to change, however, when François Mitterrand became its leader in 1971. Mitterrand forged an electoral alliance with the stronger Communists and eventually eclipsed them with a more moderate social democratic ideology. This strategy was vindicated by the 1981 election of Mitterrand to the presidency, the first (and to date only) leftist president of the Fifth Republic. Mitterrand's long presidency (1981–95) was marred by his party's loss of its legislative majority in 1986 and by his need to cohabit with a conservative prime minister during most of his two terms in office. Subsequently, the Socialist Party won a legislative majority in 1997. Though it was defeated in the 2002 and 2007 legislative and presidential elections, its fortunes have been revived with the 2012 election of President François Hollande. At present, the Communist Party, along with the Green Party and other parties of the left, command attention but relatively few seats.

THE RIGHT

Unity has also long proved elusive for the French right, though as with the left, this may now be changing. In the past, the most important force on the right consisted of those who considered themselves the political heirs of General Charles de Gaulle, often called Gaullists or neo-Gaullists. But since de Gaulle never associated himself with any party, his heirs created various competing parties of the right that were more often than not divided by personality and presidential ambitions. The two most important forces were the Rally for the French Republic, created by Jacques Chirac, and the **Union for French Democracy (UDF)**, an alliance of five center-right parties founded by Chirac's rival, former president Valéry Giscard d'Estaing. These parties differed in part over the role of the state and their view of the European Union, but over the years, the differences mostly disappeared. In 2002, President Chirac encouraged most of the center right to cohere as a single party, the Union for a Popular Movement (UMP). During the presidency of Nicolas Sarkozy, the UMP continued to move in a more liberal direction, though it still supported a relatively strong role for the state. Following Sarkozy's dramatic loss in the 2012 presidential election (no president had been turned out of office after one term since 1981) some suggest that the UMP may move in a more explicitly nationalist direction to set it apart from the Socialists.

Unity among France's two main conservative parties was partly spurred by the emergence and surprising success of the National Front, on the far right. A small if noisy party, the National Front has as its major policy focus a reduction in immigration and the expulsion of illegal immigrants. Led by the fiery **Jean-Marie Le Pen**, the FN made its first real mark in national politics when proportional representation was briefly introduced in the 1980s, enabling it to win its first seats in the lower house. The party reached its peak with 15 percent of the vote in the 1997 legislative elections, but under the SMD system, it has never won more than a single seat in the lower house. Nevertheless, in the 2002 presidential elections, Le Pen benefited from the divided votes among various leftist candidates to make it into a runoff with President Chirac. In the second round, he won less than 20 percent of the vote as voters recoiled from the possibility of a Le Pen presidency. But the factors that make the National Front a success, particularly fears over immigration, remain. To a large extent these fears have been successfully co-opted by the UMP, which has emphasized law and order and greater controls over immigration and immigrants. The National Front leadership has been revived with the election of Le Pen's daughter, **Marine Le Pen**, to the top leadership position of the party in 2011, and she has reemphasized antiglobalization and Euroskepticism as central values of the party (see "The National Front and Nationalism in France" in the "Current Issues" section, p. 191). In the 2012 presidential elections, Le Pen won 20 percent of the vote, a high for the FN, placing in third.

Civil Society

As early as the 1830s the French scholar Alexis de Tocqueville noted the weakness of French civil associations. Most scholars argue that French interest groups and associations remain weaker than those in most advanced democracies, a function of the powerful state and the emphasis on so-called mass action over organized lobbying. Nevertheless, trade unions and organizations representing private enterprise are two important elements of civil society that are worth discussing in detail.

LABOR UNIONS

Observers of French politics, particularly its numerous strikes, commonly speak of how powerful the French labor unions are. This is misleading. In fact, French labor unions have traditionally had a long history of being fractious. Less than 10 percent of the French workforce belongs to a union, one of the lowest rates in Europe. And unlike the powerful trade unions found elsewhere on the continent, French labor unions have usually been divided along partisan lines. The most powerful French union confederation includes the **General Confederation of Labor (CGT)**, historically linked to the PCF (though this is no longer the case); in contrast, the **French Democratic Labor Confederation (CFDT)** and Force Ouvrire (FO) have tended to have more centrist or anticommunist orientations. Paradoxically, it is in part the weakness and fragmentation of French unions that explain the large number of strikes that occur in France. More powerful unions could effectively engage in productive bargaining with employers or the government, but lacking this authority, they resort to public demonstrations and work stoppages as a vital tool to express discontent, something that capitalizes on the French tendency toward mass action and public protest. But despite their weakness, unions continue to play a key role in French society and in the management of the country's major welfare organizations (health care, retirement, and social security). They are also strongly represented in France's public-sector workforce and are a power to reckon with when any French government attempts to reform welfare benefits, as has been attempted of late.

PRIVATE ENTERPRISE

Compared with French labor, the business sector is well organized, with large firms represented by MEDEF (Movement of French Enterprises), and smaller firms represented by CGPME (General Confederation of Small- and Medium-Size Enterprises). Both have tended to support lower taxes on business, more flexible laws regarding the hiring and firing of workers, and a reduced role for government in the economy. Business has generally supported parties on the right

Demonstrators from the General Confederation of Labor protest against the 2010 pension reform, which raised the retirement age from 60 to 62.

such as the UMP. Since large numbers of France's business leaders are *enarques*, French business often has privileged access to the state bureaucracy. Not surprisingly, MEDEF has been a strong supporter of economic reforms; CGPME has been less enthusiastic, fearing that deregulation will remove many of the barriers that currently protect small businesses from competition.

ORGANIZED RELIGION

Unlike labor unions and private enterprise firms, organized religious institutions have had less of a role in French civil society. France is formally a Catholic nation, and despite minorities of Muslims, Protestants, and Jews, more than 80 percent of the French are nominally Catholics. Yet despite the predominance of a single religion, France has long been an anticlerical society, dating back to the revolution, when the church was seen as a tool of monarchical power. Church and state have been formally separate since 1905, under what is known as ***laïcité*** (which roughly translates as "secularism"). Under *laïcité*, no religion can receive state support, and religious education is restricted. The church continues to play a role in important social rituals (marriage, births, funerals), but not in the day-to-day lives of most

French citizens. The church lacks an important or central role in French politics, which has no Christian democratic party as found in other Catholic countries, such as Italy or Germany. The church can, however, rally to the defense of its own institutional issues: in the 1980s, church opposition forced the Socialist government to back away from plans to impose stricter government control over religious schools.

As the Catholic church has waned in power, other religions, particularly Islam, have grown. France has thus seen a rapid growth in mosques and Islamic educational and cultural institutions, something that has made many French citizens nervous. For many of these institutions, the Union of Islamic Organizations acts as an umbrella group, and in 2002 the government created the French Council of the Muslim Faith to act as an intermediary between the government and Muslim leaders. This has had limited success in building state-faith relations, and tensions remain, which we discuss next.

Society

Ethnic and National Identity

In its ethnic identity, France is a relatively homogeneous society. Historically, this was not the case, and it continues to change in the present. In centuries past, many parts of France maintained distinct ethnic identities, which included their own languages and cultures: Gascon, Savoyard, Occitan, Basque, and Breton, to name a few. Over time, these unique communities were largely assimilated into a single French identity, though certain ethnic groups, particularly Basques and Corsicans, have retained stronger language and cultural ties.

Assimilation was in part connected to the particular role the French state played in the development of national identity. One of the important facets of the French Revolution was the idea of a set of universal rights that identified people as citizens rather than subjects of the state. This form of republicanism was unlike that of the American Revolution, where democracy was predicated on an individualism that demanded federalism and a state with lower autonomy and capacity. French revolutionaries believed in the necessity of a powerful state to destroy the institutions of the past and to serve the people in building the future. A powerful state thus became a key instrument in solidifying and expressing French national identity and patriotism in a way in which it did not in the United States.[13] In contrast to U.S. policy, in France, rivals for public loyalty were eradicated or brought under control of the state.

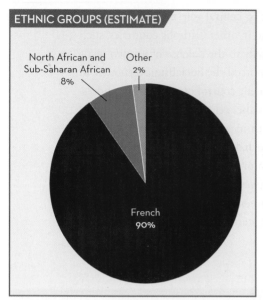

ETHNIC GROUPS (ESTIMATE)

North African and
Sub-Saharan African
8%

Other
2%

French
90%

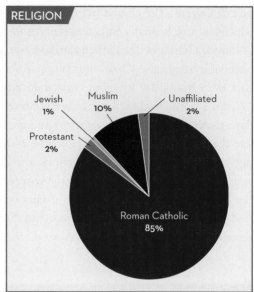

RELIGION

Jewish
1%

Muslim
10%

Unaffiliated
2%

Protestant
2%

Roman Catholic
85%

This relationship between state and nation is now being challenged by changes in both religious and ethnic identity. In the past, *laïcité* served to subordinate religious identity to the state, and ethnic identities were downgraded through assimilation and nationalism. In fact, French identity is so primary that the national census does not record such basic information as ethnicity and religion (and is forbidden by law to do so, making our data on religion and ethnic identity inexact). This became a point of debate in the 2007 presidential campaign, during which the candidates and the public were divided over whether recording such information would help address social issues or exacerbate division.

The reason this question emerged is that these ethnic and religious identities are becoming more salient. In the past few decades, France has seen an influx of people from outside Europe, notably Africa, the Middle East, and Southeast Asia. Immigrants now make up perhaps as much as 10 percent of the population. As in many countries, immigrants to France and their children often find themselves marginalized due to persistent discrimination, language barriers, and/ or a lack of education. Many immigrants are concentrated in housing projects on the outskirts of Paris and other large cities, with poor social services, employment opportunities, and access to transportation. This ghettoization compounds the sense of disconnect from French life and has led to violence. In 2005, France saw a month of heavy rioting across its immigrant suburbs, culminating in a state of emergency and approximately $200 million in damages. A second set of riots, not as large though more violent, occurred in 2007.

Within this debate over immigration, the future of the Muslim community takes center stage. Currently, France has the largest Muslim population in Europe outside Turkey, estimated to be 5 to 6 million people (approximately 10 percent of the population, including foreign born and those born in France). The growth of a large Muslim population has been disconcerting for a country that historically has been overwhelmingly Catholic, if now only nominally so. This situation is not unlike that of other Western countries but is compounded by the particular position of the French state. *Laïcité* means that Muslims are expected to place their faith below that of national and patriotic identity as part of the assimilation process. Yet many Muslims believe that the French state should be more accommodating to their needs, rather than vice versa. Furthermore, in the face of persistent

IN COMPARISON — Religion and Government

Should religion and government be kept separate? Percent saying yes:

COUNTRY	PERCENTAGE
France	72
Canada	71
Brazil	67
Germany	67
United Kingdom	66
India	58
Nigeria	57
Russia	55
United States	55
South Africa	45
Mexico	38
Japan	33
China	21

Note: Data on Iran not available.
Source: Pew Center for the People and the Press, 2007.

revolution to Napoleon to de Gaulle, French leaders have often appealed to the masses by seeking to transcend ideology and speak for the people. This populism has helped keep civil society and ideology weak by fostering an ongoing mistrust of such institutions as political parties.

The residual strength of populist ideas explains not only why ideological divisions in France are as much within groups as between them, but also why one of the most notable elements of French political culture is the tendency toward mass protests. With civic organizations being too weak to articulate public concerns and with individuals being faithful to the populist notion that the people must struggle against those in power, one of the most common forms of political activity in France is mass protest: marches, demonstrations, and strikes. For example, France regularly averages more than 1,000 workers' strikes per year, compared with fewer than 200 in the United Kingdom, and massive strikes in 2010 paralyzed much of the country for several weeks. That said, French respondents to political surveys tend to put themselves more on the left of the political spectrum than do those in the United States, United Kingdom, or Canada.

At the same time, France's populism and faith in the power of mass action is combined with a strong sense of national and patriotic identity and pride in the French state, with a belief that France is exceptional among countries—not unlike the American vision of itself. This has led to frequent conflict with the United States, a rival with a similar notion of its own exceptionalism but whose ideology of individualism runs counter to the French vision.

Political Economy

The political economy of France shares with its continental neighbors a strong state role in the economy. Part of this is a function of modern social democratic policies, whereas other elements can be traced over the course of several centuries. As far back as the sixteenth century, the absolute monarchy levied heavy taxes on the populace to support a large bureaucracy. At the same time, the French economy was highly mercantilist domestically, divided into a number of smaller markets, each subject to internal tariffs and nontariff barriers. Exports constituted a relatively small portion of the economy.[14] Although the French Revolution and the reign of Napoleon nationalized many of these structures, by the twentieth century, France was lagging behind many of its neighbors in terms of economic development. The country retained a large agricultural sector, had few large firms, and had experienced a relatively low level of urbanization. As one scholar described Paris in 1948, it was "empty of vehicles, needed neither traffic lights nor one-way streets"; electrical services and major consumer goods such as refrigerators were little known. He concluded, "France had not really entered the twentieth century."[15]

In the aftermath of World War II, the French government set out to rapidly transform the economy. This took the form of what the French termed **dirigisme**, which can be explained as an emphasis on state authority in economic development—a combination of both social-democratic and mercantilist ideas. Dirigisme involved the nationalization of several sectors of the economy (such as utilities), the promotion of a limited number of "national champion" industries to compete internationally (such as Airbus), the creation of a national planning ministry, and the establishment of the ENA and similar schools to ensure the education of bureaucrats who would be able to direct the economy.

True to its objectives, the dirigiste system helped bring about a transformation of the French economy. Economic wealth grew rapidly, along with increased urbanization. Through the help of economic subsidies from the European Union, France was also able to change its agricultural sector from one of small farms to one of large-scale production. Whereas in the 1950s France's per capita gross domestic product (GDP) was approximately half that of the United States, within 20 years it had surpassed its historical rivals, the United Kingdom and Germany.[16] Dirigisme, however, came with costs, including a large public sector, an expansive welfare system, and a heavy tax burden.

As with many other economic systems around the world, in the past 20 years this model has been put to the test. By the mid-1980s, unemployment had risen to over 10 percent, a rate that has persisted and is disproportionally concentrated among the young. Economic growth, which had been double that of the United States from the 1950s to the 1970s, fell to below 2 percent, among the lowest in the European Union. As a result of this slow growth, France's per capita GDP has stagnated, again falling below the United Kingdom and Germany and once-poorer countries such as Ireland. France also faces the European-wide dilemma of an

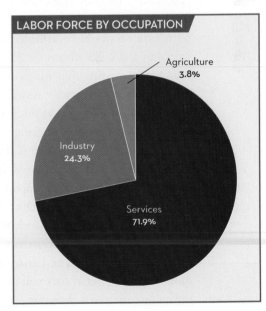

LABOR FORCE BY OCCUPATION

Agriculture 3.8%

Industry 24.3%

Services 71.9%

aging population, compounded by a large public-sector workforce that can retire early with generous benefits. As the French population has grown older, it is thus using an ever-greater share of the welfare system, while fewer young workers are available to fund those expenditures.

The French government has found it difficult to respond to these challenges. Part of the reason is a function of political culture. As the dirigiste model faces internal stresses, the French economy is also being buffeted by international competition from the United States and Asia, and from within the European Union itself. Increasing globalization presents new opportunities for France's economy, but for many French, globalization is seen as risky economic liberalism extended to the international level. Tellingly, when the French speak of economic liberalization or globalization, they speak of an Anglo-Saxon model, by which they mean the United Kingdom and the United States. Many French thus are worried that domestic economic reforms will essentially Americanize France, undermining their core identity. France is awash in discussions that the country is in decline and must carry out radical change if it is to survive in a changing world. It was Sarkozy's very call for a rupture with the past that helped him win the presidential election.

During his presidency, President Sarkozy proposed a number of changes, including pension reform, expanding the work week, lowering taxes, raising the retirement age, deregulating business, liberalizing the labor market, and cutting government payrolls. These were easier said than done. Sarkozy faced numerous protests, including the massive 2010 strikes mentioned earlier, and his emphasis on reform no doubt contributed to his defeat. Meanwhile, the global economic recession and crisis within the European Union over the future of the euro have only made reforms that much more difficult. President Hollande campaigned against Sarkozy's austerity measures, promising higher taxes on firms and the wealthy while balancing the budget. This is a tall order. In the long term, however, there may be elements working in favor of reform. First is growing consensus that reform is necessary, even if there is less appetite for the reforms themselves. Second is the fact that in spite of the structural problems of the French economy, in many ways it is highly competitive and thus amenable to reform. The United States may have a higher GDP per capita, for example, but that is due in part to the fact that Americans work much longer hours than the French. But when measured in terms of productivity, the French produce more, per hour of labor, than Germans, British, or Canadians (and only a bit less than Americans).[17] The question is whether France will be able to seize upon the recent EU crisis to turn the country in a new direction.

Another interesting facet of the debate about the future of the French economy can be seen in the struggle over agriculture. Though the percentage of the French population engaged in agriculture has shrunk dramatically in the past 50 years, agriculture still plays a central role in French identity. French culture is strongly tied to the concept of rural and agricultural life, and this is also bound up with national identity: locally or nationally produced food is central to the French self-image and to international prestige (think of French wines and cheeses). This French identity has been sustained in part, however, by large subsidies from the European Union, through what is known as the Common Agricultural Policy (CAP). Created in part to satisfy French conditions for joining the European Union, it became one of the European Union's main expenditures. The CAP consumes over

---

DECLINISM IN FRANCE

For the past few years, there has been a growth industry in France of books in the genre of what is sometimes called "declinism." Declinism is a view that decries the country's current state and predicts its demise unless steps are taken. One bestseller by historian and economist Nicolas Baverez, *La France qui tombe* (Free-Falling France), claims that the country's greatest period was in the 1970s, and that since then, it has been unable to adapt to a changing European and international environment. This crisis, Baverez argues, is not merely economic but also intellectual. Minister of Foreign Trade Pierre Lellouche's *Illusions Gauloises* (Gallic Illusions) similarly criticizes France's focus on its external forces (the United States, the United Kingdom, and the European Union) rather than emphasizing its own internal problems and need for reform. Journalists Denis Jeambar and Jacqueline Remy, in their book *Nos enfants nous haïront* (Our Children Will Hate Us), criticize the '68-ers (as baby boomers are commonly called in France) for protecting their interests above all else and thus stifling change. This discussion of declinism in the popular culture helped pave the way for a Sarkozy presidency, but whether France is "in decline" depends on what we mean by this term. France remains a highly developed and internationally competitive country with some of the highest standards of living in the world. And all countries, including the United States and the United Kingdom, have experienced their own declinist debates on numerous occasions, only to reform and rebound. However, there can be no doubt that declinism has helped contribute to the rise of the National Front of late, which has presented their party as the only one who can restore France to a position of greatness.*

*Steven Erlanger, "Focus on the French Economy Fuels Gains by Far Right," *New York Times*, February 5, 2012.

5

HEAD OF STATE:
President Joachim Gauck
(since March 18, 2012)

HEAD OF GOVERNMENT:
Chancellor Angela Merkel
(since November 22, 2005)

CAPITAL:
Berlin

TOTAL LAND SIZE:
357,022 sq km (62nd)

POPULATION:
81 million (16th)

GDP AT PPP:
$2.96 trillion (5th)

GDP PER CAPITA AT PPP:
$35,900 (32nd)

**HUMAN DEVELOPMENT
INDEX RANKING:**
10th

GERMANY

GERMANY

Introduction

Why Study This Case?

Germany commands a prominent position in the world and a pivotal position in Europe. It is the world's largest exporting nation, Europe's biggest economy, the European Union's most populous country, and an integral member of Europe's economic, political, and security organizations. Situated in the heart of the Continent, Germany today in many ways typifies the political, social, and cultural values and institutions of Europe and offers a useful window into the political institutions and public policies shared broadly by many of its European neighbors. By and large, Germans embrace social-democratic political and economic values, champion post-materialist concerns for the environment and the pursuit of leisure, and vigorously promote European integration even as they seek to enhance the competitiveness of Germany's capitalist economy and to strengthen Germany's national security. But in other fundamental ways, Germany sits apart from its European neighbors and poses interesting puzzles for the comparative political scientist.

Unlike with many of its western and northern European counterparts, the German state is federal; sovereignty and nationhood came very late to Germany. The modern institution of the nation-state finds its origin in Europe, in no small part with the 1648 Peace of Westphalia, which affirmed the principle of national sovereignty at the end of Europe's bloody Thirty Years' War. But even though this treaty was inked on German soil, it would take another 220 years before a German nation-state was established. Once forged in the nineteenth century, German nationalism took on powerful and ultimately virulent and destructive force in the twentieth century at the hands of Nazi fascists. The disastrous consequences of this hypernationalism led the allies who defeated Germany to divide the nation in 1945, a division perpetuated for over three decades by the Cold War. Despite reunification of East and West Germany in 1990, many Germans today remain hesitant to promote nationalism and are among Europe's strongest advocates of greater European integration and of the European Union. Although it can claim a thoroughly Western and European heritage, German modernization in many ways better resembles the experience of Japan than that of Britain, France, or the United States. Germany is a latecomer to both modern capitalism and democracy, with both imposed externally.

The very successes of German industrialization, democratization after World War II, and peaceful reunification have left the country uncertain about its future. Globalization poses new challenges to Germany's vaunted welfare state. Immigration has raised old questions about race and national identity; the end of the Cold War changed Germany's role as a linchpin of East-West relations; and the expansion of the European Union eastward has weakened the central role that the country historically played in that organization. Germany remains a major power, but its role in the post–Cold War international system seems muted, a reflection of a country still troubled by its past and uncertain what future responsibilities it must shoulder.

Major Geographic and Demographic Features

With an area slightly smaller than that of Montana or Japan, even reunified Germany cannot be considered large on a global scale. But its substantial population (more than 80 million), economic vitality, and location in the heart of Europe have placed it at the center of European affairs for many centuries. German topography has enhanced this centrality. Situated on the plains of northern Europe, Germany shares contiguous borders with nine European countries. With the exception of the Alps to the south and the Baltic and North seas to the north, Germany possesses no natural boundaries. Unlike England, Japan, and even France, which historically have relied upon natural barriers to offer them protection from foreign predators and to create a strong sense of national identity, Germany traditionally found itself externally vulnerable and internally divided. Its central location, accessibility, and internal incoherence meant that many of Europe's conflicts over the centuries were carried out on German soil and that Germans, unlike the British or Americans, did not have the luxury to remain aloof from the military and political affairs that surrounded and too often engulfed them. This predation by foreign armies only perpetuated Germany's continued political disunity, its sense of vulnerability, and its propensity for military preparedness.

Often the victim of foreign affairs, the German state, once it finally achieved political unity and military capacity in the nineteenth century, took its defense into its own hands and at times engaged in aggressive expansion. A lack of natural resources—with much of Germany's coal, iron, and some of its most productive farmland located in disputed border regions—also inspired German imperialism and military aggression as a means of obtaining resources. The German empire's late nineteenth-century "scramble for Africa" and Nazi Germany's call for Lebensraum (living space) were justified in these terms. This same sense of vulnerability and the bitter lessons learned from nearly a century of aggression have also propelled postwar German overtures for European integration. Just as Germans in the nineteenth century recognized that German safety and interests were well served by unification, Germans in the postwar era have concluded that German and European security and prosperity are well served by the peaceful integration of Europe.

The absence of geographical barriers also encouraged the migration of Germans and the diffusion of German culture into surrounding regions over time. These German migrants spread the German language and culture well beyond the boundaries of what now constitutes Germany. What at times became bitter conflicts over disputed territories with France (Alsace-Lorraine), Denmark (Schleswig), Czechoslovakia (Sudetenland), and Poland (Silesia) stemmed in no small part from the diffusion of ethnic groups and rival claims to these border regions.[1] The absence of natural borders has also meant that language, physical characteristics, and shared cultural values have been more important national markers in Germany than elsewhere, a cultural theme enhanced and elaborated by German intellectuals over the centuries. Although it now hosts Europe's largest immigrant population, Germany today remains quite homogeneous. Over 90 percent of the population is ethnically German, with ethnic Turks making up 2.5 percent and a variety of other European nationalities the remaining 6 percent.

Historical Development of the State

The economic, social, and political forces that swept modernization through much of Western Europe trickled far more slowly into the region we now know as Germany. National unity, industrialization, and democracy all came later to Germany than to its western European neighbors. Scholars agree that this relative backwardness profoundly shaped the German state. In France and England, feudalism gave way to states centralized by absolute monarchies that established standardized legal and administrative systems and fostered a coherent sense of nationalism. By contrast, national sovereignty and a centralized state eluded Germany until the nineteenth century. Although the German state was long in coming, once established, it loomed very large in Germany's rush to modernize.[2] As the idea of a German nation became institutionalized in a sovereign state, this unity born of national identity gained powerful force. Centuries of decentralization and disunity gave way to intense periods of authoritarian militarism and mercantilism, first under the leadership of the state of Prussia in the late nineteenth century and again under Nazi direction in the 1930s and 1940s. This relatively late unification and catch-up economic development meant that development of the state preceded industrialization, fostering state-led mercantilist development and authoritarianism.

Relative backwardness also placed Germany behind in the race for colonies and raw materials to feed industrialization, a status that fostered a voracious and aggressive imperialism that led ultimately to the **Third Reich** (empire), fascist Nazi expansionism, and military defeat. As a democratic and decentralized federal state no longer plagued by disunity, postwar Germany vigorously promoted European integration and pursued a costly program of complete German unification. As the original German and French architects of integration hoped, the success of the European Union has largely tempered fears that a reunified Germany would pursue militarist expansionism or any undue unilateral political influence.

THE ABSENCE OF A STRONG CENTRAL STATE DURING THE HOLY ROMAN EMPIRE, 800–1806

In 800 C.E., Charlemagne founded in western and central Europe what came to be known as the Holy Roman Empire. By the middle of the ninth century, a collection of German, Austrian, and Czech princes acquired nominal control of this loosely constituted empire, or **reich**. A feudal empire, it consisted of an odd assortment of hundreds of principalities, city-states, and other local political entities with varying degrees of autonomy and legitimacy, but there was virtually no allegiance to the center. This weak confederation waxed and waned in size and influence over the next 1,000 years, persisting until the time of Napoleon in the nineteenth century. Whereas comparable feudalism gave way to centralized states in England and France, the Holy Roman Empire remained politically un-unified.

TIMELINE OF POLITICAL DEVELOPMENT

YEAR	EVENT
800–900 C.E.	Loose confederation of German principalities forms Holy Roman Empire; later known as the First Reich
1871	Otto von Bismarck unifies Germany; later dubbed Second Reich
1918	Germany defeated in World War I
1919	Weimar Republic formed under difficult conditions
1933	Hitler and Nazis rise to power, establishing the Third Reich
1945	Hitler and Nazis defeated in World War II
1945–49	Germany divided among Allies into four occupied zones
1948	Berlin blockade and airlift takes place
1949	FRG founded in the west, and GDR in the east
1952	FRG joins European Coal and Steel Community
1955	FRG joins NATO, and GDR joins Warsaw Pact
1957	FRG participates in founding of European Economic Community
1961	Berlin Wall constructed
1969	FRG Chancellor Willy Brandt launches policy of Ostpolitik
1989	Berlin Wall falls
1990	Germany unified with GDR incorporated into FRG
1993	Germany becomes a founding member of the European Union

The empire took political form with the office of a weak emperor, which rotated among princes, and the imperial Reichstag, or, "Congress." This precursor to the contemporary German parliament began as a royal court composed of prominent princes and dukes who met irregularly to elect the emperor. By the fifteenth century, the Reichstag had become slightly more representative, with lesser princes and free cities also seated. However, the dominant princes, lesser princes, and urban representatives met in separate bodies, which made the Reichstag more divided, weaker, and less representative than its British counterpart. Indeterminate boundaries, centuries of entrenched localism, and mutual suspicions and prejudices among these localities hampered any efforts at unification.

Although religion had earlier served an important role in unifying much of Europe under the banner of Christianity, by the sixteenth century it, too, had become a divisive force within the Holy Roman Empire in the form of the Protestant Reformation. In 1517, the German monk and professor Martin Luther publicly displayed his writ of complaints about certain Catholic practices and doctrines. Among many other significant outcomes, this revolt split the previously religiously unified Holy Roman Empire and its German core. This religious divide took on political significance, and led to separate and often competing state churches in German locales, giving new sources of legitimacy to the local chieftains and additional justification for resisting unification. The Reformation also touched off the Thirty Years' War (1618–48), a religious conflict between Catholics and Protestants that was fought largely on German soil. For reasons beyond religion, the protracted war came to envelop most of Europe before ending with the Peace of Westphalia in 1648. This settlement affirmed the sovereignty of local political entities, thereby preserving decentralized German authority and further weakening the Holy Roman Empire.

THE UNIFICATION OF THE GERMAN STATE, THE RISE OF PRUSSIA, AND THE SECOND REICH, 1806–1918

Napoleon's invasion of Germany in 1806 effectively destroyed the empire, inadvertently began the process of German unification, and unleashed the forces of German nationalism that would ultimately lead to the rise of Nazi fascism. Napoleon's offensive wiped out many of the empire's sovereign principalities (there were some 300 at the time) and compelled others to merge with their larger neighbors for protection. Ultimately, only **Prussia** to the east and Austria to the south were strong enough to resist Napoleon's onslaught and avoid inclusion in the confederation of defeated territories he formed. After Napoleon's defeat in 1815, German allies under Prussian leadership set up a loose confederation of some 40 sovereign mini-states that created for the first time the semblance of a German state.

Over the course of the eighteenth and nineteenth centuries, the kingdom of Prussia in eastern Germany gradually acquired the autonomy, capacity, and legitimacy that allowed it to emerge as a viable core for a modern German state. A series of generally enlightened monarchs established an authoritarian state administered by an efficient and loyal bureaucratic staff, supported by a conservative and wealthy landed aristocracy known as **Junkers**, and defended by a large and well-trained standing army. (Voltaire once commented that "while some states have an army, the Prussian army has a state.") As important as the state's monopoly on violence was its mercantilist promotion of economic growth through the development of national infrastructure, the expansion of education among its subjects, and the enhancement of trade. Prussia established a customs union with neighboring German states that by 1834 included all but Austria. This highly capable and autonomous state managed to defend itself from aggressors, expand its territory, grow its economy, and thereby enhance its legitimacy beyond Prussia as it successfully competed with Austria for ascendancy in unifying Germany.

That this unification was not accompanied by greater liberalization in the political regime can be explained in part by the relative weakness of Germany's commercial and industrial middle class. Much as in China during the early twenty-first century, the educated and intellectual elite of nineteenth-century German society comprised fewer merchants and entrepreneurs and more bureaucrats, judges, and professors, largely employed by the state. Though modern in its thinking and in many ways even liberal in its outlook, this portion of society saw the state (in its hands) as a positive and essential instrument in building German national unity, wealth, and power. German intellectuals argued that individual freedom was a luxury or indeed a weakness not fit for the forging of German national identity. It would be militarist and mercantilist "blood and iron," not liberal elections, that would unify Germany.

By the 1860s, Prussia had forceful and capable leadership, a powerful military, and a growing industrial economy. Impressive war victories over Denmark, Austria, and ultimately France drew other German states into the cause and led, in 1871, to the establishment of a national German empire, or what came to be known as the Second Reich. Although the Prussian king was crowned emperor of all Germany, the key figure in the process of expansion and unification was Count Otto von Bismarck, prime minister, or chancellor, of Prussia. A politician, military officer, and member of the Junker landed class, he led a so-called revolution from above in which regime change came not from the lower, disenfranchised classes, but rather from an alliance of "iron and rye"—that is, of the industrialists and the landed aristocracy. Through the savvy use of diplomacy, war, and political machinations, the Iron Chancellor, as Bismarck came to be known, dominated German politics for two decades and brought about the first unified modern German state.

Not surprisingly, unified Germany's first national constitution established an authoritarian monarchy with only the trappings of liberal democracy. Sovereignty remained vested in the emperor, or Kaiser (derived from the Latin *Caesar*), and political power flowed from him. Although the constitution established a federal structure in which all the states were to have equal influence (a nod to the long-standing regional autonomy of the German states), it ensured the dominance of Prussia by mandating that the Prussian prime minister always become imperial chancellor. Similarly, although the constitution gave nominal deference to the notion of political equality (thus addressing the demands of the small but growing liberal middle class) by granting universal male suffrage for elections to the Reichstag, it retained aristocratic privilege in Prussian state elections. In addition, the imperial chancellor, the bureaucracy, and the military answered only to the emperor as head of state, not to the constitution. The emperor appointed the imperial chancellor, and the Reichstag could not dismiss the government. The emperor, chancellor, and their unelected administrators controlled foreign affairs and the military.

The Iron Chancellor took no chances that the constitution's nominal democratic allowances would get in the way of his forced-draft modernization drive. Bismarck bullied or circumvented the Reichstag in those few areas it did have some authority (such as the budget). He encouraged the creation of multiple political parties and then skillfully played them off one another. Through the promotion of patriotism and German culture and the expansion of national wealth and empire, Bismarck enhanced the popularity and legitimacy of his authoritarian rule. The core of this support remained the landed gentry, military, and industrial elite, but the middle and lower classes were "largely swept along" by growing prosperity and appeals to national pride as Germany's international stature grew.[3] Groups opposing Bismarck's authoritarian rule (including Catholics, liberals, social democrats, and Marxists) were met at times with coercion and other times co-optation. This policy of an "iron fist in a velvet glove" kept the peace through the deft use of both violence and the granting of social welfare benefits such as health insurance and old-age pensions.

But if democracy found infertile ground in modernizing Prussia, catch-up industrialization proved much more successful. In 1890, Bismarck was eased out of office, and Emperor Kaiser Wilhelm II assumed personal control, continuing the policy of rapid industrialization and imperialist expansion. By the early twentieth century, Germany had surpassed Britain in iron production and become a leading industrial power. Society became more complex as both the middle and working classes grew in size and political strength, with the socialist movement capturing one-third of German votes by 1912. As socialist opposition grew, some traditional sectors of German society, such as small-scale capitalists and landed aristocrats, embraced nationalism and anti-Semitism.

German patriotism, however, prevailed over these social divisions and differences. Frustrations associated with Germany's efforts to expand its empire and suspicions about the intentions of its neighbors stoked feelings of nationalism and unfulfilled destiny and contributed to German willingness to bring about World War I (1914–18). But as the war pressed on and took a particularly heavy toll on Germany, the social differences once again rose to the surface. Political liberals, Catholics, and others began to question openly why they had lent their support to an authoritarian government waging war against countries that provided their citizens democratic rights. Workers wondered why they could fight and die but not have an equal vote in the parliament. As the war ground to its bitter conclusion, the emperor made assurances of reform, but these promises offered too little and came too late. German defeat in 1918, combined with urban uprisings, prompted the emperor to abdicate and proclaim Germany a republic.

POLITICAL POLARIZATION AND THE BREAKDOWN OF DEMOCRACY DURING THE WEIMAR REPUBLIC, 1919–33

The political vacuum that followed the collapse of the Second Reich proved to be particularly infertile ground for the establishment of Germany's first republic. One scholar concluded that with radical Communists on the left, reactionary monarchists and militarists on the right, and no historical experience with liberal democracy, German society could claim "virtually no republicans."[4] No one was prepared for the sudden departure of the emperor, and few had considered how Germany ought to be constituted as a republic with no monarchy. The seeds of cynicism and elitism sown in this era would grow into the extremism and fascist totalitarianism that would spell the republic's doom in less than two decades.

In the face of these and other difficulties, politicians met in the city of Weimar in 1918 to draft a constitution. Promisingly, the majority of socialists retreated from their revolutionary goals and participated in the process. The **Weimar Republic** featured a remarkably democratic constitution that offered universal

(1949–63), who sought to integrate Germany into the Western alliance and bind it to its former military foes in Europe by joining the Coal and Steel Community and the North Atlantic Treaty Organization (NATO), and Willy Brandt (1969–74), who introduced a pragmatic policy of reconciliation with East Germany known as *Ostpolitik*. Despite political competition among thriving democratic parties, general consensus prevailed across the political spectrum, favoring domestic policies of comprehensive social welfare programs and a state-regulated marketplace, and a foreign policy promoting growing European integration and pragmatic measures to ease tensions with East Germany and ultimately embrace unification.

In the GDR, Stalinist totalitarianism replaced fascist totalitarianism. Because the Soviets blamed the capitalist system both in Germany and more globally as responsible for the Third Reich and both world wars, their first step was to eliminate East Germany's capitalist economy and replace it with a new socialist system presided over by a totalitarian Communist Party state. By the end of the 1940s, the eastern portion of Germany possessed political and economic systems almost identical to those of its Soviet mentor. With economic growth rates over the first two postwar decades nearly as impressive as those of its western counterpart, East Germany became the economic showcase of the Communist bloc. But like its Soviet mentor, the East German socialist economy ultimately could not keep pace with the capitalist West. Its failure to do so was demonstrated by the grim reality of life in the GDR. The East German state retained power by force and terror, manifested in its reliance on the *Stasi* (secret police) to squelch dissent, the construction of the fortified Berlin Wall surrounding West Berlin in 1961, and the summary execution of those caught trying to flee to the West from East Berlin.[7]

In fact, Soviet leader Mikhail Gorbachev's efforts to revitalize Communist rule and the economy in the Soviet Union through his 1980s reforms had their more immediate effects not on the Soviet Union but on its central European allies, including East Germany. These political and economic reforms threatened to undermine the Stalinist foundation on which the East German system was built. In early 1989, Hungary opened its borders with Austria, and East Germans vacationing in Hungary quickly took advantage of this breach in the iron curtain to leave for the West. Over the next six months, some 2 percent of the East German population immigrated to West Germany. This led to a rapid weakening of the GDR's legitimacy and its capacity to control events. Gorbachev urged the East German leadership to follow the Soviet reforms, further threatening the regime as the entire Communist system seemed to be crumbling around them. As public protests in East Germany grew and the pace of the exodus to the West picked up, the economy ground to a halt and the party-state lost its capacity to govern. The East German leaders stepped down and announced on November 9, 1989, the opening of the border between East and West Berlin. Crowds swarmed both sides of the Berlin Wall as the gates were opened, and this tangible and iconic image of the beginning of the end of Germany's division and the collapse of the iron curtain was televised across the world.

REUNIFICATION OF THE GERMAN STATE, 1990–PRESENT

The collapse of the East German state and the euphoria shared by all Germans propelled events much more rapidly than anyone could have anticipated. East and West German leaders prepared for a gradual process of thawing and increasing contacts, but it quickly became apparent that the only source of stability would be a quick process of unification. The flood of Germans migrating from East to West prompted hurried negotiations leading to full reunification in 1990, less than one year after the fall of the wall. In effect, **reunification** meant the incorporation of East Germany into the FRG, with the adoption of the West German Basic Law as the constitution of a unified Germany and West Germany's capitalist economic system imposed on East Germany. Although the Basic Law called for a new constitution and national referendum upon reunification, thus far, no such action has been taken.

The 1990 merger probably averted a much more disastrous political implosion of East Germany, but the long-sought reunification proved much more difficult and costly than the early optimists had predicted. The initial euphoria of national unification gave way to the cold, hard reality of bringing together two sovereign nation-states that shared a language and a pre–World War II history and culture, but little else. The huge inequality in living standards, infrastructure, and income between the western and eastern portions of Germany has been tempered in the two decades since unification, but despite huge transfers of wealth, these inequalities are still not resolved. Since reunification, the government has spent nearly $2 trillion on eastern Germany in an effort to modernize its infrastructure and stabilize its economy. Following reunification, inefficient and bloated state-owned enterprises collapsed and shrank, which led to massive layoffs. Although unemployment in the former East Germany has declined, it remains at nearly 20 percent, twice the figure of the former West Germany.

Twenty years later, reunification is viewed favorably by the vast majority of all Germans.[8]

Political Regime

For students of political science, Germany's political regime since 1949 (often called the **Bonn Republic**, since Bonn was West Germany's capital from 1949 to 1990) is a fascinating example of constitutional engineering. The republic's founders sought to prevent the breakdown of democracy that doomed the Weimar Republic. Thus, the Bonn Republic's architects sought a better balance between local and national power, between the legislature and the executive, between political stability and representative democracy, and between the power of the state and the rights of individuals. They created an innovative political system that also contained some elements of continuity with Germany's institutional past. The German political system has more checks and balances, and is thus less efficient and decisive than the British model, but to date it has proved remarkably stable and effective.[9]

Political Institutions

THE CONSTITUTION

The Basic Law (intended to serve as West Germany's temporary constitution until its unification with East Germany) was amended in 1990 to incorporate East German states and has become Germany's permanent constitution. The Basic Law is founded on five principles, designed to avoid both the chaos of the Weimar Republic and the authoritarianism of the Third Reich.[10] First, where Hitler destroyed the power of German states, the Bonn Republic Basic Law created a system of cooperative federalism, in which the federal government and state governments share power. Second, the Basic Law guaranteed an elaborate set of basic political, social, and economic rights. Third, to counter the powerful Weimar president, the Bonn Republic established a weak, indirectly elected head of state. Fourth, political power is concentrated in the head of government, the chancellor, elected by and directly responsible to the legislature. Fifth, the Bonn Republic established a powerful and independent judiciary to check the government. Each of these constitutional features will be discussed in more depth in the following sections.

- **Legislative-executive system**: Parliamentary
- **Legislature**: Parliament
- **Lower house**: Bundestag (Federal Diet)
- **Upper house**: Bundesrat (Federal Council)
- **Unitary or federal division of power**: Federal
- **Main geographic subunits**: *Länder* (states)
- **Electoral system for lower house**: Mixed single-member districts and proportional representation
- **Chief judicial body**: Federal Constitutional Court and Federal Court of Justice

The Basic Law can be amended by a two-thirds majority in both houses. In an attempt to prevent excessive concentration of state power, however, some constitutional features, such as Germany's federal system and individual rights, cannot be altered.

The Branches of Government

THE HEAD OF GOVERNMENT AND THE CABINET

German democracy is often referred to as chancellor democracy, since the **federal chancellor**, or prime minister, is the most powerful political figure and the chief executive authority in Germany. The Basic Law made the office of the chancellor far more powerful vis-à-vis the head of state to create a stronger, more stable, and more democratic regime than the Weimar Republic.

As is typical in a parliamentary system, the head of government is elected by the lower house of the legislature (the Bundestag) and has always been the leader of the largest party in the legislature. As the leader of the largest party or coalition, chancellors expect to see most of their government's policy proposals approved by the legislature. Chancellors appoint and oversee the cabinet, the group of ministers (currently 15) who head government departments. Cabinet ministers need not be members of the legislature (though most are). Chancellors may create or eliminate cabinet posts at will. Chancellor Helmut Kohl, for example, created a minister for the environment, conservation, and nuclear safety; his successor, Gerhard Schroeder, combined the ministries of economics and labor. Chancellors may fire cabinet ministers at any time, although chancellors who preside over coalition governments may threaten the stability of the government when dismissing a cabinet member from a party that is a coalition partner. Indeed,

German Chancellors and Their Coalitions, 1949–2012

BUNDESTAG ELECTION YEAR	GOVERNING COALITION	CHANCELLOR (PARTY)
1949	CDU/CSU–FDP, DP	Konrad Adenauer (CDU)
1953	CDU/CSU–FDP, DP	"
1957	CDU/CSU, DP	"
1961	CDU/CSU–FDP	" (to 1963) Ludwig Erhard (CDU)
1965	CDU/CSU–FDP (to 1966) CDU/CSU–SPD (1966–69)	Ludwig Erhard (CDU, 1965–66) Kurt Kiesinger (CDU, 1966–69)
1969	SPD-FDP	Willy Brandt (SPD)
1972	SPD-FDP	Willy Brandt (SPD, to 1974) Helmut Schmidt (SPD, to 1976)
1976	SPD-FDP	Helmut Schmidt (SPD)
1980	SPD-FDP (1980–82) CDU/CSU–FDP (1982–83)	Helmut Schmidt (SPD, 1980–82) Helmut Kohl (CDU)
1983	CDU/CSU–FDP	"
1987	CDU/CSU–FDP	"
1990	CDU/CSU–FDP	"
1994	CDU/CSU–FDP	"
1998	SPD-Greens	Gerhard Schroeder (SPD)
2002	SPD-Greens	"

| 2005 | CDU/CSU–SPD | Angela Merkel (CDU) |
| 2009 | CDU/CSU-FDP | " |

Key to Party Acronyms:
CDU/CSU: Christian Democratic Union/Christian Social Union
DP: Deutsche Partei, conservatives
FDP: Free Democratic Party
SPD: Social Democratic Party
Source: Adapted from Simon Green et al., *The Politics of the New Germany* (New York: Routledge, 2008), p. 63.

all German cabinets since 1949 have been coalitions of at least two parties, and coalition partners often designate their preferred candidates to occupy the cabinet posts allotted to them.

The actual power of German chancellors has varied over time, depending in part on their ability to dominate their own parties. Two recent German chancellors, Helmut Kohl and Gerhard Schroeder, were especially dominant political figures. Kohl was the unquestioned leader of his party, had few powerful rivals, and oversaw German reunification. Schroeder also came to dominate his party and his coalition partners, the Greens.

Chancellors have at their disposal considerable resources, including the chief of the chancellery, a chief of staff with broad powers over the government. In addition to naming the cabinet, the chancellor makes numerous political appointments to government posts.

THE HEAD OF STATE

Like most parliamentary systems, Germany's head of state (the **federal president**) is separate from the head of government. In contrast to the Weimar Republic, in which the substantial powers of a directly elected president were abused to facilitate Hitler's rise to power, the Basic Law makes the president an indirectly elected and mostly ceremonial figure who performs mainly symbolic tasks. The president may formally sign bills into law, must sign treaties, and can pardon convicted criminals—but usually takes such actions only at the behest of the chancellor. Presidents can, however, refuse to sign laws they believe contravene the constitution. (President Horst Köhler did so twice in 2006.) They formally nominate candidates to become chancellor but are expected to select the head of the majority party in the legislature or, absent a majority, the head of the largest party in the legislature. Those candidates, moreover, must receive a majority of the votes in the lower house of the legislature. In the case of a badly fragmented legislature, the president could conceivably exercise some significant discretion in deciding on a nominee, but to date, this situation has not occurred. Presidents also decide whether to dissolve the legislature and call new elections when there is no majority.

German presidents are elected for a maximum of two five-year terms by a special Federal Convention that includes all members of the lower house of the legislature and an equal number of individuals selected by Germany's state legislatures. Presidents are intended to be consensus choices who are highly respected elder statesmen, and they are expected to behave in scrupulously nonpartisan fashion once in office.

The president from 2004 to 2010, Horst Köhler, was a highly respected conservative economist and former head of the International Monetary Fund. Köhler was a somewhat controversial president.[11] In 2006 he refused to sign a consumer information law passed by the legislature because he viewed the legislation as violating states' rights as enshrined in the Basic Law. He was narrowly re-elected in May 2009, but resigned in May 2010 after he made controversial statements about Germany's overseas military deployments. He was replaced by another conservative, Christian Wulff, a former premier of the state of Lower Saxony, and a close ally of Chancellor Merkel. Wulff became Germany's youngest president (he was 51 at the time) and was the first Catholic president in more than 40 years. Allegations in 2011 that Wulff failed to disclose the receipt of a home loan from a businessman while he was a state premier, and Wulff's attempt to intimidate the newspaper that broke the story, forced him to resign. Joachim Gauck, an East German anti-communist opposition leader, was elected president in 2012. Gauck narrowly lost the 2010 presidential election as the candidate of the SPD and Greens.

THE LEGISLATURE

In parliamentary systems, the legislature is normally the center of political power. Germany's bicameral legislature, Parliament, is a powerful institution, but the Basic Law weakened the legislature's power vis-à-vis the chancellor in order to avoid the problems that had undermined the Weimar Republic. The lower house, the **Bundestag** (Federal Diet), represents the population; the upper house, the **Bundesrat** (Federal Council), represents Germany's 16 states.

The Bundestag is the more powerful of the two houses. It currently has 622 deputies, who are Germany's only directly elected public officials at the federal

German Chancellor Angela Merkel congratulates new president Joachim Gauck at his swearing-in ceremony in March 2012.

level. Deputies are elected for a maximum of four years, though elections can occur earlier. The Bundestag's chief power is its capacity to elect the chancellor. Because no German party has ever won a majority of seats in the legislature, members of the lower house select a chancellor (normally the head of the party with the most seats) who can form a majority coalition among the parties in the legislature. The current chancellor, **Angela Merkel**, was first elected after the 2005 elections, when her conservatives were able to form a majority legislative coalition with the Social Democrats. After the 2009 elections, she began a second term, this time in coalition with the centrist Free Democrats.

The Bundestag can remove the chancellor, but only through a "constructive" vote of no confidence. During the Weimar Republic, chancellors were often removed from power by the legislature, usually with votes from extreme parties of the right and left who were unable to agree on a new chancellor. The result was a succession of weak chancellors, political paralysis, and the imposition of presidential rule that facilitated the rise of Hitler. As a result, the Basic Law allows the Bundestag to remove a chancellor only if a majority of its members can (constructively) approve a replacement. There have been only two constructive votes of no

Germany is already a leader in renewable energy production, thanks in part to policies enacted under Schroeder's government, and it is the world's third-largest producer of solar panels.[31] By 2010, Germany got about 17 percent of its electricity from renewable sources (hydro, solar, wind, biomass, and biogas), but that figure is slated to increase to almost 40 percent by 2020. If Germany is going to shy away from nuclear energy in the post-Fukushima era, it will have to accelerate its already impressive pursuit of renewable energy.

Germany's Immigration Dilemma

In August 2010, Thilo Sarrazin, a prominent banker, member of the SPD, and a board member of Germany's Central Bank, published *Deutschland schafft sich ab* (*Germany Does Away with Itself*). The book, which became an instant best-seller, argued that immigration was destroying Germany because most Arab and Turkish immigrants were unwilling to integrate into German society.[32] Sarrazin was expelled from the SPD for his book and subsequent statements, and Chancellor Merkel denounced the book. However, in denouncing Sarrazin, Merkel admitted that immigration was a serious concern and claimed that multiculturalism had been a "total failure." Other politicians vigorously defended Sarrazin. Indeed, the controversy over Sarrazin's book revealed a major division among Germany's political class and German society. For example, a poll taken in September 2010 found that 36 percent of Germans agreed that the country was being "overrun by foreigners," and 58 percent thought that Germany's Muslim population should have their religious practices "seriously curbed." However, the debate about immigration and the growing resentment of immigrants may hamper Germany's ability to deal with a severe shortage of skilled labor. Since 2005, Germany has enacted legislation that requires immigrants to learn German and make an effort to integrate into German culture. Such policies are politically popular, but they may discourage skilled laborers from immigrating to Germany. Given Germany's low birthrate, a skilled worker shortage threatens to derail the growth of the German economy and drive up labor costs.

The origins of Germany's immigrant population was the wave of *gastarbeiters* (guest workers) invited to Germany in the 1950s and 1960s, initially mainly from Southern Europe, to help fuel Germany's rapid postwar economic recovery. Turkish citizens, most of whom are Muslim, soon became the largest group of immigrants, and today Germans of Turkish origin number about 4 million. Initially

Thilo Sarrazin, and a copy of his controversial book that was highly critical of immigration in Germany.

most Germans viewed the immigrants as temporary workers, and were reluctant to grant them rights as citizens, even when it became apparent that most immigrants wanted to remain in Germany. While the term *gastarbeiter* is no longer applied, Germans of foreign origin, even those who have lived in Germany for decades, are still often viewed as *Ausländers* (foreigners). In the early 1990s, an outbreak of anti-immigrant attacks heightened tensions and caused alarm among German politicians.[33]

Partly in response to this violence, Germany has made some progress in recognizing the need to better integrate immigrants into German society. Legislation passed in 2000 gives children of immigrants the right to gain citizenship. A national office of immigration and integration was opened in 2005 and now offers a variety of free courses aimed at providing immigrants with skills that can facilitate their integration into society. Still, German schools have worked poorly for children of immigrants. In 2009, only one in ten high school students of Turkish background passed the university admissions examination (half the rate of the German population at large).

NOTES

1. These disputes in many cases continue to simmer. See, for example, Mark Landler, "Lawsuit Reopens Old Wounds in Polish-German Dispute," *New York Times*, December 25, 2006, p. A1.

2. See Michael Hughes, *Nationalism and Society: Germany, 1800–1945* (London: Edward Arnold Press, 1988).

3. Monte Palmer, *Comparative Politics: Political Economy, Political Culture, and Political Interdependence* (New York: Wadsworth, 2005), p. 139.

4. Arnold J. Heidenheimer, *The Government of Germany* (New York: Crowell, 1967), p. 15. Or, as Dahrendorf describes the Weimar Republic: "a democracy without democrats." See Ralf Dahrendorf, *Society and Democracy in Germany* (New York: Doubleday, 1967).

5. On the Weimar Republic, see M. Rainer Lepsius, "From Fragmented Party Democracy to Government by Emergency Decree and National Socialist Takeover: Germany," in Juan Linz and Alfred Stepan, eds., *The Breakdown of Democratic Regimes: Europe* (Baltimore, MD: Johns Hopkins Press, 1978), pp. 34–79.

6. See Peter Katzenstein's discussion of West Germany's "semi-sovereignty," in Peter Katzenstein, *Policy and Politics in West Germany: The Growth of a Semi-Sovereign State* (Philadelphia, PA: Temple University Press, 1987).

7. For an excellent discussion of the Stasi, see Timothy Garton Ash, *The File* (New York: Vintage, 1998).

8. Pew 2009 Pulse of Europe Survey, http://pewglobal.org/2009/11/02/highlights-from 2009-pulse-of-europe-survey/, November 2, 2009 (accessed 5/25/11).

9. Dan Hough and Emil Kirchner, "Germany at 60: Stability and Success, Problems and Challenges," *German Politics* 19, no. 1 (March 2010): 1–8.

10. Adapted from M. Donald Hancock and Henry Krish, *Politics in Germany* (Washington, DC: CQ Press, 2009), pp. 80–103.

11. On the German presidency and the controversy surrounding Köhler, see Gerd Strohmeier and Ruth Wittlinger, "Parliamentary Heads of State: Players or Figureheads? The Case of Horst Köhler," in *West European Politics* 33, no. 2 (March 2010): 237–57.

12. On German federalism, see Carolyn Moore and Wade Jacoby, eds., *German Federalism in Transition: Reform in a Consensual State* (London: Routledge, 2010).

13. Brigitte Geissel, "How to Improve the Quality of Democracy? Experiences with Participatory Innovations at the Local Level in Germany," *German Politics and Society* 27, no. 4 (Winter 2009): 51–71.

14. On the German party system, see Steven Weldon and Andrea Nusser, "Bundestag Election 2009: Solidifying the Five Party System," in Eric Langenbacher, ed., *Between Left and Right: The 2009 Bundestag Elections and the Transformation of the Germany Party System* (New York: Berhan Books, 2010), pp. 69–85.

15. David Conradt, "The Shrinking Elephants: The 2009 Election and the Changing Party System," in Langenbacher, ed., *Between Left and Right*, pp. 48–68.

16. A good treatment of the CDU is Ulrich Lappenküper, "Between Concentration Movement and People's Party: The Christian Democratic Union in Germany," in Michael Geller and Wofram Kaiser, eds., *Christian Democracy in Europe Since 1945*, Vol. 2 (New York: Routledge, 2004), pp. 25–37.

17. On the SPD, see William Paterson and James Sloam, "Is the Left Alright? The SPD and the Renewal of German Social Democracy," in *German Politics* 15, no. 3 (September 2006): 233–48; and Dan Hough and James Sloam, "Different Road Maps, Similar Paths? Social Democratic Politics in the UK and Germany," *German Politics* 16, no. 1 (March 2007): 26–38.

18. Ingolfur Bluhdorn, "Alliance 90/The Greens at the Dawn of New Opportunities" *German Politics and Society* 27, no. 2 (Summer 2009): 45–62.

19. On the Left Party, see Dan Hough and Michael Kob, "Populism Personified or Reinvigorated Reformers? The German Left Party in 2009 and Beyond," *German Politics and Society* 27, no. 2 (Summer 2009): 77–91.

20. Taehyun Nam, "Rough Days in Democracies: Comparing Protests in Democracies," *European Journal of Political Research* 46, no. 1 (January 2007): 97–120.

21. "Paving the Way for a Muslim Parallel Society," *Der Speigel*, March 29, 2007.

22. David Conradt, *The German Polity*, 9th ed. (New York: Houghton Mifflin Harcourt, 2009), p. 77.

23. See, for example, the World Values Survey 1981–1999, "Views of a Changing World 2003," Pew Center for the People and the Press, www.people-press.org/2003/06/03/views-of-a-changing-world-2003/ (accessed 12/21/11).

24. Russell J. Dalton, *Citizen Politics* (New York: Chatham House, 2002), p. 84.

25. Dan Hough and Emil Kirchner, "Germany at 60: Stability and Success, Problems and Challenges" *German Politics* 19, no. 1 (March 2010): 1–8.

26. The European Central Bank reported in 2011 that since the introduction of the euro in 1999, Germany had gained competitiveness against all other euro-zone members. Reported in Floyd Norris, "Euro Benefits Germany More than Others in Zone," *New York Times*, April 22, 2011, http://topics.nytimes.com/top/reference/timestopics/subjects/c/currency/euro/index.html?scp=3&sq=Euro%20Benefits%20Germany&st=cse (accessed 5/25/11).

27. Hans Kundnani, "Germany as a Geo-economic Power," *The Washington Quarterly*, Volume 34, Issue 3: 37.

28. See, for example, Joe Nocera, "Germany Cuts off Its Nose," *New York Times,* November 28, 2011, www.nytimes.com/2011/11/29/opinion/nocera-germany-cuts-off-its-nose.html?scp=7&sq=Germany&st=cse (accessed 12/21/11).

29. M. Petrou, "Merkel Under Seige," in *Maclean's* [serial online] 124, no. 39 (October 10, 2011): 32–34. Available from: Academic Search Premier, Ipswich, MA (accessed 12/21/11).

30. Juergen Baetz, "Germany Decides to Abandon Nuclear Power by 2022," *Seattle Times*, May 30, 2011, http://seattletimes.nwsource.com/html/businesstechnology/2015187458_apeugermanynuclearpower.html (accessed 5/30/11).

31. "Renewable Energy Policy in Germany: An Overview and Assessment," published by Joint Global Change Research Institute, 2009, http://www.globalchange.umd.edu/energytrends/germany/6/ (accessed 5/27/11), and "German Lessons," *The Economist*, April 3, 2008, http://www.economist.com/node/10961890?story_id=10961890 (accessed 5/27/11).

32. An excellent overview of this controversy and the immigration issue in Germany is Tamar Jacoby, "Germany's Immigration Dilemma," in *Foreign Affairs* 90, no. 2 (March/April 2011): 8–14.

33. Mushaben J., "From Ausländer to Inlander: The Changing Faces of Citizenship in Post-Wall Germany," *German Politics & Society* [serial online], 28 no. 1 (March 30, 2010):141–164. Available from: Academic Search Premier, Ipswich, MA (accessed 12/22/11).

KEY TERMS

Basic Law Germany's current constitution

Bonn Republic The nickname for the Federal Republic of Germany, named after West Germany's capital city

Bundesrat The upper house of Germany's legislature

Bundestag The lower house of Germany's legislature

catchall parties Parties that attempt to attract voters of all classes and are, therefore, generally centrist in their platforms

Christian Democratic Union (CDU) Germany's largest conservative party

codetermination The system requiring that unions occupy half of all seats on the boards of directors of Germany's largest private firms

federal chancellor Germany's prime minister and head of government

Federal Constitutional Court The powerful court that interprets Germany's Basic Law

federal president The indirectly elected and largely ceremonial head of state

Federal Republic of Germany (FRG) The official name of democratic West Germany during the postwar division of Germany

Free Democratic Party (FDP) A small centrist party that has often formed part of governing coalitions

Gastarbeiter "Guest workers," or foreign workers allowed to reside temporarily in Germany to provide much-needed labor

German Democratic Republic (GDR) The official name of Communist East Germany during the postwar division of Germany

the Greens Germany's environmental party

Hitler, Adolf The Nazi leader during the Third Reich who led Germany to defeat in World War II

Junkers Politically powerful Prussian landed aristocrats

Länder German states

the Left The party farthest to the left of all Germany's major parties; an alliance of leftist Social Democrats and remnants of former East German Communists

Merkel, Angela Germany's current conservative chancellor, as of 2005

minister-president The governor of a German state

National Socialist (Nazi) Party Hitler's fascist party

neocorporatism A political economic model in which business, labor, and the state work within an explicit framework to guide the economy toward particular goals

Prussia The most powerful German state before Germany's unification

reich The German term for "empire"

reunification The 1990 integration of East and West Germany

Social Democratic Party (SPD) Germany's oldest party, located on the center-left

sovereign debt Debt incurred by the governments of states

Third Reich The name Hitler gave to his fascist totalitarian regime (1933–45)

Weimar Republic Germany's first democratic republic (1919–33), the collapse of which led to Hitler's totalitarian regime

Web Links

Germany's Basic Law, on-line version (www.constitution.org/cons/germany.txt)

Germany's Christian Democratic Party (www.cducsu.de)

Germany's Free Democratic Party (www.fdp-fraktion.de)

Germany's Green Party (www.gruene-bundestag.de)

Germany's Left Party (www.linksfraktion.de)

Germany's legislature (www.bundestag.de)

Germany's Social Democratic Party (www.spd.de/)

Information about Germany, a one-stop portal (www.deutschland.de/)

Major daily newspapers of Germany (www.deutschland.de/unterrubrik. php?lang=2&category1=157&category2=160&category3=199)

Russell Dalton's free online German Politics textbook (www.socsci.uci. edu/~rdalton/Pgermany.htm)

 Visit StudySpace for quizzes and other review material.
www.norton.com/studyspace

- **Vocabulary Flashcards of All Key Terms**
- **Country Review Quizzes**
- **Interactive Map Tours**

6

HEAD OF STATE:
Emperor Akihito
(since January 7, 1989)

HEAD OF GOVERNMENT:
Prime Minister
Yoshihiko Noda
(since August 29, 2011)

CAPITAL:
Tokyo

TOTAL LAND SIZE:
377,915 sq km (61st)

POPULATION:
127 million (10th)

GDP AT PPP:
$4.34 trillion (3rd)

**GDP PER CAPITA
AT PPP:**
$34,200 (38th)

**HUMAN DEVELOPMENT
INDEX RANKING:**
11th

Kurile Islands
Occupied by the Soviet Union since 1945;
today administered by Russia, but claimed by Japan

Sapporo

Akita

JAPAN

Sendai
Fukushima

Takeshima

Yokohama

TOKYO

Kobe

Hiroshima

Osaka   Nagoya

Fukuoka

Kitakyushu

Okinawa

JAPAN

Introduction

Why Study This Case?

Japan offers an important case for the study of contemporary politics, perhaps foremost to educate a Western audience about what Japan is *not*. Too much of our understanding of Japan is shaped or at least shadowed by dangerously misleading stereotypes. For example, Japan is *not*:

- *small*: It has a landmass greater than that of Germany or Great Britain; a population larger than that of all non-Asian countries other than the United States, Brazil, Nigeria, and Russia; and an economy third only to those of the United States and China.
- *defenseless*: Despite the constitution's famous **Article 9**, which renounces war, Japan possesses a **Self-Defense Force** second only to the U.S. military in terms of technical sophistication, and boasts defense expenditures comparable to or greater than those of all member countries of the North Atlantic Treaty Organization (NATO) except the United States.
- *unique, or at least no more so than any other country*: In terms of political stability, state involvement in the economy, cultural conformity, and even ethnic homogeneity, Japan may be quite different from the United States, but in these and other ways it is more often the United States that is exceptional, not Japan.

If Japan is more "normal" than we might have assumed, it nonetheless remains an intriguing case that defies generalization and begs further investigation.

Politically, an authoritarian vanguard of low-ranking nobles launched a sweeping revolution from above in the latter half of the nineteenth century, modernizing Japan under the mercantilist slogan **"rich country, strong military."** As in Germany during the same period, the aristocracy and its militarist successors waged wars of imperialist expansion in the name of the Japanese emperor during the first half of the twentieth century, which led ultimately to stunning defeat at the hands of the United States in 1945. U.S. occupiers then launched a second revolution from above, replacing authoritarian rule with a remarkably liberal and democratic constitution written entirely by the Americans (in just six days) and wholly unaltered by the Japanese in more than six decades.

For more than five of these past six decades, the conservative **Liberal Democratic Party (LDP)** governed Japan. Moreover, elected politicians have historically been subservient to Japan's nonelected career civil servants, who write most of Japan's laws. But in a momentous 2009 election, the reformist **Democratic Party of Japan (DPJ)** pushed the LDP out of power, promising, among other things, to break up this long-standing conservative alliance between nonelected bureaucrats and the LDP. The historic shift in government presents a ripe opportunity to examine questions of Japan's political development. How has Japan's externally imposed democracy evolved over the years? Does this recent change in government indicate the prospect of a more fundamental regime change? And what lessons might Japan offer for more recently imposed democratic nation building efforts elsewhere?

Economically, under conditions of state-directed industrialization, imperialism, and war, Japan's authoritarian leaders forged a highly centralized economy in the first half of the twentieth century. Concerned about Japan's economic stability in a heightening Cold War, the United States allowed the war-torn nation to retain many aspects of its state-led economic structure, even as it promoted sweeping political reforms. Japan therefore extended into peacetime its wartime mercantilist economy, which linked career bureaucrats, conservative politicians, and a big-business elite (what analysts have called neocorporatism without labor) and was spectacularly successful for several decades.[1] By the 1980s, Japan had achieved and in many cases surpassed the levels of technological prowess, commercial competitiveness, and economic prosperity of the advanced Western industrialized nations.

By the early 1990s, however, this seemingly invincible economy began a dramatic and persistent decline. If Japan's state-led expansion draws comparisons with Prussian modernization or French *dirigisme* (planned economy), Japan's more recent economic downturn invites comparisons with Great Britain's earlier postwar economic slide. Japan has entered its third decade of stagnant or slow economic growth and lagging industrial production. For much of this period, banks have been in crisis and unemployment has climbed as the stock market has plummeted. Its workforce is graying even as its population rapidly shrinks. In 2010, China surpassed Japan as the world's second-largest economy. Adding tragic and unprecedented insult to these decades of economic decline, in 2011 a devastating 9.0 earthquake and tsunami struck northeast Japan, killing tens of thousands and damaging several nuclear power plants. This catastrophe further hobbled the country's economy, threatened its energy infrastructure, exacerbated political instability, and severely strained state capacity to deal with the humanitarian disaster. Although Japan remains wealthy and most of its citizens relatively prosperous, few countries have faced such a striking peacetime turnaround in economic fortune. How does one account for this dynamic of rapid growth followed by precipitous decline? What have been the causes of Japan's economic success and its more recent failures? If its mercantilist policies persisted throughout the past century, can they be held responsible for both the rise and the decline of the nation's economy? Must Japan change, and if so, how and when?

Finally, Japan may not be unique, but its balancing of freedom and equality certainly differentiates it to some degree from many other countries. Although income inequality is rising in Japan, historically its citizens have enjoyed high levels of equality. However, this relative equity has been managed with low levels of taxation, social services, and other state measures designed to redistribute income (what one political scientist described as "equality without effort"[2]). By the same token, the civil and personal freedoms enshrined in Japan's postwar constitution are unrivaled by all but the most liberal Western regimes, yet Japanese politics remains elitist, Japan's society conformist, and its economy mercantilist.

Even the less stereotypical and more nuanced generalized features of Japan's economy and polity now face the prospect of unprecedented, if not revolutionary, change. In the wake of the country's prolonged economic downturn, long-standing corporate practices, such as lifetime employment for white-collar workers, are fading. In the face of persistent government scandal and a growing popular sense of political inefficacy, policy making in a previously harmonious Japan is becoming far more fractious and perhaps even more pluralist. Is Japan facing a third revolution, this time from below? Only by understanding this country and where it has come from will we be able to make sense of where it may be going.

Major Geographic and Demographic Features

Even though Japan may not be a particularly small country, its topography and demography certainly make it seem small and have given the Japanese a keen sense of vulnerability and dependency. Although the Japanese archipelago includes nearly 7,000 islands (including several of disputed sovereignty), few are inhabited, and nearly all Japanese citizens reside on one of the four main islands: Hokkaido, Honshu, Kyushu, and Shikoku. Even on the main islands, mountainous terrain renders only 12 percent of the land habitable, and 80 percent of all Japanese live in an urban setting, with half the population crowded into three megametropolises located on Japan's eastern seaboard: Tokyo, Osaka, and Nagoya. This means that most of Japan's 126 million inhabitants are crammed into an area about twice the size of New Jersey, making Japan one of the most densely populated countries in the world.

Land (both habitable and arable) is not the only scarce natural resource in Japan. Although it has maintained rice self-sufficiency through heroic levels of subsidies for inefficient domestic producers and through trade restrictions on foreign rice (Japanese consumers pay up to eight times the world market price for their rice), Japan remains dependent on imports for nearly three-fourths of its food. This critical dependence extends to most of the crucial inputs of an advanced industrial economy, including virtually all of Japan's oil and most of its iron ore, thus compelling modern Japan to focus on external trade relations and making it particularly sensitive to the vagaries of such trade.

Japan's external focus has sharpened at important historical junctures because of its relative proximity to the Asian mainland. The Korean Peninsula in particular served as a ready conduit to ancient and medieval Japan for importing language, technology, religion, and even the popular culture of Korea, China, and places beyond. Over time, Japan adopted (and adapted) from its mainland mentors traditions as varied as Buddhism and bowing, chopsticks and Chinese written characters. At the same time, Japan feared its vulnerability at the hands of its powerful neighbors to the west (particularly China and, later, Russia), and Japanese cartographers and rulers identified the Korean Peninsula as a dagger poised at the heart of Japan.

Japan's fears of vulnerability were not unfounded. In the thirteenth century, a formidable force of Mongols and Koreans mounted two separate attacks on Japan, both of which were repulsed in part by typhoons (named *kamikaze*, or "divine wind," by the Japanese) that blew the attacking ships off course. These incursions and subsequent struggles for power within Japan led rulers first to practice for several hundred years and then to impose for two and a half centuries a formal policy of *sakoku* (**"closed country"**), or xenophobic isolation. This ended only when Western imperialists forcibly opened Japan in the nineteenth century, reaffirming Japanese fears of weakness.

Japan's insular status has certainly contributed to its racial, ethnic, and linguistic homogeneity and its cohesive national identity. This cultural uniformity, however, should not be overstated. Although today virtually all citizens of Japan identify themselves as Japanese, this image masks the earlier assimilation of the indigenous Ainu (now found almost exclusively on Hokkaido) and the Okinawans. In recent decades, Japan has witnessed an influx of Asian migrant workers (predominantly from Southeast Asia, China, and South Asia), who continue to face varying degrees of political discrimination and social marginalization.

Historical Development of the State

Despite the many cultural oddities that European traders and missionaries discovered when they first arrived in sixteenth-century Japan, they had actually stumbled upon a nation and society whose historical development bore striking similarities to that of their own countries. As in Europe, isolated tribal anarchy had gradually given way to growing national identity and the emergence of a primitive state. Aided by clearly defined natural borders and imperial and bureaucratic institutions borrowed from neighboring China, the Japanese state grew in both capacity and legitimacy, particularly after the seventh century C.E. Imperial rule was first usurped and then utilized by a feudal military aristocracy that came to rule over an increasingly centralized and sophisticated bureaucratic state for many centuries, even as it allowed the emperors to continue to reign symbolically.

Whereas gradually weakening feudalism gave way to powerful modernizing monarchs and ultimately middle-class democracy in Europe, Japan's version of centralized feudalism persisted until Western imperialism provided the catalyst for change in the nineteenth century. Faced with external threats to their nation's sovereignty, forward-looking authoritarian oligarchs further centralized state power and consciously retained the emperor as a puppet to legitimate their forced-draft efforts to catch up with the West. During this Meiji era, the oligarchs, borrowing this time not from China but from the institutions of modern European states, established a modern Japanese state that grew in autonomy and capacity as it

TIMELINE OF POLITICAL DEVELOPMENT

YEAR	EVENT
645 C.E.	China-inspired Taika political reforms introduced
1192	Minamoto Yoritomo declared first shogun
1603	Tokugawa Shogunate established
1853–54	Japan forcibly opened by U.S. Commodore Matthew C. Perry
1867–68	Meiji Restoration takes place
1894–95	First Sino-Japanese War is fought
1904–05	Russo-Japanese War is fought
1918–31	Era of Taisho democracy
1937–45	Second Sino-Japanese War takes place
1941	Pacific War begins
1945	Japan is defeated and surrenders in World War II
1945–52	The United States occupies Japan
1955	LDP formed
1993	LDP briefly loses majority in Diet's House of Representatives
2007	LDP loses majority in Diet's House of Councillors
2009	DPJ gains majority in House of Representatives
2011	Tohoku earthquake, tsunami, and nuclear disasters take place

became a formidable military and industrial power. In further emulating the Western imperial powers, Japan also began to establish its own empire (benignly labeled the "Greater East Asian Co-Prosperity Sphere), obtaining colonies in Taiwan (after defeating imperial China in 1895) and Korea (after defeating tsarist Russia in 1905). In the 1930s, Japan continued its expansion on the Asian mainland, capturing Manchuria (1931), invading China proper (1937), and sweeping through Southeast Asia at the same time that it launched its attack on Pearl Harbor and the United States (1941). However, this course of imperial expansion and military conquest ended with defeat at the hands of the Americans in 1945, who defanged Japan's militarist state but allowed its mercantilist bureaucracy to remain intact.

Although modernization brought dramatic changes to Japan, several themes or continuities emerge from this process that are relevant to the development of Japan's modern state and its contemporary politics. First, at critical junctures in its history, outside influence or foreign pressure (what the Japanese call *gaiatsu*) has brought change to Japan. Second, in the face of this pressure, the Japanese have often chosen not to reject or even resist the external influence but rather to adopt and then adapt it, deftly assimilating what they perceive as valuable foreign innovations and achieving modernization without all of the trappings of Westernization. Third, for many centuries and arguably to the present, Japan's ruling elite has maintained a persistent division of labor between those who rule and those who reign. This division of responsibility has preserved the autonomy and strengthened the political capacity of those rulers controlling power while enhancing the continuity of the regime and the legitimacy of the state by retaining symbolic reigning authority. Fourth, Japan early on established a highly effective and respected bureaucratic leadership, which has guided the state and pursued economic development as a means of achieving national sovereignty and state legitimacy. Scholars have argued that the resulting institutional arrangements facilitated a close working relationship between national bureaucrats and private business and propelled Japan's rapid modernization throughout the twentieth century. Japan's recent economic malaise and the apparent incapacity of the Japanese state to address this challenge, however, have called into question this developmental model.

PREMODERN JAPAN: ADAPTING CHINESE INSTITUTIONS

As early as the third century C.E., shifting coalitions of tribal hunters and early rice cultivators formed a primitive state in southern Honshu under the leadership of a tribal chieftain whose legitimacy rested on a claim of divine lineage descending from the sun goddess. By the seventh century, Japan had come under the powerful cultural influence of Tang dynasty China, an influence that cannot be overstated. Among the most significant and lasting of the dynasty's cultural exports were

Buddhism, Confucianism, the Chinese written language (which by that time had become the dominant script in all Asia), and the trappings of material culture (including modes of dress, architectural styles, and even the use of chopsticks).

Tang China also had a profound influence on political reforms in seventh-century Japan, inspiring the country's leaders to establish an administrative system modeled on the Tang imperial state. To finance this new bureaucracy, the state introduced sweeping land reform, purchasing all land and redistributing it among peasants so that it could be taxed. Although Buddhist religious doctrines and Confucian social values thrived, the Tang-inspired Taika administrative and land reforms did not take hold as well as the other borrowings. The meritocratic civil bureaucracy soon evolved into a hereditary, self-perpetuating ruling elite supported by a declining tax base. Squeezed mercilessly, the peasants, either for survival or protection, were forced to sell out to local wealthy officials, who had managed to arrange tax immunity for their own lands.

From the eighth to the twelfth century, political power and wealth steadily shifted from the central government to independent rural landowners, and the urban-centered imperial system gradually disintegrated into a formalistic body concerned only with the trappings and rituals of state. The decentralized hierarchies included the territorial nobles or lords, known as daimyo, who governed the lands they occupied; the former peasants, who had become their serfs; and their warrior retainers, or **samurai**.

As their power grew, the landed aristocrats became increasingly dissatisfied with the ineffectual rule of the court. Over the course of the next 400 years, from the thirteenth through the sixteenth century, power was completely transferred to this military aristocracy. Different clans vied for supremacy, and ascendant clans established a government known as the *bakufu* (literally, "tent government," referencing its martial origins). This was a period of continual warfare based on attempts at establishing a line of succession and a semblance of unity through military conquest, during which the emperor was largely disregarded. But in Japan, unlike in Europe, the imperial household was neither "absolutely" empowered nor completely displaced. The emperor had become not so much a person as a symbol; whoever spoke in the name of the imperial chrysanthemum crest spoke with legitimate authority. The best comparison to a Western experience is perhaps that of the powerful European kings who sought claim to spiritual authority through papal anointing. The emperor became a puppet in the hands of aspiring daimyo, who never destroyed the emperor but forced him to anoint the strongest among them **shogun**, or dominant lord.

TOKUGAWA SHOGUNATE: CENTRALIZED FEUDALISM

By the end of the sixteenth century, the feudal wars had come to a head, and Japan was slowly but surely unified by the **Tokugawa** shogunate, which imposed an enforced peace for the next two and half centuries. Successive shoguns from the Tokugawa clan ruled over this feudal hierarchy in the name of the emperor, successfully shoring up the shogunate's authority and keeping the daimyo in check through an effective strategy of divide and rule at home and *sakoku*, or closed-country isolation, abroad.

The power of a local daimyo rested, in turn, on the size and productivity of the hereditary fief or feudal domain he controlled, the peasants who tilled the land, and, most important, the number of samurai the domain could support. The warrior retainers lived with their lords in the castle towns that served as the fortresses and administrative centers from which the lords governed their domains. But as the Tokugawa-enforced peace settled over the countryside, the samurai were gradually converted from warriors to civil officials with fiscal, legal, and other administrative responsibilities. These samurai-turned-bureaucrats tackled civilian tasks in the same devoted, selfless manner in which they had been trained to carry out their martial responsibilities. It is difficult to overstate the value of this cadre of efficient, skilled, disciplined, and highly respected bureaucrats as the country faced the challenges of abrupt modernization in the nineteenth and twentieth centuries.

Although Tokugawa Japan's political system was remarkably stable, its social organization and economy developed what proved to be volatile contradictions. Tokugawa society was strictly hereditary and rigidly hierarchical; individuals were born into a particular station and could neither move between classes nor, for the most part, even advance within their own class. The samurai class was at the top of the hierarchy, but not all samurai were equal. Theirs was a diverse warrior class, ranging from the wealthy and powerful shogun and daimyo to the lowly retainers barely getting by on a subsistence stipend of rice. Next down on the social rung were the peasants, who formed the bulk of the remaining subjects, followed by artisans and craftsmen, and finally, at (or near) the bottom of the social hierarchy, the merchants.[3] As in other Confucian societies, commercial activities, including moneylending, and those people who participated in them were viewed with great disdain. Despite being socially despised, however, by the nineteenth century these merchants had established sophisticated and lucrative trading networks throughout Japan. Moreover, they had established themselves as the financiers of the lifestyles of the upper ranks of the samurai, who over time grew increasingly indebted to the merchants.

When Commodore Matthew C. Perry steamed into Edo Bay with his fleet of U.S. warships in 1853, he unsuspectingly came upon this system, which was apparently stable but internally ripe for change. The ruling class had status and privilege but was heavily indebted and, in the case of many low-ranking samurai, even impoverished. The merchants were wealthy but socially disdained, lacking both political power and social status. Many Japanese, particularly among the lower ranks of the samurai, had become dissatisfied with what they saw as an increasingly ineffectual and redundant Tokugawa government and were ready for revolt. Perry did not cause this revolt, but he certainly facilitated it.

The forceful entry of American and (subsequently) European powers into Japan and the pressure they placed on the shogunate created a crisis of legitimacy for Tokugawa rule. Virtually free from foreign military threats and isolated from external innovations during the centuries of *sakoku*, the Tokugawa government lacked the military capacity to resist the unfair trade demands of the Americans and Europeans. The regional daimyo, however, judged these demands as unacceptable and thus revolted.

A decade of political chaos ensued, prompting a revolution launched not from below, by restive peasants or even aspiring merchants, but from above, by a handful of junior samurai officials. Much like Germany's nineteenth-century modernizers, this aristocratic vanguard was committed to sweeping change cloaked in traditional trappings. They recognized that the maintenance of Japanese independence required the end of the feudal regime and the creation of a modern economic, political, social, and, perhaps most important, military system capable of holding its own against the Western powers. But rather than deposing the symbolic leader of the old regime, the modernizers launched their reforms in the name of the 16-year-old emperor Meiji, ostensibly "restoring" him to his rightful ruling position.

MEIJI RESTORATION: REVOLUTION FROM ABOVE

The group of junior samurai who led the **Meiji Restoration** in 1867 and 1868 came to be known as the **Meiji oligarchs**. What began as a spontaneous rejection of the Western threat by xenophobic nationalists quickly gave way to regime change led by a handful of low-ranking samurai promoting positive reform that involved emulation of and catching up with the West. These oligarchs served as a vanguard in establishing the foundations of the modern Japanese state.

Their first priority was to make Japan a strong and wealthy state capable of renegotiating the inequitable treaties the West had imposed on the country. Under the slogan "rich country, strong military," they promoted their mercantilist view of a strong relationship between economic development and industrialization on the one hand, and military and political power in the international arena on the other. They dismantled the feudal state, deposing the shogun and converting the decentralized feudal domains to centrally controlled political units. They jettisoned the feudal economy, eliminated hereditary fiefs, returned land to the peasants, and converted samurai stipends to investment bonds. Perhaps most surprisingly, they destroyed their own class, ending samurai privileges.

In 1889, the oligarchs adopted an imperial constitution (patterned after the German constitution), which was presented as a "gift" from the emperor to his subjects. It specified not the rights and liberties of the citizens but the duties and obligations that the subjects owed the emperor and the state. The constitution created some of the formal institutions found in Western democracies, including a bicameral parliament, known as the **Diet**, though its members were chosen by a limited franchise and exercised little real authority. The constitution vested all executive power in the emperor, who appointed the cabinet ministers (just as reigning emperors had previously appointed the ruling shogun) and retained supreme command over the military. The oligarchs further legitimized this power structure by promoting an emperor-centered form of Shintoism as the mandatory state religion and by inculcating both national patriotism and emperor worship in the education system.

Buttressed by the traditional and charismatic legitimacy of a reigning emperor and the rational-legal legitimacy of an equally symbolic (and largely powerless) parliament, the oligarchs had obtained both the authority and the autonomy to promote painfully rapid development and to create a modern military. The highly capable agents for carrying out these goals were threefold:

1. *Bureaucracy*: This revolution from above was envisioned by a handful of elites, but it was carried out by a modern, centralized bureaucracy recruited on the basis of merit. Although the civil service was open to all, it was staffed almost entirely by former samurai who were literate, respected, and had served their feudal lords in similar administrative capacities for generations.
2. *Zaibatsu*: Believing they did not have the luxury to wait for the emergence of an entrepreneurial class, the oligarchs fostered and financed the establishment of huge industrial conglomerates, known as zaibatsu, or financial cliques. In so doing, Japan's leaders forged the first of the enduring ties between big business and the state that have persisted to the present.

3. *Military*: Although the military was created initially for defense, the country's resource dependency, the voracious appetite of the zaibatsu, and the example of Western imperialism soon launched Japan on its own successful path of imperial warfare.

By the end of World War I, the Meiji oligarchs had realized many of their initial goals. In foreign policy, they had successfully renegotiated the inequitable treaties with the West, which now recognized Japan as a rising world power. Japan had not only defeated both imperial China (1894–95) and tsarist Russia (1904–05), but had also acquired colonies in Taiwan (1895) and Korea (1910). Furthermore, by this time Japan had established a fragile but rapidly growing economy.

But Japan's foreign policy and economic successes were not matched in the domestic political realm. By the 1920s, Japan was becoming a nation of diverse economic and political interests that could no longer be easily subsumed under a single banner or slogan, and pressure to change the highly authoritarian system was building. The desire for change became increasingly apparent during the reign of the Taisho emperor (1912–26), particularly in the era of Wilsonian democracy after World War I. By that time, the original Meiji oligarchs had passed from the scene, and efforts by their bureaucratic and military successors to maintain the state autonomy of the Meiji political system faced challenges from a middle class demanding democratic rights, laborers organizing for better working conditions, and peasants rioting against onerous taxes.

In an era that came to be known as **Taisho democracy** (1918–31), efforts by these groups and their liberal political proponents to institute democracy were significant but short-lived and ultimately unsuccessful. Different groups increasingly sought to exercise influence in the political realm, with some success, including the election of the first commoner as prime minister in 1918; the granting of universal male suffrage by 1925; and the establishment of political parties.

THE MILITARIST ERA: IMPERIAL EXPANSION AND DEFEAT

By the end of the 1920s, a number of events had stymied Japan's first attempt at liberal democracy. The Great Depression and the rising global protectionism of the 1930s dealt trade-dependent Japan a harsh blow, bringing about increased labor agitation and political unrest as the economy weakened. This domestic instability, combined with anti-Japanese sentiment in China, spurred rising nationalist and fascist sentiments at home and reemerging militarism and adventurism abroad.

As in Europe and elsewhere, the emergence of such forces led in the early 1930s to a period of political polarization and increased political violence, with democracy the chief victim. One Western observer labeled this period an era of "government by assassination."[4]

The era of Taisho democracy ended with the Japanese army's seizure of Manchuria in 1931 and the assassination of the last elected head of the government by naval cadets in 1932. Over the next decade, the military steadily expanded its control of the state, ruling in an often uneasy alliance with the bureaucracy and the zaibatsu. Although most historians are not comfortable labeling the Japanese militarist state fascist, the emperor-based system lent itself to the establishment of a near-totalitarian state, one with many similarities to the European fascist states. The state sought to bring under its auspices or otherwise eliminate virtually all pluralist groups and autonomous organizations, censoring the press, repressing all forms of political dissent, crushing political parties and other forms of free association, and gaining almost complete control over industrial production.

Also, like its fascist allies in Europe, Japan promoted an ultranationalist ideology and expansionist foreign policy, with the intent of extending its empire. It annexed Manchuria in 1932, invaded China proper in 1937, and launched full-scale war in December 1941 with the attack on Pearl Harbor and rapid expansion into Southeast Asia. At the height of its power, Japan's so-called Greater East Asian Co-Prosperity Sphere of conquered lands included most of the eastern half of China, Sakhalin and some of the Aleutian Islands, Korea, Taiwan, the Philippines, Indochina, Thailand, Malaya, Burma, Indonesia, and portions of the South Pacific. As in Europe, Allied forces met, stemmed, and turned back the aggression by 1944. Costly and stunning defeats at sea and on land, followed by the destructive U.S. firebombing of Japanese cities in early 1945 and the atomic bombing of Hiroshima and Nagasaki in August of that year, prompted Japan's unconditional surrender on September 2, 1945.

U.S. OCCUPATION: REINVENTING JAPAN

Japan's defeat and destruction were devastatingly complete: militarily, industrially, even psychologically. One historian estimates that the war cost Japan some 2.7 million lives (nearly 4 percent of its population), and that by war's end many more millions were injured, sick, or seriously malnourished.[5] Under these conditions, it was once again foreign (specifically, American) pressure that provided the impetus for revolutionary change in Japan. Although the seven-year occupation of Japan was technically an Allied operation, it remained overwhelmingly a U.S. enterprise managed by a single individual: the Supreme Commander of the Allied Powers in Japan, General **Douglas MacArthur**.

Like the arrival of Commodore Perry's ships nearly a century earlier, the American occupation of Japan following World War II is significant both for what it changed and what it did not change. The initial plan called for demilitarization to exorcise Japan's militant feudal past, and then democratization to establish American-style democratic values and institutions. Demilitarization proceeded swiftly and included not only the purging of all professional military officers, key wartime politicians, and zaibatsu leaders, but also the disbanding of the ultranationalist associations and political parties. These thorough purges destroyed the military class and replaced entrenched politicians with technocrats (in most cases, former bureaucrats) and zaibatsu families with professional managers. Most dramatically, the new "Japanese" constitution (quickly drafted by MacArthur's staff and adopted by the Diet in 1947 almost unaltered) included Article 9, the so-called Peace Clause, by which Japan would "forever renounce war as a sovereign right" and never maintain "land, sea, and air forces, as well as other war potential."

Changing the status of the emperor—constitutionally and in the eyes of the Japanese citizens—to no longer a political force was key to MacArthur's democratization efforts. The constitution reduced the emperor's stature from godlike and inviolable to simply symbolic, and it transferred sovereignty to the Japanese people. Other measures of this regime change included extending suffrage to women; clarifying relations among the prime minister, the cabinet, and the two houses of the Diet; guaranteeing civil rights and freedoms; breaking up the zaibatsu and imposing antitrust measures; encouraging labor unions and other interest groups; redistributing land to the peasants; and reforming the education system.

The two-stage approach of demilitarization and democratization remained largely in place for the first two years of the occupation. But continued economic hardship (due in part to war reparations and an American policy of little economic aid), combined with the newfound freedom of socialist and Communist activists, pushed Japan rapidly toward the left. This political shift and the onset of the Cold War (compounded by the Communist victory in China in 1949 and the outbreak of the Korean War in 1950) led to a "reverse course" in occupation policies.

The earlier desire to refashion Japan as weak and docile in the manner of an Asian Switzerland gave way to a plan that would make Japan a full, albeit still unarmed, ally of the West. In an effort to rebuild the economy, occupation authorities scaled back the deconcentration of industry and prohibited labor strikes. They purged and in some cases (re)jailed leftist labor activists even as they released and rehabilitated numerous conservative politicians. Notably, in all of the twists and turns of occupation policy, the wartime bureaucracy of technocratic planners was left intact, in part because the American occupiers needed it, and in part because the United States saw the bureaucracy as only the instrument, not the agent, of war.

Today, some occupation reforms are universally considered to have been both successful and beneficial. Others largely failed, whereas still others remain highly controversial and even contradictory. For

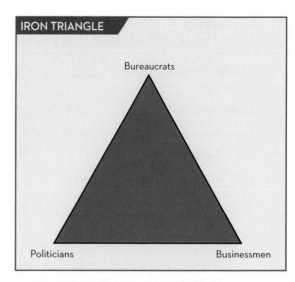

Japan's postwar corporatist and elitist state structure is often referred to as an "iron triangle," and has limited the political influence of Japanese citizens and other pluralist interests.

instance, on paper, Japan has one of the most liberal political systems in the world. But by default and design, its postwar state featured a core elite of experienced bureaucrats closely allied with conservative politicians (many of whom were former bureaucrats) and big-business executives. This ruling triad, or **iron triangle**, has remained largely intact throughout the past six decades and has been both credited for Japan's remarkable postwar development and blamed for its more recent economic troubles. We now turn to an examination of this contemporary political structure.

Political Regime

Is Japan a democracy? The continuing dominance of a ruling triad of bureaucrats, politicians, and businessmen has led to much controversy on this issue. In important ways, Japan's political structures and procedures are democratic. The rights and liberties enshrined in Japan's 1947 constitution certainly exceed those of the U.S. Constitution and are perhaps globally unrivaled. Its citizens are well protected by the rule of law, and its electoral system is probably no more corrupt than that of other advanced liberal democracies. Unlike in the United States, Japan's political arena hosts both socialist and Communist parties, arguably resulting in a greater range of political debate and choice than in the United States.

Yet these formal institutions and procedural safeguards of democracy do not tell the whole story. Although democratic practices seldom live up to the ideals of political pluralism in any democratic regime, the initial dominance and persistent power of the postwar bureaucracy and its conservative political and corporate allies have led some analysts to conclude that Japan's democracy is dysfunctional, if not an outright mockery. For more than five decades, the conservative LDP dominated the legislature, and both the LDP and its DPJ successor have in turn been overshadowed in policy making by nonelected career civil servants. Longstanding political practices and informal levers and linkages of power have constrained the full functioning of this imported democracy. This dualism becomes more apparent upon examination of the formal institutions and substantive practices of Japanese democracy.

Political Institutions

THE CONSTITUTION

"We, the Japanese people. . . ." The opening phrase of Japan's unamended 1947 constitution reveals what are perhaps the document's two most significant aspects: its American imprint and the transfer of sovereignty from the emperor to the Japanese people. Although America's allies were calling for the prosecution of Emperor Hirohito as a war criminal, General Douglas MacArthur insisted that the emperor renounce his divinity but be allowed to retain his throne, to offer continuity and legitimacy to both the occupation government and the new democratic regime. The constitution reduces the emperor's godlike stature to that of a "symbol of the State and of the unity of the people with whom resides sovereign power." In order to empower Japanese citizens, the American framers of the Japanese constitution constructed an elaborate system of representative institutions, including universal suffrage, a parliamentary legislature in which the cabinet is responsible to the Diet (rather than to the emperor), and an independent judiciary. The constitution also introduced a greater measure of local autonomy, increasing the role of local elected officials.

The Branches of Government

THE HEAD OF STATE

Although invested by the Meiji Constitution with total authority, the imperial institution was always controlled by de facto rulers. The 1947 constitution eliminated even this derivative authority, making the role of the emperor wholly

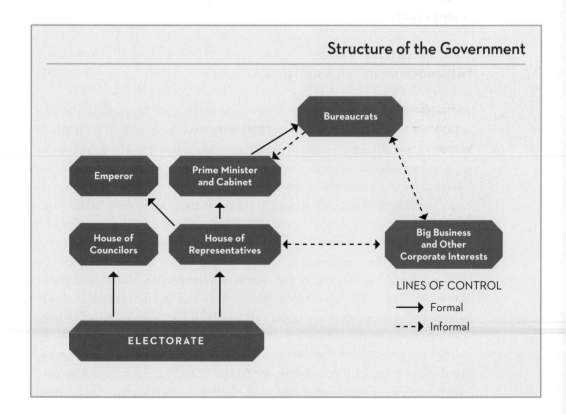

symbolic. Unlike the British monarch, the Japanese emperor is technically just a symbol of the Japanese state, not the head of state. Like the British queen, however, this standard-bearer of the world's oldest imperial dynasty continues to play a significant role in symbolizing the unity and continuity of contemporary Japan. The emperor also performs purely ceremonial tasks, such as appointing both the prime minister (once elected by the Diet) and the chief justice of the Supreme Court (once designated by the government), and he receives foreign ambassadors and represents the nation on many important ceremonial occasions at home and abroad.

The Japanese throne is both hereditary and patrilineal; therefore, no female heir is permitted to rule in her own right. Emperor Hirohito (who reigned from 1926 to 1989) was succeeded by his eldest son, Akihito, who became Japan's 125th emperor. Although polls show that recent generations of Japanese citizens, like their British counterparts, find themselves increasingly less connected to the throne, significant events, such as the passing of Hirohito and the birth of a prospective heir, generate enormous public interest and a deeper sense of attachment than the polls seem to indicate. Furthermore, Japan's royal family has faced none of the scandal that has challenged the British royals in recent years.

THE PRIME MINISTER AND THE CABINET

The prime minister serves as head of government and draws from the Diet at least the majority of cabinet members who serve as ministers, or heads, of Japan's 17 bureaucratic ministries and other key agencies. The prime minister is always chosen from the lower house or House of Representatives and is elected by the members of that chamber. Typically this has meant that the leader (president) of the political party holding a majority of seats in the House of Representatives (or leader of the dominant party in a ruling coalition) has been elected prime minister. Elections in the lower chamber must be held every four years, but prime ministers serve only as long as they can maintain the confidence of both the members of the House of Representatives and the members of their own party. This process has enhanced the role of internal factional party politics and required that successful candidates to the office of prime minister not just belong to the right party, but also curry sufficient favor and rise high enough in a dominant faction within that party. As the dominant party for over five decades from its formation in 1955, the LDP fostered prospective party leaders who were more concerned with factional ties, personal connections,

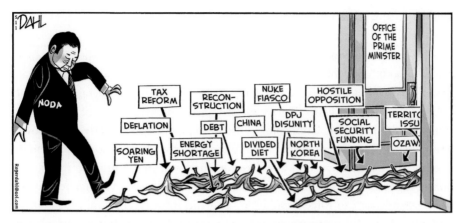

Like his predecessors, Japan's Prime Minister Noda and his DPJ government face a host of challenges, including a persistently sluggish economy and a costly clean-up of the tsunami and nuclear disasters.

and backroom bargaining than with promoting a particular ideological or policy agenda. Faction leaders typically brokered this selection process and rotated the office of LDP president (and prime minister) among various factions relatively frequently. Therefore, although Japanese prime ministers have been experienced and savvy politicians, they tend to be older, have less policy expertise, and, with notable exceptions, serve for far shorter tenures than do their counterparts abroad. The recent exception to this rule was the five-year tenure of LDP Prime Minister **Junichiro Koizumi** (2001–06). But in the five years since his departure, Japan had seven prime ministers; overall, a total of 37 heads of government have led the country since 1945 (compared to 14 for the United Kingdom and 9 for Germany). Although elected in 2009 with a mandate to reform politics as usual, the current DPJ government has followed the same pattern as the LDP, and has struggled to find a prime minister who can maintain the confidence of the party or the nation. The party's first prime minister served less than a year, and his successor served only 15 months. The prospects for current prime minister **Yoshihiko Noda**, who took office in 2011 leading a fractious party and facing a not-so-loyal opposition, are little better. In addition to party factions and what the Japanese call a "*twisted Diet*," in which no ruling party or coalition has control of both chambers of parliament, scholars also point to disgruntled voters, weak political leaders, and the rise of new media as possible reasons for the brief tenure of Japan's prime ministers.[6] But whatever the cause, this frequent turnover of elected heads of government has made these political leaders very dependent on the expertise, experience, and connections of the unelected bureaucrats within the ministries over which they ostensibly preside.

THE LEGISLATURE

The 1947 constitution declares Japan's legislature, or Diet (from the Latin *dieta*, meaning both "assembly" and "daily food allowance"), the "highest organ of state power" and claims exclusive law-making authority for the bicameral parliament. The Japanese Diet has two directly elected chambers: the House of Representatives and the House of Councillors. The **House of Representatives**, the lower house, has 480 members elected for a four-year term. As in other parliamentary systems, the government typically dissolves the lower house prior to the expiration of the term to call elections from a position of strength. Alternatively, a vote of no confidence can force dissolution, as it did most recently in 1993 (one of only four successful postwar no-confidence votes). General elections have taken place on average every two to three years since 1947. The upper chamber, the **House of Councillors**, comprises 242 members, elected for fixed six-year terms (staggered so that half the chamber stands for election every three years). Unlike the lower house, the upper house cannot be dissolved, but the House of Councillors has passed several symbolic but influential votes in recent years expressing no confidence in the party controlling the lower house as control of the upper house has shifted hands between coalitions led by the LDP and DPJ. In fact, for much of the time since 2007, parliament has faced a "twisted Diet." As in other parliamentary systems, Japan's constitution grants the lower house far more power than the upper; the House of Representatives can override any House of Councillors decision on significant legislation with a two-thirds majority vote. However, recent elections in both houses have permitted first the opposition DPJ and then the opposition LDP to use their position in the upper house to obstruct or at least slow the policies and embarrass the leadership of the party in government.

The Diet convenes for only about 80 days each year, a session roughly half the duration of that of the British Parliament. The brevity of the session has enhanced the role and responsibility of the standing committees and their members in the House of Representatives. Many veteran politicians have established both expertise in particular policy areas and close ties to bureaucrats and interest groups having jurisdiction over or interest in those policy areas. This has given individual legislators a degree of influence over policy formerly reserved for bureaucratic experts and has simultaneously weakened party discipline in voting. The importance of pursuing **pork-barrel projects** for home-district constituencies has also weakened allegiance to the government. Therefore, even though the LDP maintained single-party rule for decades and confronted growing demands for change in the face of persistent economic decline, LDP governments hesitated to promote reforms over the objections of these experienced and entrenched politicians bound to networks of bureaucrats, businesses, and local constituencies. Over the years, this has fostered conservative governments that promoted change only gradually, if at all. And even though DPJ governments promising change have in recent years ended the LDP's parliamentary monopoly, meaningful reform efforts have frequently been gridlocked by the "twisted" parliament these governments have faced.

THE JUDICIAL SYSTEM

The 1947 constitution established for Japan a court system with a high degree of judicial independence from the other branches of government. In practice, however, the LDP over the years used its political dominance, appointment powers, and other administrative mechanisms to manipulate the courts and ensure judicial decisions in accordance with its political interests. This was made easier because, unlike the dual system of federal and state courts in the United States, the Japanese system is unitary, with all civil, criminal, and administrative matters under the jurisdiction of a single hierarchy. At the top is the constitutional court, or Supreme Court, whose 15 members are appointed by the cabinet and subject to a retention referendum every ten years.

Although politicians in all democracies seek to influence the courts, this combination of a unitary judicial system dominated for many decades by a single conservative party, has rendered Japan's courts particularly subservient and, like the political party that served as its political patron, distinctly conservative. Perhaps not surprisingly, even though the Supreme Court is invested with the constitutional power of judicial review, it has seldom used this authority and has been extremely hesitant to declare policies or statutes unconstitutional. Since its creation in 1947, the Court has struck down only eight laws on constitutional grounds and has steadfastly refused to rule on matters relating to what is arguably postwar Japan's most significant constitutional issue: challenges to Japan's military and security activities under Article 9, the so-called Peace Clause.[7]

The Electoral System

As with other political institutions in Japan, the electoral system is both a cause and consequence of the LDP's long-standing reign. Postwar LDP governments maintained grossly disproportionate voting districts and established electoral rules that clearly favored the party's interests.[8] Only in the past few years have reforms enacted by a short-lived opposition coalition government in the mid-1990s begun to chip away at these LDP advantages and shift the landscape of electoral institutions and outcomes in Japan.

Representatives in the two chambers of the Diet are elected according to different rules. Although the membership of the weaker House of Councillors varied slightly during the postwar period, its electoral rules were not affected by the 1990s reforms and have remained largely unchanged. The 242 councillors serve fixed six-year terms, with half facing election every three years. Elected according to a mixed system, 96 are chosen from party lists using proportional representation (PR) in a nationwide election. The remaining 146 are elected from 47 multimember districts (MMDs) that coincide with Japan's 47 prefectures. Each district returns between one and five members, but rather than drawing from a party list, voters have a single, nontransferable vote that they cast for an individual candidate. In other words, rather than first-past-the-post in a single-member district (SMD), as in legislative elections in Great Britain and the United States, the top several-past-the-post (ranging from one to five members) are elected from each district.

Prior to 1994, the electoral system that was used to determine membership in the House of Representatives resembled the second part of the system used for the upper house.[9] Two significant consequences of the old system should be mentioned. First, because contenders ended up competing for seats not just against opposition candidates but also against members of their own party, the system produced factions or mini-parties within the LDP and other parties large enough to put forth multiple candidates. Therefore, the most important electoral battles were fought within the LDP, among individuals sharing essentially the same conservative ideology and policy positions. Second, unable to rely upon simple party or factional affiliations or even policy positions alone to succeed, candidates were compelled to form local party machines, known as *koenkai*, to generate essential votes and campaign funds and to institutionalize ties of mutual dependency.

In 1993, a series of notorious scandals, unpopular tax measures, and precipitous economic decline brought into government an opposition coalition that lost no time in reforming the rules governing lower house elections. The coalition's 1994 reforms eliminated the old system and established a new mixed system similar to that of Germany and Mexico. Under this system, the lower chamber retained 480 seats, but 300 of them are elected from SMDs. The remaining 180 are chosen by PR from 11 regional constituencies, in which seats are assigned to the parties according to their share of the total blocwide votes. As in the German system, candidates may run in their own districts and be included in a regional party list, to safeguard their seats in the event of defeat in the home SMD.

The architects of these reforms sought to shift electoral competition away from highly personalized factional politics within the LDP to national party politics between two dominant parties offering genuine policy alternatives. Although the PR portion of the ballot provides some seats for smaller parties able to garner the minimal threshold of votes, nearly two-thirds of the seats are chosen from SMDs, a system that favors well-organized and well-established parties, as in the United States and Great Britain. The 1994 reforms also reapportioned districts to reflect demographics more accurately, giving more equitable clout to the much more numerous (and typically less conservative) urban voters in an effort to weaken the disproportionate clout of rural voters, who had been among the LDP's most loyal supporters. As a testament to the importance of these kinds of formal political institutions, scholars attribute the recent tectonic political shifts that have consolidated opposition forces in the DPJ and that ended the LDP's half-century of single-party rule at least in part to these electoral reforms. Reflecting the continued elitism of Japanese politics, the reforms were less successful in dealing with (and in fact less concerned about) political corruption, which the Japanese call **money politics**—precisely the issue that the public and foreign observers most hoped would be addressed. Although anticorruption measures were implemented, as in other capitalist democracies, individual candidates and the corporations and other interest groups that woo them have discovered plenty of loopholes to keep campaign funds flowing, and campaign finance scandals continue to plague politicians from both the LDP and the DPJ.

Because the government automatically registers voters, virtually all eligible voters in Japan are registered. Accordingly, voter turnout in national elections has been relatively high, usually between 60 and 75 percent. But significantly, even as the system has become more competitive and politicians have increased their clout vis-à-vis the bureaucracy, voter turnout has declined. Although there are a number of reasons for the decline, popular distrust of politicians across the party spectrum and disillusionment with the political process and the Japanese state are paramount.

Local Government

Japan is divided into 47 administrative divisions, known as prefectures, each with its own elected governor and legislature. Japan is nonetheless a unitary (not a federal) system, in which most political power is invested in the central government. The

A common sight during Japan's election season, a white-gloved candidate for political office campaigns from her loudspeaker-equipped van.

prefectural governments decide many local issues and are able to raise sufficient taxes to cover about one-third of their expenditures (what the Japanese call 30 percent autonomy). These subnational governments depend on the central government, however, for the remainder of their budget. Central authorities delegate all local authority (at the prefectural and municipal levels) and can, and sometimes do, retract that authority. The national government can override the decision of any local governor, and has done so most notably in the case of Okinawa, whose elected local officials have attitudes toward the overwhelming U.S. military presence there that differ significantly from those of national leaders. Okinawans are not alone, however, in wishing for the devolution of more authority and increased local autonomy.

Recognizing the political value of this issue, the DPJ has garnered electoral support by promising to devolve greater authority to prefectural governments. Similarly, some regional politicians have called for the merger of city and prefectural governments in an effort to strengthen the hand of local authorities vis-à-vis Tokyo. In a nod to the American neoliberal and populist "Tea Party" movement, several of these politicians have labeled their successful political campaign a "sake" party similarly focused on cutting taxes, slashing salaries for elected officials, and wresting power from the central government.

Other Institutions: Bureaucracy and the Iron Triangle

The Japanese state's most influential, yet entirely extra-constitutional, institution of policy-making authority remains the bureaucracy. As in other liberal democracies, the Japanese bureaucracy staffs the dozen or so ministries comprising the Japanese state, but it is at once both smaller in size and greater in influence than any of its Western counterparts. Ministers appointed to head these ministries are often not experts in their assignments, but rather, obtain their appointments based on political criteria, and therefore rely almost entirely upon the career civil servants within their ministries to formulate, facilitate, and ultimately implement and enforce laws and policies. In each ministry, an administrative vice minister with some 25 to 30 years of experience in that particular ministry heads these efforts, presiding over a staff of Japan's brightest, who willingly subject themselves to grueling workweeks for relatively meager compensation (see "The Power and Prestige of Japan's Bureaucracy," p. 282).

Enduring linkages among senior bureaucrats, conservative politicians, and corporate executives form what has been referred to as an iron triangle, in which the determination and implementation of policies are often facilitated not by formal negotiations, hearings, or parliamentary votes but by informal discussion (known as **administrative guidance**) between former colleagues and during after-work drinking sessions among friends. This web of informal connections within the Japanese state consists of hundreds of triangles involving veteran politicians with particular policy expertise, bureaucrats in a particular ministry or division, and the private-sector representatives of interest groups in the given policy area. In the past, ruling bureaucrats traditionally dominated these associations, while reigning LDP governments made sure that the party's most important constituents, including corporations (from which the party received massive campaign funds) and rice farmers (on whose overrepresented vote the party depended), were well taken care of with producer-oriented industrial and financial policies and protectionist trade barriers. Representatives of Japan's large corporations in turn offered firsthand policy advice to the bureaucrats and generally accepted the business-friendly policies and guidance they received in return.

THE POWER AND PRESTIGE OF JAPAN'S BUREAUCRACY

Why are Japan's unelected civil servants so powerful? First, the Japanese state has a long-standing tradition whereby leaders who have formal authority do not necessarily exercise power. Rulers and ruled alike are accustomed to legitimate governance by those who may not be vested with formal authority. Nonelected administrators have long exercised such power in Japan. Second, whereas U.S. occupation authorities jailed wartime politicians, purged the military, and broke up the zaibatsu, the experienced bureaucrats continued to administer Japan uninterrupted and unscathed. Third, this political vacuum prompted many veteran bureaucrats to move into leadership positions in Japan's conservative postwar political parties, which gave them significant political influence. Chief among these was **Shigeru Yoshida**, a former Foreign Ministry bureaucrat who served as prime minister through most of the occupation and beyond and profoundly shaped the postwar bureaucracy-dominant political system. Fourth, the legitimacy and prestige of this dominance have been enhanced by the strictly meritocratic nature of hiring and advancement within the bureaucracy. As these bureaucrats advance, only the very best are promoted to senior leadership positions; the bureaucrats who have been passed over are dismissed from the ministry. Senior civil servants exercise extensive policy authority in potent ministries, such as the Ministry of Finance and the Ministry of Economy, Trade, and Industry (formerly and famously known as the Ministry of International Trade and Industry, or MITI).

This orderly promotion-and-dismissal policy also helps explain the willingness of the bureaucrats to work so hard for apparently so little and offers a final reason for the remarkable reach and power of the Japanese bureaucracy. Each year, a contingent of dismissed but nonetheless highly qualified bureaucrats in their 40s and 50s undergo *amakudari* ("descent from heaven"), either to try their hand in politics (overwhelmingly as LDP Diet members) or, more commonly, to take senior positions in the very corporations they previously regulated. All but a handful of Japan's postwar prime ministers were former top bureaucrats. Likewise, the corporations that employ retired civil servants gain not just their skills but also their connections. At any given time, Japan's policy elite comprise people who do not just share a common outlook but also often attended the same prestigious schools and may have worked for decades in the same ministry.

Long credited with leading the postwar economic miracle, Japan's elite bureaucracy now receives much of the blame for the country's more recent two decades of economic decline and growing political dysfunction. The bureaucracy's reputation has been badly tarnished not just by the economy's poor performance, but also by a series of scandals and gaffes, including revelations of kickbacks from politicians and corporations; a series of costly cover-ups involving HIV-infected blood transfusions, lost pension records, and nuclear accidents; and the mishandling of natural disaster recovery efforts following the 1995 earthquake in Kobe and the triple tragedy of the **2011 earthquake**, tsunami, and Fukushima nuclear catastrophe. Declining confidence in the bureaucracy and in Japan's iron triangle has led many to conclude that this "well-oiled, conservative machine" is undergoing a "regime shift," in which parliament, interest groups, and even Japanese citizens are gaining political influence. Elected politicians have pursued administrative reforms that have given the prime minister increased leverage over the bureaucracy and electoral reforms that have dislodged the long-reigning LDP from government. Politicians have also gained increasing policy expertise in their own right, which has made them less dependent on their bureaucratic counterparts in policy making.

Where, then, does power reside in the Japanese state? Even though Japan, unlike the United States, lacks the formal separation of powers between state and national government and between the executive and legislative branches, it is fair to say that there is no single locus of power in the Japanese state. Even during the era of the bureaucracy's greatest strength, from the 1950s through the 1970s, powerful prime ministers such as Shigeru Yoshida and Kakuei Tanaka still often held sway over the bureaucracy.[10] Some of Japan's most famous and successful corporations, such as Sony and Honda, achieved their status in part because they defied bureaucratic dictates. And while each bureaucratic ministry may have substantial authority within its own domain, these independent fiefdoms are subject to no overriding direction or guidance.

Scholars critical of the Japanese state have described it as headless and susceptible to the kind of uncoordinated drift that led to a quixotic war against the United States in the twentieth century, followed by unsustainable trade surpluses with virtually every industrialized country and an inability to reform sufficiently its twentieth-century mercantilist economy to cope with the challenges of a twenty-first-century globalized economy.[11] Will Japan be able to change, and if so, what will be the impetus? Because elements within the iron triangle have demonstrated little willingness or incentive to change, many observers argue that one must look beyond this ruling triad and perhaps even beyond Japan to locate the forces and pressures capable of bringing about change.

Political Conflict and Competition

The Party System and Elections

Like Mexico or South Africa, postwar Japan until recent years has offered an example of a predominant party system. The LDP dominated all other parties from the time of its formation as the merger of conservative parties in 1955 until its stunning defeat at the hands of the DPJ in upper house elections in 2007 and lower house elections in 2009. For most of this period, the Japan Socialist Party (JSP; renamed the Social Democratic Party, or SDP, in 1996), formed as a merger of leftist parties in 1955, served as its perennial loyal opposition. The JSP regularly garnered fewer than half as many votes as the LDP in parliamentary elections and, thanks to LDP gerrymandering, obtained even fewer seats. During this period of LDP dominance, several other parties joined the JSP in opposition by taking advantage of Japan's former electoral system to carve out niches in the Japanese electorate among voters who felt excluded by both the larger parties. These included the Japan Communist Party (JCP), which consistently embraced policies to the left of the JSP, and the more moderate Democratic Socialist Party (DSP) and New Komei Party (NKP), which occupied a middle ground between conservative, pro-business LDP politics and the socialist (and pacifist) platform of the JSP. These three and a couple of other short-lived parties typically accounted for roughly 20 percent of the popular vote.

This remarkably stable one-and-a-half-party system, an important component of the equally stable iron triangle, remained intact for nearly four decades. However, the bursting of Japan's economic bubble in the early 1990s, combined with the LDP government's inept and unpopular efforts to address the structural economic problems that prolonged the economy's slide, led in 1993 to a historic vote of no confidence in LDP rule and the defection of LDP parliamentarians to an opposition coalition. Two successive short-lived opposition coalitions held power long enough (just over a year) to implement electoral reforms that fostered the emergence of the DPJ, a party strong enough to legitimately and consistently challenge LDP rule, and pave the way for what some are calling a political revolution. To understand the causes and the nature of this revolt and why it was so long in coming, it is necessary to examine both the LDP and the DPJ that has emerged to challenge it.

THE LIBERAL DEMOCRATIC PARTY

Although the LDP no longer has a guaranteed lock on Japan's parliament, the party did manage to control government for over five decades since its founding in 1955. The nature of this rule has led some observers to conclude that the LDP has been woefully misnamed: It is conservative, not liberal. Its internal politics have been highly authoritarian, not democratic. And its factional divisions make it a collection of mini-parties, not a single party.

The LDP can perhaps best be understood as a collection of politicians acting as independent political entrepreneurs bound together in a highly pragmatic electoral machine in which ideological consistency has never taken priority over winning. Over the years, the party established electoral rules and engaged in campaigns and elections with the express purpose of staying in power by maintaining a majority (or at least a healthy plurality) of seats in the parliament. But the LDP became more than a political machine for members of parliament. The party's persistent control of the government meant that the campaign for the LDP presidency was in almost all cases a contest for the office of prime minister.

Two organizational features have proved key to the LDP's continued dominance, but have also caused the party significant problems and hampered effective internal reform. The first of these features is the factions, or mini-parties, that have formed within the party. Japan's former electoral system compelled contenders for seats in the parliament to compete against candidates from not only other parties but also within their own party. This intraparty competition created a clientelist system in which candidates had to vie for the support of patrons within the party who could provide members with campaign funds, official party endorsements, appointed positions within the party and the government, and other favors. These faction leaders in turn could count on the support of their faction members in the party's all-important presidential elections. Five LDP factions emerged in the mid-1950s that have been led by successive generations of LDP kingpins. And even though the electoral system has been reformed, with the elimination of the intraparty competition that generated the factions in the first place, these intra-LDP divisions have largely survived (and grown in number, if not influence) in recent years.[12]

But even unswerving factional loyalty did not guarantee LDP parliamentary candidates electoral success in their home district under the old system. In order to help individual candidates obtain enough votes and to ensure that no single contestant received too many votes (thereby "wasting them"), each candidate constructed a local support group known as a *koenkai*. The *koenkai* are made up of influential district members able to gather votes in their community or, more recently, among members of a particular professional or other special-interest group within the district. In the same way that the LDP candidates promised allegiance to their factional patron in exchange for support from above, so they promised policy favors, contracts, and other pork-barrel enticements in exchange for the votes and campaign donations delivered by their *koenkai*. And just as the party factions have outlived individual leaders, so have the *koenkai* been multigenerational. It is not uncommon for an entire *koenkai* to throw its full support behind the son, grandson, or other descendant of a retiring member of parliament.

Although these multiple levels of patron-client relations certainly contributed to the LDP's long-term political dominance, the gifts, favors, and huge sums of money required to lubricate the system and manage the LDP's intense intraparty competition (in which purse size, not policy preference, mattered) fostered a system of money politics that has made Japanese election campaigns among the most expensive in the world. Put simply, the LDP has been foremost a vote- and money-delivery system, with money being the single most powerful way of obtaining votes. Both money and votes have been secured through expanding circles of corporatist co-optation of businesses and other large interest groups, and through clientelist currying of favor among local communities and individuals by means of pork-barrel projects, favors, and gifts. As in any democracy, pork-barrel projects in the home district, such as bridges and schools, create jobs and deliver votes, and the lucrative contracts and licenses awarded to corporations to build these projects bring campaign donations. One

House of Representatives Election Results by Major Political Party, 2000–09

| | PARTY (IDEOLOGY) | | | | | |
YEAR	LDP (RIGHT)	DPJ (CENTER)	NKP (CENTER)	SDP (LEFT)	OTHERS	TOTAL SEATS
2000	239	129	29	19	64	480
2003	237	177	34	6	26	480
2005	296	113	31	7	33	480
2009	119	300	21	7	33	480

scholar notes that while residents of other democracies are certainly familiar with pork-barrel politics in their own political systems, Japan's extensive clientelist arrangements are more like an "industrial hog farm."[13] In addition, politicians and their supporters also attend the funerals, weddings, graduations, and other important family events of their loyal constituents (on average more than 30 each month), honoring them with their presence and an appropriate (monetary) gift. As a result, these campaign strategies and money politics, both hugely expensive, have plagued the LDP with scandals throughout its history and, together with other factors, have turned increasing numbers of voters away from the long-dominant party.

Persistent—indeed, mounting—corruption scandals, combined with growing dissatisfaction with LDP governance, prompted the defection of a number of LDP members of parliament to an opposition coalition that wrested power briefly from the LDP in the mid-1990s. But after a year in exile, the less-than-popular LDP nonetheless returned to office as part of a series of coalition governments. As Japan entered its second decade of economic malaise, the LDP received a boost in support as voters pinned their hopes for economic recovery and political reform on the promises of maverick politician Koizumi Junichiro, who served as LDP prime minister from 2001 to 2006. With his raffish hairdo and populist style, Koizumi represented in many ways the antithesis of the traditional LDP politician. He secured the LDP presidency without the explicit backing of any major LDP faction and won three consecutive elections with promises to halt Japan's economic malaise and take on the country's conservative bureaucratic and political elite (including his own LDP) and their deeply entrenched constituencies. In 2005, he led the LDP to a dramatic (and short-lived) victory in lower house elections in which the party won an outright majority of seats for the first time since 1990 (see "House of Representatives Election Results by Major Political Party, 2000–09," p. 286).

Although LDP party rules required the popular prime minister to step down in 2006 after five years as party president, his government managed to implement a number of modest reforms, including the privatization of Japan's postal savings system (see "Japan Post and the Iron Triangle," p. 288). But Koizumi's tenure was followed by LDP politics as usual, including factional infighting, corruption scandals, and colorless prime ministers. Following a succession of three highly unpopular LDP governments in as many years and a stunning defeat in upper house elections in 2007, the LDP finally lost control of the lower house and government in the even more dramatic 2009 election that brought the DPJ to power for the first time.

JAPAN POST AND THE IRON TRIANGLE

When Japan's Meiji modernizers looked to the West in the nineteenth century seeking to adopt institutions to promote their modernization efforts, one of the first they seized upon was Britain's postal savings system. It offered banking through neighborhood post offices and channeled deposits large and small into state coffers where the funds could be reinvested in industrial development. Although a dozen other countries also copied the British model, **Japan Post** has proven the most successful by far, with holdings growing in recent years to over $3 trillion, making it the largest bank in the world. Because Japan's powerful bureaucracy controlled the purse strings of this huge financial institution, Prime Minister Koizumi made privatization of Japan Post one of the key measures in his efforts to reform and weaken Japan's iron triangle. Not surprisingly, Koizumi's plan faced resistance not just from the Ministry of Finance and other bureaucrats, but also from the LDP old guard, who worked with bureaucrats to channel these monies into pork-barrel public works projects in their home districts. In 2005, when LDP members of parliament refused to support his privatization bill, Koizumi responded by dissolving the House of Representatives, calling snap elections, and nominating new ninja ("assassin") candidates to contest seats held by those who opposed his privatization bill, both from the opposition DPJ and his own LDP. Koizumi and his LDP "assassins" won a landslide victory (see "House of Representatives Election Results by Major Political Party, 2000–09," p. 286), giving the LDP an outright majority in the lower house and permitting Koizumi to pass his landmark bill, which authorized a ten-year privatization plan for Japan Post. The political tug-of-war over this lucrative institution was, however, far from over. In order to appease the demands and ensure the support of a junior coalition partner, newly elected DPJ prime minister Yukio Hatoyama agreed in 2010 to scale back Japan Post's privatization and increase incentives for the public to save in the institution at the expense of private banks. Critics see this move as another nod to iron triangle politics as usual and a blow to the genuine political reform promised by the DPJ.

DEMOCRATIC PARTY OF JAPAN

Capitalizing on mounting public frustration with LDP rule and anticipating the intended consequences of the recent electoral reforms favoring large, organized political parties, the DPJ formed in 1998 as a merger of several reform-minded opposition parties. Led early on by future prime ministers Yukio Hatoyama and Naoto

Kan, the DPJ received a significant boost in 2003 when former LDP kingpin and political mastermind **Ichiro Ozawa** joined his opposition Liberal Party with the DPJ. Despite (or perhaps because of) his questionable reputation as a backroom "shadow shogun," Ozawa helped the DPJ to upper house electoral victories in 2004 and 2007. In 2009, after being implicated in a fund-raising scandal, Ozawa was forced to resign as DPJ president prior to the party's victory in the 2009 House of Representatives elections that swept the LDP from power.

Despite this decisive and unprecedented victory, the DPJ fell just short of winning the two-thirds majority of seats required to override a veto from the upper house, where it held a substantial plurality of seats but not a majority. In order to ensure a majority in this weaker House of Councillors, the DPJ formed a coalition with two smaller parties, the Social Democratic Party and the People's New Party. Elected into office on a platform of bold promises and with a significant mandate for carrying out political, economic, and social reforms, the DPJ nonetheless struggled both to realize its campaign pledges and to retain the support of voters. The DPJ's first prime minister, **Yukio Hatoyama** (2009–10), came to office vowing to weaken the iron triangle by shifting political authority from bureaucrats to elected politicians and to devolve central political authority to local communities and citizens. The Hatoyama government promised to jump-start the economy by spurring consumption and reducing growing income inequality through subsidies for children and farmers. The new government also pledged to strengthen cooperation with China and reduce the American military footprint in Japan's island prefecture of Okinawa. This last highly contentious promise proved Hatoyama's demise: U.S. pressure and growing regional security concerns led the prime minister to break his campaign promise to close an American military base in Okinawa and forced him to resign after less than a year in office.

In the hope of strengthening the party's prospects in the 2010 upper house elections, the party put forth **Naoto Kan**, who had a reputation for taking decisive action, implementing bold reforms, and standing up to bureaucrats. But the DPJ and its coalition partners fared poorly in the elections, losing their upper house majority and once again giving Japan a "twisted" parliament in which the DPJ held a majority in the lower chamber but the LDP-led opposition dominated the upper house. Following that election, Kan and the DPJ government struggled to keep together its coalition, carry out reforms, or even maintain a consistent policy position. The tragic earthquake, tsunami, and nuclear disaster of 2011 further stalled hope of dramatic progress and prompted Kan's resignation later that year and the party election of Yoshihiko Noda to replace him. Voters and the media have been highly critical of the government's inept handling of the disaster in contrast with the remarkable heroism and stoicism of the people. Some are looking to Japan's civil society as the best hope for breaking the institutional inertia and path-dependency that keep Japan mired in political intransigence and economic malaise.

Civil Society

Because the reforms that brought about Westernization and democracy were imposed from above (and, in many cases, from *outside*), Japan's political system has fostered a centralized bureaucratic society rather than a civil society in which citizens independently organize and participate in political, economic, and social affairs. Like other authoritarian systems, the Meiji and militarist states fostered corporatist and mercantilist institutions to harness Japan's industrial society in the service of modernization and imperialism. Although the U.S. occupiers destroyed many aspects of Japanese authoritarianism and carried out sweeping political, social, and economic reforms, they retained the bureaucracy and, out of fear of communism, squelched many of the nascent civic groups they had initially fostered.

In pursuing economic development and political stability, the postwar Japanese state organized or co-opted interest groups that were important to these goals, such as business and agricultural associations, and formed associations for facilitating their political participation. In exchange for their support, these groups have had their interests well represented (and protected), and have prospered. During the postwar decades of economic growth, this symbiotic relationship expanded to include many other smaller groups and constituencies in a system of distributional welfare. These corporatist arrangements prolonged LDP bureaucratic rule, but did so at the increasing expense of both economic health and political flexibility. In addition, labor unions, consumers, and other groups that have often been prominent in the politics of industrialized countries have been notably absent from these arrangements and have in many ways borne the burden of the corporatist system, which is sometimes referred to as Japan, Inc. On occasion, students, environmentalists, and other groups excluded from Japan, Inc. have resorted to extra-parliamentary protests in order to be heard. Some of these protests, particularly in the 1950s, were quite violent and at times successful.

The third leg of the iron triangle after the politicians and bureaucrats is made up of Japan's large corporations and the large industrial groupings or conglomerates (**keiretsu**) to which they belong. These players have been both proponents of and participants in Japan's postwar development. Big business exercises political influence through the business association Keidanren (Federation of Economic Organizations), which voices the concerns of large corporations and offers policy recommendations to the government. Keidanren is the conduit through which most campaign contributions have been channeled from large businesses to LDP coffers and therefore has inclined the government to champion business-friendly policies, such as cheap access to capital, investment incentives, and various forms of market protection. Since the economic downturn of the 1990s, businesses have bridled at having to make these campaign contributions and have complained about the use of growing corporate taxes to subsidize inefficient farmers and pork-barrel projects. Analysts point to this divergence of interests as yet another sign of the weakening of the iron triangle.

Another key pillar of political support has been the agricultural sector, whose highly organized political interests are channeled through local agricultural cooperatives to the national "peak organization" Nokyo (Central Union of Agricultural Cooperatives). Agriculture's key political contribution has been its capacity to provide a dependable and geographically concentrated bloc of votes. In exchange, both the LDP and DPJ governments have enacted policies that favor farmers, including price supports, relatively low taxes, and protection from agricultural imports. Although urbanization and electoral redistricting have to some extent weakened the significance of the rural farm vote, Japanese farmers remain an important political force.

Big business and agriculture are not the only interest groups to have offered their campaign contributions and votes in exchange for favorable policies and a share of the benefits of Japan's postwar economic boom. Small and midsize businesses comprise the lion's share of the Japanese economy, despite their unsung status when compared with such high-profile large firms as Toyota and Sony. The smaller manufacturers and retailers have been very well organized and have parlayed their electoral support into tax breaks, subsidies, and protection from larger firms. For example, the ubiquitous mom-and-pop corner grocery stores effectively kept large retailers out of Japan's neighborhoods for many years. Another group worth mentioning comprises the half million construction firms in Japan, most of which are small, unproductive, and well cared for by an inefficient and corrupt government bidding system for public works.

Japan's faltering economy and growing corruption scandals involving both the LDP and DPJ and their supporters have cast new light on the economic and political costs of the country's corporate welfare system. Critics argue that the LDP's varied and growing host of constituencies led to distributional tyranny, fueled Japan's economic crisis, and stifled political change. Corporatist arrangements have also long excluded interests deemed potentially harmful to the goals of rapid industrialization, including trade unions, consumers, and women's groups. Because of this, Japan's major labor organizations, including RENGO (Japanese

Trade Union Confederation) and the teachers' and public employees' unions, have had long-standing adversarial relationships with the LDP and have traditionally supported the more left-leaning political parties, such as the Socialists and Communists. More recently, these unions and other groups consistently excluded from the iron triangle have thrown their support to the DPJ, confirming the influence of electoral reforms designed to produce a two-party system and enhancing the prospects of weakening and transforming the corporatist arrangements of the iron triangle. Similarly, as Japan's postindustrial and post-materialist society grows more complex, and the political marketplace more competitive, many observers hope that an increasing number of interests will use electoral competition and constitutional guarantees to establish a broader range of civic associations.[14]

Society

Ethnic and National Identity

Few national populations view themselves as racially and ethnically homogeneous as do the Japanese. With immigrants constituting only 1 percent of the population and foreign nationals comprising only 2 percent, this perception is grounded in demographic reality. Nonetheless, those of foreign ancestry in Japan make up some 5 percent of the population. The notion of a racially pure and monoethnic Japan was fostered largely by the Japanese state from the Meiji period onward as it sought to forge a Japanese nation from the culturally and even linguistically diverse feudal domains of nineteenth-century Japan and to establish Japanese racial superiority over the peoples of its far-flung empire in the first half of the twentieth century.

Japan's strong ethnic and national identity has come at the expense of several minority groups, who have been prevented from developing a Japanese identity and enjoying the full privileges of citizenship as Japanese nationals with a separate ethnic heritage. These minorities include the indigenous Ainu in the north and Okinawans in the south; descendants of Koreans, Chinese, and Southeast Asians; and the children of mixed ancestry and foreigners. Although not racially separate, the 2 to 4 million *burakumin* (social outcasts), whose ancestors worked in the "unclean" occupations such as grave digging, butchery, and tanning are also seen as a minority group and have faced intense prejudice. Discrimination in areas such as employment and marriage against these minority groups has been widespread and persistent. Those individuals who have sought to assimilate by taking

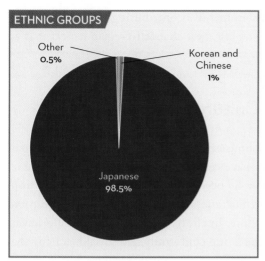

ETHNIC GROUPS

Other
0.5%

Korean and
Chinese
1%

Japanese
98.5%

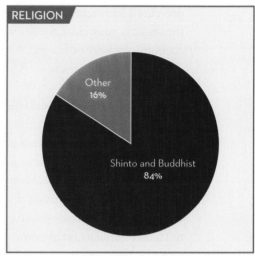

RELIGION

Other
16%

Shinto and Buddhist
84%

on Japanese names, mastering the Japanese language, and adopting Japanese cultural mores have generally remained socially marginalized and culturally scorned.

If cultural assimilation is difficult, the naturalization process is nearly as arduous. Being born in Japan does not automatically confer citizenship or voting rights. Non-Japanese can become citizens only after adopting a Japanese name and enduring a process that includes a series of interviews, home visits, and consultations with neighbors to ensure that the candidate has sufficiently assimilated Japanese culture—a process that many find invasive and humiliating. In addition, permanent residents who do not choose citizenship are fingerprinted and required to carry alien registration identification.

However, scholars note that economic necessity may eventually compel the social integration and mobility that cultural obstacles and state policy have prevented. With both a rapidly aging population and dwindling fertility, Japan faces the prospect of having some 30 percent fewer people by midcentury than it has today and a proportionally smaller workforce. Facing labor shortages during the 1980s, the government introduced policies designed to attract to Japan both skilled and unskilled migrant labor from China, Southeast Asia, and South America. But more recently these programs have faced local resistance on both economic and cultural grounds. Responding to popular discontent and persistent economic recession, the government has offered to pay migrant workers to return to their homelands in exchange for assurance that they will not return to Japan. However, economists and demographers warn that if Japan is not prepared to overcome its racism and sexism, which have prevented immigrants and women from fully contributing to the workforce, the country may close the door on its last, best chance to regain its status as an economic powerhouse.

Ideology and Political Culture

Japan's historical experiences with Shintoism, Buddhism, Confucianism, feudalism, militarism, and bureaucratism have certainly shaped the norms and values that guide Japanese political behavior. So have its experiences with the West, from imposed inequitable treaties and democratic institutions to military defeat and the embrace of Western popular culture. In efforts to attribute political behavior to culture, scholars often point to the group conformity and social hierarchy that pervade most aspects of Japanese life. The basic unit of Japanese society is not the individual but the group, as manifested in such institutions as the family, the company, the political faction, and the nation. Japanese are socialized to defer to the needs of the group and to make decisions through consensus rather than majority vote. Similarly, hierarchy governs most social relationships in Japan, and Japanese are most comfortable in settings in which their social standing in relation to that of others is clear. Inferiors yield to their superiors' authority, and superiors are obliged to care for their subordinates' needs. Promotion in firms, bureaucratic ministries, and political party factions is more often based on seniority and personalized patron-client relationships than on merit.

Japan has undergone political and economic modernization, but on its own (not fully Western) terms. Individual freedom and social equality remain less important than one's acceptance by the group and one's rightful position in that group's hierarchical division of labor. Japan's relatively equitable distribution of wealth (until recently, on par with that of the European social democracies) has had little to do with cultural norms of egalitarianism or explicit government policy. In fact, Japan has had a weak labor movement, and its conservative governments promoted the low taxation and public spending policies that typically foster inequality. Rather, Japan's relative economic and social equality can be attributed, in large part, to three factors. First, World War II reduced all of Japanese society to poverty levels. Second, postwar occupation reforms, including land reform; the breakup of the huge zaibatsu conglomerates; purges of the political, military, economic, and aristocratic elite; and empowerment of labor unions to bargain collectively for improved working conditions, fostered equality. Third, Japan's rapid and sustained postwar economic growth showered unprecedented prosperity on virtually all social groups in Japan. These factors have consistently weakened the salience of issues of redistribution of wealth as an ideological cleavage in Japan, contributing to the weakness of the Japanese left and shoring up support for the LDP and its pro-growth policies. In a recent poll, nearly three-fourths of respondents identified themselves as having a political stance ranging from conservative to neutral, whereas less than one-fourth saw themselves as progressive or close to progressive.

The recent economic malaise (combined with the forces of globalization and an ongoing generational change in values) has led to greater income inequality and economic insecurity, and may lead to greater diversity of political attitudes and perhaps even to a shift in political culture in Japan. The fading of guaranteed permanent employment (so-called lifetime employment) for Japan's corporate *sarari-man* (white-collar "salaryman") and rising unemployment among college graduates (and indeed an increasing number of college and even high school dropouts) have led to disillusionment with business and politics as usual and to mounting calls for change. Such disillusionment is particularly strong among Japanese youth, who have no memory of wartime hardship or postwar poverty and who place more value on individual fulfillment through leisure diversions and risky entrepreneurial opportunities than through long hours and long years of work for the sake of a company. Younger Japanese have less incentive to remain loyal to a company that can no longer promise them job security, and they have little patience for the corruption and authority of long-in-the-tooth bureaucratic rule. In short, change may be initiated by a younger generation far more willing and likely to switch both their jobs and their political loyalties.

But as this chapter has indicated, change does not come easily to entrenched Japanese institutions, no matter how dysfunctional. Unwilling to conform and unable to bring about change, a growing minority of Japanese are choosing to "exit" Japan's "straitjacket" society through extreme measures. Since 1990, homelessness has risen sharply, particularly among middle-aged men. Japan has regularly ranked first among industrialized countries for suicides, and suicide constitutes the leading cause of death in Japan among men ages 20 to 44. Hundreds of thousands of Japanese youth and young adults (mostly male) have elected to drop out of society, shutting

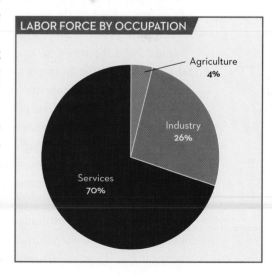

LABOR FORCE BY OCCUPATION

Agriculture 4%

Industry 26%

Services 70%

themselves in their rooms or apartments for years at a time. The antisocial behavior of the homeless, reclusive "shut-ins," and those who take their own lives speaks to the powerful institutional inertia of groupism in Japan and the drastic measures some nonconformists feel compelled to take in order to escape the system.

Political Economy

Japan's sudden introduction to the global political economy in the nineteenth century fostered the development of a mercantilist political economic system concerned with neither liberal freedom nor Communist equality. Compelled by U.S. gunships to open the country's borders to "free" trade with the West, the Meiji oligarchs recognized that Japan must either modernize quickly or, like China, be overrun by Western imperialism. State-led economic development became not a way of serving the public but rather a means of preserving national sovereignty. The oligarchs' national slogan, "rich country, strong military," reflected Meiji modernizers' awareness from the outset of the strong relationship between economic development and industrialization on the one hand, and military and political power in the international arena on the other.

Despite the tumultuous change that Japan experienced in the twentieth century, the basic structure of its catch-up mercantilist political economy persists. Forged under conditions of military rigor, refined during the U.S. occupation, and perfected under the aegis of American military and economic protection, this developmental model propelled Japan from the ashes of devastating military defeat to become the second-largest economy in the world. Not surprisingly, scholars and policy makers alike have sought to understand this developmental "miracle," and the investigation of the model of Japan's **capitalist developmental state** has become an important field of academic study and policy analysis.[15] Japan's capitalist developmental state differs significantly from the liberal capitalist system that Americans often presume to be the only "true" form of capitalism. Like France and Germany's coordinated market economies, Japan's political economic system permits a far higher level of state guidance of competitive markets and cooperation with private firms than do the liberal systems in the United Kingdom and the United States. This guidance has included a host of formal and informal economic measures often grouped under the term **industrial policy**. Industrial policies are formulated and implemented by Japan's elite economic bureaucracy after consultation and coordination with the private sector. Measures include imposing protective tariffs and nontariff barriers on imports, encouraging cooperation and limiting "excessive" competition in strategic export sectors, and offering low-interest loans and tax breaks to firms willing to invest in targeted industries and technologies.

Government guidance has not always worked well or as planned. But for many decades, state-led developmental capitalism kept Japan's economy strong, prosperous, and internationally competitive, and kept its iron triangle of bureaucrats, politicians, and business leaders closely linked. The prewar family zaibatsu were replaced by professionally managed keiretsu conglomerates with ready access to cheap capital. Workers agreed to forgo disruptive labor strikes in exchange for promises of permanent employment, ensuring management a skilled and disciplined workforce. As early heavy-handed policies of protectionism and explicit control proved unwieldy, bureaucrats came to rely more upon informal directives known as administrative guidance and on subtle incentives more suitable for the increasingly internationalized Japanese economy. After growing at an average rate of over 10 percent per year during the 1950s and 1960s, Japan's economy still managed to grow over 5 percent per year during the 1970s and 1980s. In fact, from the early 1950s to 1990, Japan's gross domestic product (GDP) grew at twice the rate of that of the other advanced industrial economies. The flagship automotive and consumer electronics companies within Japan's large conglomerates became multinational giants and household names, and the fruits of Japan's rapid growth lifted incomes and opportunities for nearly all Japanese.

By the 1980s, Japan's very prosperity was masking what now, in hindsight, is much easier to detect as serious structural problems within the model. Even as the international political economy grew ever more integrated and hypercompetitive, the costs of doing business in Japan were mounting. Japan's multinational automotive and electronics exporters felt this competitive pressure first, but kept their heads above water by shifting production overseas and drastically cutting costs at home. Most of Japan's companies were not able to react so nimbly, however; nor was the government prepared to tolerate the kind of unemployment that would have resulted from the wholesale transfer of production abroad. Rather than face global competition, inefficient industries used their influence within the iron triangle to seek protection. They obtained it from a government that had become accustomed to looking after not just economically strategic industries but also politically and socially important ones. This government assistance led to waste, overcapacity, and overpricing.

These corporate welfare measures, combined with a rapid jump in the value of Japan's currency, propelled the country's stock and real estate markets skyward in the latter half of the 1980s. This led to dangerous overvaluation of both securities and land. At one point in the early 1990s, Japan's stock market was valued at fully half of all the world's stock markets combined. At its peak value, the land under the emperor's palace grounds in central Tokyo was worth as much as the land of the entire state of California! Japan was awash in overinflated assets and easy money, which led companies, banks, the Japanese Mafia, and even the government to invest in grossly overpriced assets and risky (even foolish) business ventures. When this asset bubble burst in 1992, the value of stock and property plummeted, growth slowed, and already uncompetitive companies were left with huge debts (and dwindling assets and production with which to repay them). The Japanese labeled these firms **zombies**: essentially dead but propped up by banks and a political system unwilling to force them into bankruptcy and face the social costs of closed businesses and spiraling unemployment.

The government slid deeper into debt as it sustained not just these insolvent firms but also the banks that carried their debts (valued in the trillions of dollars), even as it attempted to stimulate consumer spending. Although a combination of government stimulus measures and liberalizing reforms have breathed some life back into the economy, Japan is now mired in its third consecutive decade of no or slow growth. The economy remains plagued by the three Ds of deflation (declining prices), government debt (twice Japan's annual GDP and the largest in the world), and budget deficits (running annually at about 10 percent of GDP). Over the course of two decades, Japan experienced a reversal of fortune unprecedented in a peacetime economy. It has slipped from its position as one of the richest and most powerful countries in the world to that of a relatively insignificant power. In 2010, China surpassed Japan as the second-largest economy in the world, and it is predicted that by 2050, India, Brazil, Indonesia, Mexico, and Turkey will also overtake Japan. While government-business cooperation and a targeted focus on economic development promoted rapid postwar economic growth, this mercantilist political economic structure proved far less successful once it had caught up and found itself pursuing cutting-edge technologies and competing in unpredictable and rapidly changing markets. Moreover, as the economy struggled, politicians and bureaucrats boosted the funding of public works and provided generous subsidies to inefficient and uncompetitive firms in order to prop up employment and preserve voter support. Although these destructive inefficiencies were tolerable during the boom years, they became a significant drag on the Japanese economy and a political albatross for the long-ruling LDP.

The DPJ came to government in 2009 promising to curtail public works and end corporate welfare, but soon backed away from its early campaign pledge to shift funding "from concrete to people." Like its LDP predecessor, the DPJ recognized that swiftly ending corporate welfare in a weak economy would be political suicide. At the same time, it has been fostering its own "pork constituencies" among organized labor, agriculture, and urban consumers.[16] However, in recent elections, voters have expressed a willingness to accept a bit higher taxes and a more open economy in exchange for a stronger social safety net. In short, just as the loosening of the iron triangle may gradually bring political competition to Japan, so, it is hoped, will the slow privatization of state-owned financial institutions, the painful weaning of firms from government protection, the loosening of the bonds of companies to their keiretsu alliances, and the weakening of employees' ties to their firms bring much-needed market competition and efficiency to the Japanese economy. But precisely because changes are painful, both the maverick LDP reformer Koizumi and more recent DPJ governments have struggled to deliver on bold promises of structural reform in the face of conservative bureaucratic, political, and corporate resistance. This resistance has led many observers to conclude that the key to substantial economic liberalization remains political reform.

Foreign Relations and the World

Despite the vicissitudes of Japan's external relations, its foreign affairs have been marked by several continuities worth noting. First, though insular, the Japanese have been inveterate adopters and adapters of things foreign. From Chinese ideograms to American popular culture, the Japanese have at key periods in their history pragmatically adopted and adapted foreign elements that they deemed beneficial. Second, they have historically maintained a hierarchical perception of the world, one in which international entities (countries, empires, races), like internal entities (family members, classes, companies), are seen and ranked in hierarchical terms. Third, Japan's island status and catch-up strategy of mercantilist development have given the Japanese a very strong and sharply delineated sense of nationalism, which has made Japanese citizens highly responsive to calls for sacrifice on behalf of the nation when faced with a foreign challenge.[17]

Japan and Asia

Given these continuities, it should not surprise us that some frustrated advocates of political and economic reform in Japan are calling for *gaiatsu* (foreign pressure) or even a "third opening" of Japan (after Perry and MacArthur) as the impetus for change. Although the country's external dealings over the past century and a half have been the source of understandable anxiety and much military disaster, they have also been the impetus for beneficial change. By the same token, Japan's substantial international stature has meant that both its earlier economic success and its more recent problems have been spilling over into the rest of the world, with a variety of consequences.

If one were to view Japan's international relations as a series of concentric circles, the most immediate and significant circle would include Japan and its Asian neighbors. These neighbors have felt most acutely both the cost and the benefit of Japan's military, economic, and cultural expansion. Under the promise (or guise) of a Greater East Asian Co-Prosperity Sphere, modern Japan in the first half of the twentieth century expanded its empire first to Taiwan and Korea, then to the Chinese mainland, Southeast Asia, and the Pacific Islands. Japan brought oppressive colonial rule, imperial exploitation, and military destruction wherever it went, but also built economic infrastructure, transferred technology and training, and exported its version of developmental capitalism to several of its longer-held colonies. Moreover, it brought much of Asia into what it termed in the 1930s a **flying geese** pattern of economic development, with Japan at the head of a flock of dependent Asian economies. Japan offered leadership by exploiting its comparative advantage in advanced industries and then passing its skills on to the next tier as newer technologies became available. The second tier would do the same for the third, providing a ladder of industrial progress for (and Japanese dominance of) all Asia.

Since Japan's World War II defeat and its embrace of American-directed pacifist prosperity, the rest of Asia has viewed Japan with understandable ambivalence. On the one hand, though its constitution renounces war, Japan has never been required to atone for or even acknowledge its colonial and wartime legacies in the way that Germany has faced and frequently reexamined its Nazi past. The Japanese Imperial Army forced thousands of Korean and other Asian so-called comfort women to serve as sexual slaves for its troops in the field, and (like most conquering armies) committed a host of other war-related atrocities. Koreans, Chinese, and other Asians are troubled that Japanese textbooks have largely glossed over these events and that many of Japan's conservative politicians and prime ministers have made annual pilgrimages to Yasukuni Shrine, a controversial Shinto shrine honoring Japan's war dead (see "Yasukuni," p. 301). Chinese and Korean patriots regularly take to the streets demanding Japanese apologies and threatening boycotts of Japanese products.

On the other hand, the past benefits and future fruits of investment in and trade with the world's third-largest economy make it difficult for the rest of Asia

YASUKUNI

Located in a peaceful wooded setting in central Tokyo, **Yasukuni Shrine** was established as a national memorial during the nineteenth century to honor soldiers and others who had lost their lives fighting on behalf of the emperor. The U.S. occupation's mandate that the emperor renounce his divinity and that there be a complete separation of church and state forced the Japanese to privatize what had been a national shrine. In accordance with Shinto beliefs, the memorial offers a permanent resting place for the spirits of the 2.5 million Japanese who died in armed conflict and are enshrined there. The shrine has stirred much controversy because it honors, among others, the spirits of those convicted of war crimes during World War II, and it operates an on-site museum honoring Japanese war heroes that presents a highly sanitized if not revisionist interpretation of World War II. Most controversially, many Japanese politicians, including former prime minister Koizumi, have paid regular visits to this "private" shrine in the face of acrimonious complaints from the leaders of foreign countries, particularly China and Korea, who see their nations as victims of Japan's aggression. Koizumi's successor, Shinzo Abe, an ardent nationalist who visited Yasukuni in the past, did not visit during his year-long tenure as prime minister, nor have any succeeding prime ministers.

Entrance gate to the controversial Yasukuni Shrine, revered by Japanese nationalists but criticized by Japan's Asian neighbors.

to turn its back on Japan. Despite memories of war, many Asians are more interested in educational opportunities in Japan or employment in a Japanese factory than they are in an apology for past offenses. Despite historical tensions, its own economic woes, and the growth of China, South Korea, and other economies in the region, Japan remains the region's largest provider of technology and investment capital, and an essential link in regional trade networks. At the same time, resource-poor Japan finds itself increasingly competing with and confronting resource-hungry China and other neighboring nations seeking to exploit regional sources of fossil fuels and other natural resources.

Japan and the United States

But Japan's very real economic clout in Asia must be placed in the broader context of growing security concerns in the region and Japan's continued economic (and, particularly, military) dependence on the United States. Within the context of Japan's overwhelming defeat in World War II and America's decades-long struggle with the Soviet Union, this patron-client relationship made good sense and good foreign policy for both the United States and Japan. The United States sponsored Japan's return as a member in good standing of the U.S.-sponsored world trading system and Cold War alliance, and Japan turned its full attention to rebuilding its economy. But by the 1970s, its very success as dutiful client had led to a divergence in Japan's economic and security relations with its American patron. Whereas both the United States and Japan have been willing to retain a relationship of military protection and dependence, Japan's rapid economic growth made it a full-fledged economic competitor. Over the past four decades, the United States and Europe have engaged in trade wars with Japan and increased their demands that Japan end its economic protectionism and shoulder the burdens of a full-fledged economic partner, demands to which Japan has acceded, albeit at times reluctantly.

Japan, the rest of Asia, and the rest of the world have changed too much to allow the persistence of Japan's status quo. Critics both inside and outside Japan express frustration over the country's split personality as economic giant and political pygmy and call for it to become a "normal" or "ordinary" country. These terms mean different things to different advocates, but typically entail liberalizing Japan's economy and society; opening the country's borders to trade, investment, immigrants, and students; and militarizing Japan, developing its ability both to defend itself and to contribute to regional and global security. We have already discussed the obstacles to and prospects for economic and social change in Japan. Here, we turn finally to Japan's security and its political role in the world.

Japan and the World

Despite a constitution that prohibits the use or threat of war in resolving conflicts (Article 9) and the presence of nearly 50,000 U.S. troops on its soil, Japan is not without its own means of defense. It currently has a Self-Defense Force of some 240,000 personnel and an annual military budget of more than $50 billion, which ranks it fifth in the world in terms of military expenditures. Although sentiment in Japan since World War II has been decidedly pacifist, neighboring North Korea's pursuit of nuclear weapons, the growing capacity of China's military (which ranks second only to that of the United States in expenditures), and growing tensions between China and Japan over competing territorial claims have shifted public opinion in Japan quite dramatically. Although only 30 percent of Japanese respondents in a 2011 opinion poll favored changing Article 9 of the constitution (down from 33 percent in 2007), this is still nearly twice the percentage advocating reform in 2003 and four times the percentage in a 2001 poll.

At the same time, the United States and other countries are pressuring Japan not only to bear more of the burdens of its own defense, but also to participate more fully in regional and global peacekeeping operations. They criticize Japan's so-called checkbook diplomacy, by which it has largely limited its participation in the Gulf, Afghan, and Iraq wars to financial contributions. However, over the past decade, conservative Japanese governments used this convergence of *gaiatsu* (foreign pressure) with their own political and ideological interests to bolster the technological sophistication of Japan's military and the capacity to project force beyond its borders. Despite a great deal of controversy at home, Japan deployed naval refueling ships in support of U.S. operations in Afghanistan in 2001 and later sent more than 500 troops to help rebuild Iraq. Domestic opponents argued, however, that both measures violated the constitution, and they succeeded in forcing the government to remove SDF troops from Iraq in 2006 and end the refueling mission in 2010.

Nowhere is Japan's ambivalence about pacifism, militarism, and its alliance with the United States more apparent than the controversy over American military bases on the Japanese island of **Okinawa**. Occupied and administered by the United States from the end of World War II to the time of its reversion to Japan in 1972, the small island continues to host over half of all U.S. military personnel in Japan on some 14 bases. Growing local opposition to this American presence has garnered national support in recent years, leading the DPJ's Hatoyama to make the campaign promise that his government would relocate U.S. troops from Okinawa. The inability of his government to deliver on this promise in the face of U.S. pressure and growing regional security concerns forced Hatoyama to resign after less than a year in office.

Although a growing minority of Japanese citizens is willing to accept a greater role for Japan's armed forces, most Japanese, and certainly most Asians, remain highly wary of Japanese militarism. Advocates of a nonmilitarized Japan argue that the country can and indeed has projected its power and influence abroad in a host of beneficial ways, and that striving for militarized "normalcy" is contrary both to the intent of Japan's pacifist constitution and to the interests of Japan and the world. They argue that Japan need not be a military power to be a global power, and they point to numerous areas in which Japan has already shown global leadership. They note that Japan has been among the world's top donors of international aid, giving over $10 billion in foreign development assistance annually. They contend that Japan ought to focus its efforts on areas of global benefit, such as technology transfers to developing countries and meeting the challenges of climate change, rather than engage in a dangerous and costly arms race with China or other countries.

Can Japan use its unique constitutional restrictions to create a new kind of nonmilitary global influence? More fundamentally, can it implement the economic and political reforms necessary to right its economic ship in time to maintain this international presence? Will these reforms come from above, from below, from the outside, or perhaps not at all (or not in time)? In this, as in other areas, Japan's capacity and willingness to change in the twenty-first century will prove crucial to its future security, and to its economic prosperity and political stability.

CURRENT ISSUES IN JAPAN

3/11: Japan's Triple Tragedy

No stranger to earthquakes or other natural disasters—Japan has experienced 15 significant earthquakes since 1995 and gave us the word *tsunami*—this island nation was wholly unprepared for the disastrous Tohoku earthquake and tsunami that struck the northeast region of Honshu, Japan's largest island, on March 11, 2011. The biggest (of many) tremors registered 9.0 magnitude on the Richter scale, making it the largest recorded earthquake ever to strike Japan and one of the five most powerful anywhere. With its epicenter 40 miles off the coast and 20 miles under the ocean's surface, the quake generated tidal waves up to 133 feet high that wreaked havoc on the coastline and traveled as far as 6 miles inland. The entire island of Honshu shifted some 8 feet to the east. The earthquake and tsunami caused an estimated 25,000 casualties and hundreds of billions of dollars in damage, and shaved roughly 5 percent off the annual GDP.

But the greatest long-term danger posed by this disaster has come from the destruction and meltdown of nuclear reactors at the Fukushima Daiichi plant and the associated nuclear accidents and radioactive fallout. Experts have judged this to be the worst nuclear catastrophe since the meltdown in Chernobyl in the former Soviet Union some 25 years earlier, estimating that the process of cooling and dismantling the three damaged reactors and decontaminating the area could take as long as a decade. This ongoing threat of radiation is particularly poignant for Japan, the only country to have experienced widespread radioactive contamination following the atomic bombing at the end of World War II.

This nuclear fallout has led growing numbers of Japanese citizens and political leaders to question the safety and wisdom of reliance on nuclear energy. Prior to the crisis, Japan met nearly one-third of its energy needs from nuclear power and had plans to boost this to fully half its power generation. But the disaster has

Scene of the extensive destruction resulting from Japan's Tohoku earthquake and tsunami.

prompted increasing calls for reducing nuclear energy dependency and has led the government to shut down a number of additional reactors. Certainly not as deadly, the political fallout from the disaster has been significant as well. Although the crisis initially provided a boost to the flailing DPJ government, its slow and inadequate response to the disaster prompted growing frustration and activism among Japanese citizens. The iron triangle of Japan, Inc. became a particular target of this popular dissatisfaction, as it became apparent that the bureaucratic ministry charged with ensuring the safe operation of the private utility corporation's nuclear plants had in fact served as its chief promoter. As is often the case in these kinds of disasters, the real heroes were its victims. The region experienced virtually no looting or other crimes in the days and weeks following the earthquake and tsunami, and the Japanese people demonstrated a remarkable degree of patience, cooperation, and national purpose.

Graying Japan

In the twenty-first century, Japan faces an additional demographic tsunami with potentially even greater consequences than the great tidal wave of 2011 or even the country's decades-long economic recession. Japan finds itself at the forefront of a problem confronting many advanced industrial societies: the convergence of an aging population and dwindling fertility rates. Although Japan is not alone in facing this challenge, it is the first large country to begin rapidly shrinking as a result of natural demographic trends and is now the world's fastest-aging society. As in Italy, Germany, and other European societies, Japan's population aged 65 and older is rapidly increasing relative to the rest of its society. As noted in the next box ("In Comparison: Percentage of the Population Over Age 65"), the ratio of Japanese senior citizens to the total population was only 12 percent in 1990, but is expected to climb to more than 35 percent by 2050. By midcentury, demographers predict, Japan will have 1 million centenarians and 30 percent fewer people overall, and nearly 1 million more people will die each year than are born.

The graying of Japan's population brings economic challenges that the United States and other countries certainly face as well, including health and financial care. But the most acute problem Japan faces, far more so than other advanced countries, is that of a declining workforce. The size of Japan's workforce peaked in 1998 and will continue to decline rapidly as fewer and fewer Japanese reach maturity each year to replace retiring and dying workers. Japan is certainly not

Percentage of the Population Over Age 65

YEAR	JAPAN	UNITED STATES	GERMANY	FRANCE	UNITED KINGDOM
1990	12.05	12.39	14.96	13.99	15.72
1995	14.54	12.47	15.47	15.09	15.74
2000	17.37	12.30	16.40	15.97	15.75
2010	22.54	12.89	20.19	16.62	16.95
2020	27.85	16.29	22.51	20.45	20.21
2030	29.57	20.17	27.70	23.85	24.34
2040	33.23	21.00	30.92	26.16	27.24
2050	35.65	21.09	30.97	26.73	27.31

Source: "International Comparison: Ratio of 65 Years Old and Over Among Total Population," Statistics, Web Japan: Gateway for All Japanese Information, http://web-japan.org/stat/stats/01CEN2C.html (accessed 7/16/05).

alone in this problem, but whereas most advanced societies have expanded their labor pools by more fully integrating women and immigrants into the workplace, Japan has been unwilling to embrace either group. In fact, experts have argued for years that one of the quickest boosts to Japan's economic slowdown would be to expand work opportunities for women, particularly in management and other professional roles. Only 40 percent of Japanese women currently work (compared with nearly 47 percent in the United States and 48 percent in Sweden). But resistance to expanding women's role in the workforce remains high in this traditionally patriarchal society.

Even if Japanese women were fully empowered, economists and demographers agree that the only long-term hope for stabilizing Japan's population and workforce is to increase and sustain immigration over many years. Absent this source of workers, consumers, and taxpayers, experts predict that Japan's economy will not just decline but may very well collapse. As its traditional views toward the role of women have kept women at home, Japan's conservative attitudes toward ethnic purity and the insular nature of Japanese society have severely restricted immigration. Whereas the United States accepted an average of 1 million immigrants a year during the 1990s, it took Japan a quarter century to absorb 1 million immigrants into its society. Moreover, most of these immigrants have been brought in from other Asian countries to fill low-paying "dirty, dangerous, and difficult" jobs. Japan has done little to attract immigrants with specialized knowledge and skills, once again handicapping its economy. All this begs the question: Is Japan willing or indeed even able to make the changes necessary to assume its global responsibilities or compete internationally in a twenty-first-century world that has changed so considerably while many aspects of Japan have not?

Territorial Tempests

An additional thorny challenge lies beyond the shores of Japan's main islands and concerns territorial disputes with each of the country's largest continental neighbors. Although the total land mass of these contested islands could easily fit within the area of metropolitan Tokyo, conflicts with Russia, China and South Korea over these mostly uninhabited (and in many cases uninhabitable) territories has been rancorous, persistent, and seemingly intractable. Ironically, the conflicts are not so much about the islands themselves, but rather a convergence of bitter historical memories, expressions of national sovereignty, and competition for access to lucrative fisheries and seabed petroleum resources.

The largest of these territories and the source of the most long-standing dispute are what the Russians call the Kurile Islands and the Japanese refer to as the "Northern Territories." Control of this chain of islands stringing northward from Hokkaido (the most northern of Japan's four largest islands) has shifted back and forth between Japan and China since the nineteenth century. However, since Japan's defeat in World War II, the entire archipelago has been occupied by the Russians. Because each country forfeited control over the islands as a result of war defeat (Russia in 1905 and Japan in 1945), neither side is willing to legitimate the claims of the other. In fact, this dispute has prevented Japan and Russia from ever concluding a peace treaty ending the Second World War. Although Japan currently lays claim to only the four southernmost islands in the chain, the two countries appear as far away as ever from resolving this issue that has festered for nearly seven decades. In 2010, Russian President Dimitri Medvedev became the first Russian political leader to visit the islands, an area valued for its highly productive fishing grounds. Choosing to tour the islet closest to Japan, he posted photos to his Twitter account, noting "how many beautiful places there are in Russia!"

Moving southward, Japan's island dispute with South Korea concerns two tiny islets whose sizes belie the degree of bitter acrimony between the two countries. The two jagged outcroppings of rock known as the Dokdo (Korea) or Takeshima (Japan) islands are located almost equidistant (just over 100 miles) from both the Korean mainland and Japan's main island of Honshu. Although each country claims sovereignty over the territory, South Korea administers the 46 acres of volcanic rock on which an octopus fisherman and his wife (both Korean citizens) comprise the entire permanent residents (guarded by 37 South Korean police officers also stationed on the island). South Korea, in particular, remains highly sensitive to this issue since Japan's claim to the territory is founded chiefly on its harsh colonization of Korea in the early twentieth century. When the Japanese prefecture laying claim to the islets launched a "Takeshima Festival" in 2005, an angry Korean mother responded in protest by severing off her own finger and that of her son. Another Korean protester set himself on fire.

Likewise, Japan's dispute with China over the Diaoyu (China) or Senkaku (Japan) islands finds its roots in Japan's imperial past. Although each country cites centuries-old historical records to justify its respective claims of sovereignty, Japan formally annexed the five islets in 1895 after its military victory against China that year. The same treaty awarded the far larger island of Taiwan (which lies some 100 miles to the south) to Japan as its first colony. The uninhabited outcroppings lie almost equidistant (approximately 200 miles) from the Chinese mainland and Japan's Okinawa. Although abundant fishing in the area has led to numerous incidents between Chinese fishing boats and Japanese patrol boats (including the intentional ramming of a Japanese coast guard cutter by a much smaller Chinese trawler in 2010), the greater stake in this dispute has been the oil and gas fields discovered in this region. Although both countries agreed in 2008 to make the East China Sea a "sea of peace, cooperation and prosperity" and to jointly exploit the seabed petroleum fields, bitter accusations and rising nationalist protests on both sides have been common.[18] In fact, while these multinational island disputes are ostensibly foreign policy issues, they remain salient in large part because of conservative nationalist groups in each country that see any show of flexibility or compromise on the parts of their own governments as a sign of weakness against the imperial designs of their neighbors. This proves that in the case of Japan, as demonstrated elsewhere in this textbook on comparative politics, perhaps all politics in the end are domestic politics.

NOTES

1. T. J. Pempel and Keiichi Tsunekawa, "Corporatism Without Labor: The Japanese Anomaly," in Philippe Schmitter and Gerhard Lehmbruch, eds., *Trends Toward Corporatist Intermediation* (New York: Sage, 1990).

2. Margaret A. McKean, "Equality," in Takeshi Ishida and Ellis S. Krauss, eds., *Democracy in Japan* (Pittsburgh: University of Pittsburgh Press, 1989), p. 203.

3. There was also an underclass or outcast segment of society known as the *eta* or *burakumin*, discriminated against for their work in the ritually impure trades, such as tanning and butchering.

4. Hugh Byas, *Government by Assassination* (New York: Alfred A. Knopf, 1942).

5. John Dower, *Embracing Defeat: Japan in the Wake of World War II* (New York: W. W. Norton, 1999), p. 45.

6. "Experts ponder reasons for Japan's rash of short-term prime ministers," *Japan Times*, January 1, 2012.

7. David S. Law, "The Anatomy of a Conservative Court: Judicial Review in Japan," *Texas Law Review* 87 (June 2009): 1545–93.

8. Although the population of voting districts was relatively balanced when districts were originally set up after the war, the LDP never reapportioned them even as the countryside became depopulated. In exchange for their voting loyalty, farmers were assured high prices for their rice and were given voting clout as much as three times greater than that of urban voters, who were less likely to vote for the LDP. In the 1990 lower house elections, for example, opposition parties won nearly 54 percent of the popular vote but garnered only 44 percent of the seats. Likewise, even though the DPJ outpolled the LDP in the 2010 upper house elections, it garnered fewer seats.

9. Under the old system, all representatives were elected from multimember districts in which voters had a single nontransferable vote (SNTV), which they cast for a specific candidate instead of a party list. This unusual MMD/SNTV system created a variety of incentives and consequences, both for the LDP, which benefited immensely from the rules, and for opposition parties struggling to compete.

10. Tanaka, the consummate Japanese politician, was perhaps also Japan's most influential and successful. He fostered a powerful LDP faction in the early 1970s and served as prime minister from 1972 to 1974 but was forced to resign and ultimately convicted of financial misdeeds involving huge sums of money.

11. See, for example, Karel van Wolferen, *The Enigma of Japanese Power* (New York: Alfred A. Knopf, 1989).

12. For a useful analysis of Japan and Italy's comparable 1990s electoral reforms with strikingly different outcomes, see Daniela Giannetti and Bernard Grofman, eds., *A Natural Experiment on Electoral Law Reform: Evaluating the Long Run Consequences of 1990s Electoral Reform in Italy and Japan* (New York: Springer, 2010).

13. See Andrew DeWit, "Dry Rot: The Corruption of General Subsidies in Japan," *Journal of the Asia Pacific Economy* 7 (2002): 355–78.

14. See Simon Andrew Avenell, "Civil Society and the New Civic Movements in Contemporary Japan: Convergence, Collaboration and Transformation," *Journal of Japanese Studies* 25 (2009): 247–83.

15. The seminal study in this field is Chalmers Johnson, *MITI and the Japanese Miracle: The Growth of Industrial Policy, 1925–1975* (Stanford, Calif.: Stanford University Press, 1982).

16. T. J. Pempel, "Between Pork and Productivity: The Collapse of the Liberal Democratic Party," *Journal of Japanese Studies* 36 (2010): 227–54.
17. Clyde Prestowitz, *Trading Places* (New York: Basic Books, 1988), pp. 82–94.
18. "Getting their goat," *Economist*, September 16, 2010.

KEY TERMS

administrative guidance Informal policy negotiations among Japanese bureaucrats and corporate executives

amakudari Literally "descent from heaven," in which retiring Japanese senior bureaucrats take up positions in corporations or run for political office

Article 9 The clause in Japan's postwar constitution that requires Japan to renounce the right to wage war; also known as the Peace Clause

capitalist developmental state Japan's modern neomercantilist state, which has embraced both private property and state economic intervention

Democratic Party of Japan (DPJ) Social democratic party formed in 1998 as a merger of reform-minded opposition parties that has held government since 2009

Diet Japan's bicameral parliament

flying geese A model of regional economic development imposed on Asia in the 1930s with Japan at the head of a flock of dependent Asian economies

Hatoyama, Yukio DPJ's first prime minister (2009–10)

House of Councillors The upper and weaker chamber of Japan's parliament

House of Representatives The lower and more powerful chamber of Japan's parliament

industrial policy Government measures designed to promote economic and industrial development

iron triangle A term describing the conservative alliances among Japan's elite bureaucrats, conservative politicians, and big-business executives

Japan Post Japan's national postal system, including the world's largest savings institution, which began privatization in 2005

Kan, Naoto DPJ's short-lived second prime minister (2010–11)

keiretsu Japan's large business conglomerates

koenkai Japan's local political support groups or political machines

Koizumi, Junichiro A populist Japanese LDP prime minister (2001–06)

Liberal Democratic Party (LDP) Japan's conservative political party, which governed Japan for over five decades since the party's inception in 1955

MacArthur, Douglas The U.S. general who presided over the seven-year occupation of Japan (1945–52)

Meiji oligarchs The vanguard of junior samurai who led Japan's nineteenth-century modernization drive

Meiji Restoration Japan's 1867–68 "revolution from above," which launched Japan's modernization in the name of the Meiji emperor

money politics An informal system of gifts, favors, and huge sums of money required to lubricate Japanese politics

Noda, Yoshihiko Current DPJ prime minister, serving since September 2011

Okinawa Japanese prefecture comprised of several island archipelagoes located southwest of Japan's four major islands and host to several controversial U.S. military bases

Ozawa, Ichiro Former LDP kingpin and important leader of the opposition until forced to resign as DPJ president in 2009 when implicated in a fund-raising scandal

pork-barrel projects Government appropriation or other policy supplying funds for local improvements to ingratiate legislators with their constituents

"rich country, strong military" The mercantilist slogan promoting Japan's nineteenth-century modernization efforts

sakoku **("closed country")** Tokugawa Japan's policy of enforced isolation, which lasted from the seventeenth to the nineteenth centuries

samurai Japan's feudal-era warrior retainers

Self-Defense Force Japan's military, ostensibly permitted only defensive capacity

shogun A dominant lord in feudal Japan

Taisho democracy The era of tentative democratization in Japan (1918–31)

Tokugawa The military clan that unified and ruled Japan from the seventeenth to the nineteenth centuries

"twisted Diet" Situation in which no party or coalition of parties controls both chambers of the Japanese parliament, common since 2007

2011 earthquake Disastrous 9.0 earthquake that struck the northeast region of Honshu, Japan's largest island, causing a destructive tsunami that resulted in the meltdown of several nuclear reactors

Yasukuni Shrine The controversial Shinto shrine honoring Japan's war dead

Yoshida, Shigeru The influential Japanese LDP prime minister who led the country from 1946 to 1954, with a brief hiatus

zombies Japanese firms rendered essentially bankrupt during Japan's recession but propped up by banks and politicians

WEB LINKS

Japanese constitution (www.gol.com/users/mi[...]
Japanese prime minister and cabinet (www.ka[...]
Japanese Statistical Data, affiliated with Japa[...]
  provides regularly updated statistical in[...]
  including aging, crime, elections, med[...]
  web-japan.org/stat/index.html)
National Diet of Japan, includes useful li[...]
  of Representatives, with extensive in[...]
  strength of parties, and electoral and legisla[...]
  .edu/ias/eac/Kokkai.htm)

 Visit StudySpace for quizzes and other review material.
www.norton.com/studyspace

- Vocabulary Flashcards of All Key Terms
- Country Review Quizzes
- Interactive Map Tours

RUSSIA

HEAD OF STATE :
President Vladimir Putin (since May 7, 2012)

HEAD OF GOVERNMENT:
Prime Minister Dimitri Medvedev
(since May 7, 2012)

CAPITAL:
Moscow

TOTAL LAND SIZE:
17,075,200 sq km (1st)

POPULATION:
138 million (9th)

GDP AT PPP:
$2.22 trillion (9th)

GDP PER CAPITA AT PPP:
$15,900 (24th)

**HUMAN DEVELOPMENT
INDEX RANKING:**
65th

RUSSIA

Introduction

Why Study This Ca[se]

For decades, Russia stood out from all other countries [...]
1917, the Soviet Union (which included present-day Russia and many of its neigh[bors])
was the world's first Communist state. The Soviet Union served as a beacon for Communists everywhere, a symbol of how freedom and equality could be transformed if the working class could truly gain power. It provoked equally strong responses among its opponents, who saw it as a violent, dangerous, and power-hungry dictatorship. The rapid growth of Soviet power from the 1930s onward only exacerbated this tension, which eventually culminated in a Cold War between the United States and the Soviet Union following World War II. Armed with thousands of nuclear weapons, these two ideologically hostile states struggled to maintain a balance of power and to avoid a nuclear holocaust. Until the 1980s, many observers believed that humanity would eventually face a final, violent conflict between these two systems.

Yet when the Soviet Union's end finally came, it was not with a bang but with a whimper. In the 1980s, the Soviet Union saw the rise of a new generation of leaders who realized that their system was no longer primed to overtake the West, economically or otherwise. The general secretary of the Soviet Union's Communist Party, Mikhail Gorbachev, attempted to inject limited political and economic reforms into the system. His reforms, however, seemed only to exacerbate domestic problems and polarize the leadership and the public. Gorbachev's actions resulted in the actual dissolution of the Soviet Union and the formation of fifteen independent countries, one of which is Russia.

How would Russia be reconstructed from the ruins? Like many of the other postcommunist countries, it had to confront the twin tasks of forging democracy

315

land that had little historical experience of either
go about creating a market economy after commu-
out building democracy? Russia proves a fascinating
ild new institutions that reconcile freedom and equality in
nt from that of the previous regime. We can learn a lot from
t meeting this awesome challenge.

rs on, the prospects for Russian democracy and development are
er an initial decade of incomplete and chaotic political and economic
the country began moving away from a liberal economic system and lib-
mocracy. Under the leadership of President (and Prime Minister) **Vladimir
tin**, Russia has seen the weakening of democratic institutions. These include
the state, where central and regional sources of political power are restricted, and
where ever-greater authority is concentrated in the hands of the president. Limitations on federalism, electoral reform, and other changes have all been directed
at reducing political power beyond the presidency. Additionally, steps have been
taken to restrict civil society, with the state bringing the mass media under federal
control and increasingly preventing independent political parties and nongovernmental organizations from functioning. Today, an incipient democratic ideology
has been replaced by a focus on Russian nationalism, reflecting a sense of humiliation that the country has lost its authoritative role in the international system.

Similarly, the economy, which in the 1990s experienced a drastic and incomplete shift to private property and market forces, has seen both institutions
increasingly curtailed. Powerful economic leaders whose fortunes rose during that
period, the **oligarchs**, have in most cases been divested of their wealth, driven
from the country, or imprisoned. Assets, particularly natural resources, have been
renationalized in many cases or transferred to individuals close to Putin. Although
economic growth has characterized the past few years, that growth is largely propelled by a rise in oil and gas prices. In economics and politics, the country has
fallen under the control of the *siloviki* (men of power), individuals who, like
Putin, have their origins in the security agencies. And yet Putin's consolidation
of power and his limitations on democracy and the market have garnered tremendous public support. Tired of the chaos of market reforms, cynical about
postcommunist politics, and angry about Russia's loss of power in the world, the
people have appreciated Putin's promise to restore order and Russian pride. To a
large extent, he has succeeded.

In 2008, President Putin stepped down from power, having served the two-
term limit on the office. His handpicked successor, Dimitri Medvedev, easily won
the presidential election and promptly appointed Putin to be his prime minister.

Given Medvedev's non-*siloviki* background and the power inherent in the presidential office, some expected that this transfer of power could represent a break with the Putin era. But this was a false hope. As prime minister, Putin still called the shots, and then returned to the presidency in 2012, appointing Medvedev as prime minister. Able to serve another two six-year terms, it appears that Putin will remain in office until 2024. At that point he will have governed Russia for a quarter of a century.

In many ways, Russia has become as opaque and resistant to change as it was under communism, a worrying sign for that country and the rest of the world. In this chapter we will look at the past, the promise, and the present of Russian politics and political change, with an eye toward where this country may be headed.

Major Geographic and Demographic Features

As we study Russia's geography, the first thing we notice is the country's vast size. Even when viewed separately from the various republics that made up the Soviet Union, Russia is nearly four times the size of the United States and covers eleven time zones. Yet much of this land is relatively unpopulated. With some 139 million people, Russia's population is far smaller than that of the United States or the European Union (with around 300 million and 500 million, respectively). Much of the Russian population is concentrated in the western, geographically European part of the country.

Russia's east, Siberia, is a flat region largely uninhabited because of its bitterly cold climate. Siberia represents an interesting comparison to the American frontier experience. While Americans moved westward toward the Pacific Ocean in the nineteenth century, to find new lands to settle, Russians moved eastward, toward the same ocean. Alaska was part of the Russian Empire until it was sold to the United States in 1867. But Russian and American experiences of the frontier were quite different. In America, the amenability of the climate and soil helped spread the population across the country and reinforce a sense of pioneer individualism. In contrast, the harsh conditions of Siberia meant that only the state could function effectively in much of the region, where it developed infrastructure and created populated communities. Many of the people who settled Siberia, before and after 1917, were political prisners sent into exile.

Because of Russia's enormous size and location, the country has many neighbors. Unlike the relative isolation of North America, Russia shares borders with no fewer than 14 countries. Many of these countries were part of the Soviet Union and are considered by Russians to remain in their sphere of influence (not unlike the way in which many Americans view Latin America). But Russia also shares a long border with China, a neighbor with whom it has often had poor relations. Russia also controls a series of islands in the Pacific that belonged to Japan until 1945, a situation that remains a source of friction between the two countries. Russia has long felt uneasy about its neighborhood. Over the centuries, unable to rely upon oceans or mountains as natural defenses, it has been subject to countless invasions from Europe and Asia. Physical isolation has never been an option.

While Russia may suffer from some intemperate climates and uneasy borders, it benefits in other areas. The country is rich in natural resources, among them wood, oil, natural gas, gold, nickel, and diamonds. Many of these resources are concentrated in Siberia and are thus not easy to extract, yet they remain important and have been central to the Russian economy.

Historical Development of the State

RELIGION, FOREIGN INVASION, AND THE EMERGENCE OF A RUSSIAN STATE

Any understanding of present-day Russia and its political struggles must begin with an understanding of how the state developed over time. While ethnically Slavic peoples have lived in European Russia for centuries, these peoples are not credited with founding the first Russian state. Rather, credit is usually given to Scandinavians (Vikings) who expanded into the region in the ninth century C.E., forming a capital in the city of Kiev. Nonetheless, the true origins of the Russian state remain open to debate. This issue is highly politicized, as many Russians reject the notion that foreigners were first responsible for the genesis of the Russian people. The dispute even involves the very name of the country. Scholars who believe in the Viking origin of the Russian state argue that the name Russia (or **Rus**) comes from the Finnish word for the Swedes, *Ruotsi*, which derives from a Swedish word meaning "rowers." Those who dispute this claim argue that the name is of a tribal or geographic origin that can be traced to the native Slav inhabitants.[1]

Whatever its origins, by the late tenth century the Kievan state had emerged as a major force, stretching from Scandinavia to Central Europe. It had also adopted **Orthodox Christianity**, centered in Constantinople (modern-day Istanbul). Orthodoxy developed distinctly from Roman Catholicism in a number of practical and theological ways, among which was the perception of the relationship between church and state. Roman Catholics came to see the pope as the central leader of the faith, separate from the political power of Europe's kings. Orthodoxy, however, did not draw such a line between political and religious authority, a situation that, some argue, stunted the idea of a society functioning independently of the state.

Another important development was the Mongol invasion of Russia in the thirteenth century. The Mongols, a nomadic Asian people, first united under Genghis Khan and controlled Russia (along with much of China and the Middle East) for over two centuries. During this time, Russians suffered from widespread economic destruction, massacres, enslavement, urban depopulation, and the extraction of resources. Some scholars view this occupation as the central event that set Russia on a historical path separate from that of the West, one leading to greater despotism and isolation. Cut off from European intellectual and economic influences, Russia did not participate in the Renaissance, feel the impact of the Protestant Reformation, or develop a strong middle class.

Not all scholars agree with this assessment, however. For some, the move toward despotism had its impetus not in religion or foreign invasion but in domestic leadership. Specifically, they point to the rule of Ivan the Terrible (1533–84), who came to power in the decades following Russia's final independence from Mongol control. Consolidating power in Moscow rather than Kiev, Ivan began to assert Russia's authority over that of foreign rulers and began to destroy any government institutions that obstructed his consolidation of personal power. In a precursor to the Soviet experience, he created a personal police force that terrorized his political opponents. Though Ivan is viewed in much of Russian history as the unifier of the country, many historians see in him the seeds of repressive and capricious rule.[2] Whatever his legacy, it is in Ivan's rule that we see the emergence of a single Russian emperor, or **tsar** (or czar, from the Latin word *Caesar*), who exercised sovereignty over the nation's lands and aristocrats.

We might argue that no one factor led to Russia's unique growth of state power and its dearth of democratic institutions. Religion may have shaped political culture in a way that influenced how Russians viewed the relationship between the individual and the state. Historic catastrophes such as Mongol rule may have stunted economic growth and cut the country off from the developments that occurred elsewhere in Europe. Political leadership might also have solidified certain authoritarian institutions. None of these conditions, individually, may have had a defining influence on the country's development, but taken together, they served to pull Russia away from the West. This interpretation of events has been reemphasized of late in Russian politics.

TIMELINE OF POLITICAL DEVELOPMENT

YEAR	EVENT
1237–40	Mongols invade
1552–56	Ivan the Terrible conquers the Tatar khanates of Kazan and Astrakhan; establishes Russian rule over the lower and middle Volga River
1689–1725	Peter the Great introduces reforms, including the subordination of the church, the creation of a regular conscript army and navy, and new government structures
1798–1814	Russia intervenes in the French Revolution and the Napoleonic Wars
1861	Edict of Emancipation ends serfdom
1917	Monarchy is overthrown and a provisional government established; Bolsheviks in turn overthrow the provisional government
1918–20	Civil war takes place between the Red Army and the White Russians, or anticommunists
1938	Joseph Stalin consolidates power; purges begin
1953	Stalin dies
1956	General Secretary Nikita Khrushchev denounces Stalin
1985	Mikhail Gorbachev becomes general secretary and initiates economic and political reforms
1991	Failed coup against Gorbachev leads to the collapse of the Soviet Union; Boris Yeltsin becomes president of independent Russia
1993	Yeltsin suspends the parliament and calls for new elections; legislators barricade themselves inside the parliament building and Yeltsin orders the army to attack parliament; Russians approve a new constitution, which gives the president numerous powers
1994–96	In a war between Russia and the breakaway republic of Chechnya, Chechnya is invaded, and a cease-fire is declared
1996	Yeltsin is re-elected

1999	Yeltsin appoints Vladimir Putin prime minister and resigns from office; Putin becomes acting president
1999	Russia reinvades Chechnya following a series of bomb explosions blamed on Chechen extremists
2000	Putin is elected president
2004	Putin is re-elected
2008	Medvedev becomes president; Putin becomes prime minister
2012	Putin returns to presidency

Ivan's death left Russia with an identity crisis. Did it belong to Europe, one of numerous rival states with a common history and culture? Or did differences in history, religion, and location mean that Russia was separate from the West? Even today, Russia continues to confront this question. Some rulers, most notably Peter the Great (1689–1725), saw Westernization as a major goal. This was typified in the relocation of the country's capital from Moscow to St. Petersburg, to place it closer to Europe (it was moved back to Moscow after the Russian Revolution of 1917). Peter consulted with numerous foreign advisers in his quest to modernize the country (particularly the military) and to carry out administrative and educational reforms. In contrast, reactionaries such as Nicholas I (1825–55) were hostile to reforms. In Nicholas's case, this hostility was so great that in the last years of his reign even foreign travel was forbidden. Reforms, such as the emancipation of the serfs in 1861, proceeded over time but lagged behind the pace of changes in Europe. As Russia vacillated between reform and reaction, there was continuity in the growth of a centralized state and a weak middle class. Industrialization came late, emerging in the 1880s and relying heavily on state intervention. This inconsistent modernization caused Russia to fall behind its international rivals.

THE SEEDS OF REVOLUTION

The growing disjunction between a largely agrarian and aristocratic society and a highly autonomous state and traditional monarchy would soon foster revolution. As Russia engaged in the great power struggles of the nineteenth and twentieth

- **Legislative-executive system**: Semi-presidential
- **Legislature**: Federal Assembly
- **Lower house**: State Duma
- **Upper house**: Federation Council
- **Unitary or federal division of power**: Federal

- **Main geographic subunits**: Republics, provinces, territories, autonomous districts, federal cities (Moscow and St. Petersburg)
- **Electoral system for lower house**: Proportional representation
- **Electoral system for upper house**: Appointed by local executive and legislature
- **Chief judicial body**: Constitutional Court

The Branches of Government

THE KREMLIN: THE PRESIDENT AND THE PRIME MINISTER

For centuries, Russians have referred to executive power, whether in the form of the tsar or the general secretary, as the **Kremlin**. Dating back to the eleventh century, the physical structure known as the Kremlin is a fortress in the heart of Moscow that has historically been the seat of state power. Today, much of the Kremlin's power is vested in the hands of the presidency, as elaborated in the 1993 constitution. That constitution created a powerful office through which the president could press for economic and political changes despite parliamentary opposition. Under Yeltsin and Putin, the result was a semi-presidential system in which the president served as head of state while a prime minister served as head of government. Power is divided between the two offices, but the president has held an overwhelming amount of executive power. Since 2012, the president is directly elected to serve a six-year term. (Prior to this, presidential terms were only four years.) The president may serve no more than two consecutive terms, and can be removed only through impeachment. Vladimir Putin was elected in 2000 after serving as Boris Yeltsin's last prime minister, and was re-elected in 2004, having faced little serious competition for the office. His successor, Dimitri Medvedev, was similarly selected by Putin to run for the office in 2008, and won easily, since other candidates were effectively barred from running for the office. Putin returned to the presidency in 2012, once Medvedev declined to run for re-election.

On paper, the president's powers are numerous. It is the president, not parliament, who chooses and dismisses the prime minister and other members of the

WHO IS VLADIMIR PUTIN?

Vladimir Putin's rapid rise to power caught virtually every observer by surprise, since not many were aware of his existence just a few years before his election to the presidency. Putin was born in 1952 in Leningrad (now St. Petersburg) and studied law at the state university there. From his early years, he showed an interest in the security services; in 1975, upon graduation, he joined the KGB, the Soviet intelligence agency. What exactly he did during his time in the KGB is unclear. It is known that from 1984 to 1990 he was stationed in East Germany, where he learned German and was charged with recruiting KGB agents and keeping tabs on opposition movements in that country.

In 1991, Putin left the KGB to work for the new mayor of Leningrad, Anatoly Sobchak, who had been one of his college professors and who supported Yeltsin during the 1991 coup. In 1994, Putin became deputy mayor of the city (by then renamed St. Petersburg) and was soon after made deputy chief administrator for the Kremlin, charged in part with helping to implement presidential decrees. In 1998, Yeltsin made Putin head of the Federal Security Service, and in 1999 he appointed him prime minister.

In December 1999, Yeltsin resigned from office, naming Putin acting president in advance of the 2000 presidential elections. During that time, Putin was viewed as a decisive actor, in contrast to the increasingly unstable (and often drunk) Yeltsin. Of particular importance for Putin's career was the Second Chechen War, which he initiated in 1999 after a series of terrorist apartment house bombings in Russia killed more than 300 people. After becoming president, Putin filled many of the top posts in his administration with the so-called *siloviki* (men of power), whose careers began in the military or the KGB. At the same time, he effectively marginalized any rivals, either inside or outside government. Even as he finished his two terms in office in 2008, he managed the election of the new president, viewing Medvedev as someone unlikely to check his own power base. In fact, while Medvedev served as president, Putin held the office of prime minister, effectively overshadowing him. After one term, Medvedev stepped aside, allowing Putin to be elected for a third presidential term. Although many Russians are dismayed by Putin's hold on power, he continues to enjoy strong support from the public for his tough leadership. (He is known for his coarse language and aggressive manner.) Many Russians believe that he saved the country from collapse and has restored its place in the world.

cabinet. The lower house of parliament, the State Duma, may reject the president's nominee, but if it does so three times, the president must dissolve the Duma and call for new elections. The president cannot dissolve the Duma in the year following parliamentary elections, however, or in the last six months of his term. The president also appoints leaders to seven federal districts that constitute all of Russia, which allows him to oversee the work of local authorities.

The president may propose and veto bills and can issue decrees, which are laws that do not require legislative approval, are often not made public, and may not be challenged by citizens in the courts. President Yeltsin frequently relied on decrees to bypass his obstreperous legislature, and even with a more compliant body, Putin has often used the power of the decree to enact law.[7]

Another source of power lies in the president's control of important segments of the state. The president has direct control over the Foreign Ministry, the Defense Ministry, and the Interior Ministry (which handles the police and domestic security), and over the armed forces. He also controls the successor to

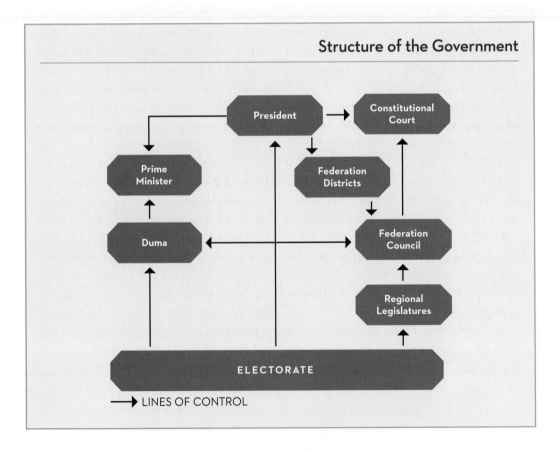

Structure of the Government

the KGB, the **Federal Security Service (FSB)**, which manages domestic and foreign intelligence. Presidential control over these ministries and services allows the office a great deal of influence in foreign affairs and domestic security.

As in the United States and other presidential or semi-presidential systems, it is difficult to remove the Russian president; impeachment is possible only on a charge of high treason or another grave crime. The impeachment process must first be approved by the high courts, after which two-thirds of both houses of parliament must vote in support of the president's removal. In 1999, the parliament attempted to impeach President Yeltsin on various charges, including his 1993 conflict with the legislature, economic reform, and the war in **Chechnya**. None of the charges passed.

In contrast to that of the president, the prime minister's role is to supervise those ministries not under presidential control and to propose legislation to parliament that upholds the president's policy goals. The Russian prime minister and other members of the cabinet, unlike their counterparts in many other parliamentary systems, are not appointed from and need not reflect the relative powers of the various parties in parliament. Because of the president's ability to choose

A 2012 protest by the Communist Party against Putin's re-election. As the banner suggests, Putin (on the left) will hold another twelve years in office, when an elderly Medvedev (right) could again return to the presidency until 2030.

the prime minister and other members of the cabinet, there is less need to form a government that represents the largest parties in parliament. During Putin's first tenure as president, Russian prime ministers were largely career bureaucrats chosen for their technical expertise or loyalty to the president rather than party leaders who had climbed the ranks in parliament. However, the appointment of Putin to be prime minister "under" Medvedev raised many questions about the nature of the semi-presidential system in Russia. In advance of the 2008 presidential elections, Putin made it clear that he expected to become prime minister in return for his selection of Medvedev to run for president, and he continued to dominate politics from what was ostensibly the weaker office. This led to a great deal of confusion as to where executive power really lay, and Medvedev's decision to step down after one term—apparently agreed to far in advance between the two men—only reinforced the sense that power is more vested in an individual than any particular office. Putin's personal authority has trumped institutional authority, rendering problematic our understanding of Russian politics through reference to the constitution.

THE LEGISLATURE

Given the power of the Russian presidency, does the national legislature have any real role? Its lack of effectiveness is certainly consistent with the Soviet past. Under Communist rule, the legislature served as little more than a rubber stamp, meeting for a few days each year simply to pass legislation drafted by party leaders. Today, Russia's parliament has little direct influence over the course of government, but it would be an exaggeration to say that nothing has changed since Soviet times.

Russia's bicameral parliament is known officially as the Federal Assembly. It comprises a lower house, the 450-seat State Duma, and an upper house, the 166-seat Federation Council. Members of the Duma, the more powerful of the two offices, serve five-year terms, while members of the Federation Council serve varied terms depending on the rules of federal territory they represent. The Duma has the right to initiate and accept or reject legislation and may override the president's veto with a two-thirds vote. The Duma also approves the appointment of the prime minister, though repeated rejections can lead to its dissolution. As in other legislatures, the Duma can call a vote of no confidence in opposition to the prime minister and his government. Should a no-confidence vote pass, the president may simply ignore the decision. If a second such vote passes within three months, however, the president is obliged to dismiss the prime minister and cabinet or call for new Duma elections.

In the instances of prime ministerial approval and votes of no confidence, then, the Duma wields unpredictable weapons. The Duma's opposition to the prime minister (and, by extension, the president) could lead to its own dissolution. Under the right circumstances, however, the Duma's opposition could lead to elections that strengthen the position of opposition parties. Of course, the exact opposite could also occur. Thus far, the Duma has not put this power to use, though in 1998 the Yeltsin administration was forced to withdraw a candidate for prime minister after he was rejected twice. In that case, the president feared new elections would only bring more anti-Yeltsin representatives into the Duma.

Another area in which the Duma can wield power is in the drafting of legislation. During the Yeltsin administration, the majority of legislation originated in the Duma, much of it dealing with substantial public issues. This changed under the Putin administration, however, and most legislation now originates with the president or prime minister, in keeping with most European parliamentary systems.

The legislature's powers have become increasingly theoretical over the past decade. As the Duma became dominated by a single party loyal to Putin (see the section "The Electoral System" on page 335), it has receded from any significant political role, to the point where some view it as little more powerful than its Soviet-era predecessor. In one telling incident, in November 2008, the president proposed changing the constitution to extend the terms of the president and Duma. He submitted the legislation within a week, and it was considered and ratified by the Duma in just ten days. More regular legislation is often passed within a day. This is not to say that its constitutional functions could not again become important should the balance of power within the Duma or between the Duma and the executive shift. For now, however, that is not the case.

As the upper house, the **Federation Council** holds even less power than the Duma. The Federation Council primarily serves to represent local interests and act as a guarantor of the constitution. The body represents each of the 83 federal administrative units, with two representatives from each. Since 2002, one representative has been selected by the governor of each region and another by the regional legislature (see the discussion of "Local Government" on page 337). Prior to that time, governors and the heads of the regional legislatures served directly in the Federation Council. Although the Federation Council does not produce legislation, it must approve bills that deal with certain issues, including taxation and the budget. The Federation Council may consider other Duma legislation if the

pipelines linking Central Asia to its own markets and growing energy needs. India has spoken of this linkage as a "New Silk Road," replacing the metaphor of the Great Game (in which India was a pawn) with the historical analogy of pathways between East and West. This vision would link Central Asia with South Asia, Europe, and the Middle East.

One of the first statements of Putin's new administration articulated Russia's ambitions in the struggle over Central Asia. In an editorial, Putin called for a "Eurasian Union" that would remove all barriers to trade, capital, and labor movements among its members. In his editorial, he asserted that the Eurasian Union was "not about recreating the USSR," but rather, about seeking "a powerful supranational union that can become one of the poles of today's world."[22] Already, Russia, Belarus, and Kazakhstan have announced plans in this direction, and Tajikistan and Kyrgyzstan have suggested that they may join as well.

What are the implications of a Russian-led Eurasian Union, and how might it affect the role of major powers in the region? First, it is not clear that even if the Eurasian Union expands and deepens, it will have the kind of power (or extend Russia's authority in the way) we might expect. While the Eurasian Union may become a vehicle for greater integration in such areas as trade, the problems of weak states, ethnic conflict, regional rivalries, and low levels of economic development that plague Central Asia are a formidable barrier to integration. That Russia has the ability and leadership to resolve these issues is uncertain. It is also not clear how much Russia itself has to offer to the member states of the Eurasian Union, given its own economic and political difficulties. That said, following from our discussion above, many Central Asian states are concerned about the rapid expansion of China into the region. China's economic influence over markets and national resources in the region, it is feared, will inevitably turn into Chinese political power, comprising the sovereignty of states in the region. Russia's smaller economy (its total GDP is less than a third of China's) may mean that states in the region see Russian influence through the Eurasian Union as less of a threat, and rather a bulwark against Chinese encroachment. Many Central Asian leaders are concerned that liberalized economic relations with China will lead to Chinese ownership over much of their economies and a migration of Chinese workers into their countries. In contrast, many Central Asians remain tightly connected to Russia through a shared history. In the long run, a successful Eurasian Union would bring Russia and China into more direct competition than they have been since the collapse of the Soviet Union. A new Great Game may define regional dynamics in the decades to come.

Russia's Demographic Future

One issue that plagues Russia—and worries its leaders—is the country's demographics. This concern is nothing new, dating back to the Soviet era, and takes several forms. The first worrisome demographic is the general level of Russian health: Russian life expectancy at birth is approximately 69 years; 75 for women and 63 for men. This is shockingly low given the overall level of development of the country. This puts Russia's life expectancy at 125th out of 194 countries, worse than in Iraq, Bangladesh, or North Korea. Why? Some of this may be due to the erosion of Russia's health care system following the collapse of the Soviet Union and the transition to capitalism, though this erosion in fact began to emerge in the 1960s. It is not a function of high infant mortality rates, which in Russia tend be similar to those in other countries within the same economic range. Rather, Russia shows an unusually high level of *adult* mortality, especially among men, whose life expectancy is about that of men in India. The primary explanation appears to be a relatively simple one: alcohol. Russian alcohol consumption, particularly among men, is extremely high, by some estimates among the top five in the world. Russia is also by far the highest consumer of hard liquor as opposed to beer or wine. This leads to two results: first, a high level of death by circulatory diseases, and second (and perhaps more striking), a very high level of death by accidents, suicides, and homicides—three times higher than in the advanced democracies. The abuse of alcohol in Russia has a long history, and we could argue it is ingrained in Russian culture, something not easily dislodged. In fact, one of Gorbachev's first reform policies in the 1980s was an anti-alcohol campaign, which provoked public discontent (though during its short time, it appeared to have a positive health effect).

A second demographic worrying Russian leaders is the country's low birth rate. Just as Russia has a low life expectancy rate, it also has an extremely low rate of fertility, even when compared to other European countries where such rates also tend to be low. Again, this dates back to the 1960s, and is marked by the high rate of abortion, a result of limited access to birth control. (Russian abortion rates are still among the highest in the world.) The high participation of women in the workforce, as well as economic stresses, contributes to an environment in which few Russians want, or can afford, to have larger families. When combined with low life expectancy, the result is a shrinking and aging population. A decade ago, Russia's population was close to 150 million; by 2050, it may be closer to 100 million. As the population ages, this puts a burden on social expenditures while reducing the workforce necessary to expand the economy and provide tax revenue. Also, though rarely addressed, the symbolism of a

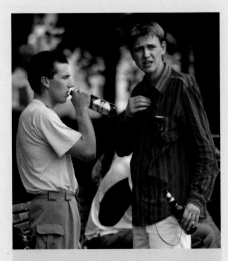

Two young men drinking beer in Moscow. The high level of alcohol consumption in Russia, especially among men, is a major factor in the country's demographic and health concerns.

"shrinking" country clashes with the self-image of a country that considers itself a major power.

Russia is struggling with how to respond to its demographic troubles. In 2009, the government announced a new campaign against alcohol abuse, relying in part on increased taxes on alcohol as a way to deter consumption. It has also offered cash bonuses for women who have more than two children. Consistent public health and pro-family policies could certainly alleviate many of these demographic concerns, but whether the Russian government and state have the will and capacity to carry out these changes is uncertain. An aging, unhealthy population is not a positive sign for the future.[23]

NOTES

1. Hakon Stang, "The Naming of Russia," Meddelelser Occasional Paper, no. 77 (Oslo: University of Oslo, 1996), www.hf.uio.no/east/Medd/PDF/Medd77.pdf (accessed 7/26/05); see also Nicholas Riasanovksy, *A History of Russia* (New York: Oxford University Press, 1963).

2. For a fascinating Soviet-era interpretation of Ivan's leadership, see the Sergei Eisenstein film *Ivan the Terrible* (1945).

3. For a discussion of this period, see Richard Pipes, *Three "Whys" of the Russian Revolution* (New York: Vintage, 1995).

4. Mary McAuley, *Soviet Politics: 1917–1991* (New York: Oxford University Press, 1992), pp. 26–27.

5. See Robert Conquest, *The Great Terror: A Reassessment* (New York: Oxford University Press, 1991), and Anne Applebaum, *Gulag: A History* (New York: Doubleday, 2003).

6. For a discussion of the last days of Soviet rule, see David Remnick, *Lenin's Tomb: The Last Days of the Soviet Empire* (New York: Random House, 1993).

7. Oleh Protsyk, "Ruling with Decrees: Presidential Decree Making in Russia and Ukraine," *Europe–Asia Studies* 56 (July 2004): 637–60.

8. Transparency International Annual Corruption Perceptions Index 2010, www.transparency.org (accessed 11/1/11).

9. For more on the courts in Russia, see Alexei Trochev, *Judging Russia: Constitutional Court in Russian Politics, 1990–2006* (Cambridge, UK: Cambridge University Press, 2008).

10. Andrei Zakharov, "Russian Federalism as a 'Dormant' Institution," *Russian Politics and Law* 49, no. 4 (July/August 2011): 8–17.
11. Andrew Konitzer and Stephen Wegren, "Federalism and Political Recentralization in the Russian Federation: United Russia as the Party of Power," *Publius* 36, no. 4 (2006): 503–22.
12. Mikhail Myagkov, Peter Ordeshook, and Dimitri Shakin, *The Forensics of Election Fraud: Russia and Ukraine* (Cambridge, UK: Cambridge University Press, 2009).
13. See the platform of Just Russia at www.spravedlivo.ru/information/party_english/english_foreword/ (accessed 2/1/12).
14. Luke March, "Managing Opposition in a Hybrid Regime: Just Russia and Parastatal Opposition," *Slavic Review* 68, no. 3 (Fall 2009): 504–27.
15. Human Rights Watch, "Choking on Bureaucracy: State Curbs Independent Civil Society Activism," February 2008, www.hrw.org (accessed 5/7/09).
16. International Religious Freedom Report 2009: Russia, U.S. Department of State (October 26, 2009) www.state.gov (accessed 11/1/11).
17. Press Freedom Index 2011, Reporters Without Borders http://en.rsf.org/ (accessed 2/2/12).
18. For more on Russian nationalism, see Marlene Laruelle, *In The Name of the Nation: Nationalism and Politics in Contemporary Russia* (New York: Macmillan, 2009).
19. See Tom Washington, "Russia Faces a New Brain Drain—Survey," *The Moscow News*, October 6, 2011, www.themoscownews.com (accessed 11/1/11).
20. Some emphasize that "resource traps" are much more complicated than simply asserting that resources lead to authoritarianism or poorly functioning state institutions. See Pauline Jones Luong and Erika Weinthal, *Oil Is Not a Curse: Ownership Structure and Institutions in Soviet Successor States* (Cambridge, UK: Cambridge University Press, 2010).
21. For a good discussion of Russian foreign policy, see Dmitri Trenin, "Russia's Post Imperial Condition," *Current History* (October 2011); available at http://carnegieendowment.org/ (accessed 11/1/11).
22. Vladimir Putin, "A New Integration Project for Eurasia: The Future in the Making," available at the web site of the Government of the Russian Federation http://premier.gov.ru/eng/events/news/16622/ (accessed 11/1/11).
23. "Russia Facing Demographic Challenges," UN National Human Development Report, Russian Federation, 2008.

KEY TERMS

asymmetric federalism A system where power is devolved unequally across the country and its constituent regions, often the result of specific laws negotiated between the region and the central government

Caucasus Southwest Russia, near the Black Sea and Turkey, where there is a diverse mixture of non-Slavic peoples with distinct languages and customs, and a much stronger historical presence of Islam than Orthodox Christianity

Chechnya Russian republic that has been a source of military conflict since 1991

Cheka Soviet secret police created by Lenin; precursor to the KGB

Commonwealth of Independent States (CIS) A loose integrationist body that incorporates most former Soviet republics

Communist Party of the Russian Federation (CPRF) Successor party in Russia to the Communist Party of the Soviet Union

Constitutional Court Highest body in the Russian legal system; responsible for constitutional review

Duma Lower house of the Russian legislature

Eurasian Union Proposed economic and political union among former Soviet states

Federal Security Service (FSB) Successor to the KGB, the Russian intelligence agency

Federation Council Upper house of the Russian legislature

glasnost Literally, "openness"; the policy of political liberalization implemented in the Soviet Union in the late 1980s

insider privatization A process in Russia where the former *nomenklatura* directors of firms were able to acquire the largest share when those firms were privatized

Just Russia A small party in the Russian Duma with a social-democratic orientation

KGB Soviet secret-police agency charged with domestic and foreign intelligence

Khodorkovsky, Mikhail Oligarch arrested and imprisoned for his opposition to the Putin administration

Kremlin Eleventh-century fortress in the heart of Moscow that has been the historical seat of Russian state power

Liberal Democratic Party of Russia (LDPR) Political party in Russia with a nationalist and antidemocratic orientation

nomenklatura Politically sensitive or influential jobs in the state, society, or economy that were staffed by people chosen or approved by the Communist Party

oligarchs Russian people noted for their control of large amounts of the Russian economy (including the media), their close ties to the government, and the accusations of corruption surrounding their rise to power

Orthodox Christianity A variant of Christianity separate from Roman Catholicism and Protestantism; originally centered in Byzantium (now roughly modern-day Turkey)

parties of power Russian parties created by political elites to support their political aspirations; typically lacking any ideological orientation

perestroika Literally, "restructuring"; the policy of economic liberalization implemented in the Soviet Union in the 1980s

Politburo Top polic...

Putin, Vladimir Cur...
  Russia from 199...

Right Cause Small ...

Rus Origin of the wo...
  region in the nint...

shock therapy A pro...

soviets Name given t...

tsar Russian word for...

United Russia Main p...

Yabloko Small party in...
  economic system

Yeltsin, Boris President...

WEB LINKS

Carnegie Endowment for ...
  Program (www.carneg...

Moscow Times (www.mosc...

Radio Free Europe/Radio Liberty (www.rferl.org)

Russia Today (http://rt.com/)

Transitions Online (www.tol.org)

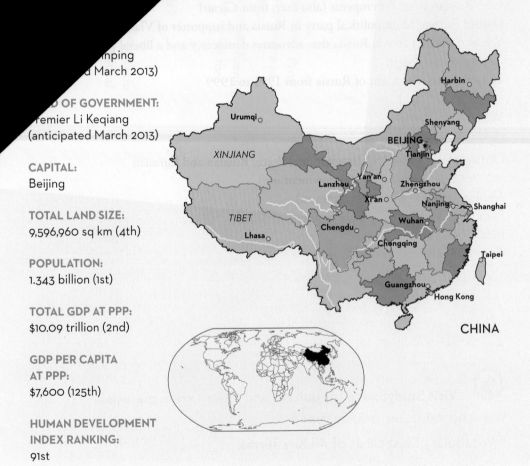

HEAD OF STATE:
...inping
(...d March 2013)

HEAD OF GOVERNMENT:
...remier Li Keqiang
(anticipated March 2013)

CAPITAL:
Beijing

TOTAL LAND SIZE:
9,596,960 sq km (4th)

POPULATION:
1.343 billion (1st)

TOTAL GDP AT PPP:
$10.09 trillion (2nd)

**GDP PER CAPITA
AT PPP:**
$7,600 (125th)

**HUMAN DEVELOPMENT
INDEX RANKING:**
91st

CHINA

CHINA

Introduction

Why Study This Case?

Napoleon Bonaparte is said to have described China as a sleeping giant. Centuries later that description continues to resonate, though with every passing year it seems less and less appropriate. Today, China is indeed stirring after centuries of slumber, with repercussions that are transforming the world. But it is not simply these changes that draw our attention; after all, China is not the first, nor the only, country to undergo dramatic change. Rather, it is that these changes are taking place in a country that we tend to speak of in superlatives, with qualities no other country can easily match.

The first of China's superlatives is its history, which extends back at least 4,000 years. Several millennia before most modern nations and states existed in even rudimentary form, China had taken shape, a relatively unified country and people. To be certain, it was torn apart innumerable times during this process by civil strife and external invasion. Yet in spite of these difficulties, a continuous Chinese civilization has existed for thousands of years and directly shapes and informs modern Chinese society and politics. The best Western equivalent to this kind of long-lived civilization would be an ancient Roman Empire that successfully conquered all of Europe and persisted for thousands of years to the present.

Second is the sheer size of China's population. China is the most populous country in the world, with more than 1.3 billion people. This is four times the population of the United States. With the exception of India (whose population also exceeds 1 billion), no other country's population even comes close to China's. China has over 50 cities with more than a million inhabitants; the United States has nine. Overpopulation has been both a source of concern for the Chinese government and a lure for foreign businesses that have dreamed for centuries of the profits that could be gained if they somehow tapped into this vast market.

This leads to a third superlative quality: China's recent and rapid development. In centuries past, China was one of the most powerful empires in the world, easily dominating its much smaller neighbors. It saw itself as the center of the world. Over time, this superiority led to isolation, and from isolation to stagnation. Foreign imperialism in the nineteenth century forced China open but also led to war and revolution. By the time of the Communist takeover in 1949, foreign powers had finally been expelled, and China once again enjoyed a period of isolation. But starting in the late 1970s, the ruling Chinese Communist Party introduced more liberal economic policies while maintaining its tight control over political power. Known as **reform and opening**, these changes launched a period of extended economic growth unmatched in the world. In the more than three decades since reform and opening began in 1978, China's gross domestic product (GDP) has grown at an average rate of just under 10 percent a year—double the rate of the other fast-growing Asian tigers, such as South Korea and Singapore, and quadruple the average growth rates of the United States, Japan, and the United Kingdom.

China's rapid economic growth can be measured in many ways, but one of the most obvious has been the country's remarkable building boom. A 2011 study found that China is completing a new skyscraper every five days and that by 2015, six of the world's ten tallest buildings will be found there. Visitors to the city of Shanghai—with its 5,000 skyscrapers, twice the number in New York City—stand awestruck before the towering buildings that line the banks of the Huangpu River. Political reform, however, has been much more limited, and public demands for change, such as the **Tiananmen Square** protests in 1989, have garnered violent reactions from the Communist regime. In this sense, China stands in contrast to Russia, whose initial transition from communism made way for greater democracy but came with the cost of economic decline and marginalization from the rest of the world.

The World Bank estimates that reform and opening has raised some 400 million Chinese out of poverty over the past several decades. At the same time, economic reforms have also led to huge income disparities and widespread social disruption. China is thus engaged in a precarious race to reform itself before the shock of these changes overwhelms the country. Economic modernization is not only transforming the physical and social landscape of the country but also reshaping international finance, trade, and the environment. China, moreover, is becoming a central factor in globalization. Indeed, the recent flood of cheap Chinese exports into the world market has displaced numerous workers outside of China, heightened concerns in advanced countries about the safety of China's food and toy exports, and substantially lowered rates of global inflation. China's voracious consumption of oil and other raw materials has become a focus of international discussions about global shortages and global warming. China now claims 16 of the world's 20 most polluted cities and is facing an environmental crisis of unprecedented proportions, spreading well beyond its borders. Now that the giant is awake, its development will have profound effects on the world.

Major Geographic and Demographic Features

In addition to boasting the largest population in the world, China, not surprisingly, is also one of the largest countries in terms of landmass, exceeded only by Russia, Canada, and the United States. Its physical size allows for a range of climates and geographic features. The southwestern portion of the country, including Tibet, is known for its mountain ranges (the Himalayas and the Altai), and most of the northwestern Xinjiang region is desert. The northeastern portion, bordering Mongolia and Russian Siberia, is marked by bitterly cold winter temperatures. Most of the Chinese population, therefore, lives in the southern and seaboard portions of the country, where the temperate climate and greater rainfall yield the majority of China's arable land. Intersecting this region are the two lifelines of China: the Yellow (Huang He) and Yangtze (Chang Jiang) rivers, which flow east toward the Pacific Ocean. The Yangtze has garnered much domestic and international attention due to the Three Gorges Dam project, which was completed in 2008. The largest dam ever constructed, it generates millions of kilowatts of electricity (something desperately needed in China) and helps prevent the flooding that has been a recurrent problem. Critics point out that the dam has destroyed countless historic sites, displaced millions of people, and caused major environmental damage. Moreover, failure of a dam this size would have catastrophic results.

Given the country's large population and landmass, the Chinese are a puzzlingly homogeneous population, with over 90 percent of the population considered part of the main ethnic group, known as Han. This stands in contrast to the persistence of ethnic diversity in Europe, Africa, and South Asia, even within individual countries. What explains the difference? The answer lies in the geography. The southern portion of the country is not only more amenable to human habitation but also free of the extreme geographic barriers, such as high mountains and deserts, that impede travel and migration. Historically, the Yellow and Yangtze rivers connected much of the country, allowing knowledge, foods, animals, and culture to spread more easily than in other parts of the world. Such connections helped foster the emergence of a single Han identity, though not always intentionally. The lack of land barriers made it much easier for early empires to develop and bring a large area under their bureaucratic control. China was first unified as early as 221 B.C.E., and with political centralization, the diverse cultures and languages of southern China were slowly absorbed into the larger Han identity. It is at this point in history that we can begin to speak of the emergence of a singular Chinese state.

Historical Development of the State

The paradox of China's political development is how a country with such an ancient civilization and such early political centralization could become such a weak state by the nineteenth century, lacking both the capacity and autonomy to resist Western imperialism. But a closer examination reveals that China's early development and later weakness are closely related. The country's first political leaders can be traced to the Shang dynasty, which reigned from the eighteenth to the eleventh century B.C.E., two thousand years before European states appeared in their earliest forms. It was during this time that written Chinese (characters) emerged. Power in the country was decentralized, however, and feudal wars among various rivals were commonplace. It was only much later, during the Qin dynasty (221–206 B.C.E.), that a single Chinese empire (and the name China) was born. During this period, China first experienced political centralization, with the appointment of nonhereditary officials to govern provinces, the minting of currency, the development of standard weights and measures, and the creation of public works, such as roads, canals, and portions of the famous Great Wall.

CENTRALIZATION AND DYNASTIC RULE

Sovereign power was centralized and expanded by the Han dynasty (206 B.C.E.–220 C.E.), a reign marked by great cultural flowering and the rise of domestic and international trade, foreign exploration, and conquest. At this time, China far outpaced Europe in its understanding of timekeeping, astronomy, and math-

TIMELINE OF POLITICAL DEVELOPMENT

YEAR	EVENT
1700 B.C.E.	Chinese civilization under Shang dynasty begins
221 B.C.E.	China unified under Qin dynasty
1839–42	First Opium War takes place
1911	Qing dynasty is overthrown
1919	May Fourth movement takes place
1921	Chinese Communist Party (CCP) is founded
1934–35	Long March takes place
1937–45	Sino-Japanese War is fought
1949	People's Republic of China (PRC) is founded
1958–60	Great Leap Forward takes place
1966–76	Cultural Revolution takes place
1978	Deng Xiaoping launches reform and opening
1989	Chinese government cracks down on protestors in Tiananmen Square Massacre
2001	China joins the World Trade Organization
2008	China hosts the Beijing Summer Olympics

ematics. The philosophy of **Confucianism** influenced the imperial leaders, with its emphasis on a fixed set of hierarchical roles, meritocracy, and obedience to authority. Confucianism also helped foster the development of the Chinese civil service, a corps of educated men chosen on the basis of a rigorous series of competitive exams testing their familiarity with Confucian thought. The notion of a meritocratic, professional bureaucracy did not emerge elsewhere in the world for centuries.

With the collapse of the Han dynasty, China was divided for nearly four centuries, until the Sui and Tang dynasties (591–907 C.E.). These dynasties restored the unity of the empire; the bureaucratic institutions of the Han period were resurrected, and economic and cultural life once again flourished. The institution-alization of the bureaucracy also helped foster the development of a gentry class made up of landowners and their children, who were groomed from birth to join the bureaucracy. This bureaucratic class became the glue that held China together. Subsequent dynasties continued to rely upon the bureaucracy to maintain Chinese unity, even when new dynasties were established by foreign conquerors, as under the Yuan (Mongols) and the Qing (Manchus). Such continuity helped foster economic development and innovation, which continued to advance faster than in Europe and other parts of the world.

AFFLUENCE WITHOUT INDUSTRIALIZATION—AND THE FOREIGN CHALLENGE

At the advent of the Ming dynasty (1368–1644), China still led the world in science, economics, communication, technological innovation, and public works. Although such knowledge offered the foundation for Chinese modernization and industrialization, these processes did not take place. During these three centuries, as Europe experienced the Renaissance, international exploration, and the beginnings of the Industrial Revolution, Chinese innovation and economic development began to stagnate. By the mid-1400s the Chinese Empire had banned long-distance sea travel and showed little interest in developing many of the technological innovations it had created. Why did this occur?

There are several possible reasons. One argument is cultural. Confucian thought helped establish political continuity and a meritocratic system in China, but over the centuries these ideas became inflexible and outdated. During the early twentieth century, bureaucratic examinations were still based on 2,000-year-old Confucian dogma. Rigidly conservative, Confucian ideology placed China at the center of the world (and universe), viewing any new or outside knowledge as unimportant and rejecting changes that might disrupt the imperial system.

A second argument is economic. During the early centuries of the Chinese Empire, entrepreneurialism was the main path to wealth. But the rise of the bureaucratic elite usurped entrepreneurialism's role and became a more powerful means of personal enrichment, particularly through rent seeking and corruption. The financial rewards of public employment led many in the upper classes to divert their most talented children to the civil service. It also concentrated economic power in the hands of the state, while business activity was stunted by a

Confucian disdain for commerce and by steep, arbitrary taxation. Naturally, the bureaucracy opposed any reforms that might threaten its privileges. Historians have also argued that the very success of China's pre-industrial economy, with relatively efficient trade and production networks and plentiful cheap labor, offered little incentive to pursue additional scientific and technical innovations. These conditions created in China a "high-level equilibrium trap" that thwarted entrepreneurial and technological impulses, circumstances that differed substantially from those in Europe that would give rise to the Industrial Revolution, where labor was more expensive, trade and production less efficient, and enlightenment thought was promoting scientific and technical exploration.[1]

A third argument is geographic and furthers the points just made. The geographic factors that facilitated early unification and continuity also limited competition, since there was less danger that a lack of innovation might lead to destruction by outside forces. In Europe, by contrast, innumerable states continuously vied for power, making isolation impossible and conservatism a recipe for economic and military defeat. No single power in Europe could ban seafaring or abolish the clock; states that resisted progress and innovation soon disappeared off the map. China, however, could reject technology and embrace isolation, since there were no rival powers to challenge such policies. In short, a combination of cultural, economic, and geographic forces allowed China's lengthy isolation.

Europe's economic and technological development continued, and its age of exploration and conquest began just as China was closing itself off to the outside world. The Portuguese first reached China by 1514, and during the sixteenth and seventeenth centuries other European traders sought to expand these initial contacts. These remained tightly controlled by the Chinese, however, and attempts to expand connections were futile. In perhaps the most famous example, a British trade mission led by Lord Macartney was rebuffed by the Chinese emperor, whose reply to King George III read in part, "I set no value on objects strange or ingenious, and we have no use for your country's manufactures."[2]

But the Chinese Empire was losing its ability to ignore the outside world, and external forces were beginning to test China's power. The First Opium War (1839–42) with Great Britain resulted in a resounding Chinese defeat, forcing China to cede Hong Kong to the British and pay restitution. Various Western powers quickly demanded similar access, and subsequent wars with the French and the Japanese only further extended the control of imperial powers over the country. Foreign pressures in turn contributed to growing domestic instability.

THE EROSION OF CENTRAL AUTHORITY: CIVIL WAR
AND FOREIGN INVASION

By the beginning of the twentieth century, the centralized authority of the Chinese state, developed over 2,000 years, effectively crumbled. In 1911, a public revolt finally swept away the remnants of the Qing dynasty, and China was declared a republic, but it soon fell under the control of regional warlords. In the midst of this chaos, two main political organizations formed to compete for power. The Nationalist Party, also known as the **Kuomintang (KMT)**, slowly grew in strength under the leadership of **Sun Yat-sen**. The party was aided by student protests in 1919 that came to be known as the **May Fourth movement**. These nationalist revolts rejected foreign interference in China and called for modernization, radical reform, and a break with traditional values and institutions, including Confucianism.

The second organization was the **Chinese Communist Party (CCP)**, formed in 1921 by leaders of the May Fourth movement. Adhering to the principles of Marx and Lenin, the CCP's founders sought to organize China's nascent working class to resist the exploitation of both foreign imperialists and domestic warlords. Though the KMT's Sun had been educated in the United States, both parties received support from the recently established Soviet Union. In fact, the Soviets saw the KMT as a more likely contender for power than the much smaller CCP and hoped to move the KMT into the Soviet orbit. Following Sun's death in 1925, relations between the KMT and the CCP unraveled. Chiang Kai-shek, head of the KMT's armed forces, took control of the party and expelled pro-Soviet and pro-CCP elements. Chiang subdued or co-opted key regional warlords and brutally suppressed the CCP in areas under KMT control. By 1928, the KMT had emerged as the effective leader of much of the country, while the CCP was pushed out of the cities and into the countryside. The KMT quickly shed any pretense of democracy, growing ever more dictatorial and corrupt.

During the repression of the CCP, power within the party began to pass into the hands of **Mao Zedong** (1893–1976). Deviating from the Marxist convention that revolutions be led by the urban proletariat, Mao believed that a Communist revolution could be won by building a revolutionary army out of the peasant class. He and the CCP established their own independent Communist republic within China, but KMT attacks forced the CCP to flee westward in what came to be known as the **Long March** (1934–35). In this circuitous retreat, the CCP and its loyal followers traveled over 6,000 miles and lost many lives. (Indeed, of the 100,000 who set out on the Long March, only 10 percent arrived at their final destination, in Yan'an.) The Long March represented a setback for the CCP but secured Mao's leadership and strengthened his idea that the party should reorient itself toward China's peasant majority. The CCP fostered positive relations with the peasantry during the Long March, engaging in actions that contrasted strongly with the more brutal policies of the KMT. The revolutionary ideology of the CCP and its call for equality drew all classes of Chinese to its ranks.

In 1937, both the KMT and the CCP faced a new threat as Japan launched a full-scale invasion of the country after several years of smaller incursions. The two parties formed a nominal united front against the invading Japanese, though they continued to battle each other even as they resisted the Japanese advance. While the war weakened KMT power, which was based in the cities, it bolstered the CCP's nationalist credentials and reinforced its ideology of a peasant-oriented communism of the masses. The war also forged a strong Communist military, the **People's Liberation Army (PLA)**, trained both to fight the enemy and to win public support. This birth of Chinese communism through peasant guerrilla warfare is quite different from the Soviet experience, in which a small group of urban intellectuals seized control of the state through a coup d'état. In fact, the CCP and PLA comprised a new state and regime in the making.

THE ESTABLISHMENT AND CONSOLIDATION OF A COMMUNIST REGIME

Japan's defeat at the end of World War II found the CCP much strengthened and the KMT in disarray. The Communists now commanded the support of much of the countryside, while the KMT's traditional urban base of support was shattered by war and weakened by widespread corruption and rampant inflation. Communist attacks quickly routed the KMT, and in 1949 the Communist forces entered Beijing unopposed and established the People's Republic of China (PRC). Chiang and the remnants of the KMT fled to the island of Taiwan, declaring *their* Republic of China as the legitimate government of all of China—which the United States recognized (rather than the PRC) until 1979. The island nation continues to claim and maintain its sovereignty, though the PRC has never recognized it and asserts that eventually the province of Taiwan will return to mainland control.

The new Communist regime faced the challenge of modernizing a country that was far behind the West and ravaged by a century of imperialism and war. The CCP's assets, forged during the war, were its organizational strength and

Youthful Red Guards gather to read aloud from Quotations of Chairman Mao *during the Cultural Revolution.*

REFORM AND OPENING AFTER MAO

With Mao's death, the incessant campaigns to whip up revolutionary fervor ended, and the party came under control of leaders who had themselves been victims of the Cultural Revolution. Most important was **Deng Xiaoping** (1904–97), a top party leader from the earliest years of the CCP who had been stripped of his post (twice) during the Cultural Revolution. In the race to take control of post-Mao China, Deng initially allied with Mao's successor, Hua Guofeng, who had outmaneuvered Mao's widow, Jiang Qing, and her allies (known as the Gang of Four). Deng then marginalized Hua and, by late 1978, had consolidated his power and set the nation on a very different course.

In contrast to Mao's emphasis on revolutionary action for its own sake, Deng pursued modernization at the expense of Communist ideology, in what became known as reform and opening. The government encouraged the gradual privatization of agriculture and then business; it also cultivated foreign relations with capitalist countries, continuing a process that began under Mao with U.S. president Richard Nixon's visit to China in 1972. It also expanded foreign investment and trade while deemphasizing ideology. To quote Deng, "Whether a cat is black or white makes no difference. As long as it catches mice, it is a good cat." Ironically, the destruction of much of the party-state under the Cultural Revolution made these pragmatic reforms easier. China began to embrace the market economy, with all of its benefits and difficulties.

GATE OF HEAVENLY PEACE

The broad plaza that fronts the Forbidden City (the former imperial palace) in the heart of Beijing known as Tiananmen, or "Gate of Heavenly Peace," Square has been the site of numerous significant political events, including the 1919 May Fourth movement, the declaration of the PRC's founding in 1949, and huge Red Guard tributes to Mao Zedong during the 1960s Cultural Revolution. In April 1989, students gathered in the square to mourn the death of Hu Yaobang, a former general secretary of the CCP who had been dismissed after student protests in 1987. The eulogy quickly grew into a general protest against corruption and a call for political reform. These were calls not for an end to Communist rule but for greater public participation in decision making, not unlike what was occurring at the same time in the Soviet Union under Mikhail Gorbachev.

The demonstrators' ranks swelled rapidly. On the historically significant May 4, an estimated 100,000 students and other citizens marched in the streets of Beijing, and by May 17 an estimated 1 million people had occupied Tiananmen Square. Martial law was declared, but many protesters remained, and on June 4 (now known in China simply as *liusi*, or "6/4," much as Americans refer to 9/11), the party leadership brought in the military. Although those gathered in the square itself were permitted to leave, hundreds of protesters were killed in clashes around Beijing that day and in other major Chinese cities. Over the next few months, thousands of students and others connected to the protests were arrested, and students throughout China were required to attend Communist ideology indoctrination courses. More than two decades later, security at Tiananmen Square remains extremely tight.

One reform that did not take place, however, was political. In spite of the downgrading of Communist ideology, the CCP still maintained complete control over political life, and attempts at public debate in the 1970s were quickly silenced. Although reform and opening has lifted millions out of poverty, by the 1980s, serious problems had emerged, among them inflation, unemployment, and widespread corruption (particularly within the CCP). As with the May Fourth movement and the Red Guards of the Cultural Revolution, students once again played a major role in expressing discontent over this situation. In the 1989 Tiananmen Square demonstration, hundreds of protesters were killed for daring to call for political reforms (see "Gate of Heavenly Peace," p. 377).

The regime's swift and violent response to the protest and its vigilant suppression of even hints of political unrest in the decades since Tiananmen have been combined with continued economic reform and opening. Deng Xiaoping and, with his passing in 1997, China's successive CCP leaders have in essence offered a social contract to their citizens: in exchange for accepting the CCP's monopoly over political power, the Chinese public has been permitted an unprecedented degree of economic freedom and the right to pursue prosperity. Most Chinese have accepted this bargain, and the Chinese economy is now in its fourth decade of white-hot growth. The question remains whether a conservative, authoritarian state can continue to preside successfully over this dynamic economy and an increasingly vibrant and restive society. We turn now to an examination of this political regime.

Political Regime

Despite China's three decades of economic reform and global trends of democratization, the country remains stubbornly authoritarian. In fact, approximately half of the world's population that does not democratically elect its leaders resides in China.[4] Certainly China's historical legacy of more than 2,000 years of centralized authoritarian rule (legitimized by Confucian precepts) has buttressed the current regime. But to understand the nature and resilience of China's Communist authoritarianism, we must examine the ways in which political control is organized and exercised in a Communist party-state. In spite of China's economic liberalization, this party-state retains the essential organizational structure that the Chinese Communist Party adopted from the Soviet Union at its founding in the 1920s. Though China's reformist leaders have almost fully rejected Marx in their embrace of market freedoms, their decision to retain a closed political system is very much in accord with Lenin's vision of the Communist party-state. Lenin contended that for the Communist revolution to succeed in Russia, a self-appointed Communist Party elite, enlightened with wisdom and imbued with revolutionary fervor, would need to serve as a vanguard on behalf of the masses. This group alone would have the organizational capacity and resolve to lead the revolutionary transitions from feudalism and capitalism to state socialism and ultimately utopian communism. The need to guide this revolutionary process, Lenin argued, justified the party in maintaining a political monopoly and serving as a "dictatorship of the proletariat."

This ideological and organizational logic has had several consequences for the exercise of political control in China (as was true in the Soviet Union and other Communist party-states) in the period of reform and opening. True to its Leninist heritage, political authority both within the party-state and from the party-state to broader Chinese society still flows largely *from* the party elite *to* those within the party, the state, and society, who are expected to submit to this authority. However, China's rapid economic growth in recent years and increasingly complex society has compelled the party-state to devolve substantial authority to regional and local officials and to ease its iron grip on society. This has had significant consequences for China's political regime and its state capacity.

Political Institutions

The CCP exercises control over the state, society, and economy through the *nomenklatura* system, by which party committees are responsible for the appointment, promotion, transfer, and firing of high-level state, party, and even public-industry personnel. (In China's case, this comprises some 10 million positions.) The party also maintains direct control over the government and bureaucracy through a political structure of "organizational parallelism," in which all government executive, legislative, and administrative agencies are matched or duplicated at every level of organization by a corresponding party organ (see the table "Parallel Organization of the Chinese Communist Party and the Chinese Government," p. 380). These CCP bureaus supervise the work of the state agencies and ensure that the interests of the party prevail. This means that although the Chinese state has a premier, a parliament, and bureaucratic ministries, party

Parallel Organization of the Chinese Communist Party and the Chinese Government

PARTY OFFICE OR ORGAN	OFFICEHOLDER OR NUMBER OF MEMBERS OR DEPARTMENTS	CORRESPONDING GOVERNMENT OFFICE OR ORGAN	OFFICEHOLDER OR NUMBER OF MEMBERS OR DEPARTMENTS
Chairman	Office abolished in 1982	President (head of state)	Xi Jinping (anticipated 2013)
General secretary	Xi Jinping (head of party)	Premier (head of government)	Li Keqiang (anticipated 2013)
Politburo Standing Committee (PSC)	9 members	State Council Standing Committee	10 members
Politburo	25 members	State Council	76 members
Central Committee (CC)	204 members	National People's Congress Standing Committee	Approximately 150 members
National Party Congress	2,987 members	National People's Congress (NPC)	2,987 members
Central Military Commission (CMC) of the CCP	11 members	Central Military Commission of the PRC	11 members (same members as CCP's CMC)
CMC Chairman	Xi Jinping (anticipated 2014)	CMC chairman	Xi Jinping (anticipated 2014)
Secretariat	Large staff of party officials	State Council General office	Large staff of civil servants
Party departments	Approximately 46 departments	Bureaucratic ministries	Approximately 46 ministries, bureaus, and commissions
Central Commission of the Discipline Inspection	121 members	Supreme People's Court	President and 8 vice presidents

Source: Updated and adapted from Melanie Mannion, "Politics in China," in Gabriel Almond et al., *Comparative Politics Today: A World View* (New York: Pearson/Longman, 2004), p. 428.

officials and organizations orchestrate the policy process and direct the votes of the party members who hold elected and appointed government and state offices (typically more than four-fifths of all officeholders). The CCP maintains this same organizational control at the regional and local levels of government and also places party "cadre," or officials, in schools, state-owned businesses, and social organizations to supervise—at least theoretically—all aspects of government, economic, and social activity.

In fact, scholars describe ruling Communist parties as "greedy institutions" that are not satisfied with simply controlling the political process, but also seek to control all aspects of public and even private life. This was particularly true during the Maoist era of mass campaigns and totalitarian penetration of society. Mao and the party-state ensured control through the ***danwei* (work unit) system**, which gave all urban-dwelling Chinese citizens a lifetime affiliation with a specific industrial, agricultural, or bureaucratic work unit that dictated all aspects of their lives, including family size, housing, daily food rations, health care, and other social benefits. This organizational plan was reinforced by the ***hukou* (household registration) system**, which tied all Chinese to a particular geographic location. Firmly in place for decades, reform and opening has erased most aspects of these hierarchical structures of state control. Today, the day-to-day choices of most Chinese citizens are governed much less by the party-state and much more by the free market. Chinese families live where they can afford to live, workers seek employment wherever they can find a job, and Chinese consumers pay cash for life's necessities and pleasures. China today has a "**floating population**" of some 150 million itinerate workers (more than the entire population of Russia) who have abandoned their rural *hukou* designation to seek employment in China's cities and who have no *danwei* affiliation.

Still, although market reforms have dramatically increased mobility and altered state-society relations, China's twenty-first-century authoritarian party-state has worked diligently to keep pace. The state has drawn on the same technologies that have aided China's rapid development and hastened social mobility to maintain and even enhance its efforts of social control through high-tech surveillance and censorship. We need to be very careful, however, not to overestimate the authoritarian grasp of China's political leaders. Despite Herculean efforts at control, the opening of the economy and the growing complexity of Chinese society have inevitably weakened China's authoritarian regime. Economic and financial decentralization has given local authorities and private firms the autonomy to resist central policies and develop greater independence. These changes, combined with the long-standing inefficiency of China's enormous bureaucracy and growing problems of corruption and nepotism at all levels of government (and the sheer size, growing complexity and persistent backwardness of much of China), also call state capacity into question. These centrifugal pressures for decentralization and the general weakening of the party's power have led scholars to label China's current political regime one of "fragmented authoritarianism."[5] Before exploring the potential consequences of this fragmentation, we first examine the political institutions of China's authoritarian rule.

THE CONSTITUTION

China is ostensibly governed by a constitution that is designated "the fundamental law of the state" and that vests formal authority in both party and state executive and legislative offices. However, under the conditions of elite authoritarian rule in China, political power has not been highly institutionalized. Just as the party always prevails over the state, Mao Zedong and his successors have been little deterred by any checks or balances inherent in the formal institutions of either the party or the state. China's supreme leaders have relied as much or more on their informal sources of power (including personal connections, age, experience, and patronage) than on their formal positions or titles. Although there has been collective agreement among current leaders to avoid a return to the tyranny of the Maoist era, political rule in post-Mao China has remained largely vested in a single "paramount" leader surrounded by a key group of 25 to 35 highly influential political elites. Though these leaders hold key positions in the party and the state, their stations for the most part affirm rather than determine their status and authority.

Historically, the personal and particular nature of political rule has meant that the Western notion of the rule of law (in which all citizens are equal under the law and are protected from arbitrary state power) has generally not prevailed in China. Most significantly, during the Maoist period (but even during the reform era), the country's legal issues were highly politicized. Most legal institutions have been subject to the ideological priorities of the party-state and the personal motivations of its leaders. But reform and opening has forced the state to seek new means of maintaining control and influence, including increased reliance on legal statutes. The growing complexity of economic and social life has required the state to adopt new laws governing the environment, contracts, labor relations, trade, and even property. China's reliance on foreign trade, in particular, has had a huge impact on legal reforms, as foreign investors, local entrepreneurs, and international bodies such as the World Trade Organization (WTO) have increased pressure on Chinese authorities to abide by contracts and to respect property rights (though not always successfully). This newfound legal adherence is spilling over into other aspects of policy making and portends an even greater role for some of China's other formal political institutions, as discussed next.

Communist Party Institutions and Organs

Although the National Party Congress "elects" its Central Committee (CC), which in turn "selects" the Politburo (short for "political bureau"), in fact, the nine or so members of the Politburo Standing Committee (PSC) make up the top political leadership of China. The PSC convenes in weekly meetings headed by the general secretary of the party, currently Xi Jinping (as of October 2012). PSC members are "elected" by the 25 or so Politburo members, but it is the PSC (that is, the Politburo's dominant senior members) that typically determines all key national policy decisions. The Politburo effectively serves as China's governing cabinet, with each member responsible for a particular set of policy areas or issues that roughly correspond to the ministerial portfolios of the government's State Council.

Technically, the Politburo, the PSC, and the general secretary are all "elected" by the CC of the National Party Congress, but in reality, party leaders determine the makeup of both the Politburo and the PSC prior to the actual casting of ballots. When the 200 or so CC members vote, they do so on a ballot on which all candidates run unopposed. The CC typically meets annually and carries out the ongoing approval and endorsement of the National Party Congress between its sessions. Despite the largely ceremonial role of the CC, its members constitute the pool of China's party officials who are groomed for top leadership. However, in this system of largely informal power, membership in the CC simply confirms the elite status that these party leaders have already earned through personal connections and patronage ties.

The CC, in turn, is elected by the **National Party Congress** which is the party's cumbersome representative body, somewhat akin to an American political party nominating convention. With well over 2,000 delegates, it is far too unwieldy and meets too infrequently to conduct any real policy making. Instead, its "plenary," or full, sessions have been used as venues for announcing changes in policies and leadership and formally endorsing the ideological "line" of the party. In recent decades, the Party Congress has regularly convened at five-year intervals. There have been a total of 18 party congresses from the founding of the party in 1921 through the 18th Party Congress, held in 2012. The 17th Party Congress marked the start of General Secretary Hu Jintao's second five-year term and unveiled his policy of "scientific development and the creation of a **harmonious society**," party-speak for the continuation of economic reform but with more concern for the growing wealth and welfare gaps between urban and rural China. The 18th Party Congress elected **Xi Jinping** for the first of what will likely be his two five-year terms as general secretary and pronounced the party's vision and direction under his leadership.

Delegates to the Party Congress ostensibly represent the more than 80 million members of the CCP, organized at the provincial and local levels. In both the Party Congress and its CC, delegates are left with few if any choices of candidates for the higher-level bodies, and their senior leaders heavily influence the choices they can make. Since 1982, however, members of the CC have been elected by secret ballot, and since the late 1980s, there have actually been more candidates than seats available for the CC.

There are several other party organs worth noting. Like the government, the CCP also staffs its own bureaucracy, known as the Secretariat. The Secretariat oversees the implementation of Politburo decisions and, just as important, the distribution of propaganda in support of these decisions through its propaganda department. Given the important political role of China's military, party leaders have used the Central Military Commission (CMC) to retain tight control over the armed forces. The CMC presides over China's military, reports directly to the Politburo, and has always been chaired by China's paramount leader or his designee. Significantly, Hu Jintao's predecessor, **Jiang Zemin**, first relinquished his position as general secretary of the CCP in 2002 and as president of the People's Republic of China in 2003, but retained his office of chairman of the CMC for another year. Likewise, **Hu Jintao** gave up his party leadership in 2012 and is anticipated to surrender his office as PRC president in 2013 and CMC chair in 2014. A final party organ, the Central Commission for Discipline Inspection, is charged with maintaining party loyalty and discipline and rooting out corruption.

China's former paramount leader, Hu Jintao (back) looks on as current leader Xi Jinping addresses China's National People's Congress.

Each of the institutions just discussed is part of the central party structure located in Beijing. Each province also has a party committee, with a secretary and a standing committee with departments and commissions in the pattern of the central party apparatus. Below this level, the party is represented by comparable organizations at the county, city, district, township, and village levels. The lower-level party leaders have often exercised a degree of autonomy, with potentially significant consequences for the devolution of authority and the political liberalization of China.

The Branches of Government

The complex hierarchy of governance of the Chinese party-state becomes even more complicated when we add the state government institutions to those of the CCP just above. Although the national constitution designates China's unicameral legislature, the **National People's Congress (NPC**, not to be confused with the National Party Congress), the highest organ of the state, government and state institutions remain subservient to party oversight. Nonetheless, day-to-day

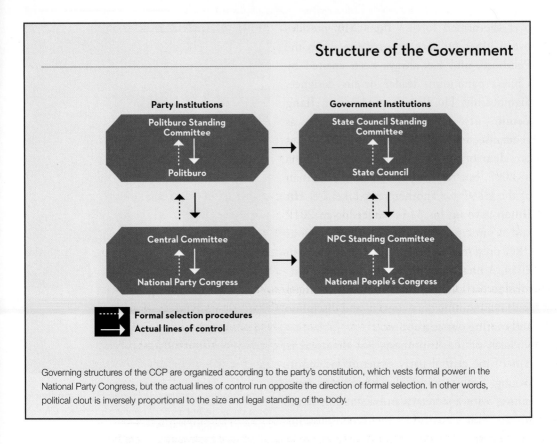

Structure of the Government

Party Institutions

Politburo Standing Committee

Politburo

Central Committee

National Party Congress

Government Institutions

State Council Standing Committee

State Council

NPC Standing Committee

National People's Congress

▸▸▸▸▸ Formal selection procedures
▶ Actual lines of control

Governing structures of the CCP are organized according to the party's constitution, which vests formal power in the National Party Congress, but the actual lines of control run opposite the direction of formal selection. In other words, political clout is inversely proportional to the size and legal standing of the body.

responsibilities for managing the affairs of the country are largely in the hands of the executive State Council's ministries and commissions.

THE HEAD OF STATE

The president of the PRC is China's head of state, an entirely titular office. During the reform era, the paramount leader or his designee has always held this office. Deng Xiaoping preferred to rule behind the scenes, designating Jiang Zemin as head of state in 1993, an office he held for two terms until 2003, concurrently with his positions as general secretary of the CCP and head of the CMC. As just noted, Jiang resigned from all three of these positions, handing them one by one to his successor, Hu Jintao, who was also designated by Deng before his death in

1997. Likewise, it is anticipated that current paramount leader Xi Jinping will serve two consecutive terms, from 2013 until 2023.

THE STATE COUNCIL

The State Council, China's executive branch, is the primary organ of daily government activity and is led by the premier (who serves as head of government). The premier is recommended by the party's Central Committee and then formally elected by the NPC, which has never yet failed to choose the recommended candidate. It is anticipated that **Li Keqiang** will assume this office in 2013, when Xi Jinping becomes PRC president, and will serve for two five-year terms in tandem with President Xi. The premier is typically the second- or third-ranking member of the PSC. With the assistance of several vice premiers, the premier and his cabinet of ministers and commissioners (collectively, the State Council) govern China. The council oversees the work of China's 40 or so bureaucratic ministries and commissions, which manage the country's economy, foreign relations, education, science, technology, and other affairs of the state. The ministers who lead each ministry or commission may also serve as vice premiers or hold party offices as members of the Politburo or even the PSC. Like the CCP's Politburo, the State Council has its own standing committee, which meets twice weekly.

Historically, the State Council's primary responsibility was the management of China's socialist economy, devising the annual and five-year economic plans and managing the state-owned enterprise system. But learning perhaps from the Soviet Union's failed efforts at perestroika, China's State Council has shown more administrative flexibility in adapting to the needs of a more open economy. Under the guidance of its party counterparts, the council's ministries and commissions formulate and implement most of China's laws and regulations.

THE NATIONAL PEOPLE'S CONGRESS

The State Council is formally appointed by China's parliament, the National People's Congress (NPC), which serves as China's unicameral legislative branch. NPC elections are held every five years, a schedule observed faithfully only since Mao's death. The NPC's nearly 3,000 delegates represent both geographic and functional constituencies (for example, industry and the military). Delegates to the NPC are elected indirectly by provincial people's congresses and typically

9

HEAD OF STATE:
President Pratibha Patil
(since July 2007)

HEAD OF GOVERNMENT:
Prime Minister Manmohan
Singh (since May 2004)

CAPITAL:
New Delhi

TOTAL LAND SIZE:
3,287,590 sq km (7th)

POPULATION:
1.205 billion (2nd)

GDP AT PPP:
$4.06 trillion (5th)

GDP PER CAPITA AT PPP:
$3,500 (162nd)

**HUMAN DEVELOPMENT
INDEX RANKING:**
134th

Kashmir
Disputed boundary with China
Line of control
with Pakistan
Srinagar
Amritsar
NEW
DELHI ★
Agra
Kanpur
Ayodhya
Imphal
Kandla
Bhopal
Kolkata
(Calcutta)
Ahmadabad
Nagpur
Mumbai
(Bombay)
Hyderabad
Vishakhapatnam
Panaji
INDIA
Marmagao
Chennai
(Madras)
Bangalore
Kozhikode
Puducherry
Madurai
Kochi
Tuticorin

INDIA

Introduction

Why Study This Case?

India presents a remarkable and instructive case for the study of comparative politics. This South Asian nation will, within two decades, eclipse China as the world's most populous country. Already it is the world's largest democracy, with more voters in a typical election than the entire population of any other country in the world except China.

Besides being the largest, India is also one of the most improbable of democracies, and herein lies one of the key puzzles of the case. Scholars most often associate democracy with critical levels of prosperity, mass literacy, urbanization, and national unity. India seemingly disproves this theory with regard to each of these factors, as large, though declining, numbers of the population remain poor and illiterate. Paradoxically, poor and illiterate Indians—most often living in rural areas, not cities—are three times as likely to vote as the national average. And despite the backwardness of rural India, where basic infrastructure remains poor, satellite dishes have brought television to a majority of the population, and over a third of the rural population now owns a cellular phone.

Most puzzling, perhaps, is how democracy can survive and thrive in a country so dangerously divided by history, language, religion, and **caste**. India has thousands of years of history as an authoritarian, hierarchical culture that has stratified, segmented, and compartmentalized its society. Today, more than 1 billion Indians speak some 325 distinct languages with more than 1,500 dialects.[1] They worship more than 5,000 gods, and six separate religions have at least 50 million adherents each. Caste divisions still segregate India socially, economically, and culturally. At times, these ethnic and social divisions have erupted into violent conflict and dramatic threats of secession. Given these circumstances, some observers marvel that the country can even stay together, let alone accommodate the cacophony of demands that present themselves.

Others argue that democracy may not be so much the puzzle as the solution. A ponderous but flexible democracy may be the only way of holding this patchwork nation together. Prior to gaining its independence in 1947, India had already been introduced to—if not allowed to participate in—the liberal practices of its British imperial master. As a sovereign nation, it adopted the political institutions of British democracy, including the parliamentary model. This system has taken root and flourished, but it remains distinctly Indian. India thus offers comparative political scientists a useful Petri dish for studying the transferability of democratic institutions to a postcolonial setting and the challenges facing such a transplant.

In recent years, the greatest challenge to Indian democracy and political stability has come from persistent religious conflict and increasing fundamentalism. As this case will demonstrate, Sikh and Muslim separatism and Hindu chauvinism have threatened the very democratic system that has sought, so far successfully, to accommodate them. India prevailed in its struggle for colonial independence in large part because of one devout Indian's ability to combine the Hindu concept of nonviolence with the liberal notions of tolerance and the separation of religion and state. The charismatic leadership of Mahatma (Mohandas K.) Gandhi and the political secularism of his followers successfully united an ethnically diverse colony in the common cause of democratic nation building.

But as has been the case in nearly all other post-imperial countries, modernization has come neither quickly nor easily to India. This huge and still-impoverished nation must juggle the maintenance of its notable democracy with the challenges of development and increasing globalization. Although India's urban centers can boast a prosperous and technically savvy elite minority that stands very much in the twenty-first century, its rapid economic development over the past two decades has left much of the rest of the nation behind. So to the many other divisions threatening India's democracy and political integrity, we must add the inequalities of income and opportunity.

To some extent, India shares with most other less-developed and newly industrializing countries the multiple and simultaneous threats of ethnic conflict, political instability, and economic inequality. In that regard, it offers insight into the challenges and opportunities that developing countries face. India is important not just because of its relative ability to manage these challenges democratically, but also because its sheer size and growing international prominence guarantee it will have increasing influence in the rest of the world.

Major Geographic and Demographic Features

India looms large in both size and population, surpassed only by China as Asia's largest and most populous country. The country can be divided into two "triangles": a northern one pointing up, and a southern one pointing down. The northern triangle is home to territorial disputes that have led to three wars with Pakistan to the west and ongoing tension with China to the east. The northernmost state of Jammu and Kashmir, at the apex of the northern triangle, is claimed by both Pakistan and India and remains a volatile tinderbox of ethnic and nationalist dispute. The southern triangle forms a huge peninsula that juts into the Indian Ocean, historically buffering the area from India's neighbors but opening the region to Western trade and, ultimately, imperial conquest.

Both India's climate and its politics have been profoundly shaped by geography. The Himalayas serve as towering sentinels on the northern border, shielding the subcontinent (comprising India, Pakistan, and Bangladesh) over the millennia from Siberian winds and Central Asian invaders. The Himalayas (Sanskrit for "abode of snow") are also the source of India's two most important river systems: the Indus, long the cradle of Indian civilization, and the Ganges, a river that Hindus value as sacred and worship as a goddess. These rivers and the sheltered climate of India's northern plains have made the north remarkably fertile, sustaining dense levels of civilization.

Crop production in southern India is no less important, but is riskier because of its dependence on the monsoons, the four summer months of heavy rains. A successful monsoon season—neither too little nor too much rain—can make the difference between drought or flood and famine or feast for many Indians. The **Green Revolution** of the 1960s and '70s, with its technologically enhanced crops and cropping methods, improved production dramatically, particularly in the arid regions of the northwest. Nonetheless, India's rapidly growing population remains highly dependent on an agricultural economy, often called a "gamble in rains."[2]

Although India possesses a wide range of natural resources, its per capita endowment of oil, timber, minerals, and petroleum reserves is relatively low. More than half of all Indians remain dependent on an agrarian livelihood; only China has more peasants. And only China has more people. The United Nations (UN) predicts that India will surpass China as the world's most populous country by 2025 and will continue to grow until around 2050, when, it is estimated, its population will peak at roughly 1.8 billion, or more than one-fourth the world's total.

The product of numerous waves of empire building, India's population is racially, ethnically, and linguistically diverse. The simplest division of Indian society is between the Aryans to the north and the Dravidians to the south, though this division is amplified by linguistic differences. In the north, most Indians speak some variety of Indo-Aryan, which is part of the Indo-European family of languages. Most common among these is **Hindi**, now one of two national languages, the other being English. Most people in the south speak one of four major dialects of the Dravidian language, which is almost completely distinct from Hindi. English has become the only universal language, but one that is spoken in large part by the elite. Even so, there are more English speakers in India than in Canada. The use of English has been a major factor in foreign firms moving some of their business transactions here, such as call centers. This **outsourcing** has become a growing part of the economy, and we will speak of it later in our section on India's economy.

Historical Development of the State

Civilization on the Indian subcontinent predates a unified Indian state by several thousand years. Three religious traditions and nearly 1,000 years of foreign domination mark the contours of the gradual formation of a sovereign Indian state.

HINDUISM, BUDDHISM, AND ISLAM

Over 3,000 years ago, nomadic Indo-Aryans began migrating eastward from Persia into the northern and central plains of present-day India, subduing the darker-skinned Dravidians, many of whom moved southward. From the fusion of the two cultures emerged the customs, philosophical ideas, and religious beliefs associated with **Hinduism**. Like other traditional religions, Hinduism governs not just worship practices but virtually all aspects of life, including the rituals and norms of birth, death, marriage, eating, and livelihood. For roughly the next 2,000 years, India enjoyed relative freedom from outside influence as Hindu traditions, such as polytheism, reincarnation, and the social and political hierarchy of caste, infused Indian society (see "Indian Caste System," p. 429).

It was under the auspices of Buddhism—a second religious tradition, originating in India in the sixth century B.C.E.—that rulers commenced India's first efforts at nation building. Spreading Buddhism's message of peace and benevolence to

TIMELINE OF POLITICAL DEVELOPMENT

YEAR	EVENT
1857–58	Sepoy Mutiny is put down, and formal British colonial rule is established
1885	Indian National Congress is created
1930	Gandhi leads a boycott of British salt
1947	India gains independence from Britain; India and Pakistan are created with partition
1948	Mahatma Gandhi is assassinated
1947–64	Jawaharlal Nehru serves as prime minister until his death
1971	India-Pakistan War leads to creation of Bangladesh
1975–77	Indira Gandhi institutes emergency rule
1984	Indira Gandhi launches military operations at Amritsar and is assassinated by Sikh bodyguards
1984–86	Rajiv Gandhi serves as prime minister
1991	Rajiv Gandhi is assassinated
1992	Ayodhya mosque is destroyed
1996	Electoral victory of the Bharatiya Janata Party (BJP) leads to the rise of coalition governments
1998	Nuclear weapons are tested
2002	Muslim-Hindu violence breaks out in Gujarat
2004	Congress-led coalition defeats BJP coalition; Manmohan Singh becomes prime minister
2005	India and United States begin negotiating controversial nuclear agreement
2007	Pratibha Patil is elected India's first female president
2008, 2011	Muslim terrorist bombings in Mumbai and other Indian cities

subjects of all ethnic groups and social ranks, dynastic rulers unified much of what is now India by the fourth century B.C.E. and remained in power for several hundred years. The development of the Silk Route by the first century C.E. spread Buddhism eastward to China and beyond. At home, however, Hinduism gradually reemerged as the state religion and has remained India's dominant faith, with over 80 percent of Indians identifying themselves as Hindu. Today, Hinduism is the world's third-largest religious tradition, after Christianity and Islam.

India's 2,000 years of relative isolation gave way to a millennium of foreign domination beginning with marauding Muslim invaders in the eighth century. (Foreign invasion and occupation did not end until India gained its independence from British imperialism and colonialism in 1947.) The arrival of this third religious tradition at the hands of martial Muslim rulers never fostered the kind of tolerance shared by Hindus and Buddhists. But the introduction of Islam to India gave birth to a new religious tradition, **Sikhism**, which combines Hindu and Muslim beliefs. It also sowed the persisting seeds of mutual animosity among India's Hindus, Muslims, and Sikhs. A final wave of Muslim invaders, descendants of Genghis Khan known as **Mughals** (Persian for "Mongol"), ruled a relatively unified India for several hundred years beginning in the sixteenth century. But by the eighteenth century, Mughal rule had weakened at the hands of growing internal Hindu and Sikh dissatisfaction and expanding Western imperialism.

BRITISH COLONIALISM

The lucrative spice trade beckoned European powers to the Indian Ocean, beginning with the Portuguese and the Spanish in the sixteenth century and then the Dutch and the British by the seventeenth century. Lacking a strong centralized state, India was vulnerable to foreign encroachment, and the British in particular made significant commercial inroads. In 1600, the British Crown granted a monopoly charter to the private **East India Company**, which over the years perfected an imperial strategy of commercial exploitation. This private merchant company first cultivated trade, then exploited cheap labor, and ultimately succeeded in controlling whole principalities. It did so through a strategy of setting up puppet Mughal governors, known as nabobs, with British merchant advisers at their side. This "**nabob game**," as the British called it, greatly facilitated the plundering of Indian wealth and resources.

The British introduced the concept of private property and the English language, and with it science, literature, and—perhaps most revolutionary—liberal

INDIAN CASTE SYSTEM

Like many other premodern societies, India's was divided and compartmentalized for thousands of years according to such categories as birth, region, occupation, and social obligations. However, its "caste" system (the term derived from the Portuguese *casta*, meaning "species" or "breed") was at once more complex and more flexible than often portrayed. The term *caste* is typically used for two different but related types of social divisions. The first of these affiliations is known as *jati*, which refers to the thousands of separate but not wholly rigid occupational and regional groups and subgroups that make up Indian society. (*Gandhi*, for instance, means "greengrocer.") Each category possessed its own detailed rules for the social behavior and interactions involved in such activities as eating, communicating, and marrying. More generally, Indian society was also divided into four broader castes, or *varnas*, including Brahmans (priests), Kshatriyas (warriors and rulers), Vaishyas (traders and merchants), and Sudras (peasants and laborers). At the bottom of—technically outside—the hierarchy were the so-called untouchables. These included two groups: those who performed duties deemed unclean, which involved handling the dead and disposing of human waste, and those aboriginals who lived outside village life, in the mountains or forests (often referred to as "tribals"). High-caste Hindus traditionally considered the touch or even the shadow of these outcastes as polluting. In an effort to enhance social order, British colonial bureaucrats painstakingly cataloged these various classifications and hierarchies long sanctioned and legitimized by the Hindu religion, rendering the castes increasingly rigid over time. In independent India, Hindu elites have used these social divisions to establish political patronage networks and to justify and enhance their dominant position in the caste system. Critics of the divisive and exploitative consequences of caste, however, have made efforts to ease the discrimination associated with it and, in particular, its deleterious effects on the untouchables. Mahatma Gandhi worked tirelessly on behalf of untouchables, referring to them as *harijans*, "the children of God." India's 1950 constitution not only banned that status but also legislated special "reservations," or affirmative action, designed to improve the lives of these "scheduled castes and tribes." Calling themselves *Dalits* (suppressed groups), they now number some 170 million people, or about 15 percent of the population.*

*For a careful and thorough discussion of the caste system, its origins, evolution, and social and political consequences for India, see Susan Bayly, *The New Cambridge History of India: Caste, Society, and Politics in India from the Eighteenth Century to the Modern Age* (Cambridge, UK: Cambridge University Press, 1999).

political philosophy. Also, as the East India Company lost its monopoly on Indian trade, a growing number of British merchants sought Indian markets for British manufactures, particularly cotton cloth. With British cotton selling at less than half the price of local handmade cloth, this "free" trade put millions of Indian cloth makers out of work. Communication and transportation technology—the telegraph, print media, the postal system, and the railroad (the British laid some 50,000 miles of track)—did much to unify India and give its colonial subjects a shared recognition of their frustrations and aspirations. This was particularly true of those native Indians employed in the colonial military and civil service who were beginning to develop and articulate a sense of Indian nationalism.

Growing economic frustration, political awareness, and national identity led to the **Sepoy Mutiny** of 1857–58, a revolt backed by the Indian aristocracy and carried out by sepoys (Indian soldiers employed by the British). Incited to arms by the revelation that their British-issued guns fired bullets greased in either pork lard or beef tallow (offensive to Muslims and Hindus, respectively), the mutinous Indians failed in large part because they were too divided, both by British design and by the long tradition of religious animosity that split the Hindu and Muslim conscripts. The failure convinced the growing number of Indian nationalists that independence from British colonialism would first require national unity. To British authorities, the mutiny signaled the weakness of nabob rule, the threat of Indian anticolonialism, and the dangers of liberal ideas and institutions in the hands of the locals. In 1858, the British Parliament passed the Government of India Act, which terminated the East India Company's control of India and placed the territory under direct and far more harsh colonial rule. Under this British **raj** (rule), civil servants and British troops replaced private merchants and puppet nabobs, and British talk of eventual Indian self-rule gave way to calls for the "permanent subjection of India to the British yoke."[3] The colony of India became the "brightest jewel in the crown of the British empire."[4]

THE INDEPENDENCE MOVEMENT

By the end of the nineteenth century, calls for self-rule had become louder and more articulate, though they were still not unified. Two local organizations came to embody the anticolonial movement: the **Indian National Congress** (**INC**, also referred to simply as Congress or Congress Party), founded in 1885, and the **Muslim League**, founded in 1906. But hopes for a gradual transfer of power after World War I were instead met with increased colonial repression, culminating in a

1919 massacre in which British troops opened fire on unarmed civilians, murdering hundreds and wounding more than 1,000 innocent Indians.

This massacre galvanized Indian resistance and brought **Mahatma (Mohandas K.) Gandhi**, a British-trained lawyer, to the leadership of Congress and the broader independence movement (see "Gandhi and the Indian Independence Movement," p. 432). Gandhi led successful protests and nationwide boycotts of British commercial imports and employment in British institutions, such as the courts, schools, and civil service. Perhaps the most successful of these protests was his 1930 boycott of British salt, which was heavily taxed by the colonial raj. In declaring the boycott, Gandhi led a group of followers on a well-publicized 200-mile march to the sea to gather salt, a violation of the British monopoly. Upon their arrival, Gandhi and many others were jailed, and the independence movement garnered national and international attention.

Gandhi's integrity and example, the charismatic draw of his remarkable strategy of nonviolence, and the increasingly repressive and arbitrary nature of colonial rule swelled the ranks of the independence movement. Among those who joined was a younger generation of well-educated leaders schooled in the modern ideas of socialism and democracy. Chief among them was **Jawaharlal Nehru**, who succeeded Gandhi as the leader of the INC and became independent India's first prime minister.

Weakened by both economic depression and war, Britain was in no shape to resist Indian independence and entered into serious negotiations toward this end following World War II. The biggest obstacle to independence became not British foot-dragging but disagreements and divisions among India's many interests, most particularly Hindus and Muslims. Fearful that Muslims, who constituted 25 percent of the population, would be unfairly dominated by the Hindu majority, Muslim leaders demanded a separate Muslim state. Negotiations collapsed as civil war broke out between militant adherents of the two faiths.

Against this background of growing violence, the British chose **partition**, creating in 1947 the new state of Pakistan from the northwest and the Muslim-dominated northeast (what would become independent Bangladesh in 1971) and forming independent India from the remaining 80 percent of the colony. This declaration led to the uprooting and transmigration (in effect, ethnic cleansing) of more than 12 million refugees—Muslims to Pakistan, Hindus and Sikhs to India—across the hurriedly drawn boundaries. It is estimated that as many as 1 million Indians and Pakistanis were killed in the resulting chaos and violence.[5] Among the victims of this sectarian violence was Gandhi himself, assassinated in 1948 by a militant Hindu who saw the leader and his message of religious

GANDHI AND THE INDIAN INDEPENDENCE MOVEMENT

Mohandas K. Gandhi, affectionately known by Indians as *Mahatma*, or "Great Soul," was born in 1869 and studied law in Britain. He first experienced racism while practicing law in South Africa, when he was thrown out of the first-class compartment of a train because of his skin color. This event prompted his tactics of revolutionary nonviolent resistance, first practiced against South African discrimination and then perfected in India after his return there in 1914. In India, he adopted the simple dress, ascetic habits, and devout worship of a Hindu holy man and developed his philosophies of *satyagraha* (holding firmly to truth) and *ahimsa* (nonviolence, or love). He argued that truth and love combined in nonviolent resistance to injustice could "move the world." He also taught that Western industrial civilization must be rejected in favor of a simpler life. He led a charismatic nationalist movement embodied in his example of personal simplicity and campaigns for national self-sufficiency. The movement was punctuated by dramatic instances of nonviolent resistance, hunger strikes, and periods of imprisonment. Though successful in his campaign to end colonialism, even the Great Soul could not prevent either Hindu-Muslim violence or, ultimately, the partition of Pakistan and India, despite his best efforts. Five months after India achieved independence, a Hindu militant assassinated Gandhi to protest his efforts to keep India unified.

tolerance as threats to Hindu nationalism. Not surprisingly, the ethnic violence that marked partition and the birth of the Indian nation continues to plague Hindu-Muslim relations in contemporary India and India's relations with neighboring Pakistan.

INDEPENDENCE

Like many of the other newly minted countries that would become part of the postwar decolonization movement, independent India faced a host of truly daunting challenges. This included settling some 5 million refugees from East and West Pakistan, resolving outstanding territorial disputes, jump-starting an economy torn asunder by partition in an effort to feed the country's impoverished millions, and creating democratic political institutions from whole cloth. This last task, promised by Nehru and his INC, had to be carried out in the absence of the prosperity, literacy, and liberal traditions that allowed democracy to take hold in advanced democracies and seemed to many an unlikely prospect in India. Given India's particular circumstances and its kaleidoscopic social, political, and economic interests—what one author called "a million mutinies now"[6]—such an endeavor seemed particularly foolish.

But unlike many other postcolonial countries, India brought to the endeavor of democratization several distinct advantages. First, its lengthy, gradual, and inclusive independence movement generated a powerful and widespread sense of national identity. Although the country had not experienced a thoroughgoing social revolution in the style of Mexico or China, most Indians had come to identify themselves not just by their region, caste, or even religion, but also as citizens of the new republic. The legacy of Gandhi's charismatic outreach to all Indians, including outcastes, Muslims, and Sikhs, brought much-needed (if perhaps ultimately short-lived) unity to its disparate population.

Second, although Indians did not control their own destiny under the British raj, the Indian intellectual class was well schooled in both the Western philosophies and the day-to-day practices of liberal democracy. Not only had generations of the Indian elite been taught in the British liberal tradition, but many of them had also served faithfully in the colonial bureaucracy. By the time of independence, Indians for most practical purposes were in fact governing themselves, albeit following the dictates of a colonial power. Indeed, their appreciation of and aptitude for the virtues of democracy made its denial under British imperial rule seem all the more unjust.

Moreover, independent India inherited not just liberal ideas and traditions, but also a sophisticated and generally well-functioning central state apparatus, including an extensive civil service and standing army. The comparison between a relatively democratic India and the more authoritarian Pakistan and Bangladesh is significant. Although all three shared a common British colonial heritage, the territories that would come to constitute Pakistan and Bangladesh did not develop India's degree of centralized state administration during the colonial period. In addition, the Muslim League was much less successful than the INC in bringing effective political organization to these regions. When it came time to assert state authority over their respective territories, independent Pakistan and Bangladesh turned more readily to an authoritarian military and bureaucracy, whereas India was able to rely, at least more frequently, upon democratic political parties and politicians.[7]

Finally, the long-standing role of the INC as the legitimate embodiment of the independence movement and Nehru as its charismatic and rightful representative gave the new government a powerful mandate. Like Nelson Mandela's African National Congress, which would take its name from its Indian predecessor and be swept to power in South Africa's first free election in 1994, Nehru led the INC to a handy victory in India's first general election in 1951. This afforded the INC government the opportunity to implement Nehru's vision of social democracy at home and mercantilist trade policies abroad. The INC would govern India for 45 of its first 50 years of independence, led for nearly all those years by either Nehru, his daughter, or his grandson.

A NEHRU DYNASTY

Uncle Nehru, as Jawaharlal Nehru was affectionately called, led the INC to two subsequent victories: in 1957 and 1962. But by his third term, he had realized the intractability of many of India's economic and foreign policy challenges and his own inability to transform the nation as quickly as he had hoped. As one scholar observed, "In India, nothing changed fast enough to keep up with the new mouths to be fed."[8] Nehru died in office in 1964, and with his death, the INC began to lose some of its earlier luster and its ability to reach across regional, caste, and religious divisions to garner support.

Within two years, Nehru's daughter, **Indira Gandhi** (no relation to Mahatma), assumed leadership of a more narrowly defined INC and became India's first woman prime minister. Far more authoritarian than her father, Gandhi's first decade of rule divided the party between her supporters and her detractors. With her popularity within the party weakening in the 1970s, Gandhi sought support from India's impoverished masses with a populist campaign to abolish poverty. Although the program was highly popular and initially successful, the global oil crisis reversed many of the early economic gains. Riots and strikes spread throughout India, with citizens of all classes complaining of the dangerous dictatorship of the "Indira raj."

Facing declining support, charges of corruption, and calls to step down, Gandhi instead chose in 1975 to suspend the constitution by declaring martial law, or **emergency rule**. The Indian constitution does authorize such a measure, and during the two years of emergency rule, riots and unrest ceased and economic efficiency improved. Nonetheless, Gandhi's swift suspension of civil liberties, censorship of the press, banning of opposition parties, and jailing of more than 100,000 political opponents (including many of India's senior statesmen) chilled Indian democracy and prompted widespread (albeit largely silent) opposition to her rule.

When Gandhi surprisingly lifted emergency rule in 1977 and called for new elections, virtually all politicians and the overwhelming majority of voters rallied to the cause of the new Janata (People's) Party in what was seen as an effort to save Indian democracy. This Janata coalition formed the first non-Congress government in 30 years of independence. Although key supporters shared a common interest in rural causes and the party drew its strength largely from rural constituencies, the coalition was unified primarily by its opposition to Gandhi's emergency rule. After two years of factional disputes and indecisive governance, the INC was returned to office—with Gandhi as its leader. Indian voters had spoken, indicating their preference for the order and efficiency of Gandhi's strong hand over the Janata Party's ineptitude.

During Indira Gandhi's second tenure, persistent economic problems were compounded by growing ethnic conflict and increasing state and regional resistance to central control. Demands for the devolution of central authority were sharpest among the Sikh-majority Punjab in northern India, whose leaders had become increasingly violent in their political and religious demands. Violence escalated, and calls for an independent Sikh state of Khalistan heightened. In 1984, Gandhi declared martial law, or **presidential rule**, in the state of Punjab. This state-level equivalent of declaring emergency rule is also constitutionally authorized, permitting the federal government to oust a state government and assume national control of that state. Gandhi then launched a military operation on the Golden Temple in **Amritsar**, Sikhism's holiest shrine. The Sikh separatists' firebrand leader and some 1,000 of his militant followers ensconced in the temple were killed in the operation, and loyal followers swore vengeance. The vengeance came months later, when Gandhi's Sikh bodyguards assassinated her. In what was to become a motif of communal violence, the assassination sparked violent retribution as angry Hindus murdered thousands of innocent Sikhs throughout India.

Indira Gandhi presided over Indian politics for almost as long as her father had (Nehru had led the INC and governed India for some 17 years). But whereas Nehru's legacy was one of national inclusion and consensus building among a wide range of regional interests, Gandhi's rule was far more divisive, intolerant, and heavy-handed. The Indian state she bequeathed to her son Rajiv, who replaced her as leader of the INC, was more centralized and its party politics far more divided. This was not, however, necessarily a negative experience for Indian democracy. For the first time, a viable political opposition was emerging, one capable of standing up to the powerful INC.

Widespread sympathy in the wake of Gandhi's assassination made it natural for the INC to select her younger son, Rajiv (her older son and heir apparent,

Sanjay, having been killed in a plane accident), and it assured the Congress Party its largest (and last) majority in the 1984 election. Rajiv Gandhi governed for five years, beginning the shift of India's economic focus away from the social-democratic and mercantilist policies of his mother and grandfather. He promoted more liberal market measures, which have been expanded in the decades since. Ethnic violence and political divisiveness persisted, with trouble simmering between Hindus and Muslims in the Punjab and in new hot spots in the border region between India and Bangladesh to the east and between Hindus and ethnic Tamil separatists to the south. During a 1991 campaign, two years after Rajiv Gandhi had been turned out of office by a weak opposition coalition, he was assassinated by a Tamil suicide bomber. The Nehru dynasty thus ended (at least for the time being), and coalition governments became the norm.

COALITION GOVERNMENTS

The decline of the INC's dominance has led to a series of coalition governments typically headed by a national party, such as Congress, but shored up by regional partners. Coalitions of all political stripes have maintained the reforms begun under Rajiv Gandhi and the INC, including economic liberalization and increased political devolution to state governments. The INC's strongest competition has come from the **Bharatiya Janata Party (BJP)**, which had potential for nationwide scope and appeal. The BJP has been able to articulate a Hindu nationalist vision, an alternative (some would say a dangerous one) to the vision of a secular India established by the INC at the time of India's founding. Drawing its strength initially from upper-caste Hindu groups, by the late 1990s the BJP was attracting Hindus of all castes under the banner of Hindu nationalism.

The event that began to galvanize support for the BJP was yet another incident of sectarian violence at a temple site. The Babri Mosque, located in the northern Indian city of **Ayodhya**, had been built by Mughals on a site alleged to be the birthplace of the Hindu god Ram. The site has been deemed sacred by Muslims and Hindus and for decades has been a point of controversy for local adherents of both faiths. By the 1990s, various Hindu nationalist groups had seized on Ayodhya as both a rallying political issue and a gathering place. In 1992, BJP supporters and other Hindu extremists destroyed the mosque, vowing to rebuild it as a Hindu shrine. This act ignited days of Hindu-Muslim rioting and violence and the killing of many Indians across the country. Repercussions have persisted. In 2002, on the 10th anniversary of the event, in the city of Godhra in the western state of **Gujarat**, Muslims set fire to railcars carrying Hindu activists back from a ceremony at Ayodhya, killing 58 people. Hindu retaliatory violence incited by religious militants in the state of Gujarat killed thousands. The issues continue to simmer, with extremist elements in both the Muslim and Hindu camps regularly taking aim at each other. The year 2008 proved particularly violent, with Muslim terrorist bombings in several of India's large urban centers and a dramatic assault on Mumbai led by a Pakistani-based group that targeted wealthy Indians, Westerners, and Jews.

This communal violence has served to harden positions on both sides and polarize political support. A BJP coalition that had come to power in 1998 remained in office until 2004, when it was turned out by a surprisingly resurgent INC and assorted coalition partners. Organizations loosely affiliated with the BJP have continued to promote divisive Hindu nationalist rhetoric to garner support and have sponsored violence and discrimination against a variety of minority religious and ethnic groups. During its six years in office, however, the BJP coalition governed relatively moderately. It did so both to retain its coalition partners and to promote India's national goals of economic growth and stable relations with neighboring countries. These current domestic and international priorities will be taken up in subsequent sections.

Significantly, the leader of the INC at the time of its surprise return to office in 2004 and re-election in 2009 was **Sonia Gandhi**, the Italian-born widow of Rajiv Gandhi. Although she would have been the logical choice to assume the office of prime minister (and extend the Nehru dynasty), the BJP made her foreign birth a divisive campaign issue. Thus, she stepped aside and allowed **Manmohan Singh** to become the country's first Sikh prime minister. It should be noted, however, that Sonia Gandhi continues to lead the INC and has a son, Rahul, who gained a Congress seat in parliament in 2004, and a daughter, Priyanka, who has also shown political ambitions. Although many judge his sister to be more politically astute, many expect that Rahul will someday lead the INC, like his mother, father, grandmother, and great-grandfather before him.[9]

Political Regime

India can easily claim title to the world's largest democracy. But is this democracy genuine? And does it work? Certainly in form it is democratic. Its constitution and other political institutions were modeled explicitly on Britain's Westminster parliamentary system, and few changes to the original blueprint have been enacted. With the exception of Indira Gandhi's authoritarian interlude of the 1970s, the institutions seem in practice to function more effectively and legitimately in India than in many other former British colonies that share a similar institutional inheritance. Indian democracy nonetheless differs in important ways from that of its colonial mentor and other advanced Western industrialized democracies.

Why has democracy fared better in India than, for example, in neighboring Pakistan, a country that shares with India many cultural and historical legacies? Although a full answer to this question is beyond the scope of this work, the well-established stability and near-universal legitimacy of the political institutions discussed next provide an important part of that answer. Three generations of Indian politicians and citizens from across the ideological spectrum have been schooled in the lessons of parliamentary democracy. They function and participate in a system that maintains civil parliamentary debate, a politically neutral bureaucracy, an independent judiciary, and firm civilian control over the military.

Political Institutions

THE CONSTITUTION

Perhaps befitting India's size and population, its constitution is one of the world's longest, enshrining in writing the fundamental principles of Britain's unwritten constitutional order of parliamentary democracy. It establishes India as a federal republic, reserving significant authority for the state governments. During its

ESSENTIAL POLITICAL FEATURES

- **Legislative-executive system**: Prime ministerial

- **Legislature**: Parliament

- **Lower house**: House of the People

- **Upper house**: House of States

- **Unitary or federal division of power**: Federal

- **Main geographic subunits**: States

- **Electoral system for lower house**: Single-member-district plurality

- **Chief judicial body**: Supreme Court

nearly 50 years of hegemonic rule, the INC limited the autonomy of state governments. The weakening of the INC and the onset of coalition governments spurred a process of devolution, allowing regional political parties and the states they represent to wrest significant authority from the **Center** (a term referring to India's national government and its capital in New Delhi).

Two controversial tenets of the Indian constitution have certainly enhanced the power of the Center. The first of these authorizes the central government to suspend or limit freedoms during a "grave emergency," when India faces threats of "external aggression or internal disturbance." This emergency rule (nationwide martial law) was invoked twice during international conflicts, with China in 1962 and with Pakistan in 1971. More controversially, Indira Gandhi invoked this clause to institute emergency rule from 1975 to 1977, using it as a blunt (but nonetheless effective) tool against her political opponents. After her defeat in the subsequent election, the constitution was amended to limit such a decree to conditions of external aggression or domestic armed rebellion.

Indira Gandhi was not the only prime minister to invoke the second measure, that of presidential rule, which allows the central government to oust a state government and assert direct rule of that state. National governments have employed this measure on more than 100 occasions, when ethnic unrest, local resistance, or simply a political stalemate rendered a state, in the judgment of the Center, ungovernable. Although these measures may seem unusual and have at times been imposed for purposes of political expediency, the violence, disorder, and corruption often associated with regional Indian politics have made presidential rule an important and generally legitimate tool of the central government.[10]

The Branches of Government

THE PRESIDENT

Because India is a republic, its head of state is a president, not a monarch; as in most other parliamentary systems, moreover, the president's role is largely symbolic. The president is authorized to appoint the prime minister, but as with the monarchs of Britain and Japan, this appointment is simply a ceremonial affirmation of the leader of the dominant party or coalition in the parliament. Similarly, while it is the president's role to declare national or state emergency rule, this declaration can be made only on the advice of the prime minister.

The substantive exception to these symbolic tasks has been the president's role following elections that have produced no majority party (which has happened more often in recent years). Under these circumstances, the president seeks to identify and facilitate the formation of a workable governing coalition. If that is not possible, the president dissolves the parliament and calls new elections. An electoral college, made up of the national and state legislators, elects presidents to five-year renewable terms, though many presidents have in effect been appointed by powerful prime ministers. The current president, Pratibha Patil, was elected in 2007 and serves as India's first woman president. Nominated by the governing Congress Coalition, she experienced an unusually contentious election because of opposition BJP fears that if an upcoming election returned no majority party, Ms. Patil would give her patron, the INC, the first chance to form a coalition government.

THE PRIME MINISTER AND THE CABINET

As in the British system, the Indian prime minister and cabinet constitute the executive branch. The prime minister, as head of the government, is responsible for managing the day-to-day affairs of government and is the state's most important political figure. The prime minister has typically been the leader of the party with a majority in the lower house of the legislature or, more recently, a leader from within a coalition of parties that can garner sufficient support to constitute a majority, or even a minority, government. To remain in office, the prime minister must retain the confidence of the lower house, but also has the power to dissolve the lower house and call elections to solidify support for the government.

The prime minister chooses members of the parliament to serve in a Council of Ministers that presides over all government ministries and departments. From this larger council, a smaller and more manageable group of the 15 to 20 most important ministers meets weekly as a cabinet to formulate and coordinate government policy. The current prime minister, Manmohan Singh, is the country's first Sikh to serve in that office. He began his tenure in 2004 and was re-elected in 2009 as leader of Congress-led coalitions.

During the years of Congress dominance, the three generations of Nehru prime ministers wielded overwhelming executive power. Although this was most apparent during Indira Gandhi's authoritarian tenure, her father and even her son were also dominant prime ministers who left their personal imprints on the office

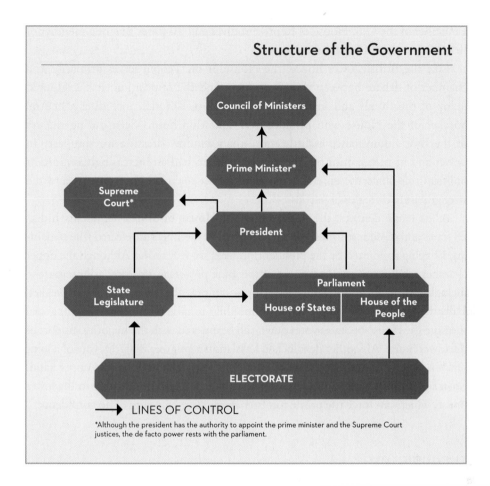

Structure of the Government

Council of Ministers

Prime Minister*

Supreme Court*

President

State Legislature

Parliament

House of States | House of the People

ELECTORATE

→ LINES OF CONTROL

*Although the president has the authority to appoint the prime minister and the Supreme Court justices, the de facto power rests with the parliament.

and on Indian politics. Even during the more recent era of coalition governments in which the prime minister's influence has weakened, the office remains the primary source of policy making and political power.

THE LEGISLATURE

As is true in many parliamentary systems, the lower house, or **House of the People**, dominates India's bicameral legislature. This lower chamber seats 545 members, all but two of whom are elected by voters for terms not to exceed five years (the final two seats are reserved for Anglo-Indians appointed by the president). Despite this chamber's enormous size, India's huge population remains relatively underrepresented. Each representative serves nearly 2 million people, four times that of a member of the U.S. House of Representatives and 20 times that of a member of Britain's House of Commons.

Like the British lower house, the House of the People serves primarily as a chamber of debate between the government and the opposition. It has adopted many of the rituals and institutions of its colonial model, including a neutral Speaker of the House who presides over "question hour." Seen during the era of the INC's dominance as little more than window dressing for the party in power and its prime minister, the lower house has had an increasingly important political role since the emergence of multiparty coalition governments and the strengthening of regional parties.

As its name denotes, the upper house, or **House of States**, represents India's 28 states and seven territories. All but 12 of its 250 members are elected (the remaining 12 being appointed by the president) to fixed six-year terms. Although the upper chamber technically possesses most of the same powers as its lower counterpart— including the right to introduce legislation—in practice it has been much weaker. Only the House of the People can introduce bills to raise revenue, and any financial measure the House of States votes down can be enacted with the majority support of the lower house. Any other deadlocked legislation is put to a majority vote of a joint session, which ensures that the more numerous lower chamber has the upper hand. Most significantly, the prime minister and cabinet are responsible only to the lower house, which can force the prime minister from office by a vote of no confidence.

THE JUDICIARY

Unlike Britain and more like the United States, India has a Supreme Court with a bench of 26 justices, who are appointed by the president and may serve until age 65. Typically, the most senior judge serves as chief justice.

India's Supreme Court is a constitutional court with the authority of judicial review (the right to rule on the constitutionality of acts of the parliament). This power to interpret the constitution is limited, however, by the comprehensive nature of the Indian constitution. Its power has also been limited by the parliament's ability to reverse court decisions by amending the constitution, as it has done on a number of occasions (92 times in six decades). With the exception of the two-year period of Indira Gandhi's emergency rule in the 1970s, when the judiciary was seen as having yielded to the prime minister's political influence both in the appointment of justices and in the suspension of constitutionally guaranteed civil rights, the Supreme Court has enjoyed (and earned) a reputation for fairness and independence.

The Electoral System

As with many of its other political institutions, India's electoral system closely resembles the British model. At the national level, voters use a plurality system to elect representatives to the House of the People, as in Britain and the United States. The country is divided into 543 single-member districts (SMDs), in which the candidate who earns a plurality of votes on the first ballot is elected. The districts are based primarily on geography and population, but some districts are reserved for the scheduled castes and tribes, or so-called **untouchables** (also called the **Dalits**). Members of the upper house are elected for staggered six-year fixed terms by the state legislatures, with seats apportioned according to each state's population.

Whereas this plurality system in the United States and Britain has favored the emergence of few or only two nationally based large parties and has penalized smaller parties, this is increasingly not the case in India. The INC certainly used the electoral system to its advantage during its period of dominance, winning clear majorities of seats in the House of the People in most elections even though it never won a majority of the popular vote (nor has any other party in India's history) and often received little more than a plurality. The largest of the other parties, including the Janata Party and the BJP, have also benefited, winning a higher percentage of seats than votes. The weakening of the INC's hegemony since the 1990s has splintered the national vote, however, and has given new significance to regional parties based on caste or on linguistic or religious identity. This has meant that while two parties tend to dominate each electoral district, these regional and caste-based parties are not nationally dominant.[11] Recent House of the People elections have seated representatives of nearly 40 different political parties, none with a majority of the seats and 10 parties with more than 10 seats each (see "House of the People Election Results, 2004 and 2009," p. 451).

Local Government

India's extensive regional diversity and the sectarian conflicts troubling the country at the time of its founding led the framers of India's constitution to establish a federal republic that preserved substantial powers for both the various states and the central government. Each of the 28 states has its own elected government consisting of a legislature (most of which are unicameral, though a few—most notably large states such as Uttar Pradesh and Maharashtra—are bicameral) and a chief minister. The **chief minister** is elected by the state legislature to serve a five-year term and can be removed from office by a vote of no confidence.

State governments in India have a great deal of power, but as in other federal systems, they have limits. In India, the Center's constitutional powers to declare a national emergency or impose presidential rule on an obstreperous state are muscular examples of central authority. The federal government is also authorized to challenge any state legislation that contradicts an act of the parliament and can even change the boundaries of states as it sees fit. But like their American counterparts, in the day-to-day management of government affairs, Indian states retain a great deal of jealously guarded autonomy. Public policies concerning health, education, economic and industrial development, and law and order are largely determined at the state level and vary significantly from state to state. The rise of coalition governments and the growing influence of regional parties in national affairs has only strengthened state power.

India's current division into 28 states and seven territories is a marked expansion from its original structure upon independence, which had 14 states and six territories. This expansion is in large part a nod to powerful state interests and speaks to an important way in which India's federalism differs from the American model. State borders in India reflect in most cases linguistic or ethno-religious differences, which pit regional interests against the Center. This conflict has been most pronounced in states such as Punjab, dominated by the Punjabi-speaking Sikhs, and **Kashmir**, where Urdu-speaking Muslims constitute a majority. However, other ethnic groups have also wielded the mechanisms of state authority to assert state interests against the federal government. India is a good example of what political scientists call **asymmetric federalism**, where power is devolved unequally across the country and its constituent regions, often the result of specific laws negotiated between a given region and the central government. This devolution has only increased over time; for example, there continue to be movements to delineate new states.

Perhaps the best comparison with Indian federalism is not the United States, but rather, the historically diverse and linguistically distinct European Union (EU).[12] Like the English and the Greeks, the Hindi speakers of Bihar in the north and the Tamil speakers of Tamil Nadu in the south converse in mutually unintelligible tongues and share little common history and equally little interaction. Like the citizens of Sweden and Portugal, their customs, cultures, and traditions vary widely, as do their social and economic profiles. Bihar is impoverished and largely illiterate, whereas Tamil Nadu is relatively more prosperous and technologically advanced. There are no similarly intense contrasts in the United States.

Comparison of India with the European Union also points to one of the crowning accomplishments of India's democratic resilience. For all of the local conflict and secessionist violence that India has experienced, the Center has held, and the strife has remained localized. With larger populations and religious, linguistic, and territorial disputes sufficient to rival any of those that led to the numerous wars of Europe (and ultimately prompted the formation of the European Union), India has for the most part managed these disputes peacefully and democratically. This is no small feat.

Political Conflict and Competition

Despite occasional heavy-handed government restrictions on civil rights and periodic demonstrations of communitarian intolerance and even violence, Indian politics remains vibrant, open, and generally inclusive. Voter turnout typically averages around 60 percent for parliamentary elections. The nonpartisan Freedom House in 2011 deemed India "free," with ratings of 2 in its political rights and 3 in civil liberties (on a scale of 1 to 7, with 1 being the most free).[13]

In fact, given India's size and diversity, some might argue that political competition has been too inclusive. As one Indian journalist complained, "Everyone in India gets a veto."[14] The competition and conflict—typically but not always healthy—reflect the dualism and diversity of India: a prosperous, cosmopolitan, and highly literate minority voting side by side with roughly two-thirds of the electorate who cannot read, have their roots in rural villages or urban slums, and may survive on less than a dollar a day. Both are important components of Indian democracy.

The Party System

During the first few decades of independence, India's party system was stable and predictable. Like Japan's Liberal Democratic Party or Mexico's Partido Revolucionario Institucional, the Indian National Congress presided over a one-party-dominant system that effectively appealed to a broad range of ideological and social groups and co-opted numerous disaffected constituencies, including the poor and minorities. More recently, this system has become far more fragmented, complex, and unpredictable, as national opposition parties and regional and even local interests have gained ground in both state and national elections.

THE CONGRESS PARTY

More than just a political party, the Indian National Congress, from its founding in 1885, became the flagship of national independence, commanding widespread appeal and support across the political and even ethnic spectrums. After independence, Jawaharlal Nehru and the INC pursued a slightly left-of-center political ideology of social democracy. This included social policies of "secularism" (more a program of religious equal opportunity than a separation of religion and state) and social reform, continuing the efforts of Gandhi to eliminate caste discrimination.

The party's economic program was marked by democratic socialism, including national five-year plans and state ownership of key economic sectors. These policies earned the support of workers, peasants, and particularly members of the lower castes. At the same time, the INC retained the support of business by respecting private property and supporting domestic industry with mercantilist policies of import substitution. It remained for decades the only party with national appeal.

The INC's dominance began to weaken after Nehru's death, as disagreements grew between Indira Gandhi and party elders in the late 1960s. These disagreements led to divisions within the party and to Gandhi's capture of the dominant faction, known as Congress (I) (for Indira) during the 1970s. Gandhi made populist promises to India's poor, vowing to abolish poverty through government programs, but never delivered on those promises. By the 1980s, the INC had begun to move away from its traditional priorities of democratic socialism and religious neutrality. Indira Gandhi began promoting Hindu nationalism, and her son Rajiv launched neoliberal economic reforms. These legacies have outlived their architects and have been embraced even more enthusiastically by other political parties.

By the late 1980s, the INC had surrendered its position of primacy, and the single-party-dominant system gave way to a regionalized multiparty system and coalition governments. During this time, the INC alternated rule with various permutations of Hindu nationalist coalitions, controlling the government in the first half of the 1990s and then returning to power in 2004. Although the INC continues to embrace in principle the neoliberal reform program first launched by Rajiv Gandhi, its most recent return to government was in large part a result of its progressive appeal to India's peasantry, a nod to both Nehru's democratic socialism and Indira Gandhi's populism.

Headquarters of the Congress Party in Uttar Pradesh state. On the top left is Sonia Gandhi, widow of former prime minister Rajiv Gandhi. At the top center is her son Rahul.

THE BHARATIYA JANATA PARTY

As opposition to the INC grew during Indira Gandhi's 1970s autocratic interlude, a number of contending parties began to emerge or take on new importance. A coalition of some of these opposition parties, under the name Janata (People's) Party, ultimately wrested the government from the INC in the late 1970s. One of the smallest of these coalition partners was Jana Sangh, a Hindu nationalist party that left the Janata coalition in 1980 and changed its name to the Bharatiya Janata Party, or Indian People's Party.

The BJP's popularity climbed rapidly as support for secularism gave way to increasing sentiment for ethnic and religious parties. The BJP won only two seats in the House of the People elections of 1984, but increasing Hindu nationalist sentiment (manifested most violently in clashes with Sikhs at Amritsar in 1984 and with Muslims in Ayodhya in 1992 and in Gujarat in 2002) allowed it to expand its representation to 161 seats by 1996 and form a coalition government, led by Atal Behari Vajpayee. Although the first BJP coalition lasted only 12 days, by 1998 the BJP had become the largest party in the parliament, and Vajpayee and his BJP-led coalition governed from 1998 until turned out of office in the 2004 elections. Despite recent decline in support (the BJP held on to only 116 seats in 2009), it remains, with the INC, one of India's two largest parties.

From its founding, the BJP has been an outspoken advocate of Hindu national identity. It is a member of a larger constellation of more than 30 loosely tied Hindu nationalist organizations known collectively as the RSS (the Hindi acronym for "National Association of Volunteers"). These religious, social, and political associations vary widely in their acceptance of violence and militancy in promoting Hindu nationalism, but all embrace **Hindutva**, or "Hindu-ness," as India's primary national identity and ideal. Whereas some of the more moderate RSS member organizations promote benign patriotism, other reactionary or fundamentalist association members teach a Hindu chauvinist version of Indian history and condone and even train their members in violent tactics of religious and racial discrimination.

Similarly, the BJP itself has both moderate and militant elements. Its elected national leaders tend to downplay the party's religious ties, promote it as a more honest alternative to the INC, and emphasize its neoliberal economic policies of privatization, deregulation, and foreign investment. This reputation of honesty and neoliberalism has appealed in particular to India's growing middle class, which is more interested in economic freedom and prosperity than in secular equality. This predominantly Hindu middle class has become frustrated with what it perceives as the reverse discrimination of the INC's secular policies of tolerance of minority religion- and caste-based affirmative action.

The extremist and fundamentalist elements in the BJP are more overtly anti-Muslim, contending that India's Muslims were forced to convert by foreign invaders and would naturally revert to their native Hinduism in an India permitted to promote its true heritage. They are more prone to violence, praising the assassin of Mahatma Gandhi and the combatants of Ayodhya and Gujarat as heroes and protectors of Indian heritage. Their leaders have been more successful politically at the local and state levels (particularly in the region of India's so-called "cow belt," in the Hindu-majority north), but have also become important allies in the BJP's efforts to form national ruling coalitions.

The most successful and controversial of the regional BJP leaders is the charismatic and outspoken chief minister (governor) of the state of Gujarat, **Narendra Modi**. Swept to power in the wake of the anti-Muslim violence in Gujarat in 2002, Modi was re-elected in 2007 and clearly has national aspirations beyond his home state of Gujarat. At the same time, the strident Hindu nationalism championed by Modi and other hard-liners is offensive to many of the allied parties that formed the BJP's governing coalition prior to 2004. National party leaders recognize that the BJP cannot win national elections on the narrow platform of Hindu nationalism, and this has led to squabbling over leadership and continued divisions within the party.

PARTIES OF THE LEFT

India's so-called Left Front consists of a collection of Communist and other left-leaning parties whose popularity seems unaffected by the declining success of Communist parties and countries elsewhere in the world. These parties together have managed to garner on average between 7 and 10 percent of the national vote and typically more than 50 seats in the House of the People. This bloc of seats has given the Communist parties a decisive role in the making and breaking of recent coalitions and therefore a certain leverage in government policy, despite their minority status. Following the 2004 general elections, the INC-led coalition required the support of four Communist parties in order to gain a voting majority in parliament. The fragile nature of this arrangement became apparent in parliamentary wrangling in recent years over a controversial nuclear cooperation treaty between India and the United States. Supported by the Congress Party, the deal was adamantly opposed by its erstwhile Communist allies, who ultimately withdrew their support from the coalition in 2008. This forced the INC to form ad hoc alliances with other small parties to assemble a majority and to avoid a vote of no confidence that would have brought the government down and forced a new election.

The leftist parties have, in large part, remained successful because of their willingness to evolve and seek alliances with other parties. Although both of the two largest leftist parties, the Communist Party of India and the Communist Party of India (Marxist), initially supported violent revolution, over the years both have ultimately embraced peaceful means to achieve communism. More recently, both have come to look and act much more like social-democratic parties, embracing a mixture of state and private ownership and even promoting foreign investment. Like nearly all other parties in India, these leftist parties rely upon strong local and regional bases of support. The lion's share of party leadership and voting strength has come from the states of **Kerala** in the far south and West Bengal in the far east.

Not all political movements on the left, however, have been willing to work within the democratic system. Chief among these radical groups is the Maoist (or guerrilla Communist) insurgency known as **Naxalism**. Named for the region in West Bengal where it originated in the late 1960s, the movement has grown in recent decades, particularly in rural areas in several of the poorest states of north-central India. Naxalite recruits are drawn primarily from the low castes, outcastes, and tribal natives largely excluded from India's recent and dramatic economic growth.

REGIONAL PARTIES

The declining dominance of the INC and the rise of coalition governments have given new prominence to regional and local political parties, which have come to dominate in many states and tip the balance in national elections. Moreover, as INC-supported secularism has waned, ethnic, linguistic, and religious identities have become increasingly important rallying points for political interests that are often concentrated by region. For example, states with predominant ethnic or religious identities, such as the Dravidian Tamils in the southern state of Tamil Nadu and the Punjabi Sikhs, have often been led by these regional and state par-ties. Other parties draw support from lower-caste Indians in several of India's poorer states. In only one of India's six most populated states does either the INC or the BJP hold a majority in the state parliament.

The localized parties also often have sufficient voting strength to control small but influential blocs of seats in the national parliament. In the 2009 election, state and special-interest parties won approximately 40 percent of the seats in the lower house. This reflects in one sense a devolution of central power that could be healthy for Indian democracy. But given the diversity of India's interests, it also speaks to the highly localized interests of Indians, and may be a sign of dangerous centrifugal forces.

Elections

Campaigns and elections are essential procedures in any viable democracy and are often dramatic theatrical events. Certainly this is true of India, where all aspects of an election must be measured in superlatives. For instance, in the spring of 2004, nearly 400 million of the eligible 690 million voters flocked to the 700,000 poll-ing stations to cast votes (using over 1 million new electronic voting machines). They selected their favored parliamentary candidates from the thousands of

House of the People Election Results, 2004 and 2009

PARTY OR COALITION	2004 SEATS	2009 SEATS
INC	145	206
BJP	138	116
INC and allies (UPA)	217	262
BJP and allies (NDA)	185	159
LF	59	24

Key to Party Acronyms:
BJP: Bharatiya Janata Party
INC: Indian National Congress
LF: Left Front
NDA: National Democratic Alliance
UPA: United Progressive Alliance

Note: UPA and NDA are party coalitions which include the INC and BJP, respectively.

choices, representatives of one of six "national" parties or the dozens of regional ones. The task was so huge that polling was spread out over four weeks as election officials and their machines migrated across the country harvesting votes. Indeed, this four-week election process was longer than the government-limited three-week campaign that preceded it.

Perhaps most amazing was the outcome itself, again testament to the authenticity of Indian democracy. Prior to the 2004 election, it was a foregone and universally held conclusion that the BJP-led coalition would retain its majority and extend its six-year tenure. With strong national economic growth and thawing relations with Pakistan over the troubled issue of Kashmir, the governing coalition called early national elections to capitalize on these successes, campaigning under the motto "India Is Shining." In the weeks prior to the election, BJP leaders were already busy divvying up potential cabinet posts, and INC leaders were offering justifications and finger-pointing for their party's anticipated weak showing.

But Indian voters had different plans, which allowed the INC to edge ahead of the BJP with just over one-fourth of total seats. With its coalition partners (known under the umbrella name of the United Progressive Alliance), the INC gained control of 40 percent of the seats, and after several days of negotiations, the INC expanded the coalition to include a number of regional, state, and left-of-center parties and secured the outside support of the Communist Party of India. The INC formed a majority coalition government, with Manmohan Singh as prime minister, and returned both the coalition and Singh to office in 2009 (see "House of the People Election Results, 2004 and 2009," p. 451).

Civil Society

As the dominance of the INC has faded and political authority has become decentralized, more—and more diverse—interests and elements of Indian society have demanded political influence. Although India has conventional civil organizations representing business, labor, and even peasants, these groups tend not to be particularly effective in influencing policy. Labor unions are organized by political party and are therefore fragmented and limited in their effectiveness, although they have done much to champion the interests of labor. Business certainly influences both politics and politicians—corruption is a serious problem among members of India's parliament—but this influence has been held in check by both traditional Hindu and more modern socialist biases against private business. Peasants are plentiful and at times vocal, but their political demands tend to be episodic and particular.

Communal interests representing ethnic, religious, and caste groups have been far more influential in Indian politics than have other factors. Hindus, Muslims, and Sikhs all have well-organized groups representing their political interests. This is also true of the Dalits, or untouchables, who have their own political party and constitute one of India's largest mass movements. Although there is good reason to be concerned about the destabilizing and divisive potential of these religious- and caste-based groups, there is also evidence that their multiple demands have often been addressed substantially (if not fully met) through the political process, thereby defusing civil discord and strengthening the legitimacy of the system.

Less traditional divisions and demands are also taking shape in contemporary Indian civil society, including significant environmental and women's movements. Environmental protests include resistance to development projects, such as deforestation and the Narmada Valley Project dam, and advocacy of redress for industrial accidents, such as the Union Carbide gas leak disaster in Bhopal in 1984. Women's movements bridging class and ethnic divisions have organized to protest so-called dowry deaths, which claim the lives of as many as 25,000 Indian women annually.

Another important voice of Indian civil society is the media establishment, arguably one of the largest and most active in the world. It comprises 40,000 newspapers and other periodicals, including some 4,000 dailies, all of which enjoy a significant degree of editorial and political freedom, especially as illiteracy recedes. India's extensive radio and television networks are even more important conduits of information and have been subject to more careful government scrutiny and control. This oversight has become increasingly difficult, however, as satellite television has introduced new competition into the market. India's substantial investment in networking the entire country with broadband cable will also certainly expand avenues for civic communication.

Society

Ethnic and National Identity

Contemporary India is a "complicated jigsaw" of astounding ethnic and social diversity pieced together by centuries of imperial conquest.[15] Independent India has sought to create from this patchwork imperial raj a unified and secular nation-state. This effort has required of India and its citizens a measure of social tolerance that has not always been available, seemingly leaving the country on the edge of disintegration. Yet for all the communitarian conflict and threats of secession, national unity has prevailed. Before noting the political culture that has at least to some degree preserved this unity, we turn first to the ethnic and social divisions that threaten it.

When the lighter-skinned Indo-Aryans migrated into what is now northern and central India thousands of years ago, they pushed the native, darker-skinned Dravidians southward. Each culture retained separate linguistic and cultural identities that persist to some extent today. Roughly two-thirds of Indians (virtually all in the north) speak some variation of the Sanskrit-based language brought by the Indo-Aryans, which now forms some 10 distinct languages. The most common of these is Hindi, one of two official national languages, which is spoken by over one-third of all Indians. Approximately one-fourth of all Indians speak one of the four main Dravidian languages. In all, the constitution recognizes 14 languages, but at least another 30 languages claim over 1 million speakers each. The only

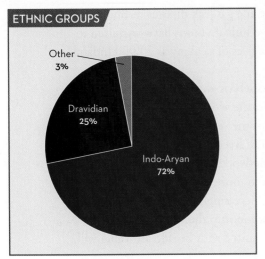

ETHNIC GROUPS

Other 3%

Dravidian 25%

Indo-Aryan 72%

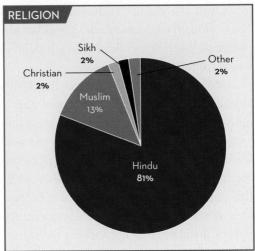

RELIGION

Sikh 2%

Christian 2%

Other 2%

Muslim 13%

Hindu 81%

other national language is English. Although only some 3 percent of the population speaks English fluently, as in other polyglot former colonies it has become an essential medium for national and international politics and commerce.

These divisions are at once exacerbated and moderated by religious differences. Although more than 80 percent of Indians share a common faith, regional and linguistic groups practice their Hinduism in different ways. The promotion of Hindu nationalism has brought a degree of unity to these groups, but at the expense of some 13 percent of Indians who are Muslim, 2 to 3 percent who are adherents of Sikhism (an amalgam of Hindu and Muslim theologies), and a comparable percentage who are Christian. These religious differences have often acquired political significance, leading at times to assassinations, violent pogroms and bitter reprisals, secessions, and threats of secession. The most dramatic flare-ups of sectarian violence have been between Hindus and Muslims, including the initial partitioning of Muslim Pakistan and Hindu India and ongoing territorial disputes in Kashmir, and the events at Ayodhya in 1992, Gujarat in 2002, and sporadic violence since then. Many Muslims, including most of the political leadership, moved to Pakistan following partition, leaving behind a weakened community in India whose loyalty is still questioned. However, Muslim and Hindu identities are more blurred than we would imagine, especially at the lower rungs of society, with Muslims incorporating Hindu rituals and Hindus praying at Muslim shrines. Religious and other identities in India are often sharper among elites than the population as a whole—a common result of modernization worldwide.

Technology and diversity in India. Muslims are a relatively small minority in India, but they have played a powerful role in the country's history. The Muslim community uses technology to link to one another and the wider Islamic world.

As if the linguistic and religious differences were not sufficiently divisive, the hierarchical separation of Indian society into castes remains the most significant of India's social divisions. Although industrialization and urbanization have made the caste system today more permeable and flexible than it once was, it remains socially, politically, and economically important. Although neither class identity nor income inequality are as severe in India as in many other developing countries, those in the lower ranks of India's caste system are typically also the poorest, with the scheduled castes and hill tribes the poorest of the poor. In an effort to redress discrimination against these suppressed groups, or Dalits, the government has established affirmative-action programs reserving for them jobs, scholarships, and even seats in the parliament. In Uttar Pradesh, the largest state in India (with nearly 200 million people) the chief minister from 2007–2012, Mayawati, is herself a Dalit, and was thus able to draw on a huge reservoir of support among other Dalits, who saw her as a harbinger of change. Her caste also allowed her to build a virtual personality cult, including a number of expensive public monuments, complete with bronze statues of important Dalit figures (including herself). For many Dalits, such extravagances, alongside related charges of corruption, were outweighed by the significance of having one of their own in charge of a major Indian state. In contrast, the rise of Mayawati and affirmative-action programs in general have angered many higher-caste Hindus, who see the measures—along with special protections afforded to minority religious groups—as reverse discrimination. The Hindu nationalist BJP has seized on this issue in expanding its constituency among the growing Hindu middle class and stirring the embers of Hindu fundamentalism.

Ideology and Political Culture

As with many other elements of Indian politics, India's political culture defies generalization. Nonetheless, two somewhat contradictory values are worth mentioning. On the one hand, Indians tend to identify themselves and their politics locally. Indians are tied most strongly to family, occupational group, and their immediate regional linguistic and religious associates. These immediate ties tend to segment and even fragment politics in India, which promotes political awareness and cooperation locally but also causes political friction and even violence between groups. Although such localization may limit the scope of conflict, it also constrains the kind of mobilization that could address pressing national needs.

On the other hand, despite their cultural diversity and contentious politics, Indians continue to identify themselves as Indians and generally support—and see themselves as an important part of—Indian national democracy. So while the bonds of national unity are less powerful than local ties, India's "bewilderingly plural population" nonetheless considers itself as "capable of purposeful collective action."[16] Gandhi and Nehru remain national heroes for most Indians who take their role as citizens seriously and see Indian democracy as legitimate.

Some find in this combined sense of local power and political efficacy a dangerous tendency toward identity politics in Indian democracy. Nehru's secular nationalism has ceded ground to political movements that mobilize supporters in the name of religion or region. Majority Hindus perceive themselves as threatened by minority religions, the prosperous middle class depicts itself as victim of India's poorest outcastes, and Kashmiri Muslims clamor for independence. Globalization has further created a sense that Indian identity as a whole is under threat and must be defended. Yet democracy and unity prevail, which speaks to India's remarkable capacity to adopt and adapt foreign institutions for its own use. An Indian adage claims that "democracy is like cricket—a quintessentially Indian game that just happened to have been invented elsewhere." There is no question that India has made democracy its own.

Fears About Foreign Influence

Our way of life must be protected from foreign influence. Percentage saying yes:

COUNTRY	PERCENTAGE
India	92
Nigeria	85
South Africa	80
Brazil	77
Russia	77
Mexico	75
China	70
Japan	64
Canada	62
United States	62
United Kingdom	54
Germany	53
France	52

Note: Data on Iran not available.
Source: Pew Center for the People and the Press, 2007.

Political Economy

By the time India finally obtained its independence from British imperialism, it had had quite enough of the West's version of liberal free trade. For nearly four decades, successive (mostly INC) governments adopted a foreign policy of mercantilist economic nationalism, promoting **import substitution industrialization** and restricting foreign investment and trade. Governments also promoted social-democratic policies domestically to limit the private sector, redistribute wealth, and give the state the leading role in guiding the economy. These policies achieved several significant results. By the late 1970s, through the technological gains of the Green Revolution, India had become one of the largest agricultural producers in the world and for most years since then has been a net exporter of food. It established a relatively large—if not broad—middle class, and some niches in the economy and some regions of the country truly prospered.

By the mid-1980s, however, frustration with poverty, corruption, and continued slow growth at home, coupled with the popularity of export-led growth and structural adjustment programs abroad, led successive governments to adopt neoliberal policies of economic reform. Piecemeal efforts during the 1980s to dismantle nearly four decades of mercantilist protectionism gave way to substantial liberalization. Although the process was gradual and the results have been less thorough than reforms in China, measures to liberalize foreign trade and investment and to privat-

THE LICENSE RAJ AND THE "HINDU RATE OF GROWTH"

Referring to India's relatively slow rate of development during its early decades of independence, an Indian economist famously compared what he called the "Hindu rate of growth" with the more rapid pace of India's East Asian neighbors. Although the phrase would seem to implicate India's culture, most observers agree that the greatest obstacle to Indian growth has been (and in important ways remains) India's huge bureaucracy with its associated red tape and corruption. India's "license raj" was the legacy of an extensive British colonial civil service superseded by independent India's far larger state bureaucracy. To carry out his social-democratic vision for India, Nehru established an interventionist state that pursued socialist and mercantilist economic policies, including protectionist measures promoting import substitution industrialization and far-reaching regulations designed to protect consumers and lift India's poorest. The result was a highly bureaucratized and politicized system of licenses, permits, and quotas governing virtually all aspects of the Indian economy.

Although some of the most stifling aspects of the license raj were reduced or eliminated with the 1991 liberalization program, the country continues to suffer from an array of bureaucratic and other barriers to business; according to the World Bank, India remains one of the most difficult places in which to set up and run a business.* Because Indians have found it so difficult to work within this system, most have little choice but to work around it by paying bribes, which have come to be expected "at almost every point where citizens are governed, at every transaction where they are noted, registered, taxed, stamped, licensed, authorized, or assessed."[†]

*World Bank Doing Business Website, www.doing business.org/ (accessed 11/28/11).
[†] Edward Luce, *In Spite of the Gods* (New York: Anchor Books, 2007), p. 78.

ize the economy have been significant. Governments weakened India's notorious **license raj**, the mercantilist holdover requiring licensing and approval processes for operating a business and importing and exporting products (see "The License Raj and the 'Hindu Rate of Growth,' " p. 458). Restrictions on foreign investment have been eased, and many state-owned companies have been sold to the private sector.

The results of the liberalization effort are impressive. In the two decades after the reforms were launched, economic growth in India averaged nearly 6 percent per year (twice the rate of the previous 20 years). In recent years, economic expansion neared the frenzied rates of neighboring China, with growth averaging closer to 8 to 10 percent per year (and inflation rates to match). Even as the population has continued to grow rapidly, the total number of poor Indians is declining. Trade and investment are up, and Western outsourcing (moving the production of goods and services to another country to take advantage of cheap labor or other savings) has brought jobs and growth to some segments of the Indian economy.

Yet huge economic problems persist. By 2015, it is expected that still one-quarter of Indians will live on less than a dollar per day—though this will be down

Modern shopping malls have sprung up in cities across India, including this one in Lucknow. Filled with Western and Indian stores, they serve the growing middle class but are far beyond the reach of most Indians.

Carter administration did not press the shah further and, in the eyes of many hopeful Iranians, even seemed to retreat from its earlier criticisms in favor of political stability.

As U.S. pressure on the shah flagged, Iranians found a second source of external opposition to his repressive rule in the form of the Ayatollah Khomeini. Still living in Iraq, in the Shiite holy city of Najaf, Khomeini had through his works elaborated a vision of an Islamic political system for Iran quite at odds with that of much of the Shia clergy. These ideas culminated in his work *Islamic Government: The Governance of the Jurist*. In this work, he argued that Islamic government should be constructed around the concept of ***velayat-e faqih***, or clerical rule; whereas a monarchy was a usurpation of Allah's rule on earth, a system of government by a clergy trained in Islamic jurisprudence would be a continuation of the political system first established by the prophet Muhammad. The clergy could serve as a regent in place of the Mahdi, who would eventually return to reestablish religious and political righteousness. Since such a form of government was the only regime consistent with the will of God, secular forms, such as those of the shah, should be overthrown. Khomeini's writings began to attract a large following in Iran, where, despite his absence, his popularity continued to grow.[6]

The shah, Khomeini, and the United States were now on a collision course. In 1978, the Iranian government attempted a smear campaign against Khomeini, which only increased support for the ayatollah and touched off a series of protests. The government responded harshly, but this in turn only sparked a new round of conflict, linked to a 40-day cycle of mourning traditionally undertaken in Islam. Finally, three important events turned public protest into revolution. First, in August 1978, a fire at Cinema Rex in Abadan killed some 400 people. Many Iranians latched on to the rumor that SAVAK had torched the theater in an attempt to frame the religious opposition. (In retrospect, it appears that Islamic radicals in fact started the fire.) The funerals for the victims became another flash point for massive public protest.

Second, in response to the public protests, the shah declared martial law. Yet the protests continued, resonating with the imagery of Ashura and Hussein. In September, a massive protest in Tehran in defiance of martial law called for the end of the monarchy and the return of Ayatollah Khomeini. The army fired on the protesters, and some fired back. Scores were killed, and the violence took on increasingly religious symbolism, with allusions to martyrdom and the coming of the Mahdi.

Third, the shah, realizing that even in exile Khomeini was a dangerous force, persuaded the Iraqi government to remove him to France. Rather than isolating him, however, the move to Europe only improved Khomeini's connections to Iran, the outside world, and the international media. By November, Tehran was racked by widespread public violence, and the shah, while increasing his reliance on force, feared for his political survival. A series of crackdowns and attempts at co-opting the opposition had no effect. The United States, too, vacillated in its support for the shah, criticizing the use of violence while continuing to give him its support.

By late 1978, the Shah's power had slipped away. In December, millions of protesters took to the streets of Tehran in defiance of a government ban on such public gatherings. Military units began to defect. The once unshakable Pahlavi dynasty rapidly fell apart, and the shah fled, replaced by a provisional government with a tenuous hold on the country. On February 1, 1979, millions gathered to welcome the Ayatollah Khomeini as he returned to Iran.[7]

THE CONSOLIDATION OF AN ISLAMIC REPUBLIC

The revolution did not automatically mean that Iran would have an Islamic regime; as in Russia in 1917, many observers expected a democratic republic, not simply a change from one form of authoritarianism to another. Many Iranian citizens did call for an Islamic regime, but it is not clear that those supporters agreed with, or even fully grasped, the kind of political system Khomeini was proposing. However, by capitalizing on the political turmoil and drawing on his own charismatic authority, Khomeini was able to undermine the secular provisional government. Outflanking the various political and religious factions that had sprung up during the revolution, he gained control of the government and oversaw the drafting of a new constitution that allowed for not only a president and prime minister but also a faqih (a religious leader with expertise in Islamic law) who would have supreme political authority. This position was filled by Khomeini until his death.

The **Islamic Republic of Iran** had a violent birth. The new government suppressed all opposition, including monarchists, members of Marxist and other secular political groups, ethnic minorities, and members of other faiths. From 1979 to 1980, perhaps thousands were executed in the name of "revolutionary justice." Student supporters of Khomeini seized control of the U.S. embassy, holding much of its staff hostage for more than a year (and leading to an ill-fated rescue attempt by the Carter administration).

Yet the violence paled in comparison with the **Iran-Iraq War**. As the Iranian Revolution unfolded, Iraq's president, Saddam Hussein, perceived these developments as a threat to his own rule over a country in which more than half the population was Shiite. Khomeini himself hoped to spread his Islamic

Revolution beyond Iran's borders, and Iraq was the logical next choice. At the same time, Iraq saw in Iran's chaos an opportunity to extend its power in the region and seize Iranian territory. In September 1980, Iraq launched a full-scale invasion of Iran, initiating the Iran-Iraq War, which lasted until 1988.

The war caused widespread destruction on both sides. Iraq had superior fire-power and the support of such countries as the United States, which feared the spread of the Iranian Revolution. Iran, in contrast, had the greater population and its revolutionary fervor—using, for example, unarmed boys to fight the Iraqis, promising them rewards in the afterlife for their certain martyrdom. In 1982, realizing that he had miscalculated his chance of success, Hussein sought to end

THE U.S. EMBASSY HOSTAGE CRISIS

On February 14, 1979, a group of Iranian students associated with a Marxist political group temporarily seized control of the U.S. embassy in Tehran. From the perspective of many Iranians, the embassy represented the power behind the throne that had propped up the shah's rule and acquiesced in his despotic ways. Khomeini denounced the takeover and forced the students' retreat. On November 4, however, the embassy was stormed a second time, and sixty-six Americans were taken hostage. On this occasion, the students were follow-ers of Khomeini and were inspired by the belief that the United States was preparing a counterrevolution that would restore the monarchy, akin to Operation Ajax in 1953. Most observers believed that the sei-zure would not be a prolonged affair; but within a matter of days Khomeini formally endorsed the takeover, helping to project the new regime's staunch anti-Americanism and sideline more moderate forces, who sought better relations with the United States. The crisis lasted for 444 days, gen-erating frustration and a deep animos-ity in the United States toward Iran while serving as a source of revolutionary pride for many Iranians. In April 1980, President Carter approved a military operation to rescue the hostages, only to have the mis-sion scuttled after sandstorms, equipment failure, and a helicopter crash that killed eight servicemen. Only after Carter had been defeated by Ronald Reagan in the 1980 presidential election did Khomeini agree to allow the hostages to leave. To this day, the United States and Iran do not have formal diplomatic relations, and the storming of the U.S. embassy is regarded by the Iranian government as a key event in the revolution.

the war; Khomeini refused, believing that this was the opportunity to carry his revolution to Iraq. In 1988, when the war finally ended, neither side emerged victorious, and nearly 1 million Iranians and Iraqis were dead. Shortly thereafter, Khomeini himself died, leaving the Islamic Republic without its founder and spiritual guide.

Political Regime

Since 1979, the Islamic Republic of Iran has sought to follow the ideas of Khomeini in creating a political system built around his notion of *velayat-e faqih*, which would replace the sovereignty of men and women with the sovereignty of God as transmitted by the clergy. Yet Khomeini came to power in the wake of a popular revolution driven by the public's demand for a political system that responded to their needs and desires, influenced by democratic, Marxist, and liberal values. The new regime would thus have to reconcile the will of the people with the will of God. Additionally, the new Iranian system was seen as a temporary set of institutions to serve until the return of the Mahdi, or true descendant of the prophet Muhammad. Some Iranians, in fact, initially saw Khomeini as this figure, or as a sign that the end of times was near. Since the death of Khomeini, however, the regime has faced the challenge of what Max Weber termed "the routinization of charisma." That is, how does a nation maintain the ideals and authority of the leader once that leader is gone? The result is a political system quite unlike any other, a mixture of institutions that seek to balance the word of man with the word of God.

Political Institutions

THE CONSTITUTION

The Iranian constitution is a product of the 1979 revolution. Since that time, the only major changes to the document were made ten years later, when Khomeini sought to ensure that the principles of the Islamic Republic would be maintained after his death. In its preamble, the constitution lays out the origins of the current regime, which is viewed as a revolt against the "American conspiracy" of the White Revolution. According to the constitution, the Islamic Republic exists not to serve the individual or mediate between diverse interests but to guide the people toward God (Allah). The Koran (the holy book of Islam) therefore serves not only as a spiritual text but also as the foundation for a unified national ideology that is embodied in the political system. Allah is sovereign over the Iranian people and state, and all political acts are expected to flow from the word of Allah. As the constitution itself states, "All civil, penal, financial, economic, administrative, cultural, military, political, and other laws and regulations must be based on Islamic criteria." This concept is consistent with religious fundamentalism in general, where sovereignty in the form of statehood and democracy is seen as blasphemous, with humans arrogating to themselves powers and rights that should reside only with God. The rule of law is heresy, as it is God's law (**Sharia**) that should reign supreme. As such, the Iranian constitution and political institutions are (at least in theory) an attempt to express God's will rather than instruments of human will.

The Branches of Government

THE SUPREME LEADER AND THE PRESIDENT

The particular nature of the Iranian constitution has resulted in a set of political institutions that are quite bewildering to outsiders but consistent with the *velayat-e faqih*. We can see this most clearly in the executive branch of the government. As in many other countries, Iran has a dual executive, with power divided between two offices. In most other cases, such divisions fall between head of state and head of government, with the former a monarch or president and the latter a prime minister. The former reigns while the latter rules.

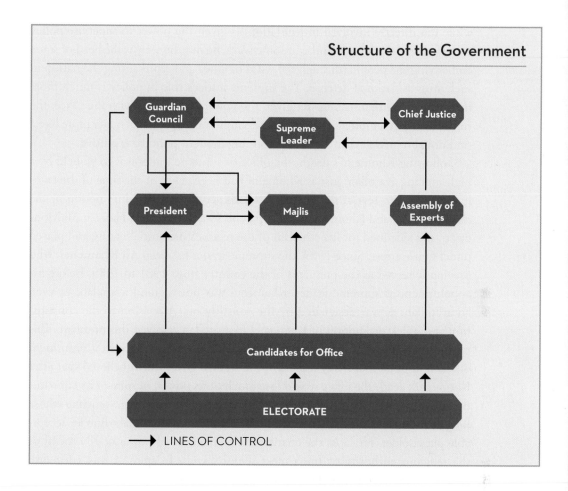

Guardian
Council

Chief Justice

Supreme
Leader

President

Majlis

Assembly of
Experts

Candidates for Office

ELECTORATE

LINES OF CONTROL

Iran's executive does not follow this pattern. The dominant executive is the **supreme leader**, a position created for Khomeini following the revolution as an expression of his charismatic power and political ideology. As befits the title, the supreme leader is the most powerful office in Iran, created to ensure that a senior cleric is at the helm of Iranian politics, directing both political and spiritual life. The supreme leader serves for life, though he can theoretically be removed for incompetence or failure to uphold his religious duty.

The powers of the supreme leader are numerous. First, he may decide who is permitted to run for the office of president, eliminating rivals in the process. He is also commander in chief of the armed forces and appoints the heads of the various branches of the military. The supreme leader also appoints the chief justice and even the directors of radio and television broadcasting. The supreme leader, while not directly involved in legislation, is given the power to supervise policy and, if necessary, call referenda. In some ways, he may be seen as the head of state, embodying the people (through the word of God) and representing the nation in such areas as national defense. The supreme leader's role in policy is much more that of reigning than ruling. Yet given the powers that reside with the office, the role is hardly ceremonial. If anything, the supreme leader looks much more like a traditional monarch than any corresponding modern political executive.

Following Khomeini's death, the office of supreme leader was to be held by a high-ranking ayatollah, just as Khomeini had been. Even at the time of the revolution, however, few of the grand ayatollahs accepted Khomeini's notion of the *velayat-e faqih*, and Khomeini's heir apparent, Grand Ayatollah Hussein Ali Montazeri, was sidelined for his criticism of the regime's dictatorial nature and placed under house arrest. Since 1989, the supreme leader has been **Ali Khamenei**, who previously served as the president of the country from 1981 to 1989. Before his appointment as supreme leader, Khamenei was not a grand ayatollah, or even an ayatollah, as was designated by the constitution. A revision to the constitution and quick promotion of Khamenei to ayatollah resolved this problem. This raises the question of why a lesser cleric would have risen to such a prominent office. It appears that many leaders in the Iranian government believed that after Khomeini's death the office would lose much of its power, in spite of its constitutional provisions. Khamenei, then, was viewed as unthreatening, someone whose long-standing loyalty to Khomeini and the revolution would make him an acceptable placeholder. He lacks the charismatic or intellectual power of Khomeini or the religious authority of Iran's most senior clerics. In spite of this safeguard, Khameini has wrong-footed many of his rivals, slowly consolidating power within the office.

How is the supreme leader chosen? In theory the role falls to the **Assembly of Experts**, a body of 86 members, all men and Islamic scholars, who are themselves popularly elected for eight-year terms. Candidates for this assembly are vetted in advance of elections, limiting the people's choice and ensuring that membership is dominated by clerics who accept the political status quo. Since Khamenei has been the only supreme leader to come to power after Khomeini, it is difficult to say how powerful a role this body will play once he passes away. Indeed, Khamenei's ascension to power in 1989 resulted from back-door negotiations among leaders in the Iranian government, and it is uncertain how the next transfer of power will occur.

If the supreme leader functions as a powerful head of state, the president is (confusingly) more akin to a head of government. Unlike the supreme leader, the president is directly elected and can serve only two four-year terms. Within his scope of responsibilities lie drafting the state budget, initiating legislation, and selecting a cabinet of ministers charged with directing various facets of policy. The president is also technically in charge of foreign policy, appointing ambassadors, signing treaties, and helping foster diplomatic relations. Given the president's lack of control over the military, however, his powers in this area remain circumscribed, and the supreme leader does not refrain from making his own foreign policy statements. In general, the president is charged with the task of executing the laws, making certain that specific policies are carried out. After 1979, there was an expectation that the president would be a nonreligious figure, more in keeping with an office concerned with "worldly" affairs. From 1981 to 2005, however, the position was held primarily by clerics. The 2005 election of President **Mahmoud Ahmadinejad**, whose background is in higher education and local government rather than theology, was a departure from this trend. Ahmadinejad's emphasis on social justice, religious piety, and confrontation with the West built him a base of support that appeared to rival Khamenei's, but over the course of Ahmadinejad's second term the supreme leader was able to check much of the president's power. The supreme leader has even suggested that he would abolish the very office of the presidency, if need be, to prevent any challenge to his own office. The president thus remains a secondary player to the supreme leader.

THE LEGISLATURE

The Islamic Republic retains one political institution from Iran's past. The legislature, or Majlis, is a unicameral body whose members are directly elected on the basis of universal suffrage of men and women over the age of 18. Its 290 members serve four-year terms. As one might suspect, this Majlis, like its predecessors, has a limited amount of power. Its powers include initiating and passing legislation, overseeing the budget, and approving the members of the president's cabinet. Cabinet members may also be removed by a vote of no confidence, though the Majlis's power in this area does not extend to the president or to the supreme leader. While the Majlis was dominated by clerics in the early years of the revolution, their participation has declined, while members associated with the paramilitary Revolutionary Guard (see the section "Other Institutions," p. 497) has risen. Currently there are eight women in the Majlis, and single seats are set aside for the Zoroastrian and Jewish communities, and three for Christians. (None of these communities makes up more than 1 percent of the population.)

The inherent supremacy of God's law in the Iranian constitution raises questions about the very functioning of the legislature. Since man-made laws are liable to deviate from God's will, the role of the Majlis is technically to legislate in accordance with divine law, and its legislation can be struck down for failing on this account (see next paragraph). In spite of this limitation, the Majlis can be an important actor. While it does not challenge the supreme leader, conflicts between the Majlis and the president over national policy is common. The Majlis is also an important instrument of local politics, utilized by representatives to gain resources for their constituents—the kind of "pork barreling" seen in most parliaments around the world.

The broader limitations of the Majlis are best seen in the presence of two additional bodies, the **Guardian Council** and the **Expediency Council**. The Guardian Council is made up of 12 individuals who serve six-year terms: 6 lawyers, who are nominated by the chief justice and approved by the Majlis, and 6 clerics specializing in religious law, who are appointed by the supreme leader. The powers of the Guardian Council are significant; among them is the power to review all legislation that derives from the Majlis, to "ensure its compatibility with the criteria of Islam and the Constitution."[8] It may send legislation back to the Majlis for revision if it finds it incompatible; if the Majlis is unable to revise the legislation to the Guardian Council's satisfaction, a third body, the Expediency Council, mediates. Members of the Expediency Council are appointed by the supreme leader for five-year terms; the council is currently headed by **Akbar Hashemi Rafsanjani**, a rival to Khamenei who served as the country's president from 1989 to 1997. The final decision of the Expediency Council cannot be overturned. The Guardian Council (and, to a lesser extent, the Expediency Council) serves as a kind of unelected upper house, with substantial powers to restrict the work of the Majlis.

THE JUDICIARY

The way in which political authority stems from religious tenets naturally has a profound effect on the nature of the law itself. The legal system in Iran, derived from religious law, or Sharia, serves to defend itself against deviation—not to interpret the law or expand its boundaries, as is often the case in secular democracies. At the apex of this branch of government is a **chief justice**, a single figure whose qualifications include an understanding of Sharia (making the appointment of a cleric necessary). The chief justice is appointed by the supreme leader for a five-year term. His role is to manage the judicial institutions and oversee the appointment and removal of judges. Beneath the chief justice is the Supreme Court, which serves as the highest court of appeal. Like the position of chief justice, this office is entirely staffed by high-ranking clerics chosen for their familiarity with religious law. This role by clerics in the judicial system extends down to the lowest level; only clerics may serve as judges. In addition to civil and criminal courts, there are also revolutionary courts, a legacy of the immediate postrevolutionary period in which elements of the monarchy and opponents of Khomeini were tried and often executed. These revolutionary courts deal with cases involving national security, such as the public protests following the 2009 presidential elections, in which numerous individuals were tried and sentenced on the grounds of *moharebeh*, or "rebellion against God." Iran executes the second-highest number of individuals in the world after China—more than 600 in 2011, which was itself over double that of the year before. (In comparison, during the same period, the United States executed 46.)

The Electoral System

In spite of the theocratic limitations, Iran seems to enjoy some elements of democratic participation. In particular, there are direct elections for the Majlis, the Assembly of Experts (which selects the supreme leader), and the presidency. The constitution gives the Guardian Council the power to oversee all elections, however, which in practice means that this unelected body may reject any candidate for elected office. In the 2008 and 2012 Majlis elections, the Guardian Council barred around 40 percent of candidates for office as "unsuitable" for elections, eliminating virtually all reformers. In the 2009 election for president, 450 individuals registered to run (including 42 women), but only 4 candidates were approved. The power of the Guardian Council to block candidates, or remove standing representatives from running for re-election, has been a major factor in the consolidation of conservative control over the Majlis and the presidency.

For the Majlis and Assembly of Experts, Iran uses a mix of single-member majority and multimember districts. The most unique element here is the multimember districts (MMD), where there are multiple seats being contested in a single district. In those cases, voters have as many votes to cast as there are seats, and any candidate who gets 25 percent of the vote acquires a seat. For seats left unfilled, there is a runoff among candidates not yet elected. A similar combination of single- and multimember districts is also used for elections to the Assembly of

Experts. For the presidency, there is a simple two-round runoff between the top two vote-getters, unless one candidate wins a majority outright in the first round.

Given the strong support for reform among the youth, the voting age has become a political tool. During the 1990s, the reformist-dominated Majlis lowered the legal voting age from 16 to 15 (the lowest in the world), seeking to enfranchise millions of young voters they hoped would help consolidate their position. As reformers lost power, conservative forces raised the voting age to 18.

Local Government

Iran's history, like that of many countries, has been one of a struggle by the state to centralize power. Though the country is currently divided into 30 *ostan*, or provinces, these bodies, like the local institutions below them, have limited authority, a condition that existed long before the current regime. Although the Constitutional Revolution of 1905–6 was driven in part by the goal of creating representative local government, this goal was never realized. The 1979 revolution similarly made claims about the need for local government, though after taking initial steps in that direction, the theocracy moved away from devolving power. The demands of institutionalizing the theocratic regime, going to war with Iraq, nationalizing industry, and quelling ethnic unrest drove the regime to centralize power even more. It rejected any notions of regional autonomy or federalism and suspended elections to the local and regional councils.

As part of a wave of reforms in 1997, the government passed a law on decentralization that moved power away from the Ministry of the Interior. Prior to that time, the ministry had been responsible for local affairs, appointing regional governors and mayors. As a result of the new law, local councils were created at the village, city, and provincial level to manage local politics and the indirect election of mayors. In a further departure from the past, these councils—more than 100,000 offices in all—were directly elected. The first elections to the newly created council positions took place in 1999, with more than 500,000 candidates competing at the local level for the first time in Iranian history.[9] Though candidates have to be approved by the Majlis, this review does not appear to be as onerous as that conducted by the Guardian Council. In 2006, a number of reform and moderate candidates won local elections and mayoral seats, in what was seen as a rebuff to President Ahmadinejad. Recently, the timing of local elections was modified so that the elections take place at the same time as the presidential election. This has been explained as necessary for streamlining the elections for the Assembly of Experts, Majlis, president, and local government. It may also be intended to limit the role of local elections as a form of midterm protest against the Majlis and president, as was the case in the recent past.

Other Institutions

THE REVOLUTIONARY GUARD AND THE BASIJ

Operating alongside the wide-reaching state power and theocratic rule in Iran are a number of institutions with political power that operate largely outside normal state authority. Of these, two merit particular mention: the Revolutionary Guard, or Pasdaran, and the Basij, or People's Militia.

The **Revolutionary Guard** is a paramilitary force that emerged from the 1979 revolution. It originally comprised several thousand men from various militias and groups that had sprung up around the revolution, and was independent of the armed forces, which Khomeini mistrusted because of their role during the Pahlavi dynasty. As a "corps of the faithful," the Revolutionary Guard was assigned the immediate task of defending the new regime and destroying rival groups and movements, such as Marxists and supporters of greater ethnic autonomy. Later, during the Iran-Iraq War, the Revolutionary Guard expanded in size to fight on the front lines as a military force. It did this by forming a large people's volunteer militia, the **Basij**, in which young boys played a notable role. With its members poorly trained and ill-equipped but imbued with religious fervor, the Basij was known for its "human wave" attacks against the Iraqi front lines, sometimes even clearing minefields with its soldiers' bodies.

The end of the war and the consolidation of the revolution undercut the justification for the Revolutionary Guard and the Basij, but both organizations have continued to play an influential and growing role in Iranian politics. Though both groups are controlled only by the supreme leader and his allies, the Revolutionary Guard has become an increasingly independent and direct player in Iranian domestic and international affairs as well, with its top leaders taking on important additional roles in the state and government. The Guard has its own ministry, army, navy, and air force units, and appears to have a hand in the development of Iran's nuclear program. It has also become deeply involved in the Iranian economy, legally and illegally. It has significant economic assets and is involved in various aspects of national development, such as construction and telecommunications. The Guard is also a major goods smuggler into Iran, circumventing sanctions and benefiting economically in the process. The Guard leadership is highly factionalized, with some having thrown their support behind Ahmadinejad in the past and others opposing him.

In contrast, the Basij is no longer a significant military force, though it has maintained its importance in other ways. Like the Revolutionary Guard (which has authority over the Basij), the organization has developed substantial economic assets. More disturbing has been its role as a public morality force, often taking responsibility for such things as preventing public displays of affection and seizing illegal satellite dishes. In the 2009 protests, the Basij was widely deployed to break up demonstrations. Basij members tend to come from poorer backgrounds, and membership is an opportunity to gain access to certain benefits, such as higher education.

In general, the trend of growing power of the Revolutionary Guard has raised concerns that Iran is moving in a more militarized direction. The Guard has become a more active player in politics and is an important tool of the supreme leader in maintaining power. At the same time, its factionalization and economic interests mean that there is a good deal of rivalry within the institution, and some worry that when Khamenei dies, the Revolutionary Guard could move to formally assert control over the government.[10]

Political Conflict and Competition

For many reasons, political competition in Iran is a confusing matter to outside observers (and insiders as well). The nature of the revolution and the role of religion in the course of that radical change constitute one factor, as they helped create political differences that do not fit easily onto our usual palette of ideologies. In addition, Iran lacks institutionalized political parties, a result of the regime's desire to stifle dissent and safeguard the revolution against "un-Islamic" policies and ideas.

It was not always this way. In the immediate aftermath of the 1979 revolution, there was an outburst of new political activity, and previously suppressed groups, such as the National Front and the Tudeh Party, reemerged. Out of this activity emerged two dominant parties. The first, the Islamic Republican Party (IRP), was closely allied with Ayatollah Ruhollah Khomeini and his desire to establish a theocracy. The second, the Liberation Movement, was more pro-Western and favored a more limited role for religion in politics. Numerous parties stood for the first postrevolutionary elections in 1980, but the electoral system eliminated virtually all groups but the IRP, which gained a majority of seats. Some independent parliamentarians and members of the Liberation Movement sought to resist this consolidation of power; others turned their weapons on the IRP, much of whose leadership was killed in a bombing in 1981. The government responded with increased repression of opposition groups, imprisoning and executing thousands of political activists while marginalizing the increasingly critical Liberation Movement.

With the 1984 and 1987 elections, the theocratic hold on the Majlis was made complete. In advance of the 1984 elections, all parties other than the IRP were banned. In 1987, even the IRP itself was eliminated.

The Rise and Fall of Political Reform

After 1987, political debate within the Majlis was limited primarily to economic concerns, with competition between those who favored a more free-market economic approach and those who supported more statist policies. (See the section "Society" on p. 503 for a discussion of these different political tendencies.) Debates on the nature of the political system itself were not allowed. Liberalization was afoot, however, made possible by the death of Khomeini in 1989 and a worsening economy. In 1992, Majlis elections saw a victory for the free-market faction, many of whom in turn supported the 1997 presidential candidacy of the pro-reform Mohammad Khatami. His victory, with over 70 percent of the popular vote, surprised Iranians and outside observers alike.

The reform period of the 1990s saw a dramatic diversification in political views and organizations, much of which called for improved relations with the outside world and democratic change, arguments spearheaded by intellectuals, students, and a number of clerics who had long opposed the idea of the *velayat-e faqih*. In 2000, reform groups coalesced to form the **Second Khordad Front** (named after the date in the Iranian calendar for Khatami's 1997 election) to compete in the following year's Majlis elections. The party went on to win a stunning 189 of the 290 parliamentary seats, and in 2001, President Khatami was again overwhelmingly re-elected, with over 70 percent of the vote. Many expected that these twin victories would solidify reformist power and pave the way for a political transition not unlike that of the Soviet Union in the 1980s.

That belief was short-lived. While reformers controlled the Majlis and the presidency, these were relatively weak political institutions. Conservatives still controlled or had the support of the Guardian Council and the Expediency Council, the Revolutionary Guard and Basij, and of course the supreme leader. Soon after the elections, a wave of repression was directed against reformists.

Numerous journalists and pro-democracy activists were arrested, and a number of pro-reform newspapers were shut down. In the Majlis, while reformers passed a wide array of legislation to limit state power and increase democratic rights, the bills were mostly vetoed by the Guardian Council. Meanwhile, President Khatami lacked the power and the political skills to contend with the conservatives. In the 2004 Majlis elections, the Guardian Council banned large numbers of Khordad candidates (including 80 standing members of parliament), and reformers called for an election boycott. As of the most recent Majlis elections, in 2012, reformers hold few Majlis seats.

The other battlefield in the struggle over reform has been the presidency. As Khatami stepped down in 2005, many expected that former president and Khatami backer Ali Akbar Hashemi Rafsanjani would return to power. However, Rafsanjani was trounced by the mayor of Tehran, Mahmoud Ahmadinejad. Ahmadinejad benefited from the fact that many pro-reform voters stayed away from the polls, dismayed by the conservative counteroffensive in the Majlis and repelled by Rafsanjani, who was widely regarded as a corrupt leader who sought reforms only to expand his power. But there was also widespread support for Ahmadinejad, especially among the poor and more conservative, who were attracted by his obvious piety and modesty. Ahmadinejad also had the support among many in the Revolutionary Guard and Basij, with whom he had close ties.

Ahmadinejad's two terms in office are characterized by several trends. The first is a more populist approach to politics, akin to values seen in the early years of the Islamic Republic. Ahmadinejad has focused on public programs aiding the poor, emphasizing the need for the government and state to address their needs. This policy is in many ways a clear challenge to government and clerical elites, many of whom have grown rich since 1979 through their roles in both politics and the market. In addition, Ahmadinejad has pursued a more openly confrontational relationship with the United States, an approach abetted by the wars in neighboring Afghanistan and Iraq. He has raised the international profile of Iran, frequently travelling and speaking against the United States, Israel, and the inequities of global politics and economic relations. He has also made the development of nuclear technology a cornerstone of his policies, though he is not in direct authority over this area. Under Ahmadinejad, the Revolutionary Guard has grown in economic and political power. Finally, Ahmadinejad has pursued a more puritanical and messianic approach to Iranian domestic politics, pursuing a crackdown on civil liberties and suggesting that the return of the Mahdi is imminent—and that he, by extension, is an agent of that return. This rising profile has put him at odds with the supreme leader.

The 2009 presidential elections pitted Ahmadinejad against several rivals, among them Mir Hussein Mousavi, former prime minister from 1981 to 1989. Long out of power, he campaigned on a strongly pro-reformist agenda, calling for such things as a liberalized press, greater rights for women, and more power for the Majlis. Young people in particular rallied around Mousavi, forming a "Green Wave" movement in favor of his election. It was widely expected that Mousavi and Ahmadinejad would face a runoff; instead, the government announced that, in fact, Ahmadinejad had won over 60 percent of the vote, thus eliminating the need for a second round. This dubious result sparked mass demonstrations around Iran and a ferocious response by the police and Basij, resulting in perhaps 150 dead, more than 1,000 detained, and an unknown number given long sentences or executed. Mousavi came under house arrest, where he remains.

The re-election of Ahmadinejad was both a victory and a loss for conservatives in Iran. The widespread demonstration of public hostility toward him weakened his position, which for a time appeared to be eclipsing that of the supreme leader himself. Ahmadinejad's attempt to anoint a successor, akin to Putin's Russia, also failed, as his associates came under attack from the judiciary and supreme leader for their corruption and "deviant" (that is, highly messianic) religious views. The question now is, who will be the next president? The supreme leader's comment that he could eliminate the presidency was not simply a threat against Ahmadinejad, but also acknowledgment that presidential elections have become a flashpoint for public protest. This is as much an institutional problem as an individual one, and will likely return to trouble the regime in 2013.

Civil Society

As might be expected, civil society in Iran has mirrored the changes and challenges of political competition. Over the past century, Iran has seen the rise of organized civil activity during periods in which the state was weak, as during the constitutional revolution in 1905–6, immediately after World War II, and during the 1979 revolution. After the creation of the Islamic Republic of Iran, the nascent civil society was again stifled, viewed as anathema to the supremacy of religious rule and a threat to national unity during the war with Iraq. Most civic organizations were either absorbed into the state or outlawed. This was consistent with the theocracy's emphasis on the notion of the *ummah*, or community, whose members were expected to act as a unified group that embodied and served the revolution. Plurality and autonomy were seen as running counter to religious rule and revolutionary ideals.

After Khomeini's death and the end of the war, however, civil society began to reemerge, though it remained marginal and beleaguered. A handful of intellectuals, clerics, and others questioned the current regime and advocated reform, but this activity was frequently met with arrest, torture, and even death. One notable example was Ayatollah Hussein Ali Montazeri, whom Khomeini had handpicked to serve as supreme leader upon his death. Montazeri eventually fell out of favor, however, having criticized the government for human rights abuses, and for many years was under house arrest. In the 1990s, President Khatami made the invigoration of Iran's civil society a major plank of his campaign platform, and this cause was soon taken up by the media. New publications rapidly proliferated at all levels of society, from academic journals and independent publishers to magazines and newspapers. In the early 1990s, for example, Tehran had five newspapers; by 2001, there were over 20. Numerous civic organizations also sprang up, dealing with such issues as local government, human rights, the environment, women's rights, and poverty. In entertainment as well, a new wave of films satirized or dramatized the country's social and political problems. Even to this day, Iranian cinema continues to produce such exceptional work as the 2012 Oscar winning film *A Separation*, which deals with divorce and contemporary family life.

As noted earlier, this flowering of civil society came under sustained attack. Supreme Leader Khamenei excoriated the press as "the base of the enemy," and numerous publications were closed or physically attacked by government-sponsored militants. A 2000 law restricted the ability of the press to operate, and many publications were closed. Dozens of journalists have been arrested, and several have been killed or have died under suspicious circumstances. Iran's press freedom, according to Reporters Without Borders, ranks 175th out of 178 countries, just above North Korea.[11]

In recent years, similar pressure has been directed against nongovernmental organizations (NGOs), with many being attacked, their offices destroyed, and an unknown number of their members detained. This intensified after the 2009 presidential election. For example, Shirin Ebadi, a human rights lawyer whose tireless work in Iran earned her a Nobel Prize in 2003, went into exile in Canada rather than face almost certain arrest.

One area of civic activity in Iran that has persevered is electronic communications. Over the past decade, Iran has been an Internet pioneer in the Middle East. Internet penetration in Iran is close to 50 percent of the population, and the country has been noted for the proliferation of blogs, which range from personal observations to online news sources that cover sensitive issues. Especially as the government has cracked down on traditional media outlets such as newspapers, the Internet has become an important environment in which alternative views can be expressed.

Many have remarked on the role of social media such as Twitter, Facebook, and YouTube in helping to galvanize public protest. Most notable was the cell phone video footage taken of the death of Neda Agha Soltan, shot during protests following the 2009 presidential elections, which was distributed worldwide via the Internet.

However, it is incorrect to say that the Internet represents some liberated space that the Iranian state cannot control. A number of Internet activists have been arrested in Iran over the past few years; in 2010, Canadian-Iranian Hossein Derakhshan, recognized as one of the pioneers of Iranian blogging, was sentenced to 20 years in prison for his writings. Numerous other bloggers and online journalists have been similarly detained, and since 2009, the government has stepped up efforts to control online activity. This includes Internet filtering, limiting data speeds in order to prevent easy access to social media sites such as YouTube, and the creation of a "cyber army" under control of the Revolutionary Guard (which has authority over national telecommunications) to track down online opposition and block web sites viewed as hostile to the regime. For Iranians, e-mail communication is relatively easy, but wider access to social networks and online media is much harder and under increased scrutiny. Online dissent remains, but has become increasingly difficult and dangerous.

Society

Ethnic and National Identity

Iran is distinct from other Islamic states in the Middle East, not only in its embrace of the minority Shia branch of Islam but also in that the majority population is ethnically Iranian (or Persian) rather than Arab. With their distinct language, history, and culture, ethnic Iranians view themselves as quite separate from people in the Arab states of the Middle East, which contributes to a sense of nationalism in many ways much stronger than that found elsewhere in the region. It was this nationalism that helped sustain Iran in its long war against Iraq, portrayed by both sides as part of a struggle between Persians and Arabs going back thousands of years.

In fact, as the legitimacy of the Islamic regime has waned, a form of Iranian nationalism has resurfaced that builds upon the myths of the pre-Islamic era, and draws on the history of the Achaemenid Empire and Zoroastrianism, a largely extinct religion that predates Islam by over a 1,000 years. Many Iranians, particularly the young, have embraced the symbols of Zoroastrianism and pre-Islamic ceremonies such as Nowruz (New Year), some going even so far as to brand Islam an alien, "Arab" faith that destroyed the Iranian empire and Iranian identity.

At the same time, Iran is not the homogeneous state that its nationalism or distinctive identity might lead us to believe it is. While Persians make up a majority of the population, it is a bare majority. The rest of the population is composed of various other ethnic groups, some close to the Persian majority, others not. Among these groups, the two largest, the Azeris and the Kurds, are particularly important not only because of their size, but also because of their connection to ethnic kin outside Iran. In both cases, turmoil and political change in surrounding countries have affected these ethnic minorities and, as a result, the way in which Iran deals with its neighbors.

The largest minority ethnic group in Iran is the Azeri, comprising around a quarter of the population (perhaps more) and concentrated in the north of the country. Like the majority Persians, the Azeris follow Shiism, but they speak a language related to those spoken in Turkey and much of Central Asia. Historically, the Azeris resided entirely within the Persian Empire, but with the expansion of Russia in the nineteenth century, their region was divided between the two countries. With the collapse of the Soviet Union in 1991, an independent Azerbaijan emerged on Iran's border, which helped foster a stronger ethnic identity among Iranian Azeris, and there have been occasional protests among Azeris in Iran over discrimination by the Persian majority. However, there is relatively little support for greater regional autonomy or unification with Azerbaijan, and Azeris have historically played a prominent role in all facets of Iranian life.

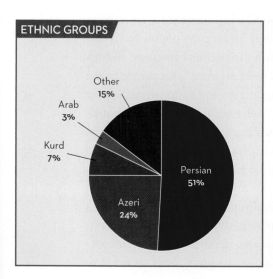

ETHNIC GROUPS

Other 15%
Arab 3%
Kurd 7%
Persian 51%
Azeri 24%

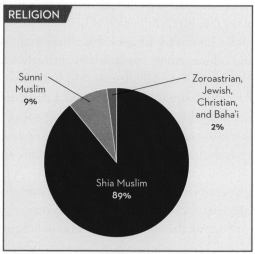

RELIGION

Sunni Muslim 9%
Zoroastrian, Jewish, Christian, and Baha'i 2%
Shia Muslim 89%

The state's relationship with the Kurds, who comprise less than 10 percent of the population, is more complicated. The Kurds carried out an armed revolt against the new Islamic Republic of Iran in 1979, gaining a degree of control of parts of northwest Iran. This revolt was ultimately suppressed by military force, though sporadic guerilla activity continued during the eighties and nineties. The rise of a largely autonomous Kurdish region in Iraq following the U.S. invasion raised hopes and fears of a sovereign Kurdish state, something that makes neighboring Iran and Turkey nervous, fearing the loss of their Kurdish regions. There have been peaceful activists as well as armed Kurdish forces operating inside Iran, often in connection with Kurdish groups in Iraq or Turkey. In the past few years, there have been several bombings and other attacks by Kurdish insurgents in the north, and the Iranian government has responded by arresting and executing several Kurdish activists. In general, the relationship between Kurds and the countries in which they reside is tense, and a recent resumption of attacks by insurgents inside Turkey may increase the degree of Kurdish activism in Iran.[12]

In addition to Kurds and Azeris, other minority ethnic groups, such as Baluchis and Arab (see chapter opening map), have complained of discrimination, which has led to protests and sporadic acts of violence and terrorism. Part of the problem may be that Iran's highly centralized political system has not allowed for a significant devolution of power that would give ethnic groups greater rights. Non-Persians have few opportunities for education in their native language, which marginalizes them. Any political change in Iran will inevitably have to confront this issue.

Ideology and Political Culture

In the absence of institutionalized political parties and free expression, it is hard to speak of any coherent spectrum of ideologies in Iran. A confusing array of terms is used: *hard-liners, radicals, conservatives, traditionalists, reformers, pragmatists, principalists, technocrats*. In spite of this confusion, we can speak of several loose political attitudes or tendencies, some of which are more ideologically coherent than others. As in other countries, the divisions tend to fall along the lines of freedom and equality, though with religion as an important institution that influences how both of those values are understood.

One major division is over the relationship between religion and the state. As we might expect, those known as "reformists" in Iran, whose political power rose and fell under the Khatami presidency, call for a reduced role for Islam in politics in favor of the rule of law and democratic reform. This group, whose orientation is more

Religion and Government

Religious leaders should not influence government.

	COUNTRY		
	TURKEY	MOROCCO	IRAN
Agree strongly	21.7%	18.1%	17.3%
Agree	47.2%	20.0%	27.2%
Neither agree nor disagree	20.0%	36.7%	27.7%
Disagree	7.5%	17.1%	22.0%
Strongly disagree	3.5%	8.1%	5.7%
Total	100%	100%	100%

Source: Values Surveys Databank.

secular, also has unexpected allies among many clerics. For many Shiite religious leaders, the very notion of the *velayat-e faqih* runs counter to the basic tenets of Shiism. Their **"quietist"** vision, which dominated Iranian Shiism before the revolution, emphasizes that worldly political power cannot be reunited with Islam until the return of the Mahdi. This belief holds that the role of the faith is to act as an intermediary between the state and society in the meantime, influencing spiritual and social values but not getting directly involved in politics. Politics is viewed as a corrupting influence on faith and thus something to be kept at a distance. In contrast, political conservatives ("principalists," as they have recently called themselves) support the *velayat-e faqih* and oppose democratization or the return of faith to a primarily social, as opposed to political, role. In their view, faith must be a central institution within the state, guiding politics and society toward God's intent. In some ways this vision implies that pious rule can hasten the Mahdi's return.

The second area of contention is over the relationship between the state and market. At the inception of the Islamic Republic there was a schism between those who saw the primary role of the revolution as bringing about a moral order and those who saw the revolution as a means to ensuring economic justice. Indeed, Khomeini emphasized both of these issues, viewing the revolution as a way to create a just social order that integrated faith, politics, and the economy. As we shall discuss shortly, however, just as religion has clashed with politics, so, too, has it led to divisions over the economy. There are those, such as former president Rafsanjani, who favor economic liberalization and better relations with the international community to increase trade and investment. Others, such as President Ahmadinejad, take a more populist line, opposing economic reform and liberalization in favor of reducing poverty and inequality (both of which have grown over the past decade). Quietists and reformers, too, while often in agreement on political change, do not necessarily see eye to eye on economic changes. Support for or hostility to capitalism does not necessarily conform to one's religious position. International sanctions have in some ways rendered this distinction moot, though there remain very real divisions over what a proper relationship between state and market should be in an Islamic society.[13]

Past these debates, we can observe more fixed elements of political culture. Iranian political culture is highly nationalist, with surveys showing that the vast majority of Iranians indicate that they are very proud of their nationality. In addition, Iranians also say that religion remains a very important part of their lives at the same time as they express support for more democracy. These views are not contradictory; Iranian religiosity appears to tend more toward the traditional, quietist view that would favor a greater separation between faith and state. This is important to consider. Many observers of Iranian politics have assumed that one result of the Islamic Republic's fundamentalism would be effectively to alienate the public from religion by politicizing it. Certainly among the younger generation and the more educated there is disaffection, as was evidenced in the Green Wave protests of 2009. But it is also clear that Islam remains a central part of Iranian culture and national identity, and political change or democratization would not necessarily mean the secularization of the country along Western lines.

Finally, another enduring part of Iranian political culture is a complicated relationship with the West. Iranian history and consequent national identity are tightly linked to the rise of the West, going back 2,000 years when Iran, Greece, and, later, Rome all commanded power and respect. In this way, Iranians may see themselves as equal participants in Western history in a way other peoples may

DEMOCRACY AND IRAN

Do you support a political system where the "Supreme Leader," along with all leaders, can be chosen and replaced by a free and direct vote of the people?

No answer/Don't know
5%

Oppose or strongly oppose
18%

Support or strongly support
77%

Source: Terror Free Tomorrow Survey, Iran, May 2009.

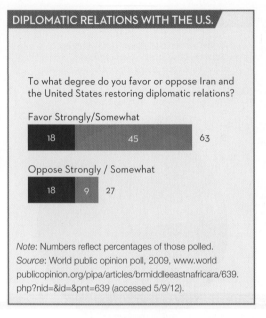

not. At the same time, the frequent Western (and Arab) interventions in modern Iranian history have created a strong tendency toward viewing international politics in conspiratorial terms, such that every political event is the product of foreign powers with seemingly limitless power. For example, while Iranians will blame the United Kingdom and the United States for the rise of the Pahlavi dynasty, they may also argue that the West was "behind" the Islamic Revolution. The United States (or Israel) is also viewed by many as the mastermind behind Al Qaeda and September 11. At an even more extreme level, many Iranians continue to believe that the United Kingdom remains the dominant world power, concealed behind its "puppet," the United States.

Indeed, Supreme Leader Khamenei singled out the United Kingdom, rather than the United States, as a mastermind of the 2009 protests. One criticism made of Iranians by outsiders is the tendency to shift blame to external actors, rather than to view themselves as also responsible for their political destiny. Even so, such views do not mean that average Iranians are opposed to better relations with the United States, even if they view American power with justifiable suspicion.

Political Economy

Iran's economic system reflects the dilemmas of late modernization, authoritarianism, and war. It is also a good example of what is sometimes called the "resource trap," the situation that occurs when a national resource paradoxically makes a country poorer rather than richer.

Iran's modern economic development lagged well behind that of the West, beginning only in the 1920s, under the Pahlavi dynasty. This was not a late embrace of liberalism, however, but rather an attempt at top-down industrialization, following the mercantilist pattern adopted by many countries in the less-developed world. Nor should such a path have been surprising; an attempt by the state to generate domestic wealth was a logical response and not unlike the Western powers' own history. Iran's mercantilist policies helped modernize the country, such that by the

1970s half the population was living in urban areas. At the same time, it led to social dislocation, as the country made a rapid jump from an agrarian, isolated, and religiously conservative society in just a few decades.

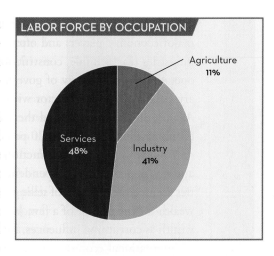

LABOR FORCE BY OCCUPATION

Agriculture 11%

Services 48%

Industry 41%

Top-down mercantilist development led to similar problems in other less-developed countries, though in Iran, the problems were compounded by the discovery of oil. At first glance, one would expect oil reserves to be the salvation of any country, providing it with the resources to develop its infrastructure and generate new industries. In reality, the opposite can be the case. Oil can be more a curse than a blessing, especially when controlled by the state. Rather than directing resources toward the goal of development, leaders give in to a seemingly irresistible temptation, which leads to corruption as they siphon off the wealth to line their own pockets or serve their own policy predilections. Moreover, since the public is eliminated as the major source of state revenue, those in power can effectively ignore the public and repress or co-opt any opposition. The resource trap may also explain the degree of women's rights; where oil is strong, the private sector is weak, limiting women's participation in the workforce and their economic independence. The issue of "taxation without representation," for both women and men, thus becomes meaningless—the state can do without either and is able to avoid having to make the trade-off. This became evident during the time of the White Revolution, when economic development coincided with growing inflation, inequality, and increased repression. Development, built on oil exports and Western imports, also fueled hostility toward Western materialism, or what was termed "Westoxication" or "Weststruckness" by one critical Iranian scholar of the era.[14]

Reflecting the economic factors that helped bring about the 1979 revolution, the new constitution explicitly stated that "the economy is a means, not an end." This stood in contrast to liberal capitalist systems, in which the quest for wealth and profit becomes "a subversive and corrupting factor in the course of man's development." The oil and other state-owned industries were to remain in the state's hands, with the profits redirected toward presumably more equitable goals. In addition, numerous private industries were nationalized after their owners fled the revolution. In many cases, their assets were turned over to several *bonyads*, or para-statal foundations. The objective of the *bonyads* is ostensibly to help the disadvantaged,

worse than Judaism or Christianity. These theological differences have limited the ability of the revolution to spread among the majority Sunni Muslim population worldwide. Only in a few countries, such as Bahrain, Iraq, Lebanon, and Afghanistan, do Shiites exist in significant numbers.[17]

A second major obstacle to Iran's international vision was ethnicity. The obvious goal of Iranian revolutionary policy was to spread the revolutionaries' vision across the Middle East, helping to overthrow secular leaders, establish Islamic states, and drive out Western influence in the process. But Iranians are not Arabs. Just as the revolution had difficulties speaking in terms of one Islam, it could not speak in terms of one Middle Eastern people. Here, too, Iran was the outlier. This status was only reinforced by the Iran-Iraq War, in which Iran relied in part upon nationalistic fervor to maintain public support, and Iraq's Arab (albeit Shiite) majority sided with their government against Iran. Although Iran failed to serve as the lodestar for revolution, many of the ideas and symbols of the revolution influenced a wave of political conflict, beginning with the war in Afghanistan in 1980 and continuing through the emergence of Al Qaeda. Though many Islamist terrorist groups view Shiism as heretical, they owe much of their ideological justification for violence to the Islamic Revolution and the Shia tradition of martyrdom.

Over the past 20 years, Iranian relations with the outside world, particularly the West, have oscillated between reconciliation and conflict. In the late 1990s, President Mohammad Khatami actively sought to improve international relations, speaking of a "dialogue of civilizations" in contrast to a "clash of civilizations." Greater domestic liberalization and an easing of tensions led to more international contact, in areas ranging from diplomatic relations and civil society to Western tourism. In addition, the terrorist attacks on the United States in 2001 and the invasion of Afghanistan on Iran's border also seemed to provide an opportunity for engagement. While President George W. Bush spoke of Iran as part of an "Axis of Evil," the Iranian government also strongly opposed the Taliban in Afghanistan (who were hostile to that country's Shia population) and their old nemesis Saddam Hussein, who had invaded Iran in 1980.

However, both domestic and international factors brought Iranian-Western rapprochement to an end. In spite of Khatami's call for improved relations, the supreme leader and many others inside the state were opposed to better relations with the United States, which they had long viewed as the "Great Satan." This limited the extent to which the Iranian president could realize his foreign policy. Second, Iran's ongoing pursuit of nuclear technology (discussed in the "Current Issues" section, p. 514) became of increasing concern after 2001, when many leaders in the international community began to worry that such technology could be transferred to terrorist or other nonstate actors. This led to increased pressure on Iran from the international community, heightening tension. Third, the election of President Ahmadinejad further changed the tenor of relations with the outside world, as Ahmadinejad took a more confrontational line, using nuclear technology as a symbol of national pride while simultaneously taking a more openly hostile tone toward Israel. Fourth, the U.S. invasion of Afghanistan and Iraq, and hostile rhetoric from the U.S. government, convinced many Iranian leaders that they were the next to be targeted—and that only a nuclear threat would deter U.S. aggression.

Iran now finds itself in a complicated international situation. At one level, its influence in the international community is greater now than perhaps at any time since 1979. Its ongoing pursuit of nuclear technology has raised its profile dramatically and generated international concern and debate over how best to engage it. In addition, while the U.S.-led invasions of Afghanistan and Iraq put the "Great Satan" on Iran's border, difficulties in both conflicts have given Iran much greater leverage than many expected. Indeed, early in the Iraq and Afghanistan wars, some observers expected that Iran would be next in the wave of regime change, with these invasions either prompting revolution inside Iran or paving the way for an invasion of Iran itself. Instead, American forces became bogged down in long-term conflicts. The Iraq War in particular seemed to play directly into Iran's hands. Not only was Saddam Hussein eliminated, but the war brought into power the majority Shiite population, who had long been under the thumb of the Sunni minority. Shiite exile groups in Iran returned to Iraq and quickly dominated politics, while domestic Shiite insurgents appeared to benefit from Iranian funding and training, inflicting heavy casualties on U.S. and coalition forces. This shift in power, combined with the nuclear standoff and growing Iranian influence in places such as Lebanon, Syria, and the Palestinian Territories, has led some commentators to speak of an emerging "Shia Crescent" of power across the region that threatens the West and Sunni Arabs alike.

In reality, the situation is more complex. Iran's increased international profile has won it some support among the Muslim world and beyond, but its nuclear program has also isolated it from much of the international community. The Arab Spring revolutions in the Middle East have also made Iran less relevant to the region, not more so. In the past, people across the Middle East could be inspired by 1979, even if the result was not necessarily what they wanted to emulate. While the Iranian government has sought to portray the Arab Spring as a culmination of 1979, in reality it means that Arab states now have their own models for removing dictatorships and building new regimes. It may be more accurate to say that Iran is more isolated now, and has less to offer ideologically,

A banner at Friday prayers, Tehran University, with a quote from Ayatollah Khomeini. Anti-Americanism remains a key facet of the Iranian regime, making diplomatic relations difficult at best.

than at any time since 1979. This does not mean the regime is in danger of collapse anytime soon. But it does mean that confrontation, rather than engagement, is one of the few tools Iran can still use to bolster its claim that the Islamic Revolution still matters.

CURRENT ISSUES IN IRAN

The Nuclear Program

One of the most critical issues confronting the international community at present is Iran's apparent nuclear weapons program. How this issue is resolved will have profound repercussions, and any solution will be complicated by Iranian domestic politics.

Before we go any further, we should recall the difference between a nuclear energy program and a nuclear weapons program. There are similarities but also important differences. In both cases, it is necessary to process, or "enrich," natural uranium, separating the uranium atoms with different numbers of neutrons (isotopes). Natural and low-enriched uranium is made up mostly of U-238 isotopes, with only a small amount composed of U-235—the fissile isotopes, or those that can sustain a chain reaction. Commercial nuclear programs enrich natural uranium to about 20 percent U-235 in order to create nuclear fuel. At this low level of enrichment, uranium can be fashioned into fuel rods, which can then be placed in a nuclear reactor to generate electricity. Weapons-grade uranium, however, requires enrichment of up to around 90 percent U-235. In other words, while peaceful nuclear programs require enriched uranium, this stockpile can be further enriched to produce a nuclear weapon. This distinction is not simply a matter of degree. Enriching uranium up to weapons grade is a major project, requiring a huge number of sophisticated centrifuges operating far beyond what is necessary for nuclear fuel. Once uranium is enriched to weapons grade, the next challenge is turning that uranium into an actual device small enough that it can be fitted onto a missile.

Even before the 1979 revolution, as part of an extensive plan to develop nuclear energy for peaceful purposes, Iran also showed interest in developing a nuclear weapon. This work was mostly halted by the revolution, the Iran-Iraq War, and international sanctions. By the early 1990s, however, Iran sought to actively restart its nuclear program, mining uranium and reaching out to various countries (such as Pakistan and North Korea) for technology and assistance in such areas as centrifuge technology. These developments began to raise alarms in the international community, and the International Atomic Energy Agency (IAEA) requested access to Iranian nuclear facilities to determine the ultimate purpose of these sites. Cooperation with the IAEA has been sporadic, as has been Iran's program. Evidence indicates that Iran has built a wide array of centrifuges, and has developed a parallel program to master the intricacies of building an actual weapon. According to observers, Iran is continuing to work on enrichment and weaponization, and already has enough low-enriched uranium that it could convert into one or more nuclear bombs. Related development in missile technology (provided in part by North Korea) has also given Iran an increasingly long reach, with the potential to strike Israel. Iran may be on the path to becoming a "virtual" nuclear state, meaning that it would have the capacity to make a bomb within a matter of months if it chose to do so.[18]

What does this mean and where do we go from here? Over the past decade there have been both international negotiations and sanctions to halt Iran's nuclear program. A diplomatic breakthrough foundered on Iran's refusal to cede control over its uranium stockpile or its right to enrichment. In return, the international community placed increasingly restrictive sanctions on Iran, limiting trade and other economic opportunities meant to harm the Iranian economy and deprive the government access to needed technology. This, unfortunately, also served to strengthen the position of actors such as the Revolutionary Guard, who benefit from the sanctions by developing their own smuggling networks and illicit economic activities. In addition, international actors have relied on espionage to slow down Iran's nuclear program. Best known is the Stuxnet computer virus, which was designed (by either the United States or Israel, or perhaps both) to attack Iran's centrifuge system. Several assassinations against top nuclear specialists in Iran also appear to have been the work of the United States or Israel. In the most optimistic assessment, such actions, combined with ongoing technical difficulties, make the Iranian nuclear threat a number of years off.

Some observers are less sanguine on this issue. Israel has long been worried about Iran's nuclear capacity, given the latter's frequent statements that the state of Israel is illegitimate. In Israel there has been an ongoing debate over whether military strikes should be used to destroy known Iranian nuclear facilities, especially given the assumption that the United States is unlikely to use this option. There is a precedent for such a strike: in 1981, Israel bombed a nuclear reactor under construction in Iraq, and destroyed a covert reactor project in Syria in 2007. And while Israel has few friends in the Middle East, it is clear that a number of Arab states also favor this option. According to a U.S. diplomatic cable published on Wikileaks, the king of Saudi Arabia called on the United States in 2008 to attack Iran's nuclear program and thus "cut off the head of the snake."[19] This is neither easy nor risk-free. First, Iran has anticipated such an attack, burying parts of its nuclear program deep underground and in various, often secret, locations. Second, it has threatened to unleash a major response to any military strike, against not just Israel but also the United States and European countries; this could include acts of terrorism. Israel itself is armed with nuclear weapons, and there are fears that such strikes and counterstrikes could escalate. Third, there is no strong belief that any attack would actually be able to bring Iran's nuclear program to a halt.

It is not certain what could resolve this impasse. Iranian agreement to greater international oversight is one clear option, but given recent political turmoil in Iran, it is unlikely that the supreme leader or those around him would be interested in any deal that showed them to be weak. Dramatic political change in Iran, along the lines of the Arab Spring, would open the door to new negotiations, though such change now seems more unlikely than ever. Further sanctions may bring the Iran government to the table or simply cause it to dig in its heels. The only thing that appears certain is that there is no obvious way for the international community to stop Iran's work on a nuclear weapon.

Alcohol and Drugs in the Islamic Republic

Alcohol and drugs have a long history in Iran. Iranian pre-Islamic history is associated with wine production, and Sufi poets such as Rumi draw frequent parallels between love and drunkenness. It is also from Iran that we get the word *assassin*, or "hashish taker," which was coined to describe a twelfth-century political and religious group, split off from Shiism, that targeted and killed a number of Sunni political leaders. (Opponents of the group claimed that its followers' fanaticism was drug-induced.) Opium, too, has a long Iranian pedigree. Many Iranian monarchies, especially the Qajar dynasty of the nineteenth century, are remembered for the drug use of their shahs (and for their prodigious consumption of wine). But such intoxicants are forbidden in Islam. Iran has veered back and forth between trying to restrict intoxicants and accepting them as an inescapable part of modern society.

In 1979, the Islamic Republic reversed the more permissive attitude that had characterized Iran over the past century, ushering in a prohibitive regime, among the strictest in the Middle East. Alcohol was banned, with limited exceptions for the country's non-Muslim minorities, such as Christians and Jews. The government also cracked down on opium, heroin, hashish, and other drugs. Penalties for drug and alcohol use were severe, including jail time, lashings, and even execution for drug and alcohol dealers. Several hundred dealers are currently on death row, and an unknown number have been executed of late—perhaps a majority of those executed in recent years.

In spite of this pressure, drug and alcohol use continues in Iran, and has perhaps even grown over time. In the case of alcohol, the destruction of Iran's own industry has simply given rise to a large smuggling network. Since the invasion of Iraq and the opening of borders between Iraq and Iran, large amounts of alcohol are brought illegally into the country, and it is easy to purchase. According to one survey, a majority of Iranian college students consumes alcohol. While this may be overstated, it is worth noting that for many young people, alcohol may be attractive particularly because of its symbolism as part of a "Western" lifestyle that the regime opposes.

As a public health concern, however, drug addiction is a far bigger problem. According to the United Nations, Iran has more than a million drug-dependent

A banner warning of the dangers of drug addiction in Sarein, Iran.

users, one of the most severe addiction problems in the world. As with alcohol, this, too, has a regional source, with drugs coming in from Pakistan and Afghanistan (the latter being the biggest producer of opium in the world). As a result, Iran has the highest rate of opium, heroin, and morphine seizures in the world, and nearly 4,000 police officers have been killed over the past three decades in counternarcotics operations. Many of these drugs only transit Iran, with Europe as their final destination. The Iranian government thus sees this issue as much as a function of Western cultural and political imperialism as a domestic problem.

In spite of what we might imagine, the Islamic Republic does not pretend that the drug problem does not exist. Realizing that severe punishments have little effect on drug users, the government has taken steps to increase the number of treatment and rehabilitation facilities. This is a rather liberal policy, more akin to that seen in Europe. However, it may reflect less a nuanced approach to drug abuse than a realization that drug addiction is such an enormous problem that punishments will have little effect. One wonders whether the social repression under the Islamic Republic is a main driver of drug addiction in Iran, or if this is a more intractable cultural problem that will remain unaffected by any future political changes.[20]

NOTES

1. Michael Axworthy, *A History of Iran: Empire of the Mind* (New York: Basic Books, 2008).

2. For a discussion of Shiism in Iran and elsewhere, see Heinz Halm, *Shi'ism* (New York: Columbia University Press, 2004), and Moojan Momen, *An Introduction to Shia Islam* (New Haven, CT: Yale University Press, 1985).

3. For a discussion of this period and the increasing U.S. influence in Iranian politics, see Kenneth M. Pollack, *The Persian Puzzle: The Conflict Between Iran and America* (New York: Random House, 2004).

4. Stephen Kinzer, *All the Shah's Men: An American Coup and the Roots of Middle East Terror* (New York: John Wiley and Sons, 2003).

5.   Ali M. Ansari, "The Myth of the White Revolution: Mohammad Reza Shah, 'Modernization,' and the Consolidation of Power," *Middle Eastern Studies* 37, no. 3 (July 2001): 1–24.

6.   Ruhollah Khomeini, *Islamic Government* (Tehran: Institute for Compilation and Publication of Imam Khomeini's Works, n.d.); see also Karen Armstrong, *The Battle for God* (New York: Alfred A. Knopf, 2000).

7.   For an analysis of these events, see Charles Kurzman, *The Unthinkable Revolution in Iran* (Cambridge, MA: Harvard University Press, 2004).

8.   From International Constitutional Law, www.servat.unibe.ch/icl/ir__indx.html (accessed 11/10/11).

9.   Kian Tajbakhsh, "Political Decentralization and the Creation of Local Government in Iran: Consolidation or Transformation of the Theocratic State?" *Social Research* 67, no. 2 (Summer 2000), and Hossein Alekajbaf and Jayum A. Jawan, *Decentralization and Local Government in Iran* (Shah Alam, Indonesia: Karisma Publications, 2009).

10. Frederic Wehrey et al., *The Rise of the Pasdaran: Assessing the Domestic Roles of Iran's Islamic Revolutionary Guards Corps* (Santa Monica, CA: RAND Corporation, 2009), www.rand.org/pubs/monographs/MG821 (accessed 11/11/11).

11. Reporters Without Borders Press, Freedom Index 2010, http://en.rsf.org/press-freedom-index-2010,1034.html (accessed 11/11/11).

12. "Iran: Human Rights Abuses Against the Kurdish Minority," Amnesty International, 2008.

13. A good discussion of different political values and positions in Iran can be found in Ray Takeyh, *Guardians of the Revolution: Iran and the World in the Age of the Ayatollahs* (New York: Oxford University Press, 2009).

14. Jalal Al Ahmad, *Weststruckness*, trans. John Green and Ahmad Alizadeh (Costa Mesa, CA: Mazda, 1997).

15. Shayerah Ilias, "Iran's Economic Conditions: U.S. Policy Issues," Congressional Research Service, June 15, 2009. http://fpc.state.gov/documents/organization/127284.pdf (accessed 2/10/12).

16. Djavad Salehi-Isfahani and Daniel Egel, "Youth Exclusion in Iran: The State of Education, Employment and Family Formation," Middle East Youth Initiative Working Paper, December 12, 2007, www.brookings.edu/papers/2007/09_youth_exclusion_salehi_isfahani.aspx (accessed 2/10/12).

17. A nuanced discussion of the role of Shia politics in the region can be found in Vali Nasr, *The Shia Revival* (New York: W. W. Norton, 2007).

18. For details, see "Implementation of the NPT Safeguards Agreement and the Relevant Provisions of Security Council Resolutions in the Islamic Republic of Iran," International Atomic Energy Agency, November 8, 2011, www.iaea.org/Publications/Documents/Board/2011/gov2011-69.pdf (accessed 2/10/12).

19. David E. Sanger, James Glanz, and Jo Becker, "Around the World, Distress over Iran," *New York Times*, November 28, 2010.

20. Roland Elliot Brown, "Chasing the Dragon in Iran," *Foreign Policy*, November 18, 2011; Faraz Sanei, "Don't Praise Iran's War on Drugs," Human Rights Watch, August 5, 2011, www.hrw.org/news/2011/08/05/don-t-praise-iran-s-war-drugs (accessed 2/10/12).

KEY TERMS

Ahmadinejad, Mahmoud Current president of Iran, as of 2005

Ashura The most important Shia religious holiday, commemorating the death of Hussein, the grandson of the prophet Muhammad

Assembly of Experts Elected body that chooses the supreme leader

ayatollah In Shiite Islam, a title in the religious hierarchy achieved by scholars who have demonstrated highly advanced knowledge of Islamic law and religion

Basij "People's militia," which serves as a public morals police

bonyads Para-statal foundations made in part from assets nationalized after the Iranian Revolution

chief justice Head of the judiciary

Expediency Council Appointed body that mediates between the Majlis and the Guardian Council over legislative disputes

Farsi Language of Iran

Guardian Council Appointed body that vets candidates for office and can overturn legislation

imams descendants of Prophet Muhammad considered by Shia to be true political and religious leaders of Islam

Iran-Iraq War The 1980–1988 conflict between the two countries, started by Iraq

Islamic Republic of Iran Name for postrevolutionary Iran

Islamism, or Islamic fundamentalism The belief that Islam should be the source of the political regime

Khamenei, Ali Current supreme leader of Iran, as of 1989

Khatami, Mohammad President of Iran from 1997 to 2005

Khomeini, Ruhollah First supreme leader of Iran, from 1980 to his death in 1989

Koran Central holy book of Islam

Mahdi In Shiism, a term for the "hidden imam," the descendant of Muhammad who will to return to earth to usher in a new age

Majlis Legislature of Iran

Mosaddeq, Mohammad Prime Minister of Iran; deposed in 1953 by Operation Ajax

Muhammad Main prophet of Islam

National Front Political party in Iran following World War II; it opposed the monarchy and favored greater Iranian control over natural resources; outlawed after Operation Ajax

Operation Ajax U.S.- and UK-backed overthrow of Iranian prime minister Mosaddeq in 1953

Pahlavi, Reza Shah Monarch of Iran from 1925 to 1941

Persia Name for Iran before 1935

quietist Description of view within Shiism that rejects theocracy and the direct role of religion in the state

Rafsanjani, Akbar Hashemi President of Iran from 1989 to 1997, current head of the Expediency Council

Revolutionary Guard Paramilitary force charged with defending the regime from domestic and internal enemies

SAVAK Secret police of prerevolutionary Iran

Second Khordad Front Reformist party that emerged in Iran to contest 2000 Majlis elections

Sharia Religious law of Islam

Shiism Minority sect of Islam that differs with Sunnism over the proper descendants of the prophet Muhammad

supreme leader Chief spiritual and political leader of Iran

theocracy Rule by religion or religious leaders

ummah Literally, "community"; meant to refer to nation or Islamic community everywhere

velayat-e faqih Rule by Islamic jurists; also, Islamic Republic's political system, which places power in the hands of clerics

White Revolution Policy of reforms enacted by Reza Shah, beginning in 1963, to rapidly modernize and Westernize Iran

WEB LINKS

Iran Daily (www.iran-daily.com)
Islamic Republic News Agency (www.irna.com/en)
Ministry of Foreign Affairs, Islamic Republic of Iran (www.mfa.gov.ir)
Press TV (www.presstv.ir/)
U.S. Institute for Peace (www.usip.org/countries-continents/asia/iran)
Web site of the Supreme Leader Ayatollah Khamenei (www.leader.ir)

 Visit StudySpace for quizzes and other review material.
www.norton.com/studyspace
- **Vocabulary Flashcards of All Key Terms**
- **Country Review Quizzes**
- **Complete Study Reviews and Outlines**

11

**HEAD OF STATE
AND GOVERNMENT:**
President
Felipe Calderón
Hinojosa (since
December 1, 2006)

CAPITAL:
Mexico City

TOTAL LAND SIZE:
1,964,375 sq km (15th)

POPULATION:
115 million (11th)

GDP AT PPP:
$1.56 trillion (11th)

**GDP PER CAPITA
AT PPP:**
$13,900 (84th)

**HUMAN DEVELOPMENT
INDEX RANKING:**
56th

Tijuana
BAJA
CALIFORNIA
NORTE
Baja California
Ciudad
Juárez
Sierra Madre Mountains
Monterrey
Torreón
San Luis
Potosí
León
Guadalajara
MÉXICO
MEXICO
CITY
Veracruz
Puebla
Mérida
MICHOACÁN
GUERRERO
Oaxaca
OAXACA
CHIAPAS
Acapulco

MEXICO

MEXICO

Introduction

Why Study This Case?

For over eight decades, stability was the feature that differentiated Mexico's political system from that of most of its Latin American neighbors and from its own turbulent pre-1917 history. Unlike the political atmosphere of most other developing countries, Mexico's post-1917 politics was relatively peaceful: power was transferred between leaders after regular elections, and the military was thoroughly subordinate to civilians. This stability resulted from a highly effective and remarkably flexible semi-authoritarian regime dominated by a single party, the Partido Revolucionario Institucional (PRI). That model delivered impressive rates of economic growth but also produced an economy plagued by severe economic inequality and massive poverty.

In July 2000, the PRI's long tenure came to a sudden end, marking the start of a new era in Mexican politics. The decline of the PRI's political hegemony began in the early 1980s, when the Mexican economy narrowly averted bankruptcy. In response to a severe economic crisis, the PRI leadership started to dismantle the prevailing protectionist and statist economic model. Mexico opened up its economy to the world and began a transition to a neoliberal political economy. It quickly became one of Latin America's most open economies. The hallmark of this new era was Mexico's 1994 entry into the **North American Free Trade Agreement (NAFTA)** with the United States and Canada.

The economic crises of the 1980s and '90s (and the PRI's response to them) created new sources of political opposition, and the party's power was seriously threatened for the first time in 70 years. In 1988, the PRI resorted to massive fraud to avoid losing the presidency, and it increased the use of fraud to prevent the opposition from taking control of state legislatures. In January 1994, armed

Mayan peasants shocked Mexicans when they seized control of a southern Mexican town. In March of that year, the PRI's presidential candidate was assassinated while campaigning for office, the first such political murder since 1928. There were allegations that the murder had been ordered by members of the governing party, and the inability of the government to solve the crime added to a sense of crisis. The emergence of a strong political challenge to the PRI, the presence of an armed guerrilla movement, and a high-profile political murder destroyed the image of Mexico's system as stable and peaceful.

The political turmoil was alarming to Mexicans and Americans alike. Participation in NAFTA only ratified a growing (but highly asymmetrical) interdependence between the U.S. and Mexican economies. Mexico and the United States share a 2,000-mile border, and Mexican immigration to the United States has long provided a steady stream of labor that is vital to the U.S. economy. In addition, the United States is the chief consumer of Mexico's oil exports, and Mexico is now the United States' third-biggest trading partner, after Canada and China.

After two decades of political and economic crisis, the July 2000 victory of **Vicente Fox**, the first non-PRI president since 1917, provided new hope for Mexico's future, even as it raised new questions. Fox took power vowing to shake up the Mexican system but soon discovered that the PRI's loss of the presidency had not given him a blank check to institute reform. The PRI maintained strongholds of political power in a variety of federal and state political institutions. The hotly contested elections of July 2006 revealed that six years after its democratic transition, Mexico was deeply polarized between left and right. The conservative **Felipe Calderón** won a razor-thin victory over a leftist candidate who was critical of free trade and whose main priority was to address Mexico's endemic poverty. The election was so close that Calderón's opponent, Andrés Manuel Lopéz Obrador, demanded a recount, launched a legal challenge to the results, and refused to concede to his opponent. As president, Calderón waged a war against Mexico's increasingly powerful drug cartels that unleashed a wave of violence that has traumatized Mexican society and raised serious questions about the power of the Mexican state.

Our study of Mexico will raise several important questions: What have been the consequences of of Mexico's transition to democracy and its embrace of a neoliberal economic model? Has democracy been able to address Mexico's endemic corruption? Has Mexico's embrace of a neoliberal economic model been a success, or has it merely exacerbated inequality and worsened poverty? How has the Mexican government dealt with the rising violence caused by the drug trade with the United States? What have been the consequences for Mexico of sharing a border with the most powerful country in the world?

Major Geographic and Demographic Features

Mexico's stunningly diverse geography includes tropical rain forests, snowcapped volcanoes, and rich agricultural regions. Historically, the two major mountain ranges that divide Mexico, the eastern and western Sierra Madres, have made transportation and communication difficult. Only 12 percent of Mexico's land is arable, and the most productive agricultural areas are in northern Mexico, close to the U.S. border. There, large and highly mechanized export farms provide much of America's winter produce. The proximity of Mexico's agricultural export to the U.S. market has been a major boost to Mexico's economic growth. Agriculture in southern Mexico is characterized by smaller farms and less efficient production. Mexico is well endowed with minerals and has major oil reserves.

With 114 million people, Mexico has the second-largest population in Latin America (after Brazil). Its population is racially quite diverse: about 60 percent are **mestizos**, people of mixed Spanish and indigenous blood; another 30 percent, living primarily in the central and southern parts of the country, are considered indigenous because they speak an indigenous language. The largest indigenous groups are the **Maya**, located in Mexico's far south (along the Guatemalan border), and the **Nahuatl**, concentrated in central Mexico. On Mexico's Caribbean coast is a large population of African descent.

Nearly three-quarters of Mexico's population lives in an urban setting, a relatively recent change. Mexico City has dwarfed all other Mexican cities: it now has about 18 million residents. Population growth has slowed with economic development, but Mexico's large population still strains the country's resources. As a result, Mexicans still migrate in very large numbers. Many have left the impoverished countryside for the cities, often leaving the poor south for the wealthier north, especially the factory towns along the U.S. border. At the same time, a steady stream of Mexicans has migrated across the border to the United States.

Historical Development of the State

The history of the modern Mexican state can be viewed as a struggle between political order, which has almost always been achieved by authoritarian rulers, and periodic outbursts of violence and political anarchy.[1]

When the Spanish conquistador **Hernán Cortés** arrived in Mexico in 1519, he encountered well-established and highly sophisticated indigenous civilizations.

The country had long been home to such peoples as the Maya, Aztecs, and Toltecs, who had relatively prosperous economies, impressive architecture, sophisticated agricultural methods, and powerful militaries. Within three years of their arrival, the Spanish conquerors had defeated the last Aztec leader, **Cuauhtémoc**; destroyed the impressive Aztec capital, Tenochtitlán; and decimated the indigenous population. By the early seventeenth century the indigenous population had been reduced from about 25 million to under 1 million. The surviving indigenous peoples of Mexico, concentrated in the central and southern parts of the country, became a permanent underclass of virtual slaves and landless peasants.

The Aztec Empire was replaced by the equally hierarchical, authoritarian, and militaristic Spanish Empire, which created a legacy very different from that imparted to the United States by British colonialism. Mexico was the richest of Spain's colonial possessions (indeed, it was far richer at the time than Britain's territories to the north), and Spain ruled the distant colony with an iron fist, sending a new viceroy to the colony every four years. Colonial viceroys were absolute dictators: armed with the terror of the Spanish Inquisition, they were able to stamp out most political dissent. Without any civilian oversight, rampant corruption thrived in the colonial administration.

INDEPENDENCE AND INSTABILITY: THE SEARCH FOR ORDER

The struggle for independence can be viewed as a conflict over control of the state between the aristocracy loyal to Spain and the increasingly powerful and wealthy **criollos** (Mexican-born descendants of the Spanish colonists). Though inspired by the French and American revolutions, the Mexican independence movement was mostly a response to the sudden blow that Napoleon's invading armies delivered to Spain. When Spain adopted a progressive-liberal constitution in 1812, conservative Mexican elites accepted independence as the only means by which to preserve order and the status quo. The leading rebels and political conservatives agreed that an independent Mexico, declared in 1821, would preserve the role of the Catholic church and implement a constitutional monarchy with a European at the head. **Mexico's War of Independence** was extremely violent, lasting 11 years and costing over half a million lives.

Mexico's independence was dominated by political conservatives who sought to preserve the economic and social status quo. As a result, independence did nothing to alleviate the poverty of Mexico's indigenous people and its large mestizo population. Indeed, the violence of the War of Independence and the elimination of the minimal protections of the Spanish Crown worsened their plight.

TIMELINE OF POLITICAL DEVELOPMENT

YEAR	EVENT
1810–21	War of Independence fought against Spain
1846–48	One-half of Mexico's territory lost in war with the United States
1910–17	Mexican Revolution takes place
1917	Revolutionary constitution adopted
1929	Official revolutionary party created, later becoming the PRI
1934–40	Presidency of Lázaro Cárdenas, during which land reform is promoted, the oil industry is nationalized, and the state is given a larger role in the economy
1939	The PAN formed as a conservative opposition to the revolution
1968	Student protest movement against the Mexican government violently repressed
1981–82	Economic collapse caused by sudden drop in oil prices and Mexico's inability to pay its foreign debt
1988	President Carlos Salinas de Gortari assumes power after elections widely viewed as fraudulent
1994	NAFTA put into effect
	Zapatistas, indigenous peasants in the southern state of Chiapas, rebel
	PRI presidential candidate Luis Donaldo Colosio assassinated while campaigning; replaced by Ernesto Zedillo
2000	PAN candidate Vicente Fox elected, marking the first defeat of the PRI in 71 years
2006	Felipe Calderón begins a six-year term as president

The power of the large landholders, or *latifundistas*, grew with independence, and the newly independent Mexico became more unequal and and politically unstable. Much of the turmoil and political chaos that plagued Mexico over the next half-century was caused by a dispute between conservatives, who wanted to maintain a monarchy, and liberals who wanted a U.S.-style democracy. With the

policies were unable to address the persistence of massive poverty in Mexico, and the more recent shift to neoliberal policies has only increased the gap between rich and poor. In 2008, the poorest 40 percent of the population earned about 12 percent of Mexico's income, while the wealthiest 10 percent earned about 40 percent, and the gap has not changed significantly since the 1980s.[29] *Forbes* magazine listed 24 Mexicans in its 1994 annual report on the "swelling roster of global billionaires." Only the United States, Germany, and Japan had more billionaires at the time. In 2011, *Forbes* listed 10 Mexicans as billionaires, including the world's wealthiest individual, entrepreneur and media mogul Carlos Slim.[30]

Poverty continues to be a serious problem for Mexico, despite significant improvements in the last two decades. Between 1992 and 2008, extreme poverty declined from about 21 percent to about 18 percent of the population, and the overall poverty rate dropped from 53 percent to 47 percent.[31] Poverty in Mexico is most pronounced in rural areas, still home to some 23 million people. Despite the legacy of land reform, most rural Mexicans cannot support themselves on their tiny plots of land, and many are forced to seek work as migrant laborers. Millions have migrated to already overcrowded urban areas, seeking employment and a better life, and millions more have emigrated to the United States for the same reasons.

Mexico's wealth is also geographically unequal. Northern Mexico is far wealthier than the central and southern regions. While the north is characterized by large-scale export agriculture (benefiting from proximity to the U.S. market), land use is much more fragmented in the south. Southern Mexico has a far poorer infrastructure, lower levels of education, and more poverty.

Another indicator of the degree of inequality in Mexico is the tremendous size and importance of the **informal sector**. It is estimated that well over one-quarter of the labor force is employed in the underground economy as informal vendors of goods and services, producing about 13 percent of the Mexico's GDP. Mexican cities are full of *ambulantes* (street vendors), which local governments have fought unsuccessfully to regulate. These workers pay no taxes on their earnings but enjoy few protections or benefits.

Efforts to redress these inequalities through increased social spending have been hampered by Mexico's inability to collect taxes, especially when compared with wealthier industrialized countries. Attempts to raise taxes meet with widespread skepticism in part because Mexico's traditionally corrupt state is simply not trusted.

Despite the myriad problems facing Mexico's economy, we would be remiss if we failed to point out the biggest change in Mexico's political economy over the last two decades. Since its recovery from the economic crisis of the mid-1990s, and under the presidencies of Zedillo, Fox, and Calderón, about half of Mexico's

CORRUPTION AS A WAY OF LIFE

The return of democracy in Mexico has brought greater transparency to some aspects of Mexican society, and has reduced corruption in some areas (such as elections), but corruption remains a signal characteristic of Mexican society.[*] Since 2001, Transparency International has been surveying Mexican households, asking them about the bribes, known in Mexico as *la mordida* (or the bite), they pay for everyday life.[†] Thirty-five types of public services were surveyed, including obtaining welfare payments, getting connected to a water or electrical supply, arranging for garbage pickup, dealing with the court system, getting a vehicle license, applying for a scholarship, dealing with a traffic cop, and obtaining a passport. The 2010 report found that households were paying bribes in about 10 of every 100 cases when accessing public services, and that the percentage has been rising since 2007. The value of those bribes in 2010 was estimated at about $3 billion, representing an informal 14 percent tax on the average household's yearly income. The dimensions of the continuing problem of corruption and the government's dire attempts to address it are exemplified by the case of Veracruz. In December 2011, the Veracruz state government fired the city's entire police force which had long been viewed as corrupt. The police force was temporarily replaced by the members of the Mexican Navy.

[*] Stephen Morris, *Political Corruption in Mexico: The Impact of Democratization* (Boulder, CO: Lynne Reinner, 2009).
[†] www.transparency.org/news_room/latest_news/press_releases_nc/2011/11_05_11_mexico_survey_corruption_worse (accessed 7/8/11).

population has entered the middle class. Several factors are responsible for this dramatic shift.[32] First, economic stability since the mid-1990s, and especially the containment of inflation, has benefited the middle class. Second, government antipoverty programs have kept many Mexicans from falling out of the middle class. Finally, Mexico's entry into NAFTA has created a more competitive economy, lowering prices of food and consumer goods for Mexicans.

Foreign Relations and the World

Mexico's foreign relations have always been heavily molded by the country's complex relationship with the United States. In the political turmoil of the nineteenth century, Mexico lost half its territory to an expanding United States. Indeed,

Mexico's humiliation at U.S. hands has been a major theme in the Mexican psyche. Even Porfirio Díaz, whose dictatorship promoted closer ties to the United States, is reported to have lamented, "Poor Mexico! So far from God and so close to the United States." One goal of the Mexican Revolution (and the aim of much of its official rhetoric) was to restore the sovereignty and power of Mexico on the global stage. The Partido Revolucionario Institucional (PRI) leadership clearly sought a system that would restore stability to the Mexican system and prevent future attacks on Mexican sovereignty. In the early years of the revolution, foreign economic interests were sharply curtailed and foreign oil companies were nationalized. Mexico under the PRI began to assert itself as an independent and autonomous state, gradually gaining the status of a regional power within Latin America.

During and after World War II, Mexico became a closer ally of the United States while still asserting an independent voice in its foreign policy. From the 1960s through the 1980s, it opposed U.S. foreign policy in Latin America, fostered a close relationship with Fidel Castro's Cuba (a U.S. archenemy), and supported revolutionary movements in the regions that often opposed the United States.

Many Mexicans were proud that their country could act so independently of the United States in the arena of foreign policy. However, the economic catastrophe of the 1980s and Mexico's decision to abandon revolutionary economic policies and liberalize its economy made clear the limits of Mexican independence in foreign affairs. In exchange for massive economic aid in the 1980s, Mexico was pressured to curtail its opposition to U.S. foreign policy in Latin America. The peso crisis of the mid-1990s only further served to emphasize Mexico's fundamental dependence on the United States.

After the election of Vicente Fox in 2000, Mexico moved closer to the United States on most foreign policy issues. Fox sought to work closely with President George W. Bush, in the hope of gaining new agreements on immigration and trade. Since NAFTA, Mexico's increased economic dependence on the United States has clearly limited its international assertiveness. However, this did not stop the Fox administration from opposing the U.S. invasion of Iraq in 2003, a stance that led to a cooling of U.S.-Mexican relations. Immediately after taking office in 2009, the U.S. administration of Barack Obama took steps to improve relations with Mexico and collaborate to stem growing drug violence in Mexico.

Though Mexico and the United States have grown closer since the end of PRI rule, the relationship remains, in the words of *The Economist*, "exquisitely sensitive," a reflection no doubt of the gigantic gap between the two partners' power.[33] Mexicans continue to resent what they view as heavy-handed intervention in Mexican domestic affairs, and unfair treatment. These feelings are well illustrated by some recent conflicts between the two neighbors. In 2009, a U.S. military report raised the specter that Mexico could become a failed state, which created an angry diplomatic response from Mexican officials, and prompted U.S. Secretary of State Hillary Clinton to travel to Mexico in order to calm the crisis. In March 2011, the U.S. ambassador to Mexico was forced to resign after cables released by WikiLeaks quoted him as questioning the Mexican government's strategy in the drug war. In July 2011, the United States finally agreed to allow Mexican trucks to carry shipments within the United States, a provision of NAFTA that the United States had refused to honor for 17 years. For years, Mexico expressed frustration with the United States's refusal to honor such commitments, and in 2001 it imposed over $2 billion in retaliatory tariffs on imported U.S. goods.

CURRENT ISSUES IN MEXICO

Mexico's Drug War: Can the Mexican State Contain Organized Crime?

The Mexican Revolution successfully strengthened state power and autonomy and ended endemic violence in Mexico. Yet the long domination of the PRI, its dependence on patron-client relations, its co-optation, and its electoral fraud all helped perpetuate a culture of corruption and lawlessness that now increasingly threatens the state and its capacity, autonomy, and legitimacy.

Over the past two decades, Mexico has seen an alarming rise in drug trafficking, driven by the growing market for illegal drugs north of the border and facilitated by a Mexican legal system that is both weak and corrupt. Mexico has experienced a dramatic growth of drug-related violence and a steady stream of corruption scandals involving drug money. The drug cartels are well funded, heavily armed, and often protected by local police forces. They intimidate local governments and have brutally executed politicians, police, and journalists who stand in their way. A series of investigations in 2008 implicated federal antidrug officials in the drug trade and further damaged the government's image.

A map of the areas controlled by Mexico's drug cartels. Much of Mexico is plagued by drug crime.

Shortly after his inauguration, President Calderón called on the army to combat the cartels, and in 2009 he sent troops to replace corrupt local police forces in some cities along the U.S. border. The military response only emboldened the drug cartels, who initiated a campaign of assassination aimed at the police and antidrug authorities. The United States has been alarmed by the growing drug traffic across the U.S.-Mexican border: it is estimated that about 70 percent of all marijuana and cocaine entering the United States arrives through Mexico. U.S. attempts to undertake antinarcotics operations in Mexico have been attacked as abridging Mexico's sovereignty, and U.S. criticism of Mexico's lackluster antinarcotics efforts has often raised tensions between the two neighbors. Mexican officals counter that drug cartels take advantage of lax U.S. gun control laws to purchase most of their weapons north of the border. In 2009, the Obama administration acknowledged that Mexico's drug wars are a shared problem and vowed to work with Mexico to address the threat.

By 2011, the drug war had claimed an alarming 40,000 victims, and the number of killings has grown rapidly. Almost 90 percent of those deaths have been execution-style killings. In some areas the rise in violent deaths has been dramatic. For example, Ciudad Juárez, on the U.S. border, had a 2010 murder rate of 229 per 100,000 inhabitants, making it more dangerous than Kandahar (Afghanistan) or Bagdhad (Iraq).[34] It is important to point out that much of the violence has been isolated in several areas and has not touched most Mexicans. It is estimated that the vast majority of killings have occurred in only 3 percent of the country's municipalities.[35] The Calderón administration can boast of the arrest of a number of top drug cartel leaders over the last few years, but there is a vigorous debate in Mexico about whether the drug war is being or ever can be won.[36] Opinion polling in 2011 suggested that Mexican voters, while generally supportive of the effort to erradicate the drug cartels, were increasingly skeptical about Calderón's ability to stop the violence. In July 2011, the president's approval rating dipped below 50 percent. Former president Vicente Fox, a member of the president's conservative PAN, called for the legalization of drugs as the most effective method of combatting organized crime.

Human Rights: Another Victim of the Drug War?

While most attention in Mexico has been focused on the battle between the Mexican state and drug traffickers, there has been growing concern about the impact of that conflict on human rights. Mexico has never had a professional, reliable police force, with corruption particularly rampant at the state and local level.[37] As a result, President Calderón relied on the armed forces to carry out his war against drug gangs. However, with the increased reliance on the military have come thousands of allegations of human rights abuses against civilians.

In November 2011, the nongovernmental organization Human Rights Watch (HRW), published a report entitled "Neither Rights Nor Security: Killings, torture and disappearances in Mexico's 'war on drugs.'" The HRW report was compiled after two years of field work by researchers, and its harsh conclusions only served to heighten the debate within Mexico about the war on drug traffickers unleashed by President Felipe Calderón.

According to the HRW report, "members of the security forces systematically use torture to obtain forced confessions and information about criminal groups. And evidence points to the involvement of soldiers and police in extrajudicial killings and enforced disappearances around the country."[38] The report was especially critical of the Mexican military, noting the "lack of impartiality and independence that results when the military investigates itself."[39] Since 2007, the military has investigated over 3,600 allegations into military human rights abuses against civilians, with only 15 soldiers (less than one half of 1 percent) being convicted. HRW called for allegations of military abuse against civilians to be investigated in the civilian justice system, rather than within the military, a view that has been echoed by Mexico's Supreme Court.

Overall, the HRW report argues that President Calderón should have reformed Mexico's law enforcement system and judiciary before launching a war against Mexican drug gangs. It claims that by increasing the law enforcement role of the unaccountable Mexican military, Calderón has weakened the rule of law in Mexico.

Calderón responded to the report by blaming criminals, not the government or army, for the decline in human rights and the increase in violence. "They are the ones who by committing serious crimes such as murder, kidnapping and extortion, systematically violate the rights of citizens and their families."[40] The governing party has rejected the conclusions of HRW, arguing that the government and the military have meticulously respected human rights, and that the government and military have reacted positively to complaints lodged by the National Human Rights Commission.[41]

In November 2011, 14 soldiers were sentenced to lengthy jail terms for firing on a family in 2007, killing two women and three children, an outcome that both defenders and critics of the military viewed as support for their positions.[42]

Migration

There is a long history of Mexicans emigrating across the 2,000-mile U.S.-Mexico border. Mexicans have long argued that the United States depends on Mexican immigrants and that the latter's right to work in the United States should be guaranteed through bilateral agreements. But many Americans have focused on the negative effects of Mexican immigration to the United States. Why has there been such a steady flow of Mexicans into the United States? Most of them come because of the higher standard of living in the United States, although the first wave of immigrants, in the early twentieth century, were also fleeing the violence of the Mexican Revolution. During the severe labor shortages of World War II, the United States established the **Bracero Program**, which allowed more than 4 million Mexicans to work temporarily in the United States between 1942 and 1964. Today, there are almost 11 million Mexicans living in the United States

The Importance of Foreign Remittances to the Mexican Economy

Do you receive money from relatives living abroad? Percentage answering yes:

COUNTRY	PERCENTAGE
Nigeria	38
Mexico	23
Russia	7
India	6
South Africa	5
Brazil	2
China	1

Source: Pew Center for the People and the Press, 2007.

(about 10 percent of Mexico's total population and 4 percent of the U.S. population). According to some estimates, the amount of foreign remittances sent to Mexico by Mexicans living outside the country has grown to almost $20 billion annually, making it the largest single source of foreign exchange (even larger than revenue earned from oil exports).[43]

From 1965 to 1986, an estimated 5.7 million Mexicans immigrated to the United States, of whom 81 percent were undocumented.[44] The United States operated a de facto guest-worker program, whereby border enforcement was tough enough to prevent a flood of immigration but not so strict as to prevent a steady flow of cheap and undocumented labor. The costs of illegal immigration were raised just enough that only about one in three undocumented Mexicans could be caught and returned. Most immigrants who tried to enter the United States succeeded, although not on the first try. The U.S. attempt to enforce border control was largely symbolic, but it never threatened the availability of cheap labor. The dramatic growth of undocumented Mexican immigrants, especially after the economic crisis in Mexico during the early 1980s, became a political crisis in the United States during the 1980s and '90s. The result was the 1986 U.S. **Immigration Reform and Control Act (IRCA)**, which imposed sanctions on employers of illegal aliens and toughened the enforcement of immigration laws.

At the same time, it provided an amnesty for longtime undocumented workers and legalized about 2.3 million Mexican immigrants. In the late 1990s, however, illegal immigration continued to skyrocket. In 2006, the U.S. administration of George W. Bush proposed tougher border controls as well as measures aimed at giving legal status to more Mexicans living in the United States.

The issue of migration continues to be a sore point in the relationship between Mexico and the United States. President Bush's promise to overhaul U.S. immigration policy fell victim to a changed U.S. domestic political atmophere after the attacks of 9/11. The policies of some U.S. states aimed at curtailing illegal emigration from Mexico have exacerbated the tensions. By 2011, a growing Mexican economy, a continuing recession in the United States, tighter border patrols, and a worsening atmosphere in the United States for Mexican immigrants had led to a reduction in the rate of illegal border crossings. However, it is a near certainty that immigration will continue to be a point of contention between the United States and Mexico for years to come.

NOTES

1. For a good overview of the development of the Mexican state, see Alan Knight, "The Weight of the State in Modern Mexico," in James Dunkerley, ed., *Studies in the Formation of the Nation State in Latin America* (London: Institute of Latin American Studies, 2002), pp. 212–52.
2. Quoted in www.libertyhaven.com/countriesandregions/latinamerica/mexicomyths.shtml (accessed 7/25/05).
3. For the best English-language overview, see Luis Carlos Ugalde, *The Mexican Congress: Old Player, New Power* (Washington, DC: Center for Stategic and International Studies, 2000).
4. Ugalde, *The Mexican Congress*, p. 146.
5. Jodi Finkel, "Judicial Reform as Insurance Policy: Mexico in the 1990s," *Latin American Politics and Society* 47, no. 1 (Spring 2005): 87–111.
6. Jorge Castañeda, *Mañana Forever? Mexico and the Mexicans* (New York: Alfred A. Knopf, 2011), p. xvi.
7. Wayne Cornelius, Todd Eisenstadt, and Jane Hindley, eds., *Subnational Politics and Democratization in Mexico* (San Diego, CA: Center for U.S.-Mexican Studies, 1999), and R. Andrew Nickson, *Local Government in Latin America* (Boulder, CO: Lynne Reinner, 1995), pp. 199–209.
8. Pamela Starr, "Fox's Mexico: Same As It Ever Was?" *Current History*, February 2002, p. 62.
9. Kathleen Bruhn, *Taking on Goliath: Mexico's Party of the Democratic Revolution* (University Park, PA: Penn State University Press, 1997).
10. Kathleen Bruhn, "López Obrador, Calderón, and the 2006 Electoral Campaign" in Jorge Domínguez et al., eds., *Consolidating Mexico's Democracy* (Baltimore, MD: Johns Hopkins University Press, 2009), pp. 169–88.
11. For a good overview, see Chappell Lawson, "Fox's Mexico at Midterm," *Journal of Democracy* 15 (2004): 339–50.

12. Joseph Klenser, "Electoral Competition and the New Party System in Mexico," paper presented at the annual meeting of the Latin American Studies Association, Washington, DC, September 6–8, 2001, and Joseph Klesner, "A Sociological Analysis of the 2006 Elections," in Domínguez et al., eds., *Consolidating Mexico's Democracy*, pp. 50-70.

13. D. Xavier Medina Vida et al., "Partisan Attachment and Democracy in Mexico: Some Cautionary Observations," in *Latin American Politics and Society* 52, no. 1 (January 2010): 68.

14. An outstanding edited volume on the 2006 presidential elections is Domínguez et al., eds. *Consolidating Mexico's Democracy*.

15. Joseph L. Klesner, "Who Participates? Determinants of Political Action in Mexico," *Latin American Politics and Society* 51, no. 2 (Summer 2009): 59–90.

16. Alberto J. Olvera, "The Elusive Democracy: Political Parties, Democratic Institutions, and Civil Society in Mexico," *Latin American Research Review* (Special Issue, 2010): 79–107.

17. Castañeda, *Mañana Forever?*, p. 9.

18. Castañeda, *Mañana Forever?*, p. 12.

19. Alan Riding, *Distant Neighbors* (New York: Vintage, 1989), p. 199.

20. Three excellent overviews are Tom Hayden, ed., *The Zapatista Reader* (New York: Thunder's Mouth Press, 2002); Lynn Stephen, *Zapata Lives: Histories and Cultural Politics in Southern Mexico* (Berkeley: University of California Press, 2002); and Chris Gilbreth and Gerardo Otero, "Democratization in Mexico: The Zapatista Uprising and Civil Society," *Latin American Perspectives* 28, no. 4 (July 2001): 7–29.

21. "The Democratic Routine" in *The Economist*, December 4, 2010, p. 61.

22. In 2009, 72 percent of Mexicans expressed little or no interest in politics, according to the Latinobarómetro survey, www.latinobarometro.org (accessed 7/6/11).

23. In the 2009 Latinobarómetro survey, 14.7 percent of Mexicans rated themselves as either 1, 2, or 3, on a 10-point scale where 1 was the most left and 10 was the most right. See www.latinobarómetro.org (accessed 7/6/11).

24. Andy Baker, "Regionalized Voting Behavior and Political Discussion in Mexico" in Domínguez et al., eds. *Consolidating Mexico's Democracy*, pp. 71–88.

25. Paul Cooney, "The Mexican Crisis and the Maquiladora Boom: A Paradox of Development or the Logic of Neoliberalism?" *Latin American Perspectives* 28, no. 3 (May 2001): 55–83.

26. Rafael Tamayo-Flores, "Mexico in the Context of the North American Integration: Major Regional Trends and Performance of Backward Regions," *Journal of Latin American Studies* 33 (2001): 406.

27. Tamayo-Flores, "Mexico in the Context of the North American Integration," pp. 377–407.

28. Quoted in Nicolas Wilson, "What's Wrong with This Picture?" *Business Mexico* 4 (April 1997): 22.

29. World Bank, www.worldbank.org (accessed 12/17/11).

30. www.forbes.com/wealth/billionaires/list (accessed 12/17/11).

31. Castañeda, *Mañana Forever?*, p. 34.

32. See the discussion in Castañeda, *Mañana Forever?*, pp. 61–2.

33. "A State of Insecurity," *The Economist*, March 22, 2011, at www.economist.com/blogs/americasview/2011/03/mexican-american_relations (accessed 6/7/11).

34. Latin American Regional Reports: Mexico and NAFTA, February 2011, ISSN 1741-444, and Howard Campbell, "No End In Sight: Violence in Ciudad Juárez," in *NACLA Report on the Americas* 44, no. 2 (May/June 2011): 19–24.

35. *The Economist*, June 20, 2011.

36. A very critical view of the drug war is Jorge Castañeda, "What's Spanish for Quagmire?" in *Foreign Policy* 177 (January/February 2010): 1.

37. See an interview with George Grayson December 23, 2011, http://www.coha.org/professor-grayson-on-exico%e2%80%99s-drug-war/ (accessed 12/26/11).

38. www.hrw.org/reports/2011/11/09/neither-rights-nor-security (accessed 12/21/11), p. 5.

39. www.hrw.org/reports/2011/11/09/neither-rights-nor-security (accessed 12/21/11), p. 10.

40. Quoted in *Latin America Weekly Report*, November 10, 2011, ISSN 0143-5280, p. 11.

41. Lilia Saúl, "Pan discrepa con informe de Human Rights Watch," *El Universal,* www.eluniversal
     .com.mx/notas/808029.html (accessed 12/18/11).

42. "Mexico: 14 Soldiers Sentenced," *New York Times,* November 5, 2011, www.nytimes.
     com/2011/11/05/world/americas/mexico-14-soldiers-sentenced.html?_r=1&scp=1&sq=14%20
     Soldiers%20Sentence%20and%20Mexico&st=cse (accessed 2/21/12).

43. "Rise Reported in Remittances to Mexico," *Seattle Times,* April 15, 2005, p. A14.

44. Douglas Massey, Jorge Durand, and Nolan Malone, *Beyond Smoke and Mirrors: Mexican Immi-
     gration in an Era of Economic Integration* (New York: Russell Sage Foundation, 2002), p. 45.

KEY TERMS

Bracero Program A World War II program that allowed millions of Mexicans to work temporarily in the United States

caciques Local military strongmen, who generally controlled local politics in Mexico in nineteenth-century Mexico

Calderón, Felipe Mexico's current president, elected in 2006

camarillas Vast informal networks of personal loyalty that operate as powerful political cliques

Cárdenas, Lázaro The Mexican president from 1934 to 1940 who implemented a radical program of land reform and nationalized Mexican oil companies

Carranza, Venustiano The Mexican revolutionary leader who eventually restored political order, ended the revolution's violence, and defeated the more radical challenges of Zapata and Villa

caudillos National military strongmen, who dominated Mexican politics in the nineteenth and early twentieth centuries

Chamber of Deputies The lower house of Mexico's legislature

Confederation of Mexican Workers (CTM) Mexico's dominant trade union confederation, which was a main pillar of the PRI's authoritarian regime

Congress Mexico's bicameral legislature

Constitution of 1917 The document established by the Mexican Revolution that continues to regulate Mexico's political regime

Cortés, Hernán The Spanish conqueror of Mexico

criollos Mexican-born descendants of Spaniards during the period of Spanish colonial rule

Cuauhtémoc The Aztec military leader defeated by the Spanish conquerors

Díaz, Porfirio The Mexican dictator who ruled from 1876 to 1910 and was deposed by the Mexican Revolution

Federal District of Mexico City A powerful Mexican district, similar to the U.S. District of Columbia; encompasses Mexico's capital city and contains most of its population

Federal Electoral Institute An independent agency that regulates elections in Mexico; created in 1996 to end decades of electoral fraud

Fox, Vicente Mexico's president from 2000 to 2006 and the first non-PRI president in more than seven decades

Immigration Reform and Control Act (IRCA) U.S. immigration legislation (1986) that toughened American immigration laws while granting amnesty to many longtime undocumented workers

import substitution industrialization (ISI) The political economic model followed during the authoritarian regime of the PRI, in which the domestic economy was protected by high tarrifs in order to promote industrial growth

informal sector A sector of the economy that is not regulated or taxed by the state

Juárez, Benito The nineteenth-century Mexican president who is today considered an early proponent of a modern, secular, and democratic Mexico

Labastida, Francisco The first-ever PRI candidate to lose a presidential election; he was defeated in 2000 by Vicente Fox of the PAN

latifundistas Owners of *latifundia* (huge tracts of land)

López Portillo, José The Mexican president from 1976 to 1982; he increased the role of the state in the economy and nationalized Mexico's banking system in an attempt to avert a national economic crisis

Madero, Francisco An initial leader of the Mexican Revolution and a landowner who sought moderate democratic reform

maquiladoras Factories that import goods or parts to manufacture goods that are then exported

Maya Mexico's largest indigenous group, concentrated in the south of the country

mestizos Mexicans of mixed European and indigenous blood, who make up the vast majority of Mexico's population

Mexican-American War The conflict between Mexico and the United States (1846–48) in which the United States gained one-third of Mexican territory

Mexican miracle The spectacular economic growth in Mexico from the 1940s to about 1980

Mexican Revolution The bloody conflict in Mexico between 1910 and 1917 that established the long-lived PRI regime

Mexico's War of Independence A bloody 11-year conflict that resulted in Mexico's independence from Spain in 1821

municipios County-level governments in Mexican states

Nahuatl Mexico's second-largest indigenous group, concentrated in central Mexico

North American Free Trade Agreement (NAFTA) A trade agreement linking Mexico with the United States and Canada

Partido Acción Nacional (PAN) A conservative Catholic Mexican political party that until 2000 was the main opposition to the PRI

Partido de la Revolucion Democrática (PRD) Mexico's main party of the left

Partido Revolucionario Institucional (PRI) The political party that emerged from the Mexican Revolution to preside over an authoritarian regime that lasted until 2000

patron-client relationships Relationships in which powerful government officials deliver state services and access to power in exchange for the delivery of political support

PEMEX Mexico's powerful state-owned oil monopoly

San Andrés Peace Accords A 1996 agreement that promised to end the Zapatista rebel uprising but was never implemented by the PRI government

de Santa Anna, General Antonio López Mexico's first great *caudillo*, who dominated its politics for three decades in the mid-nineteenth century

Secretary of Government A top cabinet post that controls internal political affairs and was often a stepping-stone to the presidency under the PRI

Secretary of the Treasury Mexico's most powerful economic cabinet minister

Senate The upper house of Mexico's legislature

Supreme Court Mexico's highest court

Televisa Mexico's largest media conglomerate, which for decades enjoyed a close relationship with the PRI

Villa, Francisco (Pancho) A northern Mexican peasant leader of the revolution who, together with Emiliano Zapata, advocated a more radical socioeconomic agenda

War of the Castes A massive nineteenth-century uprising of Mexico's indigenous population against the Mexican state

Zapata, Emiliano The southern Mexican peasant leader of the revolution most associated with radical land reform

Zapatista Army of National Liberation (EZLN) A largely Mayan rebel group that staged an uprising in 1994, demanding political reform and greater rights for Mexico's indigenous people

Zedillo, Ernesto Mexico's president from 1994 to 2000. He implemented political reforms that paved the way for fair elections in 2000

WEB LINKS

El Universal, a Mexican daily newspaper (http://english.eluniversal.com)

La Jornada, a Mexican daily newspaper (www.jornada.unam.mx)

Latin American Network Information Center, Mexico, an encyclopedic collection of links maintained by the University of Texas, Austin (www.lanic.utexas.edu/la/mexico)

Mexican government offices and agencies (www.mexonline.com/mexagncy.htm)

Reforma, a Mexican daily newspaper (www.reforma.com)

Zapatista Army of National Liberation (www.ezln.org.mx)

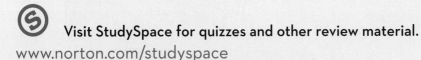 **Visit StudySpace for quizzes and other review material.**

www.norton.com/studyspace

- **Vocabulary Flashcards of All Key Terms**
- **Country Review Quizzes**
- **Complete Study Reviews and Outlines**

12

**HEAD OF STATE
AND GOVERNMENT:**
President
Dilma Rousseff
(since January 1, 2011)

CAPITAL:
Brasília

TOTAL LAND SIZE:
8,514,877 sq km (5th)

POPULATION:
203 million (5th)

GDP AT PPP:
$ 2.8 trillion (7th)

GDP PER CAPITA AT PPP:
$10,800 (103rd)

**HUMAN DEVELOPMENT
INDEX RANKING:**
73rd

Manaus
Amazon R.
Belem
Belo Monte
Hydroelectric
project
Teresina
Fortaleza
Rio
Branco
*Amazon River
Basin*
Recife
*SALVADOR
DE BAHIA*
Salvador
BRASÍLIA ★
*MINAS
GERAIS*
Belo
Horizonte
*SÃO
PAULO* São
Paulo
RIO DE JANEIRO
Rio de Janeiro
Curitiba
*RIO GRANDE
DO SUL*
Porto
Alegre
BRAZIL

BRAZIL

Introduction

Why Study This Case?

When Brazil successfully launched a rocket into space in October 2004, it became the first Latin American country to do so. Brazil has ambitious plans to sell rockets to the European Space Agency, adding to its already impressive list of high-tech exports. Brazil's successful entry into space exemplifies its greatest paradox. It is the seventh-largest economy in the world, with a dynamic industrial sector. It has strikingly modern cities, such as São Paulo and Rio de Janeiro. Recently, Brazil's export-based economy has boomed, and its economic prospects seem limitless with the 2008 discovery of large offshore oil reserves. According to the International Monetary Fund, Brazil will soon have a larger economy than the United Kingdom, and is poised to become the sixth largest economy in the world.[1] But it is also plagued by some of the worst poverty, inequality, and indebtedness on the planet, and its cities are burdened by sprawling slums and violence. One Brazilian economist dubbed Brazil **Belindia** to denote this odd combination of Belgium's modernity and India's underdevelopment.[2]

Brazil is a highly urbanized society, with over 80 percent of its population living in its cities (six of which have more than 2 million residents), but about half of its land consists of the sparsely populated **Amazon Basin**. The Amazon rain forest is often considered to be the lungs of the world, and its rapid destruction has become a major focus for environmentalists. Within Brazil, the Amazon has until recently been viewed most often as a rich resource that needs to be more efficiently exploited to help reduce inequality and poverty and to enhance Brazil's *grandeza* (national greatness).

Given Brazil's history of extreme inequality and endemic poverty, one might expect it to have experienced a mass revolution along the lines of Russia, Mexico, and China. At the very least, one might have assumed a history of political violence similar to that of South Africa during apartheid. But while violence has punctuated its history, Brazil has avoided cataclysmic revolutions or civil war. For over 150 years following its independence from Portugal in 1822, Brazil alternated between weak democratic regimes dominated by economic elites and authoritarian rule, usually presided over by the military. From 1964 to 1985, a military dictatorship quashed a growing mass movement and suspended most political freedoms. Nevertheless, Brazil experienced a gradual and remarkably peaceful transition to a more effective democracy in the mid-1980s, and today it is the world's fourth-largest democracy. Brazilian democracy is characterized by regular elections and broad civil liberties and has enabled a peaceful succession of power. In 2002, Brazilians elected a leftist president, **Luiz Inácio Lula da Silva**, known popularly as Lula, Brazil's first working-class president (see "The Legacy of Lula," p. 579). Despite fears surrounding his election, democracy has proved remarkably durable, Brazil's economy has boomed, and da Silva was re-elected to a second term in 2006. His political heir, **Dilma Rousseff**, was elected as Brazil's first female president in 2010, in Brazil's sixth democratic election since the end of military rule.

Despite this admirable political record, serious questions still remain about the long-term viability of Brazilian democracy. Can a democratic regime persist when there are extraordinarily high levels of economic inequality? Will the growing wave of crime and lawlessness erode confidence in democracy and the rule of law? Will Brazil's legacy of statism, clientelism, corruption, and political deadlock prevent democratic reforms?

Brazil is a fascinating case in part because of its relatively successful multiracial society. It has the largest African-origin population outside Africa. Despite a brutal history of slavery that lasted until relatively recently (ending in 1888) and persistent racism and race-based inequality, race has not yet polarized Brazilian politics. Nevertheless, recent attempts to redress the legacy of discrimination against Afro-Brazilians have been extremely controversial, and threaten to shatter the myth of Brazil's racial harmony.

Endowed with a gigantic and geographically insulated country and blessed with formidable natural resources, Brazilians have a strong sense of national identity that makes Brazil unlike many of its Latin American neighbors. Buoyed by its dynamic economy and its growing global influence, Brazilians feel increasingly proud of their country, a mood that has only been enhanced by Brazil's successful bid to host the 2014 FIFA World Cup and the 2016 Olympic Games.

Perceived Corruption, 2010

COUNTRY	SCORE	RANK
Germany	7.9	15
Japan	7.8	17
United States	7.1	22
United Kingdom	7.1	20
France	6.8	25
South Africa	4.5	54
Brazil	3.7	69
China	3.5	78
India	3.3	87
Mexico	3.1	98
Nigeria	2.4	134
Iran	2.2	146
Russia	2.1	154

Note: On a scale of 1 to 10, 1 = most corrupt; 10 = least corrupt

Source: Transparency International, www.transparency.org/policy_research/surveys_indices/cpi/2010 (accessed 9/8/11).

President Rousseff took power vowing to attack government corruption, but in her first year in power seven of her cabinet ministers were forced to resign over allegations of corruption, including her ministers of the presidency (her chief of staff), defense, and labor.

There are many possible explanations for the persistence of corruption in Brazilian politics, but many scholars blame the Brazilian electoral system, which favors a proliferation of weak parties in the legislature and a low level of accountability for individual legislators.

The Environment versus Economic Development

In an era of growing concern about global warming, increasing attention has been paid to the rapid deforestation of the Amazon rain forest, about 60 percent of which lies within Brazil's borders. Environmental limits on development in the Amazon have long been controversial for Brazilians, many of whom view the region as a key to their country's economic development and who resent being told by foreigners how they should manage the rain forest. In the 1960s and '70s, the Brazilian military operated under the motto "occupy so as not to surrender"— suggesting that colonization and development of the Amazon would guarantee Brazilian sovereignty over it.

The election of President da Silva, who proclaimed himself to be Brazil's first green president, was thus viewed as a watershed event. In power, however, his government bitterly disappointed environmentalists while angering pro-development forces. Upsetting the latter, Lula appointed Marina Silva, a lifelong advocate of rain forest preservation, as environment minister. The government established more than 60 forest reserves, putting vast tracts of forest off-limits to development. Laws against illegal logging were more effectively enforced. Brazil proposed a plan in which the international community would pay Brazil to preserve the area.

Yet environmentalists argued that deforestation actually increased during the da Silva administration, and they noted that forest preserves were created that could not be policed. They warned that agricultural interests increasingly dominated policy making, too readily yielding to pressure by powerful governors of pro-agricultural states. Marina Silva resigned as environment minister in 2008, to protest what she viewed as insufficient government support for environmental protection. She ran for president in 2010 as the candidate for the Green Party, winning almost 20 percent of the vote in the first round.

While Dilma Rousseff has pushed for policies to stem the deforestation of the Amazon, she oversaw a major rural electrification program as energy minister during President da Silva's first term. She became a strong advocate for the controversial Belo Monte Hydroelectric Dam, which would be the world's third-largest dam (after Brazil's Itaipu and China's Three Gorges dams). The project has drawn criticism from environmental and indigenous rights groups because it will flood 500 square kilometers of land and displace 20,000 mostly indigenous Brazilians.

The PT governments of da Silva and Roussef have always been torn by the struggle among ministers who hold very different environmental agendas. The legislative coalition supporting those governments includes many who favor more rapid development of the Amazon in order to promote agricultural exports. The rapid rise in agricultural commodity prices in 2008, which allowed the da Silva government to spend lavishly on very popular social programs, may have tilted the balance within the administration toward those who favor economic development over environmental protection.

Confronting Brazil's Authoritarian Past

As we have seen in this chapter, Brazil is unique within the context of Latin America in many ways, including its history, language, size, and its vast natural resources. As in many Latin American countries, democracy in Brazil emerged after military rule during which numerous human rights violations occurred. However, unlike Argentina, Chile, Peru, Uruguay, and others, Brazil has never formally attempted to account for and reckon with human rights violations during the 1964–1985 military regime.

In her first year as president, Dilma Rousseff created a truth commission which will spend two years investigating human rights violations during military rule. While the commission will investigate those abuses, military members are currently protected from prosecution by an amnesty law passed in 1979, when the military was still in power.

Brazil's military has long resisted attempts to examine its human rights record. President Lula da Silva abandoned his attempt to establish a truth commission when the heads of each of Brazil's three military branches threatened to resign in protest. Brazil's military has also resisted the latest attempt to come to terms with human rights violations. One top military official, accused of playing a role in torturing political prisoners, has sued to block the convening of the truth commission.[40] Some advocates for the victims of military rule have also opposed the truth commission because they feel it doesn't go far enough, and won't lead to prosecution of human rights violators. They hope that they can challenge the amnesty law, as has been done successfully in some other Latin American countries.

The debate over Brazil's military past was rekindled in December 2011, when a 1970 photograph surfaced of President Rousseff being interrogated by the military that had arrested and tortured her.

NOTES

1. "Brazilian economy overtakes UK's, says CEBR," www.bbc.co.uk/news/business-16332115 (accessed 1/4/12).

2. Marshall Eakin, *Brazil: The Once and Future Country* (New York: St. Martin's Press, 1998), p. 1.

3. Binka Le Breton, *Voices from the Amazon* (Hartford, CT: Kumarian Press, 1993).

4. For an excellent overview, see Alfred Stepan, ed., *Authoritarian Brazil* (New Haven, CT: Yale University Press, 1973).

5. The first attempt to document the abuses under military rule was conducted secretly by the Catholic Church and published as a book titled *Brazil, Never Again*, or *Brasil: Nunca Mais* (São Paolo: Archdiosis of São Paolo, 1985). It became an instant best-seller.

6. A number of prominent political scientists have argued that presidentialism has not served Brazil's relatively young democracy well because it is less flexible and responds less well to crises. See, for example, Juan Linz, "Presidential or Parliamentary Democracy: Does It Make a Difference?" in Juan Linz and Arturo Valenzuela, eds., *The Failure of Presidential Democracy* (Baltimore, MD: Johns Hopkins University Press), pp. 3–87.

7. In 1997, President Fernando Henrique Cardoso was able to push a constitutional amendment through the legislature that allows presidents and state governors to run for a second term. Cardoso became the first president to avail himself of that opportunity and was re-elected in 1998.

8. Scott Mainwaring, "Multipartism, Robust Federalism, and Presidentialism in Brazil," in Scott Mainwaring and Matthew Soberg Shugart, eds., *Presidentialism and Democracy in Latin America* (New York: Cambridge University Press, 1997), pp. 55–109.

9. Bolivar Lamounier, "Brazil: An Assessment of the Cardoso Administration," in Jorge Dominguez and Michael Shifter, eds., *Constructing Democratic Governance in Latin America* (Baltimore, MD: Johns Hopkins University Press, 2003), p. 281.

10. Angelina Cheibub Figueiredo and Fernando Limongi, "Congress and Decision-Making in Democratic Brazil," in Maria D'Alva Kinzo and James Dunkerley, eds., *Democratic Brazil: Economy, Polity, and Society* (London: Institute of Latin American Studies, 2003), pp. 62–83.

11. Juan Linz and Alfred Stepan, "Crises of Efficacy, Legitimacy, and Democratic State Presence: Brazil," in Juan Linz and Alfred Stepan, eds., *Problems of Democratic Transition and Consolidation* (Baltimore, MD: Johns Hopkins University Press, 1996), pp. 166–89.

12. Latínobarometro, online data analysis available at www.latinobarometro.org/latino/LAT AnalizeQuestion.jsp (accessed 6/24/11). On the Brazilian judiciary, see Fiona Macaulay, "Democratization and the Judiciary: Competing Reform Agendas," in Maria D'Alva Kinzo and James Dunkerley, eds., *Brazil Since 1985: Economy, Polity, and Society* (London: Institute of Latin American Studies, 2003), pp. 93–6.

13. Latínobarometro, online data analysis available at www.latinobarometro.org/latino/LAT AnalizeQuestion.jsp (accessed 6/24/11).

14. In 1989 the vote of one citizen of Roraima, a poor northern state, was the equivalent of 33 votes in São Paulo, Brazil's largest state. Timothy Power, "Political Institutions in Democratic Brazil," in Peter Kingstone and Timothy Power, eds., *Democratic Brazil: Actors, Institutions, and Processes* (Pittsburgh, PA: University of Pittsburgh Press, 2000), p. 27.

15. Scott Mainwaring, "Multipartism, Robust Federalism, and Presidentialism in Brazil," in Mainwaring and Shugart, *Presidentialism and Democracy in Latin America*, pp. 55–109.

16. David Samuels, *Ambition, Federalism, and Legislative Politics in Brazil* (Cambridge, UK: Cambridge University Press, 2003). See p. 161, on spending levels of federal and state governments.

17. Wendy Hunter, *Eroding Military Influence in Brazil: Politicians Against Soldiers* (Chapel Hill: University of North Carolina Press, 1997), pp. 42–71.

18. Anthony Pereira, "An Ugly Democracy?: State Violence and the Rule of Law in Postauthoritarian Brazil," in Kingstone and Power, *Democratic Brazil*, pp. 217–35.

19. Scott Mainwaring and Timothy Scully, "Introduction: Party Systems in Latin America," in Scott Mainwaring and Timothy Scully, eds., *Building Democratic Institutions: Parties and Party Systems in Latin America* (Stanford, CA: Stanford University Press, 1995), pp. 1–35.

20. A comparative survey in 1997 found that Brazil had the lowest level of party identification in Latin America. See J. Mark Payne, Daniel Zovatto, Fernando Cavillo-Flórez, and Andrés Allamand Zavala, *Democracies in Development: Politics and Reform in Latin America* (Washington, DC: Inter-American Development Bank, 2002), p. 136.

21. Scott Mainwaring, *Rethinking Party Systems in the Third Wave of Democratization: The Case of Brazil* (Stanford, CA: Stanford University Press, 1999), pp. 140–5.

22. On the Workers' Party, see William Nylen, "The Making of a Loyal Opposition: The Worker's Party (PT) and the Consolidation of Democracy in Brazil," in Kingstone and Power, *Democratic Brazil*, pp. 126–43.

23. Leslie Armijo, Philippe Faucher, and Magdalena Dembinska, "Compared to What? Assessing Brazil's Political Institutions," *Comparative Politics* 39, no. 6 (2006): 759–86.

24. Latínobarometro online data analysis, based on a 2008 survey, www.latinobarometro.org/latino/LATAnalizeQuestion.jsp (accessed 6/24/11).

25. On the MST, see Miguel Carter, "The Landless Rural Workers Movement and Democracy in Brazil," in *Latin America Research Review* 45 (Special Issue 2010): 186–217.

26. A good overview of race relations is Bernd Reiter and Gladys Mitchell, eds., *Brazil's New Racial Politics* (Boulder, CO: Lynne Reinner, 2010).

27. Jon Jeter, "Affirmative Action Debate Forces Brazil to Take Look in the Mirror," *Washington Post*, June 16, 2003, p. A1.

28. João Feres Júnior, Verônica Toste Daflon, and Luiz Augusto Campos, "Lula's Approach to Affirmative Action and Race," in *NACLA Report on the Americas* 44, no. 2 (March/April 2011): 34–5.

29. Rodrigo Davies, "Brazil Takes Affirmative Action in Higher Education," *The Guardian*, August 4, 2003, p. 4.

30. As reported in *The Economist*, December 2, 2010, www.economist.com/node/17627929 (accessed 6/24/11).

31. Based on 2008 survey data from Latinobarómetro, www.latinobarometro.org/latino/LAT AnalizeQuestion.jsp (accessed 6/24/11).

32. Timothy Power and J. Timmons Roberts, "The Changing Demographic in Context," in Kingstone and Power, *Democratic Brazil*, p. 246.

33. Data on extreme poverty were downloaded from Instituto de Pesquisa Econômica at ipeadata.gov.br. Data on overall poverty reduction appear in Aaron Ansell, "Brazil's Social Safety Net Under Lula," in *NACLA Report on the Americas* 44, no. 2 (March/April 2011): 23–26.

34. For an excellent overview, see Fábio Veras Soares, Rafael Perez Ribas, and Rafael Guerreiro Osório, "Evaluating the Impact of Brazil's Bosla Familia: Cash Transfer Programs in Comparative Perspective" in *Latin American Research Review* 45, no. 2 (2010): 173–190.

35. Simone R. Bohn, "Social Policy and Vote in Brazil: Bolsa Família and the Shifts in Lula's Electoral Base," *Latin American Research Review* 46, no. 1 (January 2011): 54–79.

36. *The Economist* factsheet on Brazil, 2009, www.economist.com/node/13564342 (accessed 6/25/11).

37. As reported in *The Economist*, December 2, 2010, www.economist.com/node/17627929 (accessed 6/24/11).
38. A good overview of Brazilian foreign policy is Sean W. Burges, *Brazilian Foreign Policy After the Cold War* (Gainesville: University of Florida Press, 2009).
39. On corruption in Brazil, see Matthew M. Taylor, "Brazil: Corruption as Harmless *Jeitinho* or Threat to Democracy?" in Stephen D. Harris and Charles Blake, eds., *Corruption and Politics in Latin America* (Boulder, CO: Lynne Reiner, 2010), pp. 89–111.
40. Simon Romero, "An Uneasy Search for Truth as Ghosts from Military Rule Start to Stir," *New York Times*, December 20, 2011, www.nytimes.com/2011/12/21/world/americas/brazil-uneasily-searches-for-truth-on-military-rule-abuses.html?_r=1&scp=4&sq=Brazil&st=cse (accessed 12/26/11).

KEY TERMS

abertura The gradual opening of Brazilian politics by the military during the 1970s, a process that eventually led to democratization

Amazon Basin The vast and sparsely populated area of Brazil's interior that is home to the world's largest tropical rain forest

Belindia A term combining *Belgium* and *India*; used to describe Brazil's unique combination of modernity and underdevelopment

Bolsa Família (Family Fund) A Brazilian social welfare program that pays monthly stipends to families when their children receive education and health care

Brasília Brazil's futuristic capital city that was created in the barren interior in the 1960s by urban planners

BRICS An organization of emerging developing countries that includes Brazil, Russia, India, China, and South Africa

bureaucratic authoritarian A form of authoritarian rule common in Latin America during the 1960s and '70s (in Brazil, in 1964–85) in which military leaders and civilian technocrats presided over conservative, anti-Communist regimes

caboclo Brazilian of mixed European and indigenous ancestry

Cardoso, Fernando Henrique Brazil's president from 1995 to 2002, responsible for significant economic and political reform

Chamber of Deputies (Câmara dos Deputados) The lower house of Brazil's legislature

Christian base communities Small neighborhood groups of progressive Catholics who promoted liberation theology and political activism starting in the 1960s

da Silva, Luiz Inácio Lula Brazil's two-term president from 2003 to 2010, and a member of the leftist PT

Escola Superior de Guerra (Superior War College) The elite Brazilian military academy that professionalized the Brazilian military

Estado Nôvo The populist authoritarian regime of Getúlio Vargas between 1937 and 1945

favelas Brazil's sprawling urban shantytowns

Federal Senate (Senado Federal) The upper house of Brazil's legislature

Federal Supreme Court (Supremo Tribunal Federal) Brazil's highest judicial body

Goulart, João The Brazilian leftist president (1961–64) whose removal by the military began a long period of authoritarian rule

Landless Workers Movement (MST) The large Brazilian social movement that has fought for land reform

liberation theology A radical doctrine within the Catholic church advocating that the Church should act to improve the social and political power of the poor

MERCOSUR A free-trade organization that includes Brazil and some of its neighbors

mulatto A Brazilian of mixed white and black ancestry

National Congress (Congresso Nacional) Brazil's legislature

open-list proportional representation (PR) Brazil's electoral system for legislative elections in which voters may select individual candidates instead of a party list

populist A type of leader who appeals to the masses and attacks elements of the established elite; in Brazil, the term applies to Getúlio Vargas

robust federalism A system established by Brazil's current constitution in which states enjoy very strong power

Rousseff, Dilma, Brazil's current president (since 2011), and the first female president in Brazilian history

state corporatism A political system in which citizens are encouraged to participate in state-controlled interest groups

Vargas, Getúlio The Brazilian populist dictator who presided over the Estado Nôvo (1937–45) and was later elected to office during the Second Republic

Workers' Party (PT) Brazil's most important leftist party, and the party of former president da Silva

WEB LINKS

InfoBrazil, articles on Brazilian politics and current events (www.infobrazil.com)

IUPERJ, Programa de Pós-Graduação em Sociologia e Ciência Politica, Instituto Univeristário de Pesquisas do Rio de Janeiro, an excellent source of online data (www.iuperj.br/english/pesquisas_bancodedados.php)

Landless Workers Movement (www.mst.org.br)

Latin American Network Information Center, an encyclopedic collection of links maintained by the University of Texas, Austin (Brazil lanic.utexas.edu/la/brazil)

Links to major Brazilian periodicals (newslink.org/sabra.html)

The Workers' Party (www.pt.org.br)

⑤ Visit StudySpace for quizzes and other review material.
www.norton.com/studyspace

- Vocabulary Flashcards of All Key Terms
- Country Review Quizzes
- Complete Study Reviews and Outlines

13

**HEAD OF STATE
AND GOVERNMENT:**
President Jacob Zuma
(since May 9, 2009)

CAPITAL:
Pretoria is the seat of
government;
Cape Town
is the legislative
capital; Bloemfontein
is the judicial capital

TOTAL LAND SIZE:
1,219,090 sq km (25th)

POPULATION:
49 million (25th)

GDP AT PPP:
$527 billion (25th)

GDP PER CAPITA AT PPP:
$10,700 (104th)

**HUMAN DEVELOPMENT
INDEX RANKING:**
110th

SOUTH AFRICA

Introduction

Why Study This Case?

True to its remarkable modern history of tragedy and triumph, South Africa is a nation of paradoxes. The contradictions that constitute South African history and the remarkable capacity of South Africans to face and resolve them make this an intriguing case to study.

South Africa is fascinating for several other reasons as well. Like Russia, it in fact presents to students of comparative politics two cases in one. Prior to the early 1990s, South Africa's politics, society, and economy were dominated by the racist authoritarian system known as **apartheid**, or "separateness." In **Afrikaans**, the language spoken by the descendants of the first white settlers, the term refers to policies imposed by the ruling minority regime from 1948 to 1994 that systematically segregated races and privileged white South Africans. But with the collapse of the apartheid regime, the "new" South Africa of the past decade has been a fascinating Petri dish of unfolding multicultural democracy.

South Africa's remarkable and relatively peaceful transition from oppressive minority rule to a broad-based democracy is an even more compelling reason to study this case. Refuting the mid-1990s doomsday predictions of incendiary race wars, the overwhelming majority of South African citizens chose reconciliation over revolution, opting for ballots over bullets as a means of resolving seemingly intractable political differences. This political miracle not only stands in contrast to Africa's dismal record of failed democracies and even failed states, but also offers a powerful example to other nations of the world that are plagued by racial, ethnic, and religious strife.

South Africa has taken noteworthy strides since its return to democracy in 1994. Politically, its democratically elected legislature has written and revised a constitution with broad political rights and civil liberties, and its government has convened regular nationwide elections. Socially, South Africans vanquished the world's most elaborate and overtly racist authoritarian regime and forged a common nation from its ashes. Economically, the government confounded its critics by avoiding the "easy" path of populist redistribution, instead cutting government expenditures and debt while delivering impressive gains in access to basic necessities for the country's poorest citizens. South Africa's rising international profile was evidenced when, in 2010, it became the first African country to host the FIFA World Cup and again, in 2011, when it became a member of the group of rising developing powers known as **BRICS** (Brazil, Russia, India, China, and South Africa).

Make no mistake, however; this tale of two South Africas cannot yet boast a fairy-tale ending. The decades of political violence, social partition, and economic deprivation that victimized over 80 percent of the population left some horrible and lasting scars. Compounding the legacies of racism and authoritarianism is a host of pernicious social problems, such as rampant violent crime, brooding racial tension, and the pandemic of HIV/AIDS. As if these challenges were not enough, the remarkable regime change created unmet expectations for rapid economic change and social equality, and there are concerns that democracy has been successful only because the post-apartheid government faces no serious opposition.

South Africa's leaders must attempt to satisfy rising expectations and must balance decades of pent-up social and economic demands with the requirements of lenders and investors to maintain fiscal discipline and free markets. Without economic growth, the government will lack the very means to address South Africa's social and economic problems. The political temptation to promote affirmative action in the workplace must be weighed against the demands of the marketplace. Safeguarding the political rights of all groups in South Africa can at times necessitate overruling the will of the dominant black majority and resisting the temptation to dispense with democratic niceties.

How can the current government (or any government, for that matter) fare under such challenging circumstances? As one editorial asked, "How can a black revolutionary movement, forged by 40 years of struggle against white supremacy, transform itself into a multiracial ruling party, to run a sophisticated industrial economy? How can a new generation of leaders, without the aura of struggle, restrain the pressures towards populism and maintain a tolerant democracy when so many African governments have so noticeably failed?"[1] This case seeks to address these questions and the historical puzzle of why apartheid, enforced by such a small minority, managed to persist so successfully for so long and how its collapse and replacement came about under relatively peaceful circumstances.

Despite its unique history and political experience, South Africa faces many of the same issues and dilemmas as other developing countries. These include coping with the legacies of colonialism and racism, dealing with the policy trade-offs between freedom and equality, and managing the social and economic consequences of crime, poverty, and disease. The case of South Africa offers insights into these fundamental issues.

Major Geographic and Demographic Features

Historically, South Africa has been a harsh and isolated region. Ocean currents and the dearth of natural harbors impeded early European settlement of its coastline. Much of western South Africa (with the notable exception of the area around Cape Town) remains drought stricken and unsuitable for agriculture. South Africa's eastern coast and interior are subtropical and more suitable to agriculture, though the quality of the soil is generally poor. South Africa has no navigable waterways, a fact that until modern times made transportation and communication over the vast region very difficult. These factors limited the growth of a large population in precolonial South Africa.

Today, South Africa has about 49 million inhabitants. Unlike much of the rest of Africa, South Africa has seen its birth rates decline dramatically over the past 25 years, though considerable population growth is still created by emigration from South Africa's impoverished neighbors. Due to the experience of apartheid, it is common to think of South Africa's population as being neatly divided between blacks and whites. This gross simplification obscures a much more heterogeneous ethnic makeup. Three-quarters of South Africans are black, but the ethnic composition of the black population is extremely diverse. About one-quarter of black South Africans are Zulus (the ethnic group of current president **Jacob Zuma**), another one-fifth are Xhosa (the ethnic group of former presidents **Nelson Mandela** and **Thabo Mbeki**), and about 18 percent are Sotho. The Tswana and Tsonga (and to a lesser extent the Venda and Ndebele) groups also have a significant presence in the South African population. Each of these ethnic groups has a different language and is concentrated in a different area. For example, Xhosas predominate in the western part of the country and in Cape Town and Port Elizabeth. Zulus are the dominant group in Durban.

Whites constitute about 10 percent of the population, and that population is also divided ethnically. Over half are **Afrikaners**, descendants of the Dutch, French, and German colonists who arrived in the seventeenth century and developed their own language (Afrikaans) and cultural traditions. Another 40 percent of South Africa's white population are descendants of English settlers who arrived in the eighteenth century. Even today these "English whites" favor English over Afrikaans and view themselves as somewhat distinct.

South Africans of mixed race account for 9 percent of the population. This group, largely concentrated in the Western Cape Province and KwaZulu-Natal, is widely referred to as **colored**. The majority of colored South Africans speak Afrikaans as their first language. South Africans of Asian descent, for which South Africans often use the term **Indians**, make up about 2.5 percent.

This diversity of the people is also shaped by urbanization. About half of South Africans (including most whites, Asians, and colored people) live in an urban setting. South Africa has five cities with more than 1 million inhabitants: Johannesburg (3.6 million), Cape Town (3.5 million), Durban (2.8 million), Pretoria (1.4 million), and Port Elizabeth (1.1 million). Soweto, a large black township outside Johannesburg, has 1.3 million inhabitants.

South Africa is truly a complex, polyglot nation. The 1994 constitution recognizes eleven languages, nine of which (Ndebele, Northern Sotho, Sotho, Swazi, Tsonga, Tswana, Venda, Xhosa, and Zulu) are spoken exclusively by blacks, and some of which are very closely related to one another. One characteristic of quite a few of the languages is the distinct clicking sound that eludes nonnative speakers. Quite a few blacks speak more than one African language. If there is a common language among South Africans, it is, increasingly, English. Virtually all whites, Asians, educated blacks, and coloreds can speak at least some English. Almost all Afrikaners are bilingual in Afrikaans and English, and many South Africans of English descent (and colored South Africans) also speak some Afrikaans.

But language has often bitterly divided the South African people. Blacks long resisted the imposition of Afrikaans by Afrikaners, and the 1976 Soweto Uprising was ignited by the Afrikaner authorities' attempt to make Afrikaans the official language of instruction in schools. Colored South Africans, on the other hand, along with Afrikaners, have recently fought to preserve the role of Afrikaans in the schools.

South Africa's neighbors have also been an important focal point for many South Africans. South Africa is bordered to the north by Zimbabwe (formerly Rhodesia). Zimbabwe's transition to black majority rule in 1980 was an inspiration to black South Africans, and its political crisis in recent years has created major challenges for South Africa's leaders and society. Botswana, also to the north, has been one of

TIMELINE OF POLITICAL DEVELOPMENT

YEAR	EVENT
1652	The Dutch arrive at the Cape of Good Hope
1795	Cape Town captured from the Dutch by the British
1880–81; 1899–1902	Boer Wars fought between the Afrikaners and the British
1910	The Union of South Africa formed, dominated by English-speaking South Africans
1948	Afrikaner National Party elected and apartheid begins
1960	ANC banned
1964	Nelson Mandela imprisoned
1990	Mandela released from prison
1990–93	Transition made to democracy as the result of negotiations between Mandela and President F. W. de Klerk
1994	After historic multiracial elections, ANC majority government established under Nelson Mandela
1996	Democratic constitution approved
1999	Legislative elections won by ANC; Thabo Mbeki named president
2008	Thabo Mbeki replaced as president by Kgalema Motlanthe
2009	Jacob Zuma becomes president after ANC wins a fourth consecutive election

the most economically successful African nations. On South Africa's eastern border, Mozambique and Swaziland are extremely poor. Throughout much of the twentieth century, apartheid leaders frequently pointed to these neighbors (and to much of the rest of Africa) as proof that blacks were incapable of governing themselves. Sparsely populated Namibia, a former German colony and later a UN protectorate, was long dominated by apartheid South Africa.

Historical Development of the State

The telling of history often reflects the perspective of those in power, so it is not surprising that South Africa's history has usually been told from the perspective of whites. Afrikaners often contend that southern Africa was largely uninhabited when their Dutch ancestors arrived at the Cape of Good Hope in 1652. The truth is far more complex. Hunters and herders populated South Africa when the Dutch arrived in the mid-seventeenth century. The Dutch East India Company officials who first established a fort in what is today Cape Town encountered tribes of Khoisans, whom they soon enslaved. When these native Africans died from disease and slavery, the Dutch settlers imported slaves, mostly from Southeast Asia.[2]

In the interior of South Africa, a variety of Bantu-speaking tribes were ending their centuries-long migration southward from central Africa, integrating with the hunters and herders who had long inhabited the region. Among the largest of these tribes were the Zulu, the Sotho, and the Swazi kingdoms.

DUTCH RULE

While most of the colonial "scramble for Africa" took place in the nineteenth century, European domination of South Africa began almost two centuries earlier. Cape Town was initially settled by the Dutch East India Company to resupply ships heading to and from Dutch colonies in Indonesia. The early Dutch settlers, known as **Boers** (Afrikaans for "farmer"), quickly seized the fertile land of the Cape of Good Hope. The European residents of the cape developed their own culture, based in their conservative Protestant **Dutch Reformed Church** and their unique language. The small and isolated Cape Colony was fairly prosperous until it was seized by the British Empire in 1795. The Dutch ceded formal control of the region to the British in 1814.

BOER MIGRATION

As Britain quickly began to integrate this new colony into its burgeoning empire, the arrival of waves of British settlers was seen as a threat to Boer society. Bristling under British rule, many Cape Colony Boers (and their slaves) undertook a migration into the interior of southern Africa that would later gain the status of heroic myth. During the **Great Trek** of 1835, the **Voortrekkers** (Afrikaans for "pioneers") drove their wagons northeast to regain their autonomy and preserve their way of life. They met strong initial resistance from the Xhosa and other Bantu kingdoms, though whites had important technological advantages in these conflicts and were able to exploit the numerous divisions among the indigenous tribes.

A number of bloody battles ensued, most famously the 1838 Battle of Blood River between Zulu tribesmen and Afrikaners. During that conflict, a group of heavily outnumbered Afrikaners defeated the Zulus, with legend claiming that no whites were killed. Afrikaners still consider the Blood River anniversary an important religious holiday and celebrate it each year on December 16. By the early 1840s, Afrikaners were firmly ensconced in South Africa's interior.

The exhausting exodus to escape British domination, along with the bitter fighting between Boers and blacks, was in the short term a Boer success. The Boers created two states, known as the Boer republics, in which slavery, strict segregation of races, the Afrikaans language, and the Dutch Reformed Church were protected by law.

Initially the British grudgingly tolerated the interior Boer republics. However, the discovery there of massive deposits of diamonds (in 1870) and gold (in 1886) changed everything. English speakers flooded into the interior, and the city of Johannesburg quickly became an English-speaking enclave in the Boer-controlled state of Transvaal. Transvaal president Paul Kruger attempted to limit the influence of the English by denying them the vote. In 1895, English diamond magnate Cecil Rhodes used the pretense of Boer discrimination against English settlers and the presence of slavery in the Boer republics to incite a rebellion among the English. President Kruger declared war on England in 1899.

THE DEFEAT OF THE AFRIKANERS IN THE BOER WARS

Though outnumbered five to one, the Boers fought tenaciously to defend their independence during the **Boer Wars**. To defeat the well-armed and disciplined Afrikaners, the British pioneered the use of concentration camps, in which as many as 20,000 Afrikaners and 15,000 blacks perished. By 1902, the Boers had been defeated, and the Boer republics had become self-governing British colonies. In exchange for signing a peace treaty, the Boers were promised full political rights, protections for their language and culture, and the ability to deny blacks the vote in the former Boer republics. In 1910, these agreements were formalized in the **Union of South Africa.**

THE RENAISSANCE OF AFRIKANER POWER

English and Afrikaners worked together to create a single British colony, and the first prime minister of the Union of South Africa was a former Afrikaner military leader. The Native Land Act of 1913 prevented blacks from owning land except in designated "reserves" (less than 10 percent of the total land of South Africa). Discrimination against blacks continued in the former Boer republics. Only in the largely English Cape Colony were coloreds and a small number of blacks allowed to vote. Nowhere in South Africa were rights for the black majority granted, and racial discrimination was the rule even in English-governed areas.

The first elections in the united country brought to power the South African Party (SAP), which included both English speakers and Afrikaners. But many Afrikaners, especially those in the former Boer republics, continued to resent the English deeply. The Afrikaners enjoyed full political rights, but the English controlled most of the country's wealth, especially its mineral profits and budding industry.

As has so often been the case throughout their history, the Afrikaners resisted this marginalization, but this time they did so within the political system. The formation of the **National Party (NP)** in 1914 was the most important step in their attempt to organize and mobilize the Afrikaner population. The NP demanded that Afrikaans be recognized alongside English and it called for South Africa to secede from the British Empire. In the mid-1930s, NP leader Daniel Malan articulated the policies of white supremacy that later became the hallmark of apartheid. At the same time, Malan called for Afrikaner control of the state so that wealth held by the English could be redistributed to Afrikaners. Malan's goals appealed to the mass of poor white Afrikaner workers, who felt threatened by the better-off English and by the growing number of even poorer black workers (who vied for their jobs). The NP realized that if Afrikaners could be unified, they could not be denied power. In 1948, the NP was elected to office.

THE APARTHEID ERA

What distinguishes the apartheid era were the NP's two goals: consolidating Afrikaner power and eliminating all vestiges of black participation in South African politics. To a considerable degree, apartheid simply codified and intensi-fied the racial segregation that existed in the mid-twentieth century. During an era when racial discrimination was being challenged in virtually every other country, Afrikaner leaders sought to construct elaborate legal justifications for it.

HENDRIK VERWOERD AND THE "LOGIC" OF WHITE RULE

The leading ideologue and architect of apartheid was Hendrik Verwoerd, a professor at South Africa's leading Afrikaner university and prime minister from 1958 to 1966. Verwoerd argued that the population of South Africa contained four distinct "racial groups" (white, African, colored, and Indian) and that whites, as the most "civilized" racial group, should have absolute control over the state. Verwoerd and the advocates of apartheid further argued that Africans belonged to ten distinct nations, whereas the other racial groups belonged to only one nation each. By this logic, whites were the largest nation in South Africa and were therefore justified in dominating the state.

The Population Registration Act of 1950 divided South Africa into four racial categories and placed every South African into one of those categories (see "Hendrik Verwoerd and the 'Logic' of White Rule," above). Once Africans were divided into races, the apartheid architects argued that blacks (about three-quarters of the population) were not citizens of South Africa. According to the **Group Areas Act** of 1950, blacks were deemed to be citizens of ten remote "tribal homelands" (dubbed **Bantustans**), whose boundaries and leaders were decreed by the government. The Bantustans, somewhat akin to Native American reservations, constituted only around 13 percent of South Africa's territory and were usually made up of noncontiguous parcels of infertile land separated by white-owned farms. The NP chose black leaders (often tribal chiefs) loyal to the party goals to head the Bantustan governments. All blacks in South Africa, therefore, were in effect "guests" and did not enjoy any of the rights of citizenship. The 1971 Bantu Homelands Citizenship Act allowed the government to grant "independence" to any Bantustan, and though government propagandists defended the measure as an act of "decolonization," in reality it had little impact. Over the next decade, many Bantustans became "independent," though no foreign government would recognize them as sovereign countries.

Racial segregation in the rest of South Africa went even further. Members of each of the four racial groups were required to reside in areas determined by the government. The vast majority of blacks who lived and worked in white areas were required to carry internal visas at all times. Each year, failure to carry such a pass resulted in hundreds of thousands of deportations to a "homeland" that, more often than not, the deportee had never before set foot in. The apartheid authorities created new racial categories and designed separate residential areas for South

Africans of Asian descent, or of mixed race, often forcibly relocating them. Other infamous laws reinforced racial segregation. The Prohibition of Mixed Marriages Act (1950) banned relations across racial lines, and the Reservation of Separate Amenities Act (1953) provided the legal basis for segregating places as diverse as beaches and restrooms.[3]

The apartheid system retained many of the trappings of a parliamentary democracy. Apartheid South Africa had regular elections, a fairly vigorous press, and a seemingly independent judiciary. The vast majority of South Africans, however, were disenfranchised and utterly powerless. The regime tolerated mild opposition on some issues but ruthlessly quashed individuals and groups who actively opposed apartheid itself.

FORCED RELOCATION AND THE BUILDING OF APARTHEID

One of the pillars of South African apartheid was the 1950 Group Areas Act, which prohibited South Africans of different races from living in the same neighborhoods. The practical implications were immediate and devastating: nonwhites were forcibly relocated to areas outside of South Africa's main cities. The most infamous example was Sophiatown, a vibrant black community in Johannesburg (often compared to New York City's Harlem) that was bulldozed in 1955. Its inhabitants were relocated to a settlement 13 miles outside of the city that later became known as **Soweto**. Another example was District Six, a multiracial neighborhood in Cape Town with a large mixed-race (or colored) population. It was destroyed in 1966, and its colored inhabitants were relocated to the dusty Cape Flats 15 miles outside of the city.

The apartheid regime met resistance from its very inception. The most important organization resisting racial discrimination was the **African National Congress (ANC)**. Founded in 1912, it was a largely black organization that sought the extension of suffrage to blacks. The ANC was initially nonviolent and politically moderate in its calls for multiracial democracy. Under the leadership of Nelson Mandela, it led a series of nonviolent civil disobedience campaigns against apartheid laws.[4]

Fierce repression of this protest by the apartheid regime had several consequences. First, some blacks, tiring of the nonviolent, gradualist approach of the ANC, created more radical organizations, such as the Pan Africanist Congress (PAC), founded in 1959. Second, the apartheid leaders, alarmed by the growing resistance, banned the ANC and the PAC. Third, the repression (especially the government slaughter of protesters during the 1960 Sharpeville Massacre) persuaded ANC leaders to initiate military action against the apartheid regime. The government countered by arresting Nelson Mandela and other top ANC leaders in 1963 and sentencing them to life in prison. The ongoing repression led to the incarceration and murder of thousands of South Africans who actively resisted apartheid.

Although not all whites supported the apartheid system, the NP skillfully retained the majority's allegiance. For Afrikaners, the NP dramatically improved their political and economic status, making them dependent on the perpetuation of the status quo. The NP played on English-speaking whites' fears of black rule. Moderate white critics of apartheid were mostly tolerated, as they generally held little sway among the white population at large.

Though the NP subdued most domestic resistance to apartheid, the system faced growing hostility from abroad. The end of colonialism created independent African states that supported the ANC, and the United Nations condemned apartheid as early as 1952 and imposed an arms embargo on South Africa in 1977. Nevertheless, in the context of the Cold War, South Africa was able to gain support (from the United States, in particular) by portraying its fight against the ANC as a struggle against communism. Moreover, the world's major capitalist powers had lucrative investments in South Africa and were ambivalent about promoting black rule.

THE TRANSITION TO DEMOCRACY

There was nothing inevitable about South Africa's transition from apartheid to majority rule. Five categories of factors need to be considered to explain the momentous political shift that culminated in South Africa's first free elections in 1994:

1. *Demographic pressure and growing unrest.* The growth of opposition to apartheid had at its core a demographic component. The proportion of whites in the population had dropped from a high of 21 percent in 1936 to only 10 percent in 1999. Not only was the black population growing more quickly, but it was increasingly concentrated in urban areas, which were more subject to political mobilization. Most of these newly urban blacks lived in squalid conditions in South Africa's townships, the population of which doubled between 1950 and 1980. These demographic trends meant that despite largely successful efforts to deny blacks political power, their economic power and significance were rapidly expanding.

As a result of these changes, opposition to apartheid during the 1980s assumed dimensions previously unknown in South Africa. The creation of the **United Democratic Front (UDF)** in 1983 effectively united trade unions and the major black and white apartheid opposition groups. The number of protests, strikes, boycotts, and slowdowns grew, requiring ever-greater levels of repression by the apartheid regime. In July 1985, the government imposed a virtually permanent state of emergency, which led to massive arrests of suspected opposition members. In 1988, it banned the UDF and the largest trade union confederation. The ANC, whose leadership was either in prison or in exile, waged a guerrilla war against the apartheid regime. That struggle was never able to dislodge the heavily armed white regime, but nor could the regime destroy the ANC or stop the escalating violence.

2. *Economic decline.* By the 1980s, the deficiencies in the apartheid economic model had become increasingly apparent. During this decade, South Africa's economy was among the most stagnant in the developing world, growing at an average annual rate of only about 1 percent. The apartheid economic system had clearly raised the standard of living for South Africa's whites, especially Afrikaners, but it had also led to serious distortions that were by now beginning to take a toll.

The apartheid state, with its convoluted and overlapping race-based institutions and its subsidies to the entirely dependent black "homelands," was costly and inefficient. The mercantilist apartheid policies of self-sufficiency and protectionism led to the creation of industries and services that were not competitive. The system of racial preferences and job protection that was a cornerstone of apartheid clearly hindered economic development and economic efficiency.

3. *Internal reforms.* By the mid-1970s, even leading Afrikaner politicians were convinced that apartheid was an anachronistic system that needed reform if it was to survive. The reforms that followed paved the way for a future transition to democracy. Prime Minister P. W. Botha, who took power in 1978, promised to dismantle apartheid and enacted some minor reforms that liberalized some aspects of apartheid. However, he was unwilling to push the reforms very far. The next leader, President **F. W. de Klerk** (1989–94), repealed the Reservation of Separate Amenities Act, the Group Areas Act, and the Population Registration Act. He also legalized black political parties, including the ANC and the PAC, and freed their leaders. The crisis of apartheid served to split the traditionally unified Afrikaner leadership, opening the window to even greater reform.

4. *The changing international context.* During the 1980s, many countries imposed embargoes on South Africa, limiting trade and foreign investment, though powerful nations such as the United States and the United Kingdom

NELSON MANDELA: DEMOCRATIC SOUTH AFRICA'S FOUNDING FATHER

The remarkable story of Nelson Mandela parallels the turbulent history of modern South Africa. Mandela's father was a Xhosa-speaking tribal chief in the Eastern Cape Province. Mandela was expelled from the University College of Fort Hare for demonstrating against racism but went on to earn a law degree and was one of the first blacks to practice law in South Africa. He became deeply involved in the ANC and was appointed one of its four deputy presidents in 1952.

Mandela helped move the ANC in a more radical direction after NP governments began construction of the apartheid regime in 1948. The ANC was banned in 1960 after it led nationwide protests against apartheid. In response to the Sharpeville Massacre of that same year (in which police killed 69 unarmed protesters), the ANC abandoned its strategy of nonviolent protest, and Mandela was named its first military commander. Mandela was sentenced to life in prison in 1964 and was held with other ANC leaders on Robben Island. From his cell, he was able to direct the antiapartheid struggle, learn Afrikaans, and write his autobiography.

When Mandela was released in February 1990, he immediately assumed the role of representative of the black majority in the negotiations for a democratic transition. After Mandela received the Nobel Peace Prize in 1993, his ANC won a landslide victory in the country's first multiracial elections; Mandela became South Africa's first black president. While in office, he did much to heal the racial divide, taking special pains to respect the culture of the Afrikaners. His decision to step down in 1997 and make way for a younger generation of ANC leaders was another sign of Mandela's commitment to democracy.

continued to trade with the regime into the 1990s. Of greater importance was the winding down of the Cold War in the 1980s. On the one hand, it deprived the South African regime of a key source of international legitimacy: the decline of communism weakened its claim that it was facing a communist insurgency. On the other hand, the collapse of the Soviet Union and the Soviet bloc weakened the ANC sectors that promoted Communist revolution in South Africa.

5. *Skilled leadership*. Finally, South Africa's transition would likely not have occurred (or at the very least would not have been as peaceful or successful) had skilled leaders not managed the transition. F. W. de Klerk's role in forcing Prime

Nelson Mandela greets his supporters after being released from prison in February, 1990.

Minister Botha's resignation and his courageous decisions to free Mandela and legalize the ANC were essential to the transition. De Klerk used his unblemished credentials as an NP stalwart to persuade NP die-hards to accept the transition and convince most Afrikaners that their interests would be safeguarded during and after the transition.

Likewise, Nelson Mandela risked a great deal by negotiating the terms of the transition with the NP government. Mandela and the ANC leadership agreed to power sharing and numerous guarantees in order to assuage white fears, and were able to restrain radicalized blacks who wanted quick redress for decades of abuse. Mandela's knowledge of Afrikaner language and culture (gained through decades of study in prison) undoubtedly helped him negotiate with his Afrikaner opposition. His ability to eschew bitterness and revenge after his 27-year prison term impressed even his strongest opponents. Still, the negotiations between the black leadership and the NP were protracted and difficult. De Klerk and Mandela faced serious opposition from radical sectors of their own camps. Nevertheless, an interim constitution was approved in 1993, paving the way for democratic elections and majority rule in 1994. In recognition of their important role in the South African transition, de Klerk and Mandela were awarded the 1993 Nobel Peace Prize.

Political Regime

Political Institutions

During the apartheid regime, South African whites enjoyed relatively democratic institutions. Nonwhites had much more limited political rights, or none whatsoever. As a result, few considered the country to be democratic. After the political transition in 1994, however, political rights were extended to the population as a whole, regardless of race. South Africa is now a democracy with broad political rights and civil liberties commensurate with those found in advanced democracies. South Africa's long tradition of democratic institutions, albeit highly restrictive ones, helped smooth the transition to multiracial democracy. The architects of the 1994 transition did not need to create an entirely new democratic system from scratch but merely reformed existing democratic institutions and extended them to the entire population.

THE CONSTITUTION

The new democratic regime is fundamentally enshrined in the South African constitution, approved in 1996. This document reflects the delicate nature of the country's transition to democracy, in which new democratic rights had to be provided to the black majority while those of the white minority had to be protected.

The constitution attempts to balance majority and minority concerns carefully, affirming the basic values of human rights regardless of "race, gender, sex, pregnancy, religion, conscience, belief, culture, language and birth," a list far more detailed than that of most democratic constitutions. Eleven official languages are recognized. The constitution also upholds citizens' rights to housing, health care, food, water, social security, and even a healthy environment. Reacting to decades of apartheid authoritarianism, the constitution includes unusually detailed provisions limiting the powers of the state to arrest, detain, and prosecute individuals. Finally, it enshrines the principle of affirmative action, stating that in order to achieve greater equality, laws and other measures can be used to promote or advance individuals who have been discriminated against.

The constitution also firmly protects the rights of private property, a provision added to assure the white population that their property would not be seized by a black-dominated government. Perhaps most important, the constitution defines itself as the supreme law of the land: parliament must act within its confines, and a Constitutional Court can now strike down unconstitutional behavior. This is a departure from the past, when the parliament and the government reigned supreme and could change and reinterpret laws as they saw fit, with no higher legal power to restrain them. Despite these successes, and largely as a result of the ANC's dominance in the South African political system, many scholars have begun to question the health of South Africa's political institutions. One recent report concluded that "weak institutions, a significant characteristic of South Africa's democracy, struggle to promote the effective functioning of the state, and fail to provide the checks and balances necessary for democracy to flourish."[5]

The Branches of Government

The South African government is based on British institutions, with some variations. For most of the apartheid period, South Africa had a bicameral parliament and a prime minister, with a ceremonial president as head of state. Since 1994, the South African system has been transformed into one similar to that seen in many other democracies, with a bicameral parliament and a Constitutional Court. Interestingly, as a result of historic compromises between Afrikaner and English-speaking whites, South Africa has three capitals. The seat of government is located in Pretoria, the traditional heart of Afrikaner power and the center of the former Boer republics. Cape Town, where English influence was historically strongest, is the legislative capital. South Africa's judicial capital is located in Bloemfontein.

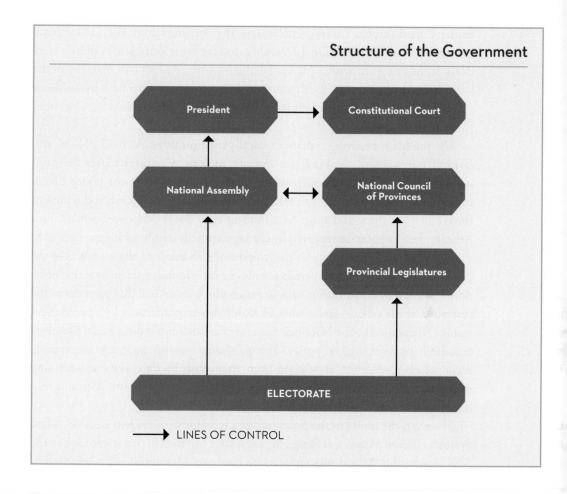

Structure of the Government

President → Constitutional Court

National Assembly ↔ National Council of Provinces

Provincial Legislatures

ELECTORATE

⟶ LINES OF CONTROL

THE PRESIDENT

The chief executive of South Africa is the president. This title is rather confusing, however, given that, like a typical prime minister, the president is chosen from the National Assembly, the lower house of the legislature, by its members, and can be removed by a vote of no confidence. Yet, there is no division between the head of state and the head of government, as is found in most parliamentary systems, so the South African president serves in both capacities. Like most prime ministers, the president chooses a cabinet of ministers, signs or vetoes legislation presented by the National Assembly, and can refer legislation to the Constitutional Court as necessary. The president may also call national referenda, dissolve the National Assembly, and (in some situations) call new elections. If the president wishes to dissolve the National Assembly, a majority of the lower house must support the dissolution and three years must have passed since it was first elected. The president is unable to call snap elections as in most other parliamentary systems.

The president is stronger than a typical prime minister. As head of state and head of government, the president can not only exert authority over the cabinet (which he selects and which he can dismiss) and government policy (like a typical head of government) but also speak on behalf of the nation and represent the country on the world stage (as a head of state does). Moreover, while South African presidents can be removed by the legislature, it is only with great difficulty. A vote of no confidence requires the support of two-thirds of the members of the National Assembly and can be taken only on the grounds of a substantial violation of the law or constitution, serious misconduct, or an inability to perform the functions of the office—circumstances akin to an impeachment in a presidential system. Theoretically, the National Assembly cannot simply dismiss the president because it opposes a given policy. This provision remains untested, however, as a vote of no confidence has not yet been attempted. To date, the overwhelming power of the ANC in the National Assembly has given the South African presidency a great deal of authority.

However, the limits to the power of the president were evident in 2008, when President Thabo Mbeki was forced to resign after he failed to win re-election to the ANC leadership. Mbeki was replaced by Kgalema Motlanthe, a caretaker president who served until the 2009 general elections. As is the case in all parliamentary systems, South Africa's head of government serves at the behest of his political party and can be replaced by the party at any time.

THE LEGISLATURE

South Africa has a bicameral parliament. The lower and more powerful of its two houses, the **National Assembly**, currently has 400 members. Members serve for five-year terms, and they are charged with electing and removing the president, preparing and passing legislation, and approving the national budget. As in the United Kingdom, the lower house has a weekly "question time," when members can question the cabinet and the president. Question time can become a heated affair, with members of the opposition parties grilling the cabinet and casting aspersions on one another. Given the racial divisions in the country, however, such debate is also limited. (For example, when one white member of parliament commented that a black member of the cabinet lacked intelligence, he was rebuked for using a racial stereotype.)

For a variety of reasons the National Assembly has not often demonstrated its independence vis-à-vis the president. The dominance of the ANC and rules enforcing strict party discipline have limited the independence of members of parliament.[6]

The upper house is the National Council of Provinces, and it is considerably weaker than the lower house. Its 90 members are indirectly elected by the nine provincial legislatures and include the premier of each province. Each province, regardless of its size or population, sends ten delegates, who cast their votes as a bloc. The power of the National Council depends on the type of legislation under consideration. When the National Assembly is dealing with national policy (such as foreign affairs or defense), the National Council has relatively little influence. When proposed legislation affects the provinces, however, the National Council can amend or reject measures, forcing the two houses to form a mediation committee to hammer out a compromise. Ultimately, the National Assembly can override the upper house with a two-thirds vote. In short, the National Council exists to ensure that local interests are heard at the national level, which is especially important when the provinces are distinguished by ethnicity, language, and culture.

THE JUDICIARY

Another important component of the transition to democratic multiracial rule in South Africa is the Constitutional Court. This body hears cases regarding the constitutionality of legislation on the separation of powers among the branches of government. Its 11 members serve 12-year terms and are appointed by the president on the basis of the recommendations of a judicial commission. The commission is made up of government and nongovernment appointees who evaluate candidates' qualifications and take racial and gender diversity into account. To date, the court has shown a tendency for activism and independence; in 1997, for example, it struck down the country's death penalty despite public sentiment in favor of capital punishment, and in 2002 it ruled that the government was obligated to provide treatment for persons with HIV/AIDS.[7] In 2011, the Constitutional Court overturned several key decisions by President Zuma and issued a ruling that Zuma's disbanding of the elite anticorruption force known as the "Scorpions" was unconstitutional. In response, Zuma warned the judiciary against encroaching on the powers of the executive and the legislature.[8]

The Electoral System

The current electoral rules in South Africa mark a significant departure from the past. Under apartheid, the country used the British single-member district (SMD), or plurality, system. As part of the transition to democracy, South Africa had to decide what election method would best represent the needs of a diverse public and help consolidate democratic legitimacy by creating an inclusive system. The result was the creation of an electoral system based on pure proportional representation (PR). Voters now cast their votes not for individual candidates but for a party, which is designated on the ballot by name, electoral symbol, and a picture of the head of the party (to ensure that illiterate voters are not excluded). To ensure the greatest possible proportionality, representatives are elected from a single nationwide constituency, and there is no minimum threshold for receiving seats in the legislature. The number of seats a party wins is divided proportionally to reflect the percentage of the total vote it receives. At elections, voters are given two ballots: one for the national legislature and one for their provincial legislature.

Overall, the electoral system in South Africa has successfully created an inclusive political atmosphere and has averted conflict and violence. Electoral turnout has been very high, and in the 2009 elections turnout was over 77 percent. However, some critics have argued that the use of PR has created a disconnect between the National Assembly and the citizens. Because members of parliament are tied to their party instead of their constituency, they are not accountable to local communities. Political parties, most notably the governing ANC, have stifled internal dissent and limited the independence of legislators by threatening to remove them from the party electoral list if they stray too far from the party's wishes. Critics inside South Africa, including the **Congress of the People (COPE)**, a party that split from the ANC in 2009, have suggested that the country consider adopting a mixed electoral system, in which some percentage of the seats are filled by plurality while the remaining are filled by PR. This would give voters a local representative with whom they could identify, and the ability to cast their vote for a particular party. However, after some discussion on electoral reform in recent years, such suggestions have faded and the current system has become institutionalized. The ANC, in particular, has been unwilling to change an electoral system that has so far delivered it a huge majority.

Local Government

Below the national level, South Africa is divided into nine provinces, each with its own elected assembly. Members are elected for a term of five years (with elections for the national and provincial legislatures occurring simultaneously) and, in turn, elect a premier to serve as the province's chief executive. The provincial assemblies have their own constitutions, pass legislation, and send delegates to the National Council of Provinces.

It is difficult to call South Africa a federal state, however, and the concept itself is a politically charged issue. During the transition to democracy, the ANC in particular looked upon federalism with a great deal of suspicion. At that time, the NP, architects of apartheid, favored federalism as a way to limit the ANC's power, while some Afrikaners in fact hoped that a federal right to self-determination could pave the way for outright secession. The Zulu-based **Inkatha Freedom Party (IFP)** also called for self-determination—and an independent Zulu state. The 1996 constitution reflects these concerns by supporting regional and ethnic diversity. Still, the constitution gives the central government the ability to overturn local legislation relatively easily, and any powers not delimited by the constitution reside with the central, not the local, government. Provinces also have limited power to levy taxes, giving them little financial autonomy.[9]

Since democratization, municipal governments have become increasingly important. The ANC has suffered its most important defeats at the local level, where complaints about the delivery of services have boosted the fortunes of the opposition. In the 2009 provincial elections, the ANC lost control of Western Cape Province, and **Democratic Alliance (DA)** leader Helen Zille became premier. An increasing number of protests against ineffective local governments, some of which turned violent, set the stage for a major increase in the DA vote in the May 2011 municipal elections. In addition to retaining control of the Western Cape Province, the party won almost a quarter of the national vote and made its first inroads into areas that had previously been bastions of ANC support. A public opinion study conducted by the country's Independent Electoral Commission showed that South Africans held local governments in lower esteem than any other levels of government.[10]

Political Conflict and Competition

The Party System and Elections

During apartheid, few political parties existed, and the NP dominated politics from 1948 until 1994. The main opposition was the weak Progressive Federal Party (PFP), which peacefully opposed apartheid laws and favored multiracial democracy within a federal framework. The enfranchisement of the nonwhite population has dramatically changed the political spectrum, though as in the past it remains dominated by one major party. The dominant party since 1994 has been the ANC, which led the struggle against white rule starting in 1912. During the ANC's long period underground and in exile, it developed an ideology strongly influenced by Marxism, favoring the nationalization of land and industry. Economic equality was seen as a necessary mechanism for overcoming racial discrimination. The ANC cultivated relations with Communist countries, such as the Soviet Union and China, and at home formed an alliance with the much smaller South African Communist Party, the SACP, (which still operates within the framework of the ANC). Many white South Africans, including some opponents of apartheid, were troubled by the ANC's demands for radical political and economic change. Since winning power in 1994, however, the ANC has stood for racial and gender equality and a strong state role in the expansion of economic opportunities for nonwhites, but it has also embraced property rights that it views as essential for economic growth and a prerequisite for the provision of jobs, education, and social services to the poor black majority. As such, its ideology is unclear and often contradictory, encompassing a mixture of social-democratic and liberal views, a lingering radicalism, and an emphasis on unity. The ANC increased its share of the vote in each of the first three democratic elections, but saw its share of the vote decrease slightly in 2009.

The overwhelming preponderance of ANC power raises concerns. Some observers fear that the party so easily embraced democracy after its long struggle in part because it has done so well with democracy. Were the ANC to face losing power, it might not look upon the democratic process so favorably. These concerns were heightened in particular by Thabo Mbeki's tenure in office, as his rhetoric and that of the ANC grew increasingly intolerant of those who challenged it. ANC leaders, including current president Jacob Zuma, have at times made statements that portray the ANC as the only truly patriotic political party, and that envision the ANC as the only party capable of governing.[11]

In general, however, the ANC's record in office has been positively evaluated by most South Africans, who give it high scores for managing the economy, improving health care, and promoting racial equality. South Africans have been most critical of the ANC's record on job creation, crime reduction, and a reduction in the gap between rich and poor.

A political schism emerged in late 2007 between ANC "populists," led by trade unions and the party rank and file, and the more technocratic wing, dominated by former president Mbeki. The populist challenge within the party helped propel Jacob Zuma's victory over Mbeki in the bitterly contested party leadership election of December 2007. After winning the ANC leadership, Zuma began to replace Mbeki loyalists with his own supporters in key party posts. Zuma was able to force the resignation of Mbeki in September 2008, but he could not become president, because he was not a member of the legislature. The ANC appointed Kgalema Motlanthe, an ally of Zuma, as a caretaker president to serve until the 2009 general elections.

Zuma's rise to the leadership of the ANC, and his ability to force Mbeki's resignation, prompted the creation of COPE, a breakaway party led by Mosiuoa Lekota, a former defense minister under Mbeki. COPE has the potential to become the first genuine black opposition party to the ANC, but in the 2009 elections it was hurt by internal divisions, a flawed political campaign, and lack of funds. Despite these problems, COPE was able to win more than 7 percent of the vote and 30 seats in the legislature, making it South Africa's third-largest political party. Its success, along with that of the DA, deprived the ANC of a two-thirds majority in the lower house, weakening the ANC's ability to amend the constitution and pass certain types of legislation. COPE suffered a stunning setback in the 2011 municipal elections, when it won under 3 percent of the vote, a result that cast serious doubt on its political future.

The overwhelming presence of the ANC in parliament dwarfs the opposition parties. Among them is the DA, successor to the old PFP. The DA is primarily liberal, favoring a small state, individual freedoms, privatization of state-run firms, and greater devolution of power to local governments. In the 2004 elections, the DA won 12 percent of the votes and 50 seats. In the 2006 local elections, it beat the ANC in Cape Town (the only local municipal council not controlled by the ANC), winning about 15 percent of the vote nationally. **Helen Zille**, a liberal journalist during apartheid and the white mayor of Cape Town, became DA leader in 2007. Under her leadership, the DA has been an increasingly outspoken opposition to the ANC. Public support for the DA has grown since the 1994 elections, but its primary base of support remains the white and mixed-race

Under Helen Zille's leadership, the DA has become a more outspoken opponent of the ANC, though it still trails far behind at the polls. Here, Zille casts her vote in the 2011 municipal elections.

population. To become a viable challenger to the ANC, it will have to broaden this base dramatically. In 2008, just under 8 percent of South Africans said they identified with the DA, and the DA continued to draw most of its support from whites and mixed-race voters. In the 2009 elections, the DA increased its votes to over 16 percent and won control of Western Cape Province (the only province not controlled by the ANC). It enjoyed its strongest showing to date in the May 2011 municipal elections, when it polled almost a quarter of the national vote.

The IFP played an ambiguous role in apartheid and post-apartheid politics. The IFP, founded in 1975 by Zulu chief Mangosuthu Buthelezi, challenged apartheid institutions but also participated in local government in the KwaZulu "homeland," one of the remote areas created to remove blacks from desirable areas and deprive them of basic citizenship. During the 1980s, animosity grew between the IFP and the ANC: the ANC saw the IFP as having been co-opted by the government, while the IFP viewed the ANC as dominated by ethnic Xhosas who did not represent Zulu interests. The animosity soon erupted into violence, which was abetted by the apartheid regime as a way to weaken both sides. After

JACOB ZUMA AND THE "NEW" SOUTH AFRICA

South Africa's current president is a strik-ing contrast from the aloof, intellectual Thabo Mbeki. Jacob Zuma is the ANC's most prominent Zulu politician. Unlike the scholarly Mbeki, Zuma grew up poor and received no formal education. He became involved in the ANC in the 1960s, and was sentenced to ten years in prison in 1963. (He served time at Robben Island with Nelson Mandela.) After his release, he became a top ANC leader in exile. After the return of democracy, Zuma quickly rose within the ANC hierarchy, an ascent that culminated in his 1997 appointment as executive dep-uty president (Mbeki's number two). While often portraying himself as being the victim of the ANC power elite, Zuma is the con-summate ANC insider.

Zuma's rise to power within the ANC was clouded in controversy. In 2005, he was charged with raping a young woman in his home. He admitted to having unprotected sex with the woman, whom he knew to be HIV-positive, but claimed the relationship was consensual. Zuma was acquitted of the charges, but his statement under oath that he had showered after the intercourse to reduce his risk of contracting HIV infuriated many South Africans.

In 2005, Zuma was fired after he was accused of corruption and racketeering in a government arms-procurement scan-dal. Charges were brought against him in 2007, but they were dropped in April 2009, shortly before the elections. Zuma has claimed that the corruption charges were politically motivated. He rose to power with strong support from South Africa's labor unions, those frustrated with the pace of change under Mandela and Mbeki. Some feared that Zuma might become an economic populist who could reverse the pro-business and pro-growth economic policies long pursued by the ANC.

In December 2007, Zuma easily defeated Thabo Mbeki in elections for the ANC pres-idency (he won two-thirds of the internal party vote), which virtually guaranteed that he would become president after the April 2009 general election.

Zuma's personal life continues to be the source of some controversy. Zuma is a polygamist who married his fifth wife in 2010. After taking office, he apologized for father-ing a child with a friend's daughter to whom he was not married. In short, Zuma's outward image appears to be a dramatic departure from those cut by Mandela and Mbeki. His more down-to-earth image has helped South's Africa's poor majority relate to him. But appearances can be deceiving. Below the surface there has been considerable con-tinuity between Zuma's policies and those of his two more circumspect predecessors.

the first democratic elections, however, the ANC was careful to bring members of the IFP into the government cabinet, which helped to diffuse much of the tension between the two parties. The IFP was embarrassed in 2004, however, having failed to do well even in the elections for KwaZulu's provincial legislature, and the party left the national government. Fears that the IFP could represent a threat to the stability of the country have disappeared. The long-term viability of a Zulu political party is doubtful since Jacob Zuma, a Zulu, became president in 2009. In the 2009 elections, the IFP continued its steady decline, winning under 5 percent of the vote and only 18 seats in the lower house. In the 2011 municipal elections, the IFP was able to win only about 2 percent of the vote.

Aside from those four main parties, few actors have much influence in South African politics. The now-defunct NP, which created apartheid and ran the country for over four decades, tried unsuccessfully to recast itself as a multiracial party and renamed itself the New National Party (NNP), and eventually merged with the DA.

National elections are held at least every five years, and according to survey data from 2008, about 68 percent of South Africans identify with a political party. Since 1994, the basis of South African political parties has been heavily influenced by race. In the words of one leading scholar, "[P]ost-apartheid South African elections bear an unmistakable racial imprint: Africans vote for one set of parties, whites support a different set of parties, and, with few exceptions, there is no cross-over voting between these groups."[12] In the 1999 elections, for example,

THE POLITICAL DOMINANCE OF THE ANC

The 2009 election was another reminder of the dominance of the ANC and the weakness of the opposition. That election witnessed the emergence of COPE, the first breakaway party from the ANC, and the opposition DA made some gains, but the ANC still easily crushed its opponents. Does the continued dominance of a single party threaten democracy in South Africa? Other democracies, such as Japan, have been dominated by a single political party. Nevertheless, the dominance of a single party may threaten

democracy in the long run by encouraging corruption, contributing to political apathy, and insulating the governing party from public criticism. Moreover, some observers have argued that the ANC's internal structure is particularly centralized and hierarchical, and have argued that many in the ANC view its opposition as unpatriotic and disloyal.*

*Kebapetse Lotshwao, "The Lack of Internal Party Democracy in the African National Congress: A Threat to the Consolidation of Democracy in South Africa," *Journal of African Studies* 35, no. 4 (December 2009): 901–14.

South African National Assembly Elections, 1999, 2004, and 2009

PARTY	1999		2004		2009	
	% OF SEATS		% OF SEATS		% OF SEATS	
	VOTE	WON	VOTE	WON	VOTE	WON
ANC	66	266	70	279	66	264
DA	10	38	12	50	17	67
COPE	-	-	-	-	7	30
IFP	9	34	7	28	5	18
NNP	7	28	2	36	-	-
Others	8	34	9	36	7	21
Total	100	400	100	400	100	400

Source: Independent Electoral Commission of South Africa, www.elections.org.za (accessed 4/25/09).

Key to Party Acronyms:
ANC: African National Congress
COPE: Congress of the People
DA: Democratic Alliance
IFP: Inkatha Freedom Party
NNP: New National Party

95 percent of blacks voted for the ANC, IFP, or other predominantly black parties, while 81 percent of whites supported the DA or other mostly white parties. Only colored and Indian voters more evenly split their votes among black and white parties. (Forty percent of coloreds and 34 percent of Indians backed white parties.)[13]

Civil Society

The exclusionary nature of the apartheid regime was built upon the policy of destroying black opposition, which it carried out by weakening any form of organized resistance. Black civil society in South Africa was crushed to an extent not seen elsewhere in colonial Africa, with traditional institutions under-mined, co-opted, and repressed wherever possible. Yet even with such pressure, anti-apartheid nongovernmental organizations (NGOs) continued to form and were vital in organizing the resistance that would help bring about democracy.

Since democratization, South Africa has developed a civil society that, in the words of one scholar, is "vigorous, effective, and shallow."[14] After 1994, the ANC attempted to co-opt many civil society groups, bringing them under its direction. Nevertheless, a whole host of groups has formed to pressure ANC-led governments on a wide gamut of issues, from the provision of basic services to the protection of minority groups. Perhaps the best example of an effective civil society group is the Treatment Action Campaign (TAC), which successfully pressured the government into an about-face in its HIV/AIDS policies. Founded in 1998 by HIV-positive activ-ists, the TAC used a variety of tactics, ranging from legal action to civil disobedience.

Despite the proliferation of civil society groups, some see South African civil soci-ety as shallow because engagement remains restricted to the relatively well-off minor-ity. Moreover, from a comparative perspective, and with the exception of political protest, other forms of public activism (including membership in pressure groups) remain low in South Africa. A 2010 study of 20 African countries showed that South Africans' civic and political participation was among the lowest in the region.[15]

One major actor in civil society is organized labor, in particular the **Congress of South African Trade Unions (COSATU)**, formed in 1985 to promote work-ers' rights and oppose apartheid. In post-apartheid South Africa, COSATU remains powerful in defending labor interests.[16] Like many other organizations that were involved in the battle against apartheid, COSATU is strongly tied to the ANC, through what is known as the Triple Alliance, which links COSATU, the ANC, and the SACP. In spite of this alliance, COSATU has been openly hostile to the ANC's liberal economic policies, and this hostility has generated friction. COSATU has complained about the consistently high rate of unemployment that has weakened the union movement. (Only a small minority of South Africa's workforce is unionized.) It has also been vocal in opposing the government's weak criticism of the Mugabe regime in neighboring Zimbabwe. COSATU has consid-ered severing its ties to the ANC, but like other civic actors, it fears that doing so will result in its political marginalization. While COSATU backed Jacob Zuma's challenge to Thabo Mbeki, relations between Zuma and COSATU soon soured. A wave of COSATU-led strikes in 2010, mainly over demands for higher wages, crippled South Africa's economy. COSATU eventually compromised over the issue, sensitive to criticisms that excessive wage demands might worsen South Africa's very high unemployment rate.

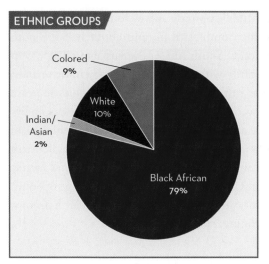

ETHNIC GROUPS

Colored 9%

White 10%

Indian/ Asian 2%

Black African 79%

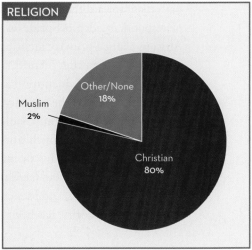

RELIGION

Other/None 18%

Muslim 2%

Christian 80%

A second important element of civil society is the media. Since 1994, electronic and print media have expanded substantially, making for a relatively well-informed public. South Africans place a high degree of trust in the media, more so than they place in any of the state institutions, perhaps due in part to the ethnic integration of television and other outlets. In 2008, concerns were raised when individuals close to the ANC leadership purchased one of South Africa's four main media groups. Opposition grew when the ANC introduced and passed proposals aimed at countering what it viewed as an excessively critical media. Some of those measures were interpreted as attempts at muzzling South Africa's vibrant and independent media (see "Civil Liberties in a Dominant-Party Political System" in the "Current Issues" section, p. 675).

Society

Given the ethnic diversity of South Africa's inhabitants, and the colonial and national policies of systematic racial discrimination, it is no surprise that South African society has been (and in many ways remains) significantly divided along racial and ethnic lines. In fact, one of the most tragic effects of apartheid was that the social policy of racial segregation was compounded—indeed, reinforced—by political persecution and economic discrimination.

What is surprising is the extent to which both groups and individuals in contemporary South Africa identify with the South African nation and express patriotism toward the state. A recent public opinion survey found that 83 percent of respondents express pride in being South African, and about half of South Africans claim a primary identification as South African, versus about 10 percent of South Africans who identify primarily with an ethnic group.[17] Unfortunately, this shared national identity has not easily been translated into domestic peace or tolerance among the country's various groups. Despite South Africa's ability to avoid much of the ethnic violence and civil war that plagues other portions of the continent, there is much truth to former president Thabo Mbeki's indictment that South Africa remains in many ways two nations: one, wealthy and largely white; the other, poor and largely black. And, alarmingly, the percentage of South Africans who express confidence that South Africa can achieve racial harmony, though still a majority, has been declining.

Racism in the Rainbow Nation

Race relations have come a long way since Nelson Mandela issued his famous call for a multiethnic "rainbow nation." Public opinion research demonstrates that in the first decade of democracy, most South Africans thought that race relations had improved. More recently, however, a number of highly publicized recent incidents have challenged the idea of a rainbow nation. In 2008, after the administration of the formerly all-white Afrikaner University of the Free State decided to integrate dormitories, angry white students produced a video of a mock initiation in which black students (portrayed by black staff members) were humiliated. A discovery of a whites-only restroom in a police station, a shooting rampage by a racist youth gang (in which four blacks were killed), and a number of anti-Afrikaner slogans employed by Julius Malema, leader of the ANC Youth League, were disturbing examples that racism and racial tensions have not been eradicated. Malema, closely associated with President Jacob Zuma, made a series of statements that appeared to incite violence against Afrikaners, and that led to his 2010 conviction on charges of issuing hate speech, and his expulsion from the ANC in 2012.

Ethnic and National Identity

As should be clear, South Africa is truly a multiracial and multiethnic society. Under apartheid, the government not only enforced policies of separate racial development but also used its "homelands" policy to divide and conquer the

THE EDUCATION CRISIS IN SOUTH AFRICA

Perhaps the most enduring legacy of apartheid can be found in South Africa's woefully inadequate education system.* While its schools are formally integrated, de facto segregation by race remains the norm. Most schools serving blacks lack basic amenities such as textbooks, libraries, and science laboratories, while schools serving mostly white students have vastly superior facilities. Half of all students in South Africa drop out of high school before taking their "metric" exam, which is required for graduation. Only about half of blacks pass their metric exams, while 99 percent of whites, 92 percent of Indians, and 76 percent of coloreds get passing grades. As a result, while far more blacks attend university today than during apartheid, and despite numerous affirmative action programs designed to increase the presence of blacks in traditionally white South African universities, only 5 percent of blacks receive a university degree. This massive education deficit has created a major shortage of skilled black labor and is a serious impediment to the ANC's goal of integrating blacks into South Africa's business elite.

* *The Economist*, "South African Schools: Desegregation and investment have yet to boost black schoolchildren," January 13, 2011, http://www.economist.com/node/17913496 (accessed 12/19/11).

country's many ethnic and tribal groups. Although Bantustans (homelands) were legally dissolved in 1994, many citizens (particularly urban blacks) had never identified with or even visited their alleged homeland. Nonetheless, black Africans, particularly rural blacks, retain strong ethnic identities.

Like black South Africans, the white population has a long history of ethnic division, stemming from the colonial-era conflict between the Afrikaners and the British. A century of sporadic violence between the Afrikaners and the English culminated in the 1910 establishment of the Union of South Africa. The English minority dominated the Union politically, economically, and culturally. In fact, it was the fear of English dominance that inspired the formation and growth of the Afrikaner National Party and its policies of cultural and racial purity during the first half of the twentieth century. Apartheid allowed Afrikaners to separate the minority whites from the majority blacks and to culturally dominate the white English subculture.

But whereas ethnic groups were fastidiously segregated under apartheid, language has rendered the multiethnic fabric of South Africa far more complex.

Indeed, linguistic differences have brought groups together and pushed them apart. Nine languages spoken exclusively by blacks are now enshrined in the constitution. Though violently resisted by blacks during apartheid, Afrikaans remains the preferred tongue of not only Afrikaners but also most colored South Africans. As is true in many polyglot former colonies, the English language serves to some extent to unify the country's citizens. However, because English is not the first language of most blacks, to the extent that it becomes the dominant language in South Africa, blacks are placed at a disadvantage vis-à-vis the white minority.

Similarly, religion has both unified and divided South African society. More than two-thirds of all South Africans, including most whites and coloreds and nearly two-thirds of blacks, identify themselves as Christian, and over three-quarters describe themselves as religious.[18] The Dutch Reformed Church (sometimes called "the National Party in prayer") played a particularly important role in unifying Afrikaners (first against the British, then against black Africans) and providing divine justification (at least in the eyes of its members) for their separate and superior status.

As with racial discrimination in America, the dismantling of legal racism in South Africa and the national strides taken toward reconciliation have not fully eliminated racial prejudice or distrust. Levels of black-on-white violence and even black-on-black violence climbed during the 1990s, particularly in the townships, with murder rates in South Africa now nearly nine times higher than those in the United States.

Despite persistent racial tensions, South Africans enjoy a remarkably high level of nationalism and patriotism. And while the apartheid state essentially excluded all nonwhites from political life, citizenship is now universally shared. However, the legacies of division and exclusion, combined with a perceived inability of the ANC government to deliver socioeconomic benefits, have dampened citizen participation and increased levels of political apathy since the dissolution of apartheid. Recent polls show that support for democracy remains very strong in South Africa, but trust in government and satisfaction with government policy have declined in recent years.

Ideology and Political Culture

Although it may be troubling for the future of South African democracy, a relative decline in levels of political interest since the tumultuous early 1990s should not be surprising. Since the fall of apartheid, political ideologies have also become less pronounced and more pragmatic. In the old South Africa, Afrikaner politicians and intellectuals combined and refined political and theological ideas to form an ideology of racist authoritarianism. Like many other movements of resistance in colonial and postcolonial settings, the ANC and other revolutionary opponents of apartheid (including the SACP) adopted radical socialist principles of economic egalitarianism and revolutionary political violence. Now the ANC government has reached out to both white capitalists and black voters, embracing liberal capitalism, promoting electoral democracy, and handily winning three national elections.

Likewise, differences among the very disparate political cultures of apartheid South Africa—between not just ruling whites and oppressed blacks but also the subcultures of Afrikaners and English, and even the Zulu and the Xhosa—have narrowed. Many South Africans have genuinely embraced the new culture of social inclusion and political participation and have supported efforts to integrate former adversaries and divided communities.

Certainly the highest-profile effort of bridge building was the **Truth and Reconciliation Commission**. Convened in 1995 and led by **Archbishop Desmond Tutu**, the commission was charged with two goals: first, establishing the

Levels of Trust in South Africa, 2006 and 2008

Percentage expressing a lot or some trust in:

	2006	2008
President	69	43
Parliament	55	49
Electoral agency	57	59
Ruling party	61	54
Courts	68	64
Police	48	44

Source: Data available at www.afrobarometer.org (accessed April 4/15/11).

"truth" of crimes committed (on all sides) from the time of the 1960 Sharpeville Massacre through the outlawing of apartheid in 1994; and second, using that truth as the essential foundation for healing the deep wounds of the era. The commission was given the authority to hear confessions, grant amnesty to those who were deemed to have told the complete truth, and provide recommendations for promoting long-term reconciliation (including reparation payments). While the commission uncovered a great deal of horrific "truth," much controversy surrounded the final report (some alleged it was too critical of apartheid, others suggested it was too quick to condemn actions by the ANC). Though it is not surprising, given the enormity of the crimes, genuine reconciliation has remained elusive.

Nonetheless, many observers remain optimistic that ANC-governed South Africa can overcome the tragedies of the country's history and its current social and economic woes, including endemic crime and violence. They argue that both the South African people and political culture have shown a remarkable capacity to avoid conflict even in the face of serious economic and social problems. Scholars note "countervailing sources of stability" in South Africa's political culture, including a pervasive tradition of collective decision making (known as *ubuntu*), the ANC's proven pragmatism and political discipline, and the "prudential caution" of whites and blacks that was forged during the period of transition. Perhaps most important, with the rise of a new black capitalist class, the country has seen the gradual emergence of a multiracial elite.[19]

There are many signs that South Africa's political culture supports democracy. According to a 2008 public opinion study, about half of South Africans are satisfied with how democracy works (down from about 65 percent in 2006), and most think democracy is preferable to all other systems.[20] South Africans express strong support for the protection of civil liberties and minority rights, and a large majority of South Africans rejects the notion of one-party rule. South Africans are split fairly evenly between those who believe that the government is responsible for improving the well-being of the population and those who believe that individuals are primarily responsible for themselves.

Political Economy

One cannot separate the political and social challenges confronting South Africa today from its economic challenges. Having vanquished the demon of apartheid, South Africa faces massive unemployment, growing income inequality, and persistent poverty among its poorest citizens.

The impoverished area of Langa, a sprawling slum outside of Cape Town.

The ANC government must adopt policies that can both ameliorate these problems without alienating its broad and disparate constituencies and preserve South Africa's nascent democracy and civil liberties. Moreover, successful democratic transition has not guaranteed the transformation of South Africa. In fact, it has in some ways made it more problematic, as issues of equality—delayed in the name of promoting political freedom—have taken on more significance.

To its credit, the government has made strides in improving the economy by curtailing debt, reversing inflation, and expanding exports. It has also improved employment opportunities and income for the growing black middle class; for South Africa's poor, it has greatly expanded access to basic necessities, such as water, electricity, and housing (see "What Difference Did Democracy Make?," p. 665). By African standards, the South African economy is highly developed, and its companies have become major investors elsewhere in the region. South Africa's economy is also highly diversified, although still fairly dependent on the country's large mineral resources, particularly gold and diamonds.

Historically, both British- and Afrikaner-controlled governments sponsored political-economic systems that favored their own ethnic constituents. In the early twentieth century, government policy facilitated English ownership and control of

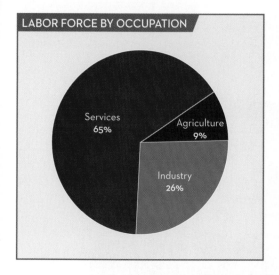

LABOR FORCE BY OCCUPATION

Services 65%

Agriculture 9%

Industry 26%

mines and other industries, even in Afrikaner-dominated regions of the country. Squeezed by wealthier and more highly skilled English workers from above and by cheaper black labor from below, Afrikaners sought political power in large part to redress what they saw as economic oppression.

With this power, the NP promoted essentially mercantilist policies of import substitution to promote local and, more specifically, Afrikaner industry. Though those policies were initially adopted to nurture an Afrikaner capitalist class, by the 1970s the international economic sanctions imposed on South Africa gave the state little option but to substitute local production and markets for those lost abroad. During its tenure, the NP government intervened extensively in the marketplace, imposing high tariffs and other trade barriers on imports; bestowing lucrative government contracts on favored firms; establishing state-owned enterprises (SOEs) in such key industries as weapons, steel, and energy production; and using oligopolist profits from industries ranging from gold and diamond exports to fuel industrialization.

Throughout the 1970s, the South African economy thrived and Afrikaners prospered. At the same time, the absence of economic opportunity for black Africans and the prohibition against the formation of black trade unions kept black labor costs artificially low, encouraging foreign investors eager to take advantage of the cheap labor and relative stability that authoritarian South Africa promised. During the 1980s, however, foreign firms and countries faced growing moral and legal pressures to divest their South African interests. At that time, too, multiracial trade unions (including COSATU) were legalized and began demanding higher wages. Finally, the government began to face a shortage of skilled labor. Limiting access to education for blacks meant that the economy could not depend on a large pool of educated workers. These pressures dealt severe—and some would say ultimately fatal—economic blows to the apartheid regime.

Given the history of policies benefiting the English and the Afrikaners, many observers expected the victorious ANC to adopt statist policies to redress the discrimination and exclusion that blacks had experienced for generations. Not only would such policies have promised to be popular with the ANC's majority black constituency, but this kind of progressive state intervention,

What Difference Did Democracy Make?

Percentage of South African households with:

	1994	2009
Formal dwelling	64	75
Access to clean piped water	62	89
Flush toilets	51	60
Landline telephone or cell phone	29	85
Electricity for lighting	51	83

Source: Data from *The Economist*, June 3, 2010.

designed to redistribute wealth and promote greater equality, would also have been in harmony with the long-standing socialist ideological heritage of the ANC and its allies. White property owners feared that a great share of their economic assets would simply be seized by the state. This, then, would be state manipulation of the market by the left rather than the right—but state intervention all the same.

The ANC's approach to the economy was much less radical than expected, and in many ways the ANC ultimately pursued a liberal political-economic model. In 1994, Nelson Mandela announced the Reconstruction and Development Programme (RDP), which focused on meeting the basic needs of South Africans living in poverty. The ANC argued that housing, electricity, jobs, safe drinking water, affordable health care, and a safe environment had to take precedence over economic growth.

Within two years, however, the ANC government had recognized that the huge costs of the RDP were unsustainable in the absence of substantially more foreign investment and greater rapid economic growth. In addition, the recent failure of communism in Eastern Europe and the Soviet Union and the increasing popularity of neoliberal market solutions within international development circles helped turn the ANC leadership away from its socialist roots. In 1996, the government adopted a plan of liberal macroeconomic structural adjustment known as **Growth, Employment, and Redistribution (GEAR)**. GEAR called for opening trade, privatizing SOEs, and otherwise limiting the role of the state in the marketplace in an effort to stimulate growth and attract foreign investment. These policies have paid dividends: growth rates under the ANC have been steady, if not spectacular, and a vast improvement over apartheid-era governments.

Not surprisingly, this dramatic shift in redistributive priorities and interventionist policies has angered the ANC's longtime allies on the left, COSATU and the SACP. In labor protests against GEAR, COSATU leaders have called the GEAR privatization of the SOEs "born-again apartheid" and have predicted devastating consequences for South Africa's working poor. The government finds itself in the position of, on the one hand, being praised by the International Monetary Fund for promoting GEAR privatization and delivering steady rates of economic growth, while, on the other hand, being under attack from its erstwhile anti-apartheid allies.

Facing this catch-22, the government is trying to please all sides: The ANC remains committed to land reform and basic health care, and funds programs to provide water, electricity, phones, and housing to the poor; it also continues to woo foreign investment by cutting inflation, lowering taxes, and keeping a lid on its spending in order to promote economic growth. It has targeted key industries and manufacturing sectors, offering low-interest loans and other incentives for investment. As in other developing economies, the government has promoted microcredit, or small-loan, initiatives designed to assist the very poorest in starting businesses. So far, GEAR and related policies have borne some fruit, in the form of increased growth rates that, it is hoped, will help reduce unemployment over the coming decade. But there are still serious obstacles to be overcome.

Chief among these is persistent income inequality (see "In Comparison: Gini Index of Economic Inequality," p. 667). Despite the ANC government's affirmative action efforts and the emergence of a small but growing black middle and upper class, the white minority still dominates the economy. South Africa has one of the highest levels of income inequality in the world. Moreover, while the rising income of some blacks and the government's redistribution efforts have led to a decline in inequality among races, overall inequality among all South Africans continues to increase. The danger is that a white economic elite will simply be replaced by a black one, with income redistribution no better (and perhaps worse) than before apartheid. The ANC has been especially unsuccessful in redistributing land, which remains overwhelmingly concentrated in the hands of the white minority; by 2007, only 5 percent of land had been redistributed to blacks, far short of the goal of 30 percent initially established by the ANC.[21]

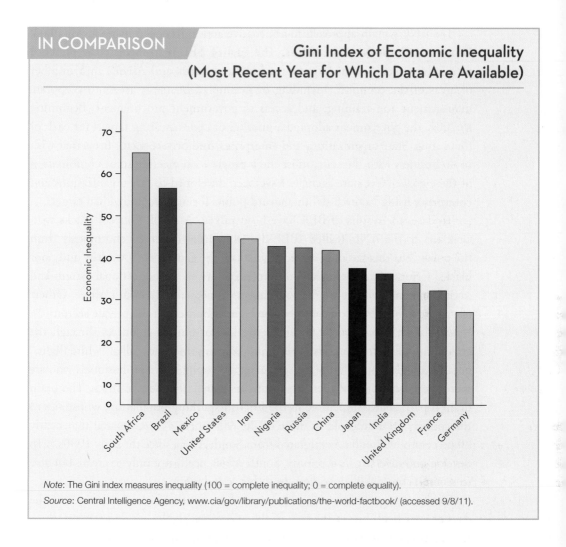

Gini Index of Economic Inequality
(Most Recent Year for Which Data Are Available)

Economic Inequality

70 —
60 —
50 —
40 —
30 —
20 —
10 —
0

South Africa, Brazil, Mexico, United States, Iran, Nigeria, Russia, China, Japan, India, United Kingdom, France, Germany

Note: The Gini index measures inequality (100 = complete inequality; 0 = complete equality).

Source: Central Intelligence Agency, www.cia/gov/library/publications/the-world-factbook/ (accessed 9/8/11).

South Africa continues to suffer from extremely high rates of unemployment. In 2011, the rate was about 25 percent, but the figure for young blacks was closer to 40 percent. While some have blamed South Africa's rigid labor laws, COSATU and others have questioned the government's commitment to job creation. South Africa's growth rate has simply not been high enough to generate enough employment. The persistence of massive levels of poverty is an equally vexing problem facing South Africa. About half of all South Africans are below the official poverty level. When asked to identify the greatest problem facing South Africa, the largest percentage of respondents (36 percent) cited unemployment, followed by the persistence of poverty (10 percent).[22]

The ANC's main approach to affirmative action has been its policy of **Black Economic Empowerment (BEE)**. The goal of BEE is to increase the presence of disadvantaged South Africans (including coloreds and Asians) in a number of areas of the economy, including ownership of business, access to corporate management and training, and access to government procurement. Beginning in 2007, the government adopted a number of codes creating targets for each of these areas. State organizations and enterprises, and private-sector firms that wish to do business with the state, must show progress on meeting some combination of these goals. New state agencies have been developed to rate organizations and enterprises using "scorecards" that award points for meeting individual targets.

To date, the results of BEE have been mixed. A small group of blacks with close ties to the ANC (called "BEE-llionaires") has benefited enormously from the policy, but this has only served to increase the gap between wealthy and poor blacks. Critics of the policy claim that inequality in the educational system and massive unemployment are the root causes of inequality in South Africa. Others fear the system will become cumbersome and a burden on the private sector.

A final challenge worth noting is the loss of human resources through the emigration of skilled workers. This brain drain is sometimes called "white flight," because a high proportion of those leaving are young white professionals who are increasingly skeptical of their prospects in their native South Africa. The brain drain is particularly noticeable in the English-speaking population, whose ties to the country are not as old as those of the Afrikaners. It is estimated that nearly 20 percent of whites have emigrated from South Africa since the early 1990s.[23] To develop and diversify its economy, South Africa needs not only to create but also to retain its most skilled workers, both black and white.

Democratic governments have reoriented the South African economy since the days of apartheid, but in the face of the enormous challenges that remain, there is a growing disillusionment with the state of South Africa's economy. According to a recent public opinion study, a steadily growing number of South Africans (61 percent in 2008, up from 45 percent in 2004) feel that the government's economic policies have "hurt most people and benefitted only a few."[24]

Foreign Relations and the World

Under apartheid, South Africa was largely isolated from the outside world, limited in its economic and diplomatic ties. This isolation helped reinforce a siege mentality among the white population and directed much of the politics of the country inward.

Relations with the rest of Africa were particularly hostile, often limited to military skirmishes with neighboring countries that harbored or supported the ANC. With the move to multiparty rule, South Africa was able to break out of its isolation, rebuilding ties in the region and in the international community as a whole.

As can be expected, however, the realities of this transition have been somewhat more complicated. For most observers, this has been most obvious in the often prickly relationship between the ANC and members of the international community, whether they are other governments, intergovernmental organizations, or NGOs. Former president Thabo Mbeki bristled at suggestions that his government was derelict in its response to the HIV/AIDS crisis and in addressing some of the main issues involved, such as sexual assault. ANC leaders have accused the international community of double standards and racism, and of treating South Africa as if it were still a colony of the imperial powers. Ironically, in some ways this defensiveness is reminiscent of the rhetoric of the apartheid-era NP, which also angrily rejected criticism from the international community. Yet when we shift our focus from the international community to Africa alone, our perspective of South Africa changes. In the international community, South Africa is still a struggling country that confronts a series of major obstacles. But in Africa, South Africa is a regional powerhouse. On the economic front, its economy alone makes up nearly half of all of sub-Saharan Africa's gross domestic product (GDP). By virtue of this large GDP and the country's vibrant private sector, South Africa has become central to trade and investment on the continent. South African exports to other African countries have risen substantially over the past decade, fostered in part by the lowering of trade barriers across the region. South Africa has also become a major investor in many neighboring countries. South African multinationals now play an important role in retail, banking, telecommunications, and other sectors in the region. As a result of this dominant economic presence, there has been a growing resentment of what is seen as a kind of South African imperialism, the effects of which are thought to be undermining local African businesses and increasingly controlling the regional economy. Inside South Africa, these actions have also been criticized as running counter to the goals of economic development within South Africa itself. Furthermore, at the other end of this relationship, the far better economic conditions in South Africa have attracted millions of illegal immigrants over the past decade, fueling xenophobia among the South African population and mistreatment of immigrants by the police, immigration officials, and the public as a whole.

South Africa's regional power has expanded in the diplomatic sphere as well. An important element of this growing influence is the country's role in the formation of the **African Union (AU)**, which replaced the Organization of African Unity (OAU) in 2002. In many ways inspired by the European Union, the AU seeks to depart from the OAU in pursuing greater political and economic integration across the continent. As the first head of the AU, Thabo Mbeki sought to position the organization as a mediator between African states and the advanced democracies. He also helped create the **Southern African Development Community (SADC)**, a 15-member body that is also concerned with regional economic integration and cooperation in southern Africa.

A cornerstone of regional integration and cooperation has been the **New Partnership for Africa's Development (NEPAD)**. NEPAD proposes that the developed world's support for African countries, unlike past aid or loan programs, be tied to commitments to the rule of law and democracy. Progress toward this goal is to be monitored by the AU. If the AU is able to show progress in tying aid to economic and political progress in the region, it will no doubt boost its own power, and with it the regional and international authority of South Africa.

Finally, South Africa has been directly involved in peacekeeping and peacemaking efforts in the region. In recent years, the South African government has worked at brokering an end to civil conflicts in the Angola, Burundi, Congo, and Liberia, and it has troops on the ground as peacekeepers or observers in several African countries.

Thus South Africa's role in the region has been transformed from pariah to continental leader and mediator with the advanced democracies. But this power comes with its own costs. In many ways, South Africa has become a regional hegemon—that is, a dominant power able to set the rules for the region, adjudicate disputes between countries, and punish those who fail to go along. That South Africa has not only the most powerful army on the continent but also a sophisticated arms industry (as a legacy of apartheid) only reinforces this authority.

That power comes with a certain degree of contradiction is true for any important actor in the international system; in that respect, South Africa is no different from any other country with more power than its neighbors. What complicates matters for South Africa, however, is the way in which its new regime has been built on moral authority: that is, the need for democracy, multiethnicity, and tolerance. As a result, South Africa has been at the forefront of promoting democracy in the region through its own diplomatic efforts and through participation in the AU and the SADC. Yet its efforts have often been viewed in the region as patronizing, not unlike the behavior of the advanced democracies toward South Africa that Mbeki often condemned. This view is reinforced by the perception of double standards. In the economic realm, some observers see South Africa's economic relations with the continent as one of domination. The formation of NEPAD, too, has been criticized by some Africans as an attempt to bring a neoliberal version of GEAR to the rest of Africa, thereby primarily benefiting South African economic interests.[25]

In the diplomatic sphere as well, South Africa's calls for greater democracy in the region have rung hollow in the face of the country's support for Zimbabwe, whose deepening authoritarianism was facilitated, in part, by South African diplomatic and economic support (see "Zimbamwe: South Africa's Troubled Neighbor" in the "Current Issues" section, p. 672). As with many other countries around the world, South Africa has found that its increased international power has led to a clash of morality, stability, and self-interest.

However, there can be little doubt that democratization has enhanced the international power and prestige of South Africa. In 2007, and again in 2010, South Africa was elected as a nonpermanent member of the UN Security Council. In April 2011, it was formally inducted into the BRIC group of emerging regional powers, which is now known as BRICS (Brazil, Russia, India, China, and South Africa).

Under President Zuma, South Africa's foreign policy has continued to be difficult to predict. While Zuma called for the resignation of Egyptian president Mubarak in 2011, and was one of the few government leaders to congratulate Chinese dissident Liu Xiabo for his Nobel Peace Prize, his government initially took a hands-off approach to a civil war in Côte d'Ivoire, maintained good relations with Libyan dictator Muammar Qaddafi, and continued to take a conciliatory approach to the Mugabe government in Zimbabwe.

CURRENT ISSUES IN SOUTH AFRICA

Crime and Corruption

Crime is regularly cited by South Africans as among the most serious problems facing the country. Crime rates skyrocketed after the transition to democracy, but started to drop after peaking in 2003. Pernicious inequality and endemic poverty have certainly contributed to the serious crime problem. The rate of violent crime in South Africa, including murder, rape, and carjackings, is extremely high. Nearly 20,000 South Africans are murdered each year, a rate nine times greater than the U.S. average. Carjackings, often resulting in death or serious injury, are commonplace and have increased dramatically since 1994. Unemployment and poverty, particularly in the townships, and corruption in the police force exacerbate this problem. Crime not only undermines the social fabric but also deters domestic and international investment and diverts security resources that could be spent elsewhere.[26]

Public opinion research has shown a steady growth in public concern about corruption since 1994, fueled in part by a number of high-profile corruption scandals that affected the governing ANC.[27] The data show that local governments in particular are viewed as corrupt (almost half of respondents view them as corrupt), while about a quarter of respondents view the president and the legislature as corrupt.

Faced with growing public concern over corruption, in 1999 President Mbeki established an elite crime-fighting unit: the Directorate of Special Operations, popularly known as the Scorpions. The unit, whose motto was "loved by the people, feared by the criminals," was well funded and highly trained, and had its own staff of investigators and prosecutors. It quickly became a popular and highly effective unit, achieving conviction rates much higher than those of the regular police force. The Scorpions ran into trouble, however, when the force began to investigate corruption within the ANC government. When they brought corruption charges against then former deputy president Jacob Zuma that led to his firing, Zuma's supporters claimed that the Scorpions were merely attempting to limit opposition within the ANC. A bitter political rivalry and turf war broke out between the police and the Scorpions. Despite widespread public opposition in 2008, Zuma's supporters passed legislation that reintegrated the Scorpions into the police force, effectively disbanding the unit. Zuma pledged to crack down on corruption by creating a performance, monitoring and evaluation cabinet post within the government. Nevertheless, in 2011 the ANC was rocked by numerous scandals that called into question Zuma's commitment to fighting corruption.

Zimbabwe: South Africa's Troubled Neighbor

Since the fall of apartheid, South Africa has sought to develop a role as an important regional actor, leading by both economic and moral example. But over the past decade, this position has been compromised by its complex relationship with its neighbor Zimbabwe.

Residents of Pretoria protest corruption in local government and the lack of delivery of basic services.

Like South Africa, Zimbabwe (previously known as Rhodesia) is a former British colony in which a small white elite once dominated the black majority. Just as the ANC fought a guerrilla campaign against the South African government, in Zimbabwe a movement known as Zimbabwe African National Union (ZANU), led by Robert Mugabe, struggled to end white rule. After years of violent conflict, the government agreed to open elections in 1980, which ZANU won. As in South Africa, the transition from white rule was predicated on guarantees that white-held private property would be protected. Unlike in South Africa, however, the transition led to conflict among different indigenous African ethnic groups, resulting in thousands of deaths.

The ZANU victory served as an inspiration for South Africans opposed to apartheid. Over time, however, it also became a more negative example. During the 1980s, ZANU (merged with its main rival, the Patriotic Front, to become ZANU-PF) consolidated power in the hands of the party and President Mugabe. Economic mismanagement and corruption followed, undermining political authority. In the late 1990s, as public opposition grew, a new party rose to challenge ZANU-PF, known as the Movement for Democratic Change (MDC). Fearing the MDC and seeking to shore up his own authority, Mugabe turned on both the MDC and the white landowners, who controlled most of the farmland in Zimbabwe. He encouraged his supporters to seize white-owned land and to harass and kill members of the MDC. The international community condemned these tactics, but Mugabe dismissed the criticism as the machinations of imperialist oppressors.

The South African government, however, took a different position. President Thabo Mbeki and the ANC expressed its support for Mugabe even in the face of increasing repression, and the South African government extended financial assistance when the rest of the international community had withdrawn its aid. In 2005, Zimbabwe held parliamentary elections that were widely regarded as rigged. Yet the South African government declared the elections free and fair, as it had done in response to similar elections in 2002. After Mugabe refused to accept his apparent defeat in the 2008 presidential elections, insisting on a second round of elections, he again began to harass the opposition. In response, South Africa's government continued to advocate constructive engagement and quiet diplomacy and appeared to many to be coddling Mugabe.[28] When MDC leader Morgan Tsvangirai withdrew from the second round of presidential elections because of state-sponsored violence against his party, South Africa opposed UN sanctions against its neighbor. While Jacob Zuma had been critical of Mbeki's conciliatory approach toward Mugabe, his government has continued the "quiet diplomacy"policy of its predecessor. ANC Youth League leader Julius Malema created a controversy when in 2010 he traveled to Zimbabwe and publically supported Mugabe, appearing to contradict the official ANC strategy.

South Africa has long received immigrants from its poorer neighbors, and the flow increased after the end of apartheid. The crisis in neighboring Zimbabwe resulted in the arrival of hundreds of thousands of new legal immigrants, and an estimated 3 million to 5 million who reside mostly illegally in South Africa and who find employment in the informal sector. The growing visibility of immigrants has caused resentment among South Africans, and in 2008 a wave of anti-immigrant violence shocked the nation. Dozens of immigrants were killed, and foreign-owned shops were destroyed.

Why would democratic South Africa coddle a neighboring dictatorship? Different factors may be at work. Some observers argue that the ANC and the ZANU-PF share a bond in the struggle against white rule. Both have since chafed at what they see as the lecturing of the international community, a reaction that also characterized Mbeki's intransigence on HIV/AIDS. Some critics have explained the ANC's support for Mugabe by emphasizing that the South African government, concerned about the complete breakdown of authority in Zimbabwe, would rather back Mugabe than face chaos on its border.

But the South African government's position is not shared by everyone in the ANC. COSATU has strongly supported the MDC and such national figures as

Nelson Mandela and Archbishop Desmond Tutu have called for Mugabe to step down, and have indirectly or directly challenged ANC policies on the matter.

The Devastation of HIV/AIDS

It is estimated that nearly 14 percent of South Africans are HIV positive, one of the highest rates in the world, and some 1,000 South Africans die of AIDS every day.[29] Despite increased access to affordable drugs, most of those infected will die of the disease. Besides being a human and social tragedy, this situation will have, and already has had, huge consequences for the economy. The HIV/AIDS pandemic will cut an estimated 5 percent from South African GDP growth each year over the next ten years, and South Africa's life expectancy has dropped from age 60 to age 47 in the past two decades. The healthcare system is underfunded and grossly inadequate, and corporations are increasingly wary of investing in personnel, given the mortality odds facing their employees. Compounding this problem is a high degree of stigma attached to those with HIV/AIDS, not to mention the questionable handling of the issue by Thabo Mbeki and other ANC politicians: they cast doubt on the causal link between HIV and AIDS and resisted conventional drugs and drug protocols prescribed in the West, citing scientifically dubious theories and charging the West with racist views of African sexuality. Pressure from international and domestic activist groups and from Nelson Mandela (whose son died of AIDS) is slowly raising awareness and the level of treatment, but treatment remains limited in the face of this devastating epidemic.

Under President Zuma, South Africa has begun to make gains in the fight against HIV/AIDS. His government has initiated the world's largest HIV testing and treatment program. (Zuma publically announced that he had been tested.) There is now evidence that the rate of HIV/AIDS infections has leveled off, but attempts to stem the tide are hampered by the reluctance of South African men to use condoms and the alarmingly high rate of rape.

Civil Liberties in a Dominant-Party Political System

This chapter has underscored the growing concern that the ANC's position of political dominance, and the weakness of the opposition political parties, could pose a challenge to the consolidation of South African democracy. These concerns form the context for the controversy surrounding the November 2011 legislative approval of the Protection of Information Bill.

Since coming to power in 1994, the ANC has been embarrassed by a series of allegations of corruption by government officials, published in and publicized by South Africa's vigorous press. Some of these allegations have targeted top ANC leaders, including Jacob Zuma, who lost his job as deputy president in 2005 as a result of allegations of influence peddling, and most recently, Mac Maharaj, a legendary ANC leader and President Zuma's spokesperson. In March 2010, President Zuma's government introduced the Protection of Information Bill. In its original form the bill gave any government agency the power to classify all documents deemed to be in the national interest. It called for prison sentences of up to 25 years in jail for anybody who publically disclosed classified information. The initial language led to widespread opposition from civil libertarians, and many within the ANC. Over the next year the bill was heavily amended, and the version approved in November 2011 limited the ability to classify documents to police, security, and intelligence services, and significantly reduced prison sentences for most illegal disclosures of information. But the ANC rejected calls to include an exception protecting the release of information that can be shown to be in the public interest.

Despite these changes, there has been a vigorous public debate over the approved legislation. Critics claim it resembles apartheid-era restrictions on reporting. After the measure was approved, demonstrators took to the streets throughout South Africa, and a number of prestigious South Africans expressed their alarm. Archbishop Desmond Tutu, a legendary anti-Apartheid leader and head of South Africa's Truth and Reconciliation Commission, said the bill would "outlaw whistle-blowing and investigative journalism." COSATU, South Africa's major trade union confederation and a close ally of the ANC, claimed the legislation would make it harder to uncover corruption. Amnesty International called approval of the law "a dark day for freedom of expression."[30]

After decades of apartheid authoritarianism, South Africans are sensitive to any perceived erosion to their hard-won civil liberties. The Protection of Information bill and the ANC's plan to create a special tribunal to adjudicate complaints about unfair media coverage are signs of the governing party's increasingly defensive posture vis-à-vis South Africa's media. But the controversy also reveals a number of strengths in South Africa's democracy. The government was forced to heavily amend the legislation. Public protest and debate was vigorous and was a sign that South African civil society is not easily intimidated by the government.[31] Finally, opponents have vowed to challenge the new law in South Africa's Constitutional Court. That body has shown a willingness to overturn legislation.

NOTES

1. Anthony Sampson, "Men of the Renaissance," *The Guardian* (London), January 3, 1998, p. 19.
2. For a discussion of South African history, see Leonard Thompson, *The History of South Africa* (New Haven, CT: Yale University Press, 2001).
3. African History: Apartheid Legislation in South Africa, http://africanhistory.about.com/library/bl/blsalaws.htm (accessed 12/30/08); contains a detailed list of the apartheid legislative acts.
4. For more on the emergence of the struggle against apartheid and Mandela's role in it, see Nelson Mandela, *Long Walk to Freedom: The Autobiography of Nelson Mandela* (Boston: Little, Brown, 1996).
5. Neeta Misra-Dexter and Judith February, eds., *Testing Democracy: Which Way Is South Africa Going?* (Capetown: ABC Press, IDASA, 2010), p. vii.
6. Pierre de Vos, "Key Institutions Affecting Democracy in South Africa," in Misra-Dexter and February, eds., *Testing Democracy*, pp. 94–116.
7. J. L. Gibson and J. A. Caldeira, "Defenders of Democracy? Legitimacy, Popular Acceptance, and the South African Constitutional Court," *Journal of Politics* 65, no. 1 (February 2003): 1–30.
8. *The Economist*, "Presidents v Judges," December 10, 2011, www.economist.com/node/21541450 (accessed 12/23/11).
9. Vinothan Naidoo, "The Provincial Government Reform Process in South Africa: Policy Discretion and Developmental Relevance," *Politikon* 36, no. 2 (August 2009): 259–74.
10. Celia Dugger, "South Africa Exults Abroad but Frets at Home, *New York Times*, April 19, 2011, p. 4.
11. For one account, see Andrew Feinstein, *After the Party: A Personal and Political Journey Through the ANC* (Johannesburg: Jonathan Ball Publishers, 2007).
12. Karen E. Ferree, "Framing the Race in South Africa: The Political Origins of Racial-Census Elections (New York: Cambridge University Press, 2011), p. 1.
13. The data are taken from Karen Ferree, "The Microfoundations of Ethnic Voting, Evidence from South Africa," Afrobarometer, Working paper no. 40, June 2004, www.afrobarometer.org (accessed 12/17/11).
14. Steven Friedman, "Beneath the Surface: Civil Society and Democracy After Polokwane," in Misra-Dexter and February, eds., *Testing Democracy*, p. 117.
15. Anne-Sofie Isaksson, "Political Participation in Africa: Participatory Inequalities and the Role of Resources," Afrobarometer, Working Paper no. 121, September 2010, available at www.afrobarometer.org (accessed 6/3/11).
16. On COSATU, see Sakhela Buhlungu, "Gaining Influence but Losing Power? COSATU Members and the Democratic Transformation of South Africa," *Social Movement Studies* 7, no. 1 (May 2008).
17. Misra-Dexter and February, eds., *Testing Democracy*, p. 153.
18. Ronald Inglehart et al., eds., *Human Beliefs and Values: A Cross-Cultural Sourcebook Based on the 1999–2002 Value Surveys* (Mexico City: Siglo XXI Editores, 2004).
19. Daniel O'Flaherty and Constance J. Freeman, "Stability in South Africa: Will It Hold?" *Washington Quarterly* 22 (Autumn 1999); and "Africa's Engine," *The Economist*, January 15, 2004.
20. 2008 Afrobarometer data at www.afrobarometer.org (accessed 4/18/11).
21. *The Economist*, "Land Reform in South Africa," December 3, 2009, www.economist.com/node/15022632 (accessed 12/19/11).
22. Afrobarometer data www.afrobarometer.org (accessed 4/18/11).
23. Dominic Griffiths and Maria L.C. Prozesky, "The Politics of Dwelling: Being White in South Africa." *Africa Today* 56, no. 4 (summer 2010): 28.

24. Misra-Dexter and February, eds., *Testing Democracy*, p. 162.
25. Henning Melber, "South Africa and NEPAD—Quo Vadis?" *Policy Brief* 31 (June 2004), Centre for Policy Studies, www.cps.org.za/cps%20pdf/polbrief31.pdf (accessed 8/3/05).
26. For more on murder, see Rob McCafferty, *Murder in South Africa: A Comparison of Past and Present* (Claremont, South Africa: United Christian Action, 2003); and www.christianaction.org.za/newsletter_uca/murder_southafrica.doc (accessed 12/30/08).
27. "Resurgent Perceptions of Corruption in South Africa," Afrobarometer, Working Paper no. 43, June 2006 (accessed 6/7/11).
28. James Hammill and John Hoffman, "Quiet Diplomacy or Appeasement? South African Policy Towards Zimbabwe," *The Round Table* 98, no. 402 (June 2009): 373–84.
29. *The Economist*, "South Africa and Aids: Getting to Grips," December 2, 2010, http://www.economist.com/node/17633289 (accessed 12/17/11).
30. *The Economist*, "Don't Blow the Whistle," November 26, 2011, www.economist.com/node/21540312 (accessed 12/23/11).
31. For a good example of the debate surrounding the legislation see the *Mail and Guardian's* "Media Under Fire" report at http://mg.co.za/specialreport/media-under-fire (accessed 12/23/11).

KEY TERMS

African National Congress (ANC)   South Africa's major anti-apartheid liberation movement, and the governing party since the return of democracy in 1994

African Union (AU)   An organization of African nations pursuing greater political and economic integration across the continent

Afrikaans   The language of South Africa's Dutch settlers (Afrikaners)

Afrikaners   White South Africans who speak Afrikaans and are descendants of Dutch, French, and German colonists

apartheid   The policy of segregation put in place by the Afrikaner-dominated racist authoritarian regime in South Africa that was in power from 1948 to 1994

Bantustans   Tribal "homelands" established by the apartheid regime to deprive the black majority of South African citizenship

Black Economic Empowerment (BEE)   South Africa's affirmative action program that aims to create a new class of black owners and management through a series of quotas and targets

Boers   The early Dutch settlers in South Africa; the term is also used to describe Afrikaners

Boer Wars   The two epic wars fought between the Boers and the British that culminated in the defeat of the Afrikaners and their integration into the Union of South Africa

BRICS An organization of emerging countries in the developing world that includes Brazil, Russia, India, China, and South Africa

colored Widely used term in South Africa to describe citizens of mixed race, largely concentrated in and around Cape Town

Congress of South African Trade Unions (COSATU) South Africa's most important trade union confederation, closely linked to the governing ANC

Congress of the People (COPE) A new South African political party formed by defectors from the ANC

de Klerk, F. W. Final president of the apartheid regime; he negotiated the transition to democracy with the ANC

Democratic Alliance (DA) South Africa's main opposition party

Dutch Reformed Church Conservative Protestant Church that has historically been central to Afrikaner culture

Great Trek The epic migration of Afrikaners (Voortrekkers) into the interior of South Africa in 1835 to escape British colonization

Group Areas Act The centerpiece of apartheid legislation that divided South Africans into four racial categories and required strict segregation of housing along racial lines

Growth, Employment, and Redistribution (GEAR) The 1996 liberal macroeconomic structural adjustment plan that moved the ANC toward a more market-friendly political policy

Indians The term used by South Africans to describe citizens of Southeast Asian origin

Inkatha Freedom Party (IFP) The small Zulu political party that is currently the party of the opposition to the ANC

Mandela, Nelson The long-imprisoned leader of the ANC who became South Africa's first post-apartheid president

Mbeki, Thabo South Africa's former two-term president who was forced to resign in 2008 when he failed to win the election as the ANC leader

National Assembly South Africa's legislature

National Party (NP) The now-defunct party that created apartheid and dominated politics during the apartheid era

New Partnership for Africa's Development (NEPAD) The African Union program that attempts to tie foreign development aid to a commitment to democracy and the rule of law

Southern African Development Community (SADC) A 13-member African regional economic and cooperation community, of which South Africa was a founding member

Soweto A township created during apartheid to house blacks who were forcibly removed from Johannesburg

Truth and Reconciliation Commission The post-apartheid body established to document apartheid-era human rights abuses and to give reparations to victims and amnesty to perpetrators who confessed to crimes

Tutu, Archbishop Desmond The anti-apartheid activist and leader of South Africa's Anglican Church who chaired the Truth and Reconciliation Commission

Union of South Africa The 1910 name given to the British colony that integrated British and Afrikaner colonists after the Boer Wars

United Democratic Front (UDF) The unified anti-apartheid coalition created in 1983 from the major black and white opposition groups

Voortrekkers The Afrikaner pioneers who migrated into South Africa's interior to escape British colonists

Zille, Helen The current leader of South Africa's main opposition party, the Democratic Alliance

Zuma, Jacob South Africa's current president, as of 2009

WEB LINKS

African National Congress (www.anc.org.za)

African Studies Internet Resources: South Africa, Columbia University Libraries (www.columbia.edu/cu/lweb/indiv/africa/cuvl/SAfr.html)

Afrobarometer (www.afrobarometer.org)

Democratic Alliance (www.da.org.za)

Inkatha Freedom Party (www.ifp.org.za)

Institute for Democracy in South Africa (www.idasa.org.za)

Mail and Guardian (www.mg.co.za)

South African Broadcasting Corporation (www.sabcnews.co.za/portal/site/SABCNews/)

South African government (www.gov.za)

S Visit StudySpace for quizzes and other review material.
www.norton.com/studyspace

- Vocabulary Flashcards of All Key Terms
- Country Review Quizzes
- Complete Study Reviews and Outlines

14

HEAD OF STATE AND GOVERNMENT:
President Goodluck Jonathan (since February 9, 2010)

CAPITAL:
Abuja

TOTAL LAND SIZE:
923,768 sq km (32nd)

POPULATION:
170 million (7th)

GDP AT PPP:
$377.9 billion (31st)

GDP PER CAPITA AT PPP:
$2,500 (174th)

HUMAN DEVELOPMENT INDEX RANKING:
142nd

NIGERIA

Introduction

Why Study This Case?

Nigeria stands out in ways both impressive and disheartening. First, it is noteworthy for its sheer size: it is the most populous country in Africa and is predicted by century's end to trail only India and China as the world's third-largest nation. Second, unlike many other African countries, Nigeria is blessed with a great deal of natural wealth, from oil to agriculture. Following independence from British rule in 1960, those assets would have been expected to make Nigeria a major regional, if not global, actor.

Yet exactly the opposite happened, and Nigeria has become renowned for all that can go wrong with political misrule, social unrest, economic inequality and environmental degradation. For much of the time since independence, the country has been under military rule. These long periods of military dictatorship have coincided with widespread corruption, with substantial portions of the country's oil revenues and other resources channeled to those in power. In spite of earning billions of dollars in oil exports each year, Nigeria has become one of the poorest and least-developed countries in the world. It would seem to be an excellent example of a country in which natural resources have been used by those in power to buy supporters and repress the public.

Yet the long era of military rule may now be at an end. In 1999, Nigeria returned to civilian rule, and since then a fragile democratic system has taken hold. Still, much remains to be done. Nigeria lacks the rule of law and continues to be recognized as one of the most corrupt countries in the world. The state also has questionable control over the monopoly of violence, both in terms of civilian authority over the military and the capacity to contain the country's widespread criminal and political violence. The standard of living for the average Nigerian remains very low, with more than 80 percent of the population surviving on less than two dollars per day, far below what the country's wealth should ensure.

If the legacy of its military rule were not enough of a challenge for Nigeria, a second concern derives from its sheer size and diversity. Nigeria is made up of more than 250 ethnic groups, whose local interests and differences have been sharpened by a perniciously corrupt form of federalism. Although nearly three decades of military rule kept this fractiousness in check, democratic rule has allowed these tensions and violence to surface. Most disturbing is a growing ethnic rift between the Muslim north and the Christian and animist south. At a time when many global conflicts center on religion and religious fundamentalism, the prospect of increasing tension among faiths in Nigeria leads some observers to worry that in the long run the country will be ungovernable and will return to authoritarianism, civil war, or both. Is Nigeria doomed to be a partitioned or failed state?

Nigeria thus provides a fascinating, if daunting, example of the possibilities and potential limits of state power and democracy under conditions of postcolonialism and vast natural resource wealth. Can the change from military rule to democracy help bring stability and prosperity to Nigeria? Or are the problems of state capacity and autonomy such that democracy cannot help improve them—and might even make them worse? We will consider these tensions as we investigate Nigeria's political heritage, current institutions, social challenges, and political prospects.

Major Geographic and Demographic Features

One of Nigeria's most impressive features is its sheer size. With more than 150 million people, Nigeria has the largest national population in Africa and currently ranks seventh in the world. Lying along the western coast of the continent, Nigeria has a diverse climate and geography. The Niger-Benue river system divides the country into distinct regions. The north is relatively arid and known for its grasslands, while the south is characterized by tropical forests and coastal swamps. Nigeria's geography and climate (particularly in the south) are favorable to agriculture, such that nearly a third of the land is arable—compared with only 15 percent of the land in China and 20 percent in the United States. Until oil became a major export commodity in the 1960s, cocoa and nuts were a major source of foreign trade.

Nigeria's best-known region is the **Niger Delta**. The Niger River enters the sea at that point, creating a vast, swampy area of over 5,000 square miles. It is the third-largest wetland in the world, after the Netherlands and the Mississippi Delta, and host to an enormous range of plants and animals. The Niger Delta is also home to approximately 30 million people, traditionally engaged in farming and fishing. The complicated topography of the area has limited interaction, integration, and assimilation, thus fostering a large variety of ethnicities. By some estimates, over a dozen groups speaking some 25 languages inhabit the Delta. It is also one of the poorest regions of the country, with limited infrastructure and development.

But the Niger Delta is also the source of Nigeria's oil, which comprises the lion's share of the country's exports. And while oil production in the Delta has been a mixed blessing at best for the country as a whole, contributing to both national wealth and national corruption, its local consequences are just as profound but almost entirely negative. The first and most commonly cited local effect is environmental degradation. In the half century since oil production began, there have been more than 4,000 spills, whose effects on the wetlands and population are a source of intense domestic and international controversy.[1] Oil production has also abetted ethnic conflicts in the region, with groups competing for access to siphoned oil and on occasion attacking oil facilities in order to draw attention to their demands or to seek ransoms. Finally, oil production has exacerbated intergroup hostility in the Delta, as some groups have perceived others as having benefited disproportionately from the industry.[2] Given the importance of oil to Nigeria, the problems of this region significantly affect the security of the country as a whole.

The diversity marking the Delta is mirrored across the country as a whole. Nigeria is home to some 250 ethnic groups. Dominant among them are the **Hausa** and the **Fulani**, who are overwhelmingly Muslim and concentrated in the north; the **Igbo** (also spelled "Ibo"), who are predominantly Christian and concentrated in the southeast; and the **Yoruba**, who inhabit the southwest and whose members are divided among Christian, Muslim, and local animist faiths.

Nigeria's large population is a function of its fertility rate. In the past 20 years, the country's population has doubled, with the result that nearly half the population is now under the age of 14. According to some projections, the country will grow by another 40 million people in the next decade, with Lagos becoming one of the 10 largest cities in the world.[3] The presence of a large, rapidly growing, ethnically and religiously diverse population will continue to complicate development, stability, and governance.

Historical Development of the State

Like most other developing countries, Nigeria's history progressed from local political organization to imperial control to recent independence and instability. Contrary to common assumptions, precolonial Nigeria was neither undeveloped nor poorly organized. Rather, the region contained varying degrees and kinds of political and social organization, some of which were highly complex and wide ranging. Although we cannot explore each of them in depth, we can point to some of the earliest and most powerful examples.

Nigeria was the setting for several early kingdoms. Over 2,000 years ago, the members of the Nok society, located in what is now central Nigeria, fashioned objects out of iron and terra-cotta with a degree of sophistication unmatched in West Africa, though little else is known about their civilization. As the roots of today's dominant ethnic groups began to take shape, new forms of political organization emerged. Around 1200 C.E., the Hausa to the north established a series of powerful city-states, which served as conduits of north–south trade. In the southwest, the Yoruba kingdom of Oyo extended its power beyond the borders of modern-day Nigeria into present-day Togo. This kingdom grew wealthy through trade and the exploitation of natural resources, facilitated by its location along the coast. In the southeast, the Igbo maintained less-centralized political power, though they, too, had a precedent of earlier kingdoms and would come to play a central role in modern Nigerian politics.

ISLAM AND THE NIGERIAN NORTH

The fortunes of these three dominant ethnic groups (the Hausa, Yoruba, and Igbo) and other peoples in what is now Nigeria changed dramatically as contact with peoples, politics, and ideas from outside West Africa increased. The first important impact came not from Europe, however, but from the Middle East, with the spread of Islam. By the eleventh century, Islam had found its way into the Hausa region of northern Nigeria, carried along trade routes linking the region to North Africa and beyond. By the fifteenth century, Islam had brought literacy and scholarship to the region through the Arabic language, though the religion and its influences remained largely confined to the Hausa elite. By the late eighteenth century, however, an increase in contact with Islamic regions led to an increase in conversions to the faith. The religion's growing influence was solidified by the leadership of Usman dan Fodio (1754–1817). A religious scholar, Usman played an important role in spreading Islam among the Hausa and Fulani. He found widespread support among the peasantry, who felt oppressed under the city-states' warring monarchies and who saw in Islam's message a promise of greater social equality. Their embrace of Islam in turn alarmed those in power, eventually precipitating a conflict between the city-states and Usman. Following an initial conflict, Usman declared jihad against the Hausa city-states in 1804 and by 1808 had overthrown the ruling monarchs, establishing what became known as the Sokoto caliphate. The Sokoto caliphate became the largest empire in Africa at the time and provided a uniform government to a region previously racked by war. Islam would now play a central role in western Africa and in the eventual establishment of an independent Nigerian state.

EUROPEAN IMPERIALISM

As Islam and centralized political organization spread across the north, the south experienced similarly dramatic effects with the arrival of the European powers. As far back as the late fifteenth century, Europeans had begun arriving along Nigeria's coast, purchasing from indigenous traders agricultural products and slaves (often captives from local wars). From the seventeenth to the nineteenth century, Europeans established several coastal ports to support the burgeoning trade in slaves, with the United Kingdom becoming the major trading power. During that time, more than 3 million slaves were shipped from Nigeria to the Americas. In 1807, the United Kingdom declared the slave trade illegal and established a naval presence off Nigeria's coast for enforcement, though an illegal trade continued for another half century. The precipitous decline in the region's major export contributed to the collapse of the Yoruba's Oyo Empire and to divisions and warfare among its people, which in turn paved the way for an expanded British presence in the interior. The colonial presence further expanded as British industrialization generated ever-greater demand for resources, such as palm oil, cocoa, and timber. That demand radically changed the nature of agricultural production and encouraged greater reliance on local slavery to produce these goods. At the same time, British missionaries began to proselytize in the coastal and southern regions, converting large numbers of Igbo and Yoruba to Christianity.

By 1861, the British had established a colony at Lagos, and by the 1884–5 Berlin Conference, other European powers had recognized the United Kingdom's "sphere of influence" along the coast. Fearing French and German encroachment in the interior, the United Kingdom quickly joined the European powers' **"scramble for Africa"** by asserting its authority far inland. Through a combination of diplomacy, co-optation, and force, the United Kingdom established control over both the north and the south. In many areas, the British relied upon a policy of indirect rule. For example, as the Sokoto caliphate was brought under

TIMELINE OF POLITICAL DEVELOPMENT

YEAR	EVENT
300s B.C.E.	Jos plateau is settled by the Nok people
1100s C.E.	Hausa kingdom is formed in the north; Oyo kingdom is formed in the southwest
1472	Portuguese navigators reach the Nigerian coast
1500s–1800s	Slave trade develops and flourishes
1807	United Kingdom bans the slave trade
1809	Sokoto caliphate is founded
1861–1914	Britain acquires Lagos and establishes a series of Nigerian protectorates
1960	Nigeria achieves independence and creates the First Republic
1966	After a military coup, the Federal Military Government is established
1967–70	In Nigerian Civil War, Biafra fails to win independence
1976	General Olusegun Obasanjo comes to power and initiates a transition to civilian rule
1979	Elections bring Shehu Shagari to power, establishing the Second Republic
1983-93	Military rulers again seize power
1993	Transition to civilian rule (the Third Republic) fails; Sani Abacha seizes power
1995	Activist Ken Saro-Wiwa is executed
1998	Abacha dies; Abdulsalam Abubakar succeeds him as the military head of government
1999	Military rule ends and the Fourth Republic is established; Olusegun Obasanjo is elected president
2000	Sharia law is adopted by 12 northern states
2000–02	Ethnic and religious clashes leave several thousand dead

(Continued)

TIMELINE (Continued)

YEAR	EVENT
2007	Obasanjo steps down; Umaru Yar'Adua comes to power in a fraudulent election, marking Nigeria's first civilian transfer of power
2009	Yar'Adua negotiates an amnesty with Niger Delta militants
2010	Yar'Adua dies in office and Vice President Goodluck Jonathan is named president
2011	Jonathan is elected president in a relatively clean democratic election

British control, local leaders were allowed to keep their positions, co-opted as part of the new state bureaucracy. Furthermore, the British colonial administration respected **Sharia**, or Islamic law, in noncriminal matters, and prohibited Christian proselytizing in the region. Such policies helped limit local resistance but increased the power of some ethnic groups over others, giving them greater authority within the imperial administration. In areas where indirect rule was less successful, as among the Igbo, resistance was much more significant. In 1914, the various protectorates in the area under British control were unified under the name "Nigeria," though the country remained highly decentralized administratively, which reflected and reinforced distinct regional differences.

Following unification, Nigeria experienced dramatic change under British imperial rule. The British developed a modern infrastructure, constructing ports, roads, and railways to facilitate economic development and extraction. Agricultural production continued to play an important role in exports. Within Nigerian society, development meant the establishment of Western educational policies and institutions, especially in regions where Christian missionaries were active. In general, indirect rule meant the development of a new local elite more Westernized and more conscious of the complexities of imperialism. The creation of a colonial legislative council, with local elections for some of the seats, introduced the idea of democratic representative institutions, no matter how limited.

It might be thought that the development of a Westernized elite would help perpetuate imperial control. Instead, as in other British colonies such as India, exposure to Western ideas served as the foundation for resistance, as Nigerians embraced the heretofore alien concepts of nationalism, sovereignty, and self-rule. Such ideas, however, were not easily planted in Nigeria's complex political terrain. For some activists, anticolonialism meant a greater role for Nigeria and other

Nigeria inherited a colonial legal system that combined British common law with an assortment of traditional or customary laws that the colonial government had permitted to handle local matters (including Sharia, which predominated in the Northern Region). This legacy fostered a court system and rule of law that historically, even during periods of military rule, retained a degree of independence and legitimacy. However, the Abacha military dictatorship (1993–8) flouted this independence, routinely ignoring legal checks and using an intimidated judiciary to silence and even eliminate political opponents. Although Abacha frequently used the courts to persecute many of his enemies (including those alleged to have plotted coups against him in 1995 and 1997), the most infamous case of "judicial terrorism" was the 1994 Abacha military tribunal that resulted in the aforementioned execution of the noted playwright and activist Ken Saro-Wiwa (see "Ken Saro-Wiwa: Playwright and Environmental Activist," p. 703).[9]

With the return to democratic rule, an effort has been made to reestablish the legitimacy and independence of the judiciary. The 1999 constitution established a Supreme Court, a Federal Court of Appeals, and a single unified court system at the national and state levels. The rule of law has been further strengthened under the Fourth Republic, with successive governments launching anticorruption campaigns. But although the courts have had some success prosecuting former state officials for enriching themselves while in office and addressing electoral fraud, these anticorruption efforts have typically faltered as they've drawn closer to those who are still in office or who remain politically influential.

The constitution also permits individual states to authorize traditional subsidiary courts, giving these customary legal systems significant judicial clout. The most controversial of the traditional systems have been the Islamic Sharia courts, which now function in 12 of the predominantly Muslim northern states. As discussed later in this case, Nigerians have debated heatedly and, in some cases, violently over the role and jurisdiction of the Sharia courts.

The Electoral System

As in other presidential systems, Nigerians directly elect their president and separately elect members of both chambers of their legislature, the National Assembly. But unlike the U.S. system, in Nigeria, presidents, senators, and representatives all serve four-year terms, with elections for all three offices held in the same year.

KEN SARO-WIWA: PLAYWRIGHT AND ENVIRONMENTAL ACTIVIST

Kenule Benson Saro-Wiwa was born in 1941 to an Ogoni family, members of an ethnic minority of southern Nigeria, on whose land in the Niger Delta rich oil reserves were discovered. By the 1980s, Saro-Wiwa had become known internationally for his novels and plays, many written in Nigerian pidgin, or "rotten," English. At the same time, he became increasingly involved in political efforts to force the Shell oil company and the Nigerian government to take greater responsibility for the environment and share a greater portion of the oil wealth with the Ogoni, whose lands the oil rigs were despoiling. In 1990, with others, Saro-Wiwa founded the Movement for the Survival of the Ogoni People (MOSOP). MOSOP challenged the government's revenue-sharing formulas, which kept the bulk of the oil wealth flowing to national government coffers. With allied groups, MOSOP also disrupted production, compelling Shell first to curtail oil extraction in the Ogoni region and ultimately to abandon its operations there altogether. By interfering in this "stream of petroleum revenues that fed the dictatorship,"* MOSOP raised the ire of General Sani Abacha's military government, which in 1994 ordered a brutal crackdown on Ogoni activists and sympathetic Ogoni villages. Saro-Wiwa and other activists were arrested on trumped-up charges and brought before a special military tribunal. The show trial returned a verdict of guilty, and in November 1995 the government hanged all nine of the defendants, despite an international outcry and the efforts of international human rights groups and the leaders of dozens of countries to intervene.

*Howard French, *A Continent for the Taking* (New York: Alfred A. Knopf, 2004), p. 38.

In an effort to ensure that the president serves with a national mandate, Nigeria's constitution requires that the winning presidential candidate obtain both an overall majority of votes nationwide and at least 25 percent of the ballots cast in at least two-thirds of the states.[10] This distribution requirement became an issue of contention in the 1979 election, when the Supreme Court was called upon to determine what constituted two-thirds of Nigeria's then 19 states (there are now 36). Ultimately, the court ruled that Shehu Shagari's victory in 12 states—not the 13 demanded by the opposition—sufficed, and Shagari was named president. The constitution holds that if no candidate succeeds in winning a majority of total votes and obtaining the two-thirds threshold in the first round, a second round of voting takes place a week later, pitting the top two candidates against each other in a runoff.

Nigeria's dominant **People's Democratic Party (PDP)** put in place another informal arrangement designed to enhance the legitimacy of presidential elections when the country returned to democracy in 1999. Christian politicians from the south feared that democracy would always favor the more numerous Muslim population in the north and that southern candidates would thereby be shut out of power (not to mention insider access to the country's vast oil revenues). As reassurance, PDP leaders established a system of presidential rotation known as "**zoning**," in which the party would alternate every two terms nominating candidates from the north and the south. While this agreement facilitated support for reestablishing democratic rule, it limited the pool of qualified presidential candidates and exacerbated ethnic divisions by framing issues and policy priorities in terms of alternating regions and religions. Moreover, like the distribution requirement just noted, this plan also ran into problems when President Yar'Adua (a northern Muslim who succeeded a southern Christian) died in office in 2010. As directed by the constitution, he was succeeded by the vice president, Goodluck Jonathan, who happened to be a Christian from the south. Jonathan's successful bid for a full second term in 2011 angered many northern politicians, who saw it as a violation of the zoning system, which should have given a northern president a full two terms. Jonathan's election prompted substantial post-election protest and violence in the north. Even though he has promised not to run again in 2015, it remains to be seen if this informal accommodation will continue.

All 360 seats in the House of Representatives are contested in single-member districts (SMDs) apportioned roughly equally by population. The 109 members of the Senate are also elected from single-member districts, with each of 36 states divided into three districts. The federal district, or "capital territory," of Abuja elects one senator in a single-seat constituency for the 109th seat. These winner-take-all single-member districts have allowed just three parties to dominate both chambers of the National Assembly. Several other smaller parties have managed on occasion to win seats in the House. The success of the smaller parties reflects the geographic concentration of ethnic groups willing to vote in blocs large enough to win a plurality of votes in the less-populous lower-house electoral districts, such as the districts dominated by the Kanuri minority of northeastern Nigeria.

Local Government

Constitutionally, Nigeria is a federal republic with national, state, and local levels of governance. Although Nigeria's military governments sought to establish a unitary system, the gaping ethnic divisions within the country have prevented governments of all stripes from truly unifying the nation and centralizing political authority. These divisions reflect the ethnic diversity of Nigeria and the legacy of colonial rule.

In 1970, the Federal Military Government divided the republic into 12 states following the Nigerian Civil War, which nearly split the country permanently. The number of states grew to 19 in 1976, 30 by 1991, and 36 by 1996, plus the Federal Capital Territory. The number of local government units has varied even more substantially, reflecting the uncertainty of how federalism should be constituted in Nigeria. The democratic government elected in 1979 doubled the number of local authorities to more than 700. In 1983, the military government downsized the number to 300, but it has since increased to nearly 800.

With a history of interregional instability and suspicion and relatively weak state capacity, Nigeria will certainly see the countervailing demands of centralization and devolution persist. On the one hand, the national government's control of the bulk of oil revenues has provided the patrimonial glue that keeps the local regions dependent upon the center. But as increasingly diverse and articulate voices have entered a progressively democratic political arena, the calls for enhanced state and local autonomy have grown louder. Those demands range from expanded state control over the budget (and for the oil-rich Niger Delta, local control over its oil revenues), to a separate military for each region, to full-fledged dismemberment of Nigeria.

To date, local and even state governments have enjoyed little autonomy from the national government and have no means of generating revenue. Put simply, the central government controls the purse strings, and the Nigerian purse depends almost completely upon oil revenues. (The non-oil sector makes up just 4 percent of the private sector.) Not surprisingly, as oil revenues have expanded, so has the public sector at all levels, as have the degrees of corruption associated with that patronage. At the same time, the expansion of oil revenues has led to increased disputes over the percentage of these funds—known as the **derivation formula**—that should accrue to the oil-producing localities.[11]

Other Institutions

THE MILITARY

Although the Fourth Republic has managed to sponsor four successive and relatively peaceful democratic elections, independent Nigeria's tumultuous history cautions us not to become too confident that the military will remain in its barracks. Nigeria's nearly three decades of experience with military rule (1966–79 and 1983–99) left a deep impression on Nigerian politics. It is not a coincidence that most of Nigeria's most powerful leaders (including former coup leader and recent president Obasanjo) boast a military background. As is the case elsewhere in postcolonial Africa and in much of the developing world, the military has served as one of the few stable avenues of meritocratic social mobility; it has long been able to attract many of Nigeria's best, brightest, and most ambitious. This avenue has been particularly important for the ethnic Muslims of northern Nigeria, who have been educationally and economically disadvantaged in comparison with southern Nigerians. Although the south is the source of Nigeria's oil, for many years the north controlled the army and used that control, in the form of military dictatorships, to redistribute oil wealth.

Scholars have offered a number of explanations for the military's nonintervention in Nigeria's Fourth Republic.[12] They point to President Obasanjo's legislation in the early 2000s requiring the retirement of all military officers who previously held political offices during the period of military rule. They also note the government's seizure of senior military officers' corruptly acquired money and properties and the growing professionalization of the younger cohorts of officers. That said, a military coup plot was preempted in 2004, and persistent corruption and the inefficacy of civilian rule, combined with the vast spoils of office, remain tempting justifications for the military once again to try to usurp control. Only time will tell if Nigeria's military is prepared to make its most recent withdrawal from public life permanent.

Political Conflict and Competition

The Party System

Politics in oil-rich, patrimonial Nigeria has been described as a "contest of self-enrichment."[13] Whether these political contests have been fought with ballots or bullets, the stakes have indeed been high, the competition fierce, and corruption and violence all too common.[14] Not surprisingly, political parties and the party system have fared best under democratic regimes and have withered during periods of military rule. Political parties first began forming during the colonial period and did so quite naturally along ethnic lines, even as early advocates of democracy sought to establish multicultural and issue-based platforms. Although the names of the dominant parties have changed over time, those that emerged during each era continued to reflect the ethnic divisions, despite efforts of democratic and even some military regimes to establish cross-ethnic national parties.

Until recently, it has made more sense to discuss Nigeria's parties in terms of their ethnic identity and, therefore, their geographic location than to try to place them on a left–right political continuum. This regional party identity has exacerbated ethnic tensions and complicated efforts to establish democratic institutions and legitimize national party politics. Moreover, most state and local contests are also dominated by the region's dominant party, a circumstance that allows that party to control the state assembly and effectively capture the seats in the national Senate and House of Representatives as well. This reminds us that in Nigeria, all politics is in the first instance local, and that in these local communities, ethnicity and clientelist networks have traditionally meant everything.

Although recent democratic elections under Nigeria's Fourth Republic have offered hope for the establishment of cross-ethnic parties with national appeal, strengthened democracy has also given stronger voice to persistent sectarian and even local separatist demands. The centrifugal pull of communal violence between the Muslim north and the Christian south and growing violent contention over the spoils of the oil-rich Niger Delta continue to weaken the centripetal push of national electoral contests too often plagued by political corruption and ethnic-based patronage networks.

Elections

Colonial-era parties survived through the First Republic (1960–66) but were banned from the onset of military rule until Olusegun Obasanjo came to power in 1976. Obasanjo legalized the establishment of political parties in 1978, and some 150 parties were formed in that year alone. In 1979, Obasanjo's elected successor, Shehu Shagari, sought to impose order on this political cacophony by compelling the formation of nationwide parties. The constitution of the Second Republic specified that any successful presidential candidate must win at least one-fourth of the vote in at least two-thirds of the states. The election commission required that all parties open membership to all Nigerians and that the parties' leadership come from at least two-thirds of the states. In all, five parties were deemed viable contenders in the 1979 and 1983 elections. Military coups in 1983 and 1985 (in part the result of the widespread corruption and failure of the Second Republic) once again banned political parties.

Ibrahim Babangida, the military ruler from 1985 to 1993, charged his National Election Commission with reforming the party system to produce a two-party system. But fears that such a system would lead to a dangerous political division between the Muslim north and the Christian south led the commission once again to approve five parties. Dissatisfied, Babangida dissolved the commission and established two national parties, one neatly placed "a little to the left of center and one a little to the right."[15] The government built headquarters for each party, gave each one start-up funds, and even named them (the Social Democratic Party and the National Republican Convention). Babangida called for local elections in 1990 and announced plans to hand over power to civilians with a presidential election in 1992.

Although the election was postponed until 1993, it took place fairly. But because the winner was a southern (Yoruba) civilian distrusted by the northern military generals, the military nullified the results and charged the apparent victor with treason. The military installed an interim puppet president, who was quickly pushed aside by General Sani Abacha. Abacha called for elections in 1996, and his military government certified five parties—all loyal to him. Not surprisingly, all five nominated Abacha as their candidate for president.

Abdusalam Abubakar, Abacha's military successor, dissolved the five parties and called for presidential elections in 1999. In another effort to foster political parties with a national, or "federal," character, the election commission approved only parties that maintained well-established national organizations. Nine parties qualified for local elections, and the three parties with the highest votes in those elections were permitted to participate in the national legislative and presidential elections. Not surprisingly, each of those parties once again reflected its regional base in one of the country's main ethnic groups: the People's Democratic Party, representing the northern Hausa; the All People's Party (APP), representing the eastern Igbo; and the Alliance for Democracy (AD), representing the western Yoruba.

Democracy advocates are hopeful that the 1999 election marked a watershed for Nigerian national politics. In that election, PDP supporters—with strength in the Muslim north, home of many of Nigeria's military leaders—chose to support Obasanjo, a retired general but a southern Christian Yoruba. The AD chose to throw its support behind the APP contender rather than field its own candidate. Obasanjo won with nearly two-thirds of the vote, and a "relieved public" overlooked the many flaws in the election and largely accepted the results that ushered in the Fourth Republic.[16]

The subsequent three elections have followed this trend of growing democracy and declining regional base for party affiliation, but also of continued PDP dominance and persistent concerns over electoral corruption. The 2003 election, the first sponsored by a civilian government in 20 years, returned Obasanjo to office. In 2007, he stepped down as required by the constitution, marking the first ever succession of democratically elected executives in Nigerian history. This cleared the way for **Umaru Yar'Adua**, Obasanjo's handpicked candidate, to succeed him, winning a landslide victory with purportedly 70 percent of the vote. As in the 2003 elections, the PDP swept not only the presidential election but also contests for the two chambers of the legislature and state assembly races, held in the same month. The victory was marred, however, by opposition and foreign observer charges of widespread corruption and fraud in electoral contests at all levels. Yar'Adua's two chief rivals for the presidency sought to annul the election results,[17] and even foreign observers concluded that the elections were so badly rigged that they "lacked even the pretense of democratic plausibility."[18] After a nearly yearlong investigation, an appeals court concluded that the margin of victory was wide enough that, despite shortcomings, even a fully clean election would still have brought Yar'Adua to office.

Coming to office as a result of what was arguably Nigeria's most corrupt election, Yar'Adua in many ways redeemed himself in the eyes of the electorate. He battled political corruption and negotiated a cease-fire in the Niger River Delta, but fell ill and died in his third year in office. His vice president, Goodluck Jonathan, assumed the presidency and the right to finish out Yar'Adua's four-year term. As a southern Christian, Jonathan was initially seen as simply a caretaker until the 2011 election would permit the PDP's northern political bosses to resume their "turn" in the rotating "zoning" system. But he lost no time in pursuing his predecessor's reform agenda and promising to tackle three of Nigeria's biggest problems: rigged elections, woefully inadequate electricity, and the insurgency in his native Niger Delta. Significantly, he sacked the powerful but corrupt head of the Nigerian election commission and replaced him with an impeccably honest academic, who oversaw Nigeria's cleanest election in 2011. Despite his southern and Christian credentials, Jonathan won both the heavily contested PDP nomination for the presidency and a hard-fought election against the popular northern former dictator Muhammadu Buhari, who represented the newly formed Congress for Progressive Change (CPC) party (see the table "Results of Nigeria's Recent National Elections," p. 711).

In spite of four consecutive affirmations of the democratic process in Nigeria and the high expectations of the Nigerian people, endemic government corruption, communal and gangster violence, and persistent economic misery continue to test Nigerians' patience for democratic rule. Much of the $400 billion in oil

An election worker marks the finger of a Nigerian voter in the 2011 presidential election, judged by observers to be Nigeria's cleanest polling to date.

revenues earned during the PDP's control of government has been neither invested nor distributed, but rather has found its way into the hands of both regional and national PDP elite, in spite of the professed and increasingly genuine efforts of top leaders to stem this corruption. Despite the vast wealth that oil has generated, 80 percent of Nigerians still live on less than two dollars a day, and critics of the ruling party have called it the "Poverty Development Party." Nigeria's ethnic and religious fault lines also remain starkly apparent; in the 2011 election, Jonathan earned nearly 60 percent of the popular vote, but failed to win in any of the 12 northernmost states. Buhari won over 30 percent of the vote, but obtained less than one-fourth of the votes in each of the 20 southernmost states. When asked in 2005 if the present system of elected government "should be given more time to deal with inherited problems," only 55 percent of Nigerians said yes, compared with 58 percent in 2003 and nearly 80 percent in 2000. When asked in 2008 how satisfied they were with how democracy works in Nigeria, over two-thirds of respondents indicated they were not very (29 percent) or not at all (38 percent) satisfied. Support for a democratic system remains strong, but governments of the Fourth Republic must start delivering on promises of better times if they hope to avoid the fate of earlier republics.

Results of Nigeria's Recent National Elections

Region	North	East Igbo	West		
Ethnicity	Hausa	APP/ANPP/	Yoruba	Other	
Party	PDP	CPC*	AD/ACN†	parties	Total

ELECTION YEAR		PRESIDENTIAL VOTE (%)			
1999	62.8	37.2	no candidate	—	100
2003	61.9	32.2	no candidate	5.9	100
2007	69.8	18.7	7.5	5.0	100
2011	58.9	31.9	5.4	3.8	100

		SENATE SEATS			
1999	65	24	20	0	109
2003	73	28	6	0	107‡
2007	87	14	6	2	109
2011	71	CPC:7; ANPP:7	18	6	109

		HOUSE SEATS			
1999	212	79	69	0	360
2003	213	95	31	7	346‡
2007	260	61	31	4	356‡
2011	199	CPC:37; ANPP:27	69	22	354‡

*The APP renamed itself the All Nigeria People's Party (ANPP) after a merger with a smaller independent party in 2003. The Congress for Progressive Change (CPC) formed in 2009 to support Buhari's candidacy and drew most of its supporters from the ANPP, though the latter has continued as a separate party.
†The Action Congress of Nigeria (ACN) is the result of the 2006 merger of the Alliance for Democracy and several smaller parties.
‡Contested returns from some districts reduced the total number of candidates seated in some Senate and House elections.

Civil Society

Neither the British colonial government nor the series of military authoritarian regimes was able to squelch Nigeria's rich tradition of activism and dissent. Even Abacha's oppressive dictatorship in the 1990s could not fully muzzle what one foreign observer referred to as Nigerian citizens' "defiant spunk."[19] In Nigeria's relatively short postcolonial history, a wide variety of formal interest groups and informal voluntary associations has emerged and persisted. Under the relaxed environment of the Fourth Republic, these groups and organizations have proliferated and strengthened. Some of them, particularly professional associations and other NGOs, have drawn their support from across Nigeria's cultural spectrum and have functioned in ways that promote national integration. Others, particularly those based on ethnic and religious identities, are among the most resilient of groups and in some cases serve to fragment Nigerian society.

Formal and informal ethnic and religious associations have always played an important role in Nigerian society. Some of these groups have long served as important vehicles of mutual trust for promoting the economic interests of their members: for example, by mobilizing savings or investing in a business. Others formed to protect or promote the ethnic or local interests of a particular minority group. In the early years of independence, some groups provided the foundation for the subsequent formation of political parties. Among the most important of these issue-based minority associations were those that emerged in the Niger Delta to protect the interests of ethnic and other groups in the region. The **Movement for the Survival of the Ogoni People**, or **MOSOP**, established by Ken Saro-Wiwa in the 1990s to defend the interests of the Ogoni, employed a variety of legal and extra-legal political tactics to secure more financial benefits with fewer environmental costs from foreign-operated oil interests in the Niger Delta. As conditions in the region have worsened and more and broader constituencies feel they have a right to a portion of the oil revenues, groups in the Niger Delta have more readily turned to violence. Most notorious among these is the **Movement for the Emancipation of the Niger Delta (MEND)**, which has developed a reputation for "bunkering" (illegally siphoning off) oil, kidnapping foreign oil workers, and even launching daylight attacks on oil facilities in the region. Former president Yar'Adua negotiated a 2009 truce and amnesty that, unlike previous efforts, brought a significant drop in violence in the region, but certainly not an end to it. The lines dividing ethnic and environmental political associations, insurgent separatist move-

Choosing Between a Good Democracy and a Strong Economy

	GOOD DEMOCRACY (PERCENTAGE)	STRONG ECONOMY (PERCENTAGE)
Nigeria	59	40
India	56	41
Mexico	53	41
China	50	44
Brazil	50	46
South Africa	40	58
Russia	15	74

Source: Pew Center for the People and the Press, 2007.

ments, youth fraternities (or cults), and common criminal gangs are blurring in this complex and troubled region.

If political violence has subsided in recent years in the Niger Delta, conflict between Christian and Muslim religious institutions and groups in the northern interior has increased, and Muslim extremism in on the rise. The radical Islamist sect Boko Haram (literally "Western education is a sin"), which is pressing for wider application of Sharia law, has presented the single largest threat to peace, claiming responsibility for hundreds of terrorist attacks. These included a series of bombings and shootings during Christmas Day services in the region in 2011 and brutal attacks on government security buildings that killed nearly 200 people in the northern city of Kano in 2012. A 2011 suicide bombing at the UN headquarters in the capital, Abuja, raised fears about the group's ties to organized terrorist organizations outside of Nigeria. It is important to note, however, that sectarian conflict has been mitigated by the numerous divisions and differences within each religious tradition. Although Muslims of the north share a common faith and have banded together in defense of certain interests (such as the maintenance

in Nigeria's Muslim community, however, and could play directly into the hands of terrorists.[26] Nigeria will undoubtedly become more connected to the globalizing world in the coming decade, but such a connection will require balancing domestic tensions with regional and international pressures. It will not be easy.

CURRENT ISSUES IN NIGERIA

Niger Delta

Nowhere do Nigeria's multitude of complex political, social, economic, and environmental problems and prospects converge more acutely than in the oil-producing Niger Delta. Home to some 31 million Nigerians, who comprise more than 40 distinct ethnic groups and speak more than 250 dialects, this region also produces over 2 million barrels of crude oil a day and has the potential to produce up to 3 million barrels. Tragically, corrupt national and local politicians steal or squander the lion's share of oil revenues; local militias and gangsters siphon oil, kidnap oil workers, and wreck production facilities; and millions of gallons of oil and other effluents contaminate the Niger's delicate tropical ecosystem. A 2011 UN report estimated that drinking water in some areas of the Delta contains some 900 times the amount of benzene (a carcinogen) that is deemed safe by the World Health Organization and predicted that cleaning the crude oil residue in the area will take decades and billions of dollars. The wasteful and illegal "flaring," or burning off, of natural gas alone is by some estimates the world's single largest contributor of greenhouse gas and wastes $500 million in potential gas revenues each year.

Although the region has been troubled for many decades, in recent years impoverished communities in the Delta have become increasingly angry, organized, and restive. With the reestablishment of democracy in 1999, politicians began to arm local gangs to rig elections for them. International oil producers who operate in Nigeria, such as Shell and Chevron, have worsened matters by regularly providing payments to local leaders as tribute for operating in their communities. This practice has increased conflict among ethnic groups in the Delta and between community leaders and unemployed youth, with each group vying

A transfer station pumps crude oil out of the Niger Delta. Oil has brought wealth, corruption, conflict, and pollution to Nigeria.

for a share of the funds. A result has been the spread of armed militias, frequently linked to political parties, battling, often violently, over oil. Among their activities are "bunkering" (illegally siphoning oil from pipelines—easily 10 percent of all that is produced), seizing or destroying facilities, kidnapping foreign oil industry workers for ransom, and staging attacks on rival groups. The militant group MEND has become the largest and best-organized of these groups, launching frequent and increasingly brazen attacks since 2006.

Both authoritarian and elected governments have tried a variety of schemes to calm the region, including military operations and offers of amnesty. Most successful of these has been a truce negotiated in 2009 in which thousands of militants surrendered in exchange for unconditional pardon, a monthly stipend, and the promise of retraining and education. The government also promised to adjust the derivation formula, allocating more oil revenues directly to Delta communities. Although the promised retraining has been slow to materialize, and violence in the region has once again been on the rise, the fact that current president Goodluck Jonathan is an Iijaw, the largest ethnic group in the Delta, and grew up in the region has raised hopes that he will deliver on the government's promises of rehabilitation and redress. A lasting solution to this conflict, however, will not be easy; it will require more effective policing, local governance, central control over the actions of foreign oil producers, and acknowledgment of the economic and environmental demands of the local population most directly affected and deeply harmed by these activities.

The Costs of Democracy

Winston Churchill once famously concluded that democracy had proven to be "the worst form of government, except for all those other forms that have been tried from time to time." Having suffered through decades of brutal military authoritarianism, some might conclude that Nigerians have perhaps been equally cursed under democratic regimes. Rather than delivering good governance, Nigerian democracy has too often brought corruption, violence, and generally weak and incompetent leaders.

Not surprisingly, oil revenues have been the primary lubricant in making democracy "work" in this postcolonial state comprising some 250 highly diverse ethnic groups. National political leaders have co-opted regional and local elite with the promises of cash and political appointments in exchange for delivering votes. This patronage system has given great electoral advantage to the incumbent, who has had control of the "excess crude account," the giant slush fund of surplus oil revenues. During the notoriously corrupt 2007 elections, this fund of some $20 billion practically evaporated as Obasanjo worked to ensure that the PDP and his handpicked successor, Yar'Adua, would secure victory.

But things are improving. If the 2007 elections were Nigeria's most corrupt, the 2011 elections were arguably Nigeria's cleanest. In 2010, President Jonathan sacked the corrupt director of Nigeria's election commission, largely responsible for rigging past elections, and replaced him with a highly respected academic who pledged to clean up Nigeria's electoral politics. In the run-up to the 2011 elections, the newly led commission fingerprinted all 73.5 million eligible voters, required that all ballots be printed abroad, and established an "open secret ballot system" in which voters' fingerprints were scanned at the polls and voters were asked to remain at the polling stations until all votes were tallied locally. Although the process cost nearly $600 million, outside observers and voters alike have concluded it was worth the cost. In addition, following the 2011 election, the Jonathan government established the Nigerian Sovereign Investment Authority. This trust is designed to insulate oil revenues from the hands and pockets of politicians, instead directing the funds toward economic development. Addressing Nigeria's poverty, inequality, and unemployment will likely do more to consolidate democracy than any other measures.

If Nigeria's elections are becoming more transparent, sadly, they have not become less violent. A journalist reporting on Nigeria's 2011 presidential election concluded that the tallies for Nigerian elections "come in two separate columns. One records the votes cast at polling stations; the other the number of people killed around the time of the election."[27] In the weeks leading up to the elections, several politicians arranged to have their opponents murdered, while others hired gangs to intimidate rivals' campaigns. On election day, groups threw hand grenades to dissuade would-be voters, and others stole ballot boxes or snatched tally sheets. The worst period was that immediately following the election, as dissatisfied voters, in many cases stirred up (or even paid) by losing candidates, went on looting and killing sprees. Some 800 Nigerians died in just the week following the elections, as simmering ethnic and religious tensions merged with electoral disappointment and economic deprivation. The greatest violence occurred (and persists) in Nigeria's Muslim north, where incomes and literacy rates are a fraction of those in the south and where poverty drives young men into the arms of criminal gangs and militant Islamic groups.[28] As with corruption, solving electoral and ethnic violence and promoting democracy will require in the first instance alleviating Nigerian poverty. Perhaps Nigerians are patient enough to wait for this. Asked about the corruption and violence that accompanied the 2011 election, one voter concluded, "We have anger, but we have even more hope."

NOTES

1. Judith Burdin Asuni, *Blood Oil in the Niger Delta* (Washington, DC: United States Institute of Peace, 2009).
2. *The Niger Delta: No Democratic Dividend* (New York: Human Rights Watch, 2002).
3. *World Urbanization Prospects: The 2003 Revision Population Database* (New York: United Nations, 2004).
4. Charles R. Nixon, "Self-Determination: The Nigeria/Biafra Case," *World Politics* 24, no. 4 (July 1972): 473–97.
5. Blaine Harden, *Africa: Dispatches from a Fragile Continent* (Boston: Houghton Mifflin, 1990), p. 247.
6. For a useful discussion of the Nigerian constitutional process, see Julius O. Ihonvbere, "How to Make an Undemocratic Constitution: The Nigerian Example," *Third World Quarterly* 21 (2000): 343–66.

7. The 1999 constitution states that the "composition of the Government of the Federation or any of its agencies and the conduct of its affairs shall be carried out in such a manner as to reflect the federal character of Nigeria and the need to promote national unity, and also to command national loyalty thereby ensuring that there shall be no pre-dominance of persons from a few states or from a few ethnic or other sectional groups in that government or in any of its agencies." See E. Ike Udogu, "Review of Rotimi T. Suberu's *Federalism and Ethnic Conflict in Nigeria*," *Journal of Third World Studies* (Spring 2004):296–300.

8. "A Reporter's Tale," *The Economist*, February 26, 2004.

9. For the term *judicial terrorism*, see Shu'aibu Musa, "Shades of Injustice: Travails of Muslim Activists in Nigeria in the Hands of Successive Regimes," paper presented at the International Conference of Prisoners of Faith, London, February 17, 2002 (London: Islamic Human Rights Commission, 2002), www.ihrc.org.uk/file/02feb17drmusaSHADES%20OF%20INJUSTICE.pdf (accessed 11/3/05).

10. Matthijs Bogaards, "Ethnic Party Bans and Institutional Engineering in Nigeria," *Democratization* 17 (August 2010): 730–49.

11. Udogu, "Review of Rotimi T. Suberu's *Federalism and Ethnic Conflict in Nigeria.*"

12. William Ehwarieme, "The Military Factor in Nigeria's Democratic Stability, 1999–2009," *Armed Forces & Society* 37 (2011): 494–511.

13. Howard French, *A Continent for the Taking* (New York: Alfred A. Knopf, 2004), p. 27.

14. Ike Okonta, "Nigeria: Chronicle of a Dying State," *Current History* (May 2005): 203–8.

15. Harden, *Africa: Dispatches from a Fragile Continent*, p. 306.

16. Peter M. Lewis, "Nigeria: Elections in a Fragile Regime," *Journal of Democracy* 14 (2003): 133.

17. These two opposition candidates were Muhammadu Buhari from the All Nigeria People's Party (formerly the APP) and Atiku Abuabakar from the Action Congress (a party resulting from the 2006 merger of the Alliance for Democracy and other small parties).

18. "It All Looks Horribly the Same," *The Economist*, February 28, 2008.

19. French, *A Continent for the Taking*, p. 42.

20. Vincent O. Nmehielle, "Sharia Law in the Northern States of Nigeria: To Implement, or Not to Implement, the Constitutionality Is the Question," *Human Rights Quarterly* 26, no. 3 (2004): 730–59.

21. Chinua Achebe, *The Trouble with Nigeria* (London: Heinemann, 1983).

22. Afrobarometer, "Summary of Survey Results, Nigeria" (East Lansing: Michigan State University, 2008), http://afrobarometer.org/index.php?option=com_content&view=category&layout=blog&id=22&Itemid=49 (accessed 2/10/12); Bratton and Lewis, "The Durability of Political Goods?" Afrobarometer Working Paper no. 48 (April 2005).

23. "A Tale of Two Giants," *The Economist*, January 13, 2000.

24. Peter Lewis, "From Prebendalism to Predation: The Political Economy of Decline in Nigeria," *Journal of Modern African Studies* 34, no. 1 (March 1996): 79–103.

25. International Monetary Fund, "Nigeria: 2005 Article IV Consultation Concluding Statement," International Monetary Fund, March 25, 2005, www.imf.org/external/np/ms/2005/032505.htm (accessed 2/27/06).

26. Princeton N. Lyman and J. Stephen Morrison, "The Terrorist Threat in Africa," *Foreign Affairs* (January/February 2004), pp. 75–86.

27. "Ballots and Bullets: Political Violence Reaches New Heights," *The Economist*, April 14, 2011.

28. Brandon Kendhammer, "Talking Ethnic but Hearing Multi-Ethnic: The PDP in Nigeria and Durable Multi-Ethnic Parties in the Midst of Violence," *Commonwealth & Comparative Politics* 48 (February 2010): 48–71.

KEY TERMS

Abacha, Sani Oppressive Nigerian military dictator from 1993 to 1998 who came to power in a military coup

Babangida, Ibrahim Military ruler of Nigeria from 1985 to 1993 who sought to establish the failed Third Republic

derivation formula Formula for distributing percentage of oil revenues between national and local government in Nigeria

federal character principle Nigerian quota system designed to ease ethnic tension by requiring the president to appoint ministers and civil servants from each Nigerian state

First Republic Nigerian parliamentary democratic regime that followed independence (1960–66)

Fourth Republic Nigeria's current presidential democratic regime, established in 1999

Fulani Predominantly Muslim ethnic group located in northern Nigeria

Hausa Predominantly Muslim ethnic group concentrated in northern Nigeria

House of Representatives Lower house of Nigerian parliament

Igbo (Ibo) Predominantly Christian ethnic group concentrated in southeast Nigeria

Jonathan, Goodluck Current president, as of 2010

Movement for the Emancipation of the Niger Delta (MEND) Militant separatist group from the Niger Delta

Movement for the Survival of the Ogoni People (MOSOP) Ethnic association founded by Ken Saro-Wiwa to promote interests of ethnic Ogoni in the Niger Delta

National Economic Empowerment and Development Strategy (NEEDS) A wide-ranging Nigerian reform program designed to stem government corruption and enhance economic infrastructure

Niger Delta World's third-largest wetland and source of Nigerian oil and economic and ethnic conflict

Obasanjo, Olusegun Military ruler from 1976 to 1979 and two-term elected president, from 1999 to 2007

patrimonialism Arrangement whereby a ruler depends on a collection of supporters within the state who will gain direct benefits in return for enforcing the ruler's will

People's Democratic Party (PDP) Political party that has dominated Nigerian politics since its 1998 formation; its base was originally the Hausa Muslim ethnic group of northern Nigeria

Republic of Biafra   Igbo-dominated Eastern Region that tried, and failed, to secede from Nigeria in 1967

resource curse   Affliction caused by abundant natural resources distorting an economy by preventing diversification

Saro-Wiwa, Ken   Noted Nigerian playwright and environmental activist, executed in 1995 for his defense of the land and peoples of the Niger Delta

"scramble for Africa"   Late nineteenth-century race by European countries to expand influence and establish imperial control over the majority of African territory

Second Republic   Short-lived Nigerian democratic regime, from 1979 to 1983, in which the former parliamentary system was replaced by a presidential system

Sharia   System of Islamic law

Third Republic   Democratic regime proposed by General Ibrahim Babangida in 1993, but precluded by General Sani Abacha's military coup in the same year, following annulled elections

Yar'Adua, Umaru   Former elected president (2007–10) of Nigeria, who died in office

Yoruba   Ethnic group largely confined to southwest Nigeria whose members are divided among Christian, Muslim, and local animist faiths

zoning   A PDP system of presidential rotation in which the party would alternate every two terms nominating candidates from Nigeria's north and south

WEB LINKS

African Studies Internet Resources: Nigeria, Columbia University Libraries (www.columbia.edu/cu/lweb/indiv/africa/cuvl/Nigeria.html)

Economic and Financial Crimes Commission (www.efccnigeria.org)

The Guardian (Nigeria) (www.ngrguardiannews.com)

IRIN News.org, a service of the UN Office for the Coordination of Humanitarian Affairs (www.irinnews.org)

Niger Delta Development Commission (www.nddconline.org/The_Niger_Delta)

Nigeria Direct: Official Government Gateway (www.nigeria.gov.ng)

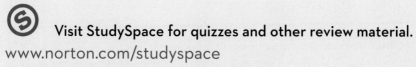

Visit StudySpace for quizzes and other review material.
www.norton.com/studyspace

- Vocabulary Flashcards of All Key Terms
- Country Review Quizzes
- Complete Study Reviews and Outlines

CREDITS

INDEX

Page numbers in *italics* refer to charts and maps. Page numbers in **boldface** refer to keyword definitions.

Arab Spring, 416, 513, 516
Argentina, 45, 50, 82, 591,
    614, 615
Arizona, 102
Article 9 (Japanese constitution),
    257, 270, 277, 302,
    303, 311
Articles of Confederation (1781;
    U.S.), **101**, 106, 116,
    145
Aryans, 426
Ashura, **478**, 519
Asia, 45, 125, 136–37, 366, 722
    Japan and, 299–301
Aso Taro, *256*, 301
Assembly of Experts (Iran), **492**,
    495–97, 520
Association of Southeast Asian
    Nations (ASEAN), 412
asymmetric federalism, **337**,
    361, **444**, 469
Atlantic Ocean, 96
atomic bomb, 136, 269
Australia, 79
Austria, 206, 212, 214, 238
autarky, 510
authoritarian regimes, **9**, 10,
    15–17, 32, 149, 290,
    528
    in Brazil, 584, 586–87,
        590–91, 592, 600
    bureaucratic, 590–91, **590**,
        624
    in China, 378–79, 388,
        389, 393, 402
    economics of, 24
    in Germany, 204, 208,
        211–12
    in Iran, 484–85
    in Mexico, 523, 525,
        531–32, 555–56, 557
    in Nigeria, 694–95
    Pakistan and, 433
    in South Africa, 629,
        636–42, 661
autobahn, 230
ayatollahs, 479, 485, 492
Ayodhya, 436–37, **436**, 447,
    448, 454, 467, 469
Azerbaijan, 504
Azeris, 504–5

Azikiwe, Benjamin Nnamdi,
    690, 692, 693
Aztecs, 526

Babangida, Ibrahim, 693, **693,**
    708, 718, 729
Babri Mosque, 436
Bachmann, Michele, 121
backbenchers, 55, 56
Bahia, 581
Baja California del Sur, 544
Baja California Norte, 540
bakufu, 264
Balkans, 137
Baluchis, 505
Bangalore, 466
Bangladesh, 425, 431, 433, 436,
    462, 464
Bank of Britain, 50
Bantu Homelands Citizenship
    Act (1971; South
    Africa), 637
Bantustans, 637, **637**, 640,
    658–59, 678
Basic Law (Germany), **213**,
    215, 216–17, 219, 220,
    221, 223–24, 226–27,
    234, 254
Basij, 497–98, 499–501, 520
Basques, 177
Bastille, 154
Bavaria, 238–39
Baverez, Nicolas, 185
Beijing, *364*, 373, 377, 385,
    402, 404, 405, 408
"Beijing consensus," **411**, 412
Belarus, 358
Belgium, 187
Belindia, **577**, 624
Belo Monte Hydroelectric Dam,
    620
Belo Monte hydroelectric
    project, 613
Benedict XVI, Pope, 238
Berlin, *200*, 212, 213
Berlin Airlift, 213
Berlin Wall, 137, 214,
    215, 229
Beslan, Russia, 347
Bharatiya Janata Party (BJP;
    India), 436–37, **436,**

    440, 443, 447–49, 450,
    451–52, 456, 469
Bhopal, 453
Biafra, Republic of, 691–92,
    691, 721, 730
bicameral legislatures, 7, **10**, 32,
    108, 112, 210, 332,
    441, 644
Bill of Rights (1689; UK), 44,
    49
Bill of Rights, U.S., **101**, 106,
    107, 145
bipolar, **172**, 196
Bismarck, Otto von, 207, 208
Black Economic Empowerment
    (BEE; South Africa),
    668, 678
blacks:
    in Brazil, 578, 581–82,
        605–7
    in South Africa, 630, 631,
        636–38, 639, 655, 658,
        660, 661, 662, 663,
        664, 666, 668
Black Sea, 346
Blair, Tony, **40**, 48, 50–51, 54,
    55, 56, 61, 63, 67, 68,
    75, 86, 87, 91
blocked vote, **166**, 196
Bloemfontein, *628*, 644
Blood River, battle of (1838),
    635
Boers, 634–35, **634**, 678
Boer Wars, **635**, 678
Bolivia, 615
Bolsa Familia (Family Fund),
    612–13, *612*, **612**, 624
Bonn Republic, **216**, 254
bonyads, 509–10, **509**, 511, 520
Bosnia, 246, 353
Boston Massacre (1770), 100
Botha, P. W., 640, 641–42
Botswana, 632–33
Bracero Program, **568**, 572
Brahmans, 429
branches of government:
    in Brazil, 593–96
    in China, 385–89, *386*
    in France, 162–68, *163*
    in Germany, 217–24
    in India, 439–42, *441*

capital punishment, 77
Cárdenas, Cuauhtémoc,
543–44, 548–50
Cárdenas, Lázaro, **542**, 543,
558, 572, 586
Cardoso, Fernando Henrique,
598, 600, **603**, 604,
606, 610, 611–12,
615, 618, 625
Caribbean, 45, 96
Carranza, Venustiano, 529–30,
529, 572
Carter, Jimmy, 485, 487, 488
Castañeda, Jorge, 556
castes, **423**, 429, 443, 446, 450,
452, 455, 467, 469
Castes War, **528**, 574
Castro, Fidel, 137, 564
catch-all parties, **228**, 254
Catholics, Catholicism, 43–44,
64, 73, 76, 110, 125,
151, 152, 155, 176–77,
179, 181, 206, 209,
213, 220, 228, 237,
238, 318–19, 345, 479,
529, 530, 545, 585,
605, 607
Caucasus, *346,* **346,** 355, 356,
361
caudillos, **528**, 572
Celtic fringe, **43**, 91
Center (India), **439**, 444, 469
Central Asia, 355, 400, 425,
476, 478, 504
oil resources of, 357
and Russia, 356–58
Central Commission for
Discipline Inspection
(China), 385
Central Committee (CC;
China), 383–84, 387
Central Military Commission
(CMC; China),
384–85, 386, 391, 392
CGPME (General Confederation
of Small and Medium-
Size Enterprises;
France), 175
Chamber of Deputies (Câmara
dos Deputados; Brazil),
593, 602, 625

Chamber of Deputies (Mexico),
535, *548*, 572
chancellor (Germany), 207–8,
210, 211, 213–14,
217–19, **217**, *218–19*,
221–22, 254
Channel Tunnel, 41
charismatic legitimacy, **7**, 32
Charlemagne, 152
Charles I, King of England, 44
Charles II, King of England, 44
Chávez, Hugo, 587, 615
Chechnya, 329, **331**, 337, 344,
346–47, 361
checks and balances, 109, 113,
129, 216
Cheka, **323**, 361
Chernomyrdin, Victor, 339
Cherokees, 99
Chevron, 724
Chiang Kai-shek, 372, 373, 417
Chiapas, 546
chief justice (Iran), 494–95,
494, 520
chief minister, **444**, 469
Chile, 137, 591, 615
China, 4–5, 9, 11, 22, 45, 155,
244, 261–63, 270, 296,
298, 364–421, 428,
650, 722
agriculture in, 367, 374,
377, 406, 407
as authoritarian regime,
378–79, 381–82, 388,
389, 393, 402
birth rate in, 97
branches of government in,
385–89, *386*
bureaucracy in, 369–70,
379–81, 406
capitalism in, 379, 391,
392, 394–95, 404,
409–11
Central Asia and, 357
civil society in, 393–99
civil war in, 372–73, 406
collectivization in, 374,
406, 407
Communist regime of, 17,
24, 137
constitution of, 381–82

corruption in, 378, 390, 410
cultural and economic
stagnation in, 370–71
Cultural Revolution in,
375, **375**, 376, 377,
390, 392, *394*, 403,
407, 411
democracy in, 390, 397,
404–5
early history of, 365,
368–71
economic growth in, 30,
366, 406, 407, 408,
460
economic inequality in,
134, 408–9
education in, 409, 460
ethnicity in, 19, 20, 367,
399, *403*
European contact with, 371
executive in, 387
floating population of, 381,
397, 409
foreign investment and
trade in, 377, 383, 406,
408, 409–11, 413, 414,
415–16
foreign relations of, 411–13
GDP of, 25, 26, 131, 358,
364, 366, 391, 408
geography of, 367, 371
Gini index in, 408
in global economy, 134–35
globalization and, 366–67
government-party
parallelism in, 379–81,
380–81, 389
Great Leap Forward in,
374–75, **374**, *394*,
403, 406–7, 419
head of government in,
364, 387
head of state in, *364*,
386–87
health care in, 406, 409
Hong Kong and, 45, 371,
417–18
Human Development Index
ranking of, 27, *29, 364*
human rights abuses in,
388–89, 397, 415–16

electoral college, 110, 114–16,
167
in India, 440
electoral districts, 13–14
electoral systems, 13, **13**, *16*, 33
in Brazil, 13, 596–97,
618–19
in France, 14, 169
in Germany, 224–27,
278–79
in India, 14, 440, 443
in Iran, 495–96
in Japan, 14, 277–79,
284–85
in Mexico, 14, 278, 538–39
in Nigeria, 14, 702–5
in Russia, 335–36
in South Africa, 648–49
two-round, 169, 172, 181
in UK, 14, 59–62, *60*,
70–71, 75, 279
in U.S., 14, 96, 114–16,
279
Elizabeth II, Queen of England,
38, 52, 53
emergency rule (India), **434**,
439, 442, 469
ENA (École Nationale
d'Administration), 171,
171, 183, 194, 197
Enabling Act (Germany), 211
enarques, 171, 176
Engels, Friedrich, 157
England, 40, 44, 51, 75
American colonies of,
97–100
judicial system in, 12
legislature of, 63
party system in, 65
religion in, 73
see also United Kingdom
English Channel, 40
English Civil War (1640–1649),
44, 92
Enlightenment, 155
environmentalism, 577
in Brazil, 620–21
in Germany, 201, 229, 230,
231, 241
in India, 452–53
in Mexico, 550

in Nigeria, 703
in U.S., 105, 117, 122, 127
equality of opportunity, *131*,
128, 424
Escola Superior de Guerra (ESG;
Brazil), **587**, 599, 625
Estado Nôvo (Brazil), 586–88,
586, 589, 598, 608, 625
Estates General (France), **153**,
197
Estonia, 353
ethnicity, **19**, *20*, 33
in Brazil, 578, 605–7, *606*
in China, 19–20, 367,
399, *403*
in France, 177–81, *178*
in Germany, 203, 238–40,
239
in India, 19, 20, 426,
453–56, *454*
in Iran, 7, 19, 20, 473–74,
475, 503–5, *504*
in Japan, 19–20, 261,
292–94, *293*, 307
in Mexico, 20, 553–54, *554*
in Nigeria, 7, 19, 20, 684,
685–88, 706–7, *708*,
715–16, *716*, 723,
724, 726
in Russia, 19–20, 337,
345–47, *345*
in South Africa, 631–33,
657, 658–60
in UK, 19, 40–41, 72,
73–75, *74*, 78
in U.S., 125, *126*
"Eurasian Union," **355**, 358
Europe, 111, 580, 722
Brazil and, 580
China's contact with, 371
voter turnout in, 70
European Central Bank, 248
European Commission, 248
European Constitution, 170
European Convention on
Human Rights, 51, 58
European Union (EU), 30, *84*,
130, 158, 191, 243,
244, 412, 616, 721, 722
debt crisis and, 247–49
Eastern Europe in, 353–54

economic inequality in, 134
euro as common currency
of, 80–81, 83, 189–90,
247
France and, 82, *84*, 151,
170, 174, 186–87
Germany and, *84*, 187,
202, 243, 244, 246–47
Greece and, 247
India compared to, 444
Nigeria and, 694
population of, 317
Russia and, 246–47,
353–54
UK and, 41, 50, 51, 68, 70,
75, 80, 82–83, *84*, 187
Euroskepticism, 174
Eurozone debt crisis, 247–49
Events of May, **159**, 197
Exchequer (UK), 56
executive, 10–11, **10**, 12, 33
in China, 387
in France, 10, 156, 159–60
in India, 10, 440–41
in Iran, 490–93
in Nigeria, 10–11,
697–701, 715
in Russia, 328–32
in U.S., 11, 108, 110–11
Executive Office of the
President, 111
Expediency Council (Iran), 494,
494, 499, 520
exports:
of Brazil, 577, 613–14,
615, 617
of Germany, 242, 244
of Mexico, 559, 560–61,
562, 569
of Nigeria, 683, 684, 692,
717–18, 722
of Russia, 352

Fabianism, 65
failed states, **8**, 33
Falklands War (1982), 45,
50, 54, 82
Falun Gong, **389**, 395,
406, 419
faqih, 487
Farsi, **473**, 475, 476–77, 520

fascism, **22**, 33, 149, 157, 158,
586, 587
in Germany, 201, 206, 209,
211–12, 240
in Japan, 268, 269
Fatherland-All Russia, 339
favelas, **580**, 610, 611, 617–18,
625
Federal Assembly (Russia), 332
Federal Association of German
Employers (BDA), 235
federal chancellor (Germany),
217, 254
see also chancellor
(Germany)
federal character principle,
699–701, **699**, 729
Federal Constitution Court
(Germany), 223–24,
223, 234, 254
Federal Court of Appeals
(Nigeria), 702
Federal District of Mexico City,
536, 539, 573
Federal Electoral Institute
(Mexico), 538, 573
Federal Electoral Tribunal
(Mexico), 538, 544
Federal Executive Council
(Nigeria), 699
federalism, **107**, 146, 322, 389
asymmetric, **444**, 469
in Brazil, 8, 585–86, 592,
598, 602
in Germany, 201, 208, 213,
216
in India, 438, 444
in Mexico, 529, 533, 539,
540
in Nigeria, 690, 691,
696–97, 705
in Russia, 8, 337–38
South Africa and, 649
in U.S., 106, 107, **107**,
117, 177
Federalists, **101**, 102, 107, 146
Federal Judicial Police (Mexico),
546
Federal Military Government
(FMG; Nigeria),
692, 705

federal president (Germany),
219, 254
Federal Republic of Germany
(FRG), 213–14, **213**,
243, 254
Federal Reserve System (U.S.),
103
Federal Security Service (FSB;
Russia), 329, **331**, 362
Federal Senate (Senado Federal;
Brazil), **594**, 597, 625
federal states, **8**, 33, 201, 322,
337
Federal Supreme Court
(Supremo Tribunal
Federal; Brazil), **595**,
625
Federation Council (Russia),
333–34, **333**, 334,
337, 362
Federation of German Industry
(BDI), 235–36
Federation of German Labor
(DGB), 235
feudalism, 43, 152, 204, 379
in Germany, 204
in Japan, 261, 265, 267,
270, 292, 294
Figueiredo, João, 591
Fillon, François, *148*
First Opium War (1839–1842),
371
first past the post (FPTP)
system, 59–62, 225,
278
Fischer, Joschka, 232
527 organizations, 124
floating population, **381**, 397,
409, 419
Florida, 100, 102, 122
flying geese, **300**, 311
Forbes, 562
Forbidden City, 377
Force Ouvrire (FO; France), 175
foreign direct investment, **30**, 33
see also specific countries
foreign influence, fear of, *457*
Foreign Office (UK), 56
foreign relations:
of Brazil, 615–17
of China, 411–13

of France, 186–90
of Germany, 244–47
of India, 461–64
of Iran, 511–14
of Japan, 299–304
of Mexico, 563–66
of Nigeria, 721–24
of Russia, 352–56
of South Africa, 668–71
of UK, 50–51, 81–85
of U.S., 95, 110, 135–38
419 (advance-fee) scams, 719,
720
four-party, two-block-system,
172, 197
Fox, Vicente, **524**, 533, 535, 537,
538, 540, 543, 546–47,
548–49, 551, 554, 558,
562, 564, 573
France, 4–5, 40, 148–98
absolutism in, 152–54,
156–57
affluence of, 27
agriculture in, 151, 183,
185–86
Algeria and, 158, 170, 192
in American Revolution,
100
aristocracy in, 152, 156
branches of government in,
162–68, *163*
bureaucracy in, 111, 156,
171–72, 176, 183
cabinet in, 161, 162, 165
changing political regimes
of, 149
civil liberties in, 149, 154,
177
civil society in, 174–77
class in, 152
Constitutional Council
of, 12
constitutions of, 149, 150,
159, 161–62, 163,
166–67, 170
Council of Ministers in,
162, 196
dirigisme system in, **183**,
196, 296
economic decline in,
183–84, 185

France (*continued*)
  economic growth in, 30, 183
  economic reform in, 184
  education in, 178, 194–95
  1848 revolution in, 156
  election of 2007 in, 159, 178
  elections in, 163, 170, 193
  electoral system in, 14, 169
  ethnicity in, 177–81, *178*
  EU and, 82, *84*, 151, 170, 174, 186–87
  Events of May in, **159**, 197
  executive in, 10, 156, 159–60
  Fifth Republic of, **150**, 159–95, 197
  First Empire of, 156
  First Republic of, 156
  foreign relations of, 186–90
  Fourth Republic of, 158, 159, 160, 161, 172
  GDP of, *148*, 183, 184
  geography of, 150–51
  Germany and, 190, 203, 206, 244, 246
  globalization and, 184, 186, 188
  head of government in, *148*
  head of state in, *148*, 162
  headscarf controversy in, 180, *180*
  Human Development Ranking of, *29*, *148*
  immigrants in, 192–93
  immigration in, 30, 160, 174, 178–81
  Iraq War and, 188
  judiciary in, 11, 168
  labor force in, *183*, 184–85
  labor unions in, 173, 175
  land size of, *148*, 150
  left in, 172, 181
  legislature in, 161, 162, 163, 165, 166–68
  in Libyan conflict, 188–89
  local government in, 170–71
  map of, *148*
  mass protest in, 182
  military of, 150, 152, 154

  monarchy in, 149, 152–55, 182
  Muslims in, 192–93
  national identity in, 151, 177–81, 185–86
  nationalism in, 191–94
  nationalization in, 183
  NATO and, 159, 186–89
  natural resources of, 150
  party system in, 172–74
  political conflict and competition in, 172–77
  political development of, 151–60, *153*
  political economy in, 24, 182–86
  political ideology and culture in, 24, 181–82, 184
  political institutions in, 10, 12, 13, *16*, 161–62, *161*
  political regime in, 161–72, *161*
  population of, *5*, *148*
  populism in, 181
  post-revolutionary era in, 156–57
  postwar modernization of, 191
  presidents of, 156, 159–60, 162–65, *164*, 166, 173
  prime ministers of, **159**, 161, 162, *164*, 165–66, 197
  private enterprise in, 175–76
  racism in, 180
  referenda in, 170
  religion in, 176–77, 178, *178*, 179–80
  revolutionary era in, 149–50, 154–56, 177, 197
  right in, 172, 173–74, 181
  rule of law in, 151, 156
  rural vs. urban conflict in, 151, 155
  Second Empire of, 157
  Second Republic of, 156–57
  as secular society, 21

  as semi-presidential system, 13, 149, 161, **162**, 168, 181, 198
  separation of church and state in, 154, 176, 178, 179, *179*, 197
  society in, 177–82
  Soviet Union and, 186–87
  standardization and reform in, 155
  as strong state, 152, 154, 155, 177
  suffrage in, 156
  taxes and taxation in, 152
  Third Republic of, 157–58, 159, 161, 172
  transportation in, 151
  as unitary state, 170
  U.S. and, 188
  U.S. relations with, 167, 182, 186–89
  Vichy regime in, 158
  Vietnam and, 160, 192
  voter turnout in, *18*
  welfare in, 159, 183, 184
  in World War I, 150–51, 157
  in World War II, 151, 157–58, 172–73
France qui tombe, La (Falling France) (Baverez), 185
Franco, Itamar, 598
Franco-Prussian War (1870–1871), 157
Franks, 152
Free Democratic Party (FDP; Germany), 225, 231, **231**, 254
Freedom House, 8, 9–10, 445
freedoms, individual, *see* civil liberties
Free French, 160
free markets, 103, 229, 231, *351*, 547, 603
free trade, 135, 560, 615
French Communist Party (PCF), 172–73, 175, 197
French Council of the Muslim Faith, 177
French Democratic Labor Confederation (CFDT), **175**, 197

French Empire, 97, 99–100, 101, 156
French Enterprise Movement (MEDEF), 175
French Revolution (1789–1799), **149**, 154–56, 177, 181–83, 186, 197
French Socialist Party (PS), 167, 169, 172–73, **172**, 197
Fuentes, Carlos, 561
Fukuda Yasuo, 301
Fukushima Daiichi nuclear plant disaster, 249, 304–6
Fulani, **685**, 697, 714, 715, 729
fundamentalism, **23**, 33

Gabriel, Sigmar, 231
gaiatsu, 299–300, 303
Gandhi, Indira, 434–35, **434**, 438, 439, 440, 442, 446, 447, 470
Gandhi, Mahatma (Mohandas K.), 424, 429, 431, **431**, 432, 433, 448, 456, 466, 470
Gandhi, Priyanka, 437
Gandhi, Rahul, 437
Gandhi, Rajiv, 435–36, 437, 440, 446
Gandhi, Sanjay, 435–36
Gandhi, Sonia, **437**, 470
Ganges River, 425
Gang of Four, 376
gastarbeiter, **239**, 250254
gay marriage, 120
GDP per capita, **24–25**, *26*, 33, *38*, *79*, *94*, 183, 184, *200*, *256*, *314*, 352, *364*, 408, *422*, *472*, 510, *522*, *576*, 610, *628*, *682*
General Agreement on Tariffs and Trade (GATT), 558
General Confederation of Labor (CGT; Germany), **175**, 197
General Confederation of Small and Medium-Size Enterprises (CGPME; France), 175

general secretary (China), 383–84, 386
general secretary (Russia), 324–25, 328
Genghis Khan, 319, 428
George I, King of England, 44–45
George III, King of England, 371
George VI, King of England, 53
Georgia, 353, 354–55
Georgia, Russia and, 246, 353, 354–55
German Democratic Republic (GDR), 213–14, **213**, 229, 254
Germany, 5, 22, 189, 200–255
  anti-Semitism in, 209, 211
  authoritarian regimes in, 204, 208, 211–12
  Basic Law in, 213, **213**, 215, 219, 220, 221, 223–24, 226–27, 234, 254
  branches of government in, 217–24
  business in, 235, 242–43
  cabinet in, 217–19
  capitalism in, 201, 202, 213–14, 215, 241, 242
  chancellor of, 207–8, 210, 211, 213–14, 217–19, *218–19*, 221–22
  checks and balances in, 216
  civil liberties in, 231, 241
  civil rights in, 216
  civil society in, 235, 242
  coalition governments in, 217–19, *218–19*, 221, 226, 230–35
  collective rights in, 242
  constitutions of, 208, 209–10, 216–17
  democracy in, 202, 209–11, 213–14, 241
  devolution in, 213
  division of, 202
  economic decline in, 210, 211–12
  economic growth in, 30, 213, 215, 235, 238, 240, 241, 242, 242–43

  economic inequality in, 215
  economic reform in, 235, 242–43
  elections in, 210–11, 220–22, 223, 224–27, 230–31, *232*, 232-33, 234
  electoral system in, 224–27, 278–79
  emigrants from, 203
  energy in, 249–50
  environmentalism in, 201, 229, 230, 231, 241
  ethnicity in, 203, 238–40, *239*
  EU and, *84*, 187, 202, 243, 244, 246–47
  and Eurozone debt crisis, 247–49
  executive in, 10
  expansionism of, 202
  exports of, 242, 244
  fascism in, 201, 206, 209, 211–12, 240
  federalism in, 8, 201, 208, 213, 216
  feudalism in, 204
  foreign relations of, 244–47
  France and, 190, 203, 206, 244, 246
  GDP of, *200*
  gender gap in, 237
  geography of, 202–3
  globalization and, 202, 243
  head of government in, *200*, 210, 217–19, 227
  head of state in, *200*, 210, 217, 219–20, 227
  health care in, 208, 210, 229
  Holy Roman Empire and, 204–6
  Human Development Index ranking of, *29*, *200*
  immigrants in, 250–52
  immigration in, 203, 229, 238–40
  imperialism in, 204
  industrialization in, 208–9
  inflation in, 210
  in international system, 244, 246

Germany (*continued*)
judiciary in, 223–24
labor force in, 240, 242, *242*, 243
labor unions in, 235, 242, 243
land size of, *200*
language and culture in, 203, 215, 238
legislature in, 10, 205–6, 210, 217, 220–23, 225, *226*, 227–28, 229, 230, 231
local government in, 226–27
map of, *200*
mercantilism in, 204, 207, 211
middle class in, 208, 210, 231
military of, 207, 208, 244–46
monarchy in, 208
Muslims in, 240
national identity in, 204, 207, 238–40, 240–41
nationalism in, 201–2, 206, 209, 210, 211, 240–41, 244
NATO and, 244, 244–46
natural resources of, 203
Nazism in, 201, 204, 206, 211–12, 213, 235, 242
neocorporatism in, 235, 242–43, **242**
nuclear power in, *236*, 237, 238, 249
pacifism in, 244
as parliamentary system, 11–12, 15, 217, 219
party system in, 213–14, *226*, 227–34
political conflict and competition in, 227–38
political development of, 203–16, *205*
political economy in, 24, 241–44
political ideology and culture in, 24, 240–41
political institutions in, 10, 12, 15, *16*, 216–17

political regime in, 216–27, *217*
population of, *5*, *200*, 202
postmaterialist values in, 241
postwar occupation and division of, 212–15
presidents of, 210, 219–20
privatization in, 233
referenda in, 227
religion in, 238, *239*
renewable energy in, 250
reunification of, 202, 204, 215–16, **215**, 229, 230, 234, 238, 244, 255
Russia and, 246–47
Second Reich in, 207–9
as semi-presidential system, 210
socialism in, 214, 239
society in, 238–41
Soviet Union and, 212–15
suffrage in, 208, 209–10
Third Reich in, 17, 151, 157–58, 172, 202, **204**, 206, 211–12, 214, 216, 255, 300, 483
totalitarianism in, 214
Turks in, 240
unemployment in, 210, 215, 235
unification of, 206–9, 239, 240
U.S. and, 213, 242, 244
voter turnout in, *18*, 228, 235
Weimar Republic in, 209–11, **209**, 216, 217, 219, 220, 221, 224, 225, 227, 230, 235, 255
welfare in, 202, 208, 210, 214, 230, 231
women in, *236*, *237*
in World War I, 209, 210
in World War II, 201–2, 212, 235, 238, 239, 244
gerrymandering, **114**, 146
Gini index, **25**, 33, 134, 408, *667*
Giscard d'Estaing, Valéry, 174

glasnost, 214, **325**, 343, 362
globalization, 28–30, **28**, 33
China and, 366–67
France and, 184, 186, 188
Germany and, 202, 243
India and, 424, 456, 460–61
Japan and, 283, 297
Mexico and, 560–61
U.S. and, 135, 140, 141
global warming, 367, 724
Glorious Revolution, 44
"Golden Shield," 398
Golden Temple, 435, 467
Good Friday Agreement (1998; UK), **64**, 74, 76, 92
Good Hope, Cape of, 634
goods and services, 24
Google, 398
Gorbachev, Mikhail, 214, 315, 325–26, 334, 353, 359, 377
Gore, Al, 115, 122
Goulart, João, **589**, 591, 625
government, 4, 33
Government of India Act (1858), 430
Gowon, Yakubu, 692
Great Depression, 104, 120, 140, 210, 268
Greater East Asian Co-Prosperity Sphere, 300
Greater London Assembly, 63
Greater London Council, 63
"Great Firewall of China," 398
Great Game, 356–57
Great Leap Forward, 374–75, *374*, *394*, 403, 406–7, 419
Great Trek (1835), **635**, 679
Greece:
debt crisis in, 248
EU and, 247
greenhouse gases, 409
Green Party (Brazil), 620
Green Party (France), 173
Green Party (U.S.), 122
Green Revolution, **425**, 457, 470
Greens (Germany), 219, 223, 230, 231–33, **231**, *232*, 232-33, 234, 236,

241, 244, 249–50, 254,
277–28
gross domestic product (GDP),
24–25, **24–25**, *25*,
26, 33
of Brazil, *576*, 610
of China, 25, 26, 131, 358,
364, 391, 408
of Costa Rica, 352
of France, *148*, 183, 184
of Germany, *200*
growth rate of, 26, *27*
of India, 25, 26, *422*
of Iran, *472*, 510
of Japan, 25, *256*, 305
of Mexico, 408, *522*
of Nigeria, *682*
of Russia, *314*, 349, 350,
352, 358, 408
of South Africa, *628*, 669
taxes as percentage of, *132*
of UK, *38*, 79
of U.S., *94*, 104, 131, 134,
184–85, 408
see also GDP per capita
Group Areas Act (1950; South
Africa), **637**, 638,
640, 679
Group of 8 (G8), 30
Growth, Employment, and
Redistribution Program
(GEAR; South Africa),
666, 671, 679
Guangdong Province, 408
Guardian Council (Iran),
494, **494**, 495, 496,
499–500, 520
Guatemala, 137, 553
Guerrero, 540, 544
Gujarat, **437**, 447, 448, 454,
467, 470
Gulf War (1991), 303

Haiti, 583, 615
Hamilton, Alexander, 101
Han Chinese, 367–68, 399, 400
handguns, 77
Han dynasty, 368–70
harmonious society, **384**, 419
Hatoyama Yukio, 287–88, **289**,
303

Hausa, **685**, 686, 690, 697, 708,
714, 715, 729
Hawaii, 96, 136
head of government, **10**, 12, 33
in Brazil, *576*, 593
in China, *364*, 387
in France, *148*
in Germany, *200*, 210,
217–19, 227
in India, *422*, 440
in Iran, *472*, 490–93
in Japan, *256*, 274–75
in Mexico, *522*
in Nigeria, *682*, 697–701,
698–99
in Russia, *314*, 328
in South Africa, *628*, 645
in UK, *38*, 52, 55, 56
in U.S., *94*, 110, 162
head of state, **10**, 12, 33
in Brazil, *576*, 593
in China, *364*, 386–87
in France, *148*, 162
in Germany, *200*, 210, 217,
219–20, 227
in India, *422*, 439
in Iran, *472*, 490–93
in Japan, *256*
in Mexico, *522*
in Nigeria, *682*, 697
in Russia, *314*, 328
in South Africa, *628*, 645
in UK, *38*, 52, 55, 162
in U.S., *94*, 110
headscarfs, 180, *180*
health care, 24
in Brazil, 611
in China, 406, 409
in Germany, 208, 210, 229
in India, 461
in Russia, 359
in South Africa, 666
in UK, 79, 86
in U.S., 95, 116, 117, 118,
118, 121, 134, 141
Henry VIII, King of England,
43, 44
hereditary peers, **57**, 92
Hezbollah, 511
Hidden Imam, 478
Himalayas, 367, 425, 463

Hindenberg, Paul von, 211
Hindi, **426**, 444, 453, 470
Hinduism, Hindus, 424, 425,
426, **426**, 428, 430,
431, 435–37, 447–49,
452, 454, 456, 462,
466–67, 470
Hindutva, **448**, 470
Hirohito, Emperor of Japan,
272, 274
Hiroshima, 269
Hispanics, 125, 134, 138–39,
146
Hitler, Adolf, 160, 210, 211–12,
211, 216, 219, 221,
254
HIV/AIDS, 630, 647, 653, 669,
675
Hokkaidō, 260, 261
Hollande, François, **160**, 173,
180, 184, 189
Holocaust, 212, 239
Holy Roman Empire, 152,
204–6
Home Office (UK), 56
homosexuality, 77, 129
Honda, 283
Hong Kong, 45, 371, 417–18
Honshū, 260, 263
household responsibility system,
407, 419
House of Commons (UK), **46**,
50, 51, 53, 54–55, 58,
59, 65, 70, 85, 87,
92, 442
House of Councillors (Japan),
276, **276**, 278, 311
House of Lords (UK), 11, **46**,
50, 55, 56, 57, 58,
92, 168
House of Representatives
(Japan), 276, **276**, 278,
311
House of Representatives
(Nigeria), 690, 691,
701, 704, 707, 729
House of Representatives (U.S.),
11, **108**, 112, 114,
141, 146, 442
House of States (India), 442,
442, 470

health care in, 461
Human Development Index
   ranking of, 27, *29, 422*
identity in, 467–68
illiteracy in, 433, 444, 445,
   453, 460
independence movement in,
   430–34
industrialization in, 424,
   455, 460
inequality of opportunity
   in, 424
information industry in,
   460–61
judiciary in, 438, 442
labor force in, 446, *460*, 461
labor unions in, 452
land reform in, 461
land size of, *422*, 425
legislature in, 10, 441–42,
   449
liberal ideology in, 428–30,
   433
linguistic diversity in, 423,
   426, 444, 453–54
literacy in, 423
local government in,
   443–45
map of, *422*
media in, 453
mercantilist trade policies
   of, 434, 436, 446,
   458–59
middle class in, 448, 456,
   458, 461
military in, 433, 438
modernization in, 424
national identity in, 430,
   433, 448, 453–56
nationalism in, 431, 432,
   436, 446, 448, 449,
   454
natural resources of, 425
Nehru dynasty in, 434–36,
   440
nonaligned movement and,
   461
Nuclear Non-Proliferation
   Treaty and, 464, 465
as nuclear power, 462,
   463, 464

outsourcing in, **426**, 459
Pakistan and, 357–58, 425,
   431–32, 439, 451, 454,
   462–63, 464, 465, 466
as parliamentary system,
   11–12, 424, 437–38,
   440–42
partition of, 431, **431**, 454,
   461–62, 470
party system in, 445–50
peasants in, 425, 446, 452
political conflict and
   competition in, 445–52
political development of,
   426–37, *427*
political economy in,
   457–61
political ideology and
   culture in, 456
political institutions of, 10,
   12, 14, *16*, 438–39
political regime in, 437–53,
   438
pollution in, 460
population of, *5*, 96,
   365–66, 412, *422*, 423,
   425–26, 459, 460
poverty in, 423, 432, 434,
   444, 446, 455, 458,
   459–60, 461
presidential rule in, **435**,
   439, 444, 471
presidents of, 439–40
prime minister in, 437,
   439, 440–41, 442
privacy and anonymity in,
   467–68
privatization in, 459
regional diversity of, 444
regional parties in, 450, 467
religion in, 423, 426, 428,
   450, 452, 454, *454*
resettlement in, 431
sectarian conflict in, 424,
   431, 435, 436–37, 439,
   445, 448, 453, 454,
   466–67
secularism in, 446, 448,
   450, 453, 456, 466–67
separatism in, 424, 435,
   436, 453, 455, 466–67

society in, 453–56
terrorist attacks in, 437,
   463, 466–67
U.S. and, 462, 464
U.S. nuclear cooperation
   agreement with,
   464, 465–66
voter turnout in, *18*, 423,
   445, 450
women in, 453, 460, 461
Indian National Congress
   (INC), 430–31, **430**,
   432, 433–35, 437, 440,
   442, 443, 445, 446,
   449, 450, 451–52, 457,
   461, 465, 470
Indian Ocean, 425, 428
Indian Removal Act (1830;
   U.S.), 99
Indians (South Africans of Asian
   descent), **632**, 679
individualism, 126–27, 129
Indo-Aryans, 426, 453
Indochina, 269
Indonesia, 269, 298
Indus River, 425
industrial policy, **296**, 311
Industrial Revolution, 39, 46,
   79, 371
inflation, **27**, 33, 210
   in Brazil, 589, 591, 609,
      610
   in China, 378
   in Germany, 210
   in Russia, 349
informal sector, **562**, 573
information technology (IT),
   460–61
Inkatha Freedom Party (IFP;
   South Africa), 649,
   652–54, 679
insider privatization, **349**, 362
intergovernmental organizations
   (IGOs), **30**, 33
International Atomic Energy
   Agency (IAEA),
   465–66, 515
International Monetary Fund,
   135, 220, 560, 611,
   666, 693
International Red Cross, 30

Macartney, Lord, 371
McCain, John, *124*
McGuinness, Martin, 76
Madero, Francisco, **529**, 573
Madrazo, Roberto, 543
Maginot Line, 150–51
Magna Carta, **43**, 44, 49, 92, 152
Maharaj, Mac, 676
Mahdi, **478**
Majlis (Iran), **480**, 483, 484,
    493–97, 499, 520
Major, John, 53, 63
majoritarian representation, **48**,
    59–61, 64, 92, 169
Malan, Daniel, 636
Malaya, 269
Malema, Julius, 658, 674
Manchuria, 262, 269
Manchus, 370
Mandarin, 399
Mandela, Nelson, 434, 579,
    631, 638–39, 641,
    642, *642*, 653, 658,
    665, 675, 679
manifest destiny, **136**, 137, 146
Maoism, 403–4, 449–50
Mao Zedong, 17, 372–73, **372**,
    374–77, *376*, 377,
    382–83, 388, 390–92,
    394, 399–404, 406–7,
    411, 421
    personality cult of, 375
maquiladoras, **560**, 573
Marbury v. Madison, 113
markets, 24, 34
    China and, 381
    free, 50, 103, 229, 231,
        351, 547, 603
    Iran and, 507
    Russia and, 348, 352
    states and, 24, 120, 133,
        507
    UK and, 50
    U.S. and, 120, 133, 140
Marshall Plan (1947–1952), 136
Marx, Karl, 73, 157
Marxism, 173, 230, 378, 392,
    650
Mary II, Queen of England, 44
Massachusetts, 97
Mauer im Kopf, 241

Maximilian, Emperor of Mexico,
    528
Maya, **525**, 528, 553, 573
Mayawati, 455–56
May Fourth Movement, 372,
    372, 377, 378, *394*,
    420
Mbeki, Thabo, **631**, 646,
    651–52, 653, 658,
    669, 670, 672, 674,
    675, 679
Mecca, 479
MEDEF (French Enterprise
    Movement), 175
media:
    in India, 453
    in Iran, 501, 502–3
    in Mexico, 531, 549,
        552–53
    in Nigeria, 695
    in Russia, 344, 350
    in South Africa, 638, 657
Medicaid, 118
Medicare, 118
Medvedev, Dmitri, *314*,
    316–17, 328, 335,
    338, 354
Medvedev, Dmitry, 308
Meiji Constitution, 267, 273
Meiji oligarchs, 261, 266–68,
    266, 296, 312
Meiji Restoration, 266–68, **266**,
    290, 312
melting pot, **125**, 146
members of Parliament (MPs;
    UK), **53**, 55, 56, 57,
    59, 69, 70, 71, 92
mercantilism, 258, 263, 267,
    283, 290, 296, 298,
    299
    in Germany, 204, 207, 211
    in India, 434, 436, 446,
        458–59
    in Iran, 508–9
    in Mexico, 560, 561–62
    in South Africa, 640, 664
MERCOSUR, **615**, 625
Merkel, Angela, *200*, 220, *221*,
    221, 229, 231, 236,
    237, 247, 248, 249,
    250, 254

mestizaje, 553
mestizos, **525**, 526, 529, 553,
    573
metric system, 155
Mexican-American War
    (1846–1848), **102**,
    136, 146, **528**, 573
Mexican Green Party (PVEM),
    547–48
Mexican miracle, **559**, 574
Mexican Revolution, 529–30,
    529, 557, 564, 568, 574
Mexico, 96, 102, 135, 298, 445,
    522–75
    agriculture in, 525, 557,
        558, 560–61, 562
    branches of government in,
        534–38, *536*
    bribery in, 563
    business in, 542, 551–52,
        559
    cabinet in, 535
    capitalism in, 557
    civil liberties in, 531
    civil society in, 550–53
    colonial era of, 525–28
    confidence in, *555*
    constitution of 1917 in,
        529–30, **529**, 533,
        534, 536, 554, 558,
        572
    co-optation in, 17
    corporatism in, 550
    corruption in, 532, 538,
        540, 546, 554, 556,
        562, 563, 565
    crime in, 564, 565–67
    democracy in, 527–28,
        557, 563
    dictatorship in, 17
    drug trafficking in, 547,
        554, 557, 564, 565–68,
        566
    economic crises in, 532,
        533, 542, 551, 559–60,
        564, 569
    economic growth in, 523,
        525, 528, 559, 564,
        570
    economic inequality in, 25,
        559–60, 561–62, 564

in India, 437, 439, 440–41, 442
in Iran, 484
in Japan, *256*, 268, 270, 274–75, 282, 283, 285
in Russia, 328–32, 333
in UK, **45**, 50–51, 52, 53–55, 70, 92
private enterprise, in France, 175–76
private property, 22, 127, 348
privatization, 50, 77, 79, 233, 349, 376–77, 381–82, 407, 459, 484, 598, 610, 666, 718
Progressive Era (1903–1920), **103**, 146
Progressive Federal Party (South Africa), 650
Prohibition of Mixed Marriages Act (1950; South Africa), 638
property, 35, 643–44, 650
collective, 22
private, 22, 127, 348
proportional representation (PR), 13–14, **13**, 35, 62, 169, 174, 224–25, 278, 279, 336, 534, 539, 597, 648
protectionism, 268, 291, 297, 299, 302, 544
in Brazil, 587, 610
Protection of Information Bill (South Africa), 676
Protestant Reformation, 206
Protestants, Protestantism, 43–44, 64, 73, 74, 76, 97, 110, 125, 176, 206, 213, 228, 237, 238, 345, 607
Prussia, 204, 206–9, **207**, 238, 255
public goods, **24**, 35
Punjab, 435, 436, 444, 450, 456
purchasing-power parity (PPP), **24–25**, *25*, *26*, 35, *38*, *94*, *148*, *256*, *314*, 408
Puritans, **97**, 146
Putin, Vladimir, *314*, **316**, 326, 328, 329, 333, 335,

336, 337, 338, 339, 342, 344, 347, 350–52, 355, 358, 363
Pyrénées, 150

Qaddafi, Mu'ammar, 188, 671
Qajar dynasty, 478–80, 481, 510
Qin dynasty, 368
Qing dynasty, 370, 372
Qom, 485
quangos, **71**, 92
"quietist" Shiism, 506, **506**, 520
Quotations from Chairman Mao, 375, *376*

racial equality, 129
racism, 180, 432, 578
in South Africa, 629, 630, 636, 658
radical attitudes, 22, **22**, 35
Rafsanjani, Ali Akbar Hashemi, 494, 500, 506–7
raj, **430**, 431, 433, 453, 471
Rally for the French Republic (RPR), 172, 173–74, 198
rational-legal legitimacy, **7**, 35
reactionary attitudes, 22, **22**, 35
Reagan, Ronald, 105, 133, 488
Reconstruction and Development Plan (RDP; South Africa), 665
red capitalists, **395**, 420
Red Guard, **375**, *376*, 377, 378, 390, 420
"Reds versus experts," **406**, 420
referenda, 170
in France, 170
in Germany, 227
in South Sudan, 6
in UK, 62, 67, 69
Reform Act (1832; UK), 47
reform and opening, 366, **366**, 376–78, 381–82, 383, 389, 391, 394, 408, 416
regime, 149, 198
see also political regimes
reich, **204**, 255

Reichstag (Germany), 205–6, 208, 210
Reichstrat (Germany), 210
Reign of Terror, 155–56, **155**, 198
religion, 22, *179*
in Brazil, 605, *606*, 607
in China, *403*, 406
diversity of, *20*
in France, 176–77, 178, *178*, 179–80
in Germany, 238, 238, *239*
in India, 423, 426, 428, 450, 452, 454, *454*
in Iran, 503, *504*, 505–6, *506*, 507
in Japan, 264, 267, *293*
in Mexico, *554*
morality and, 129, *130*
in Nigeria, 22, 684, 685, 686–88, 687–89, 690, 702, 704, 706, 707, 708, 713–14, 715–16, 723
in Russia, 343–44, 345, *345*
in South Africa, *657*, 660
in UK, 43–44, 72, 73–74, *74*, 77, 87
in U.S., 22, 95, 120, *126*, 129–30
Remy, Jacqueline, 185
RENGO (Japanese Trade Union Confederation), 291–92
rent seeking, **17**, 35
Reporters Without Borders, 344, 502
repression, 17
Republican Party (U.S.), 103, 105, 119, 120, 121, 133, 135, 141–43
Reservation of Separate Amenities Act (1953; South Africa), 638, 640
resource curse, resource trap, 508–9, **718**, 730
reunification, 215–16, **215**, 255
revolutionary dictatorship, 149, 161
Revolutionary Guard, 493, 497–98, 499–500, 503, 516, 520

Union for a Popular Movement
(UMP; France), 172,
174, 175–76, 198
Union for French-Democracy
(UDF), **174**, 198
Union of Islamic Organizations
(France), 177
Union of Right Forces (URF;
Russia), 363
Union of South Africa, **635**,
659, 680
see also South Africa
unitary states, **8**, 36
China as, 389
France as, 170
Japan as, 279–80
South Africa as, 649
UK as, 62, 86
United Democratic Front (UDF,
South Africa), **640**, 680
United Kingdom, 4–5, 7–8, 22,
38–93, **40**, 93, 189,
356, 417
affluence of, 27
aristocracy in, 50, 57, 78, 152
branches of government in,
53–59, *54*
cabinet in, **45**, 52, 53, 54,
55–56, 91
capitalism in, 65
Celtic fringe of, **43**, 91
and Central Asia, 356
civil liberties in, 77, 88
civil rights in, 51, 58
civil society in, 71–72
Civil War in (1640–49), **44**
class in, 72–73, 78
collectivist consensus in, **47**,
50, 79, 91
common law in, **43**, 59, 91
as constitutional monarchy,
7, 44, 46–47, 49–53
currency of, 80–81, 83
democratization of, 46–47,
57, 65, 68
devolution in, 62
devolution of power in, 62,
75, 85
early history of, 41–44
economic decline in, 40, 46,
47, 50, 77, 79

economic growth in, 30,
80, 81
economic inequality in, 80
education in, 73
elections in, 53–54, 56, 62,
66–67, 70–71
electoral reform in, 61, 69
electoral system in, 14,
59–62, *60*, 75, 279
ethnicity and, 19, 40–41,
72, 73–75, *74*, 78
EU and, 41, 50, 51, 68, 70,
75, 80, 82–83, *84*, 187
executive in, 10
in Falklands War, 45, 50,
54, 82
foreign relations of, 50–51,
81–85
GDP of, *38*, 79
geography of, 40–41
head of government in, *38*,
53, 55
head of state in, *38*, 52,
55, 162
health care in, 79, 86
Human Development Index
ranking of, *29*, *38*
immigration in, 30, 41, 70,
74–75
imperialism of, 45, 79, 82,
480
individual freedoms in, 77
Industrial Revolution in,
39, 46, 79
Iran and, 480–81, 483–84,
508
Iraq War and, 50, 54, 55,
56, 69, 82, 84, 86
judiciary in, 11, 52, 57,
58–59
labor force in, *78*
labor unions in, 50, 66, 67,
71–72, 80
land size of, *38*, 40
legislature in, 39, 43–47,
51, 52, 53, 56–58,
63–64, 65, 75, 76, 77,
86–87, 92, 100, 276,
430
liberal ideology in, 40,
77–79, 82, 85

local government in, 63
as majoritarian system, **48**,
59–61, 64, 92
map of, *38*
military of, 82, 150
monarchy in, 7, 39, 41,
43–46, 52–53, 55,
75, 274
Muslims in, 75, 87, 180
national identity in, 72, 75
nationalization in, 47, 79
Nigeria and, 687–89, 721
old-boy networks in, 73
as parliamentary system,
11–12, 15, 56, 58, 64,
112, 437–38
party system in, 46–48, 53,
56, 64–70, 122
Persia and, 480–82
political conflict and
competition in, 64–72
political development of,
41–47, *42*
political economy in, 24,
78–81
political ideology and
culture in, 23, 24, 40,
51, 77–78
political institutions in, 10,
12, 14, 15, *16*, 49–53
political regime in, 48–64
political scandal in, 66–67
population of, *5*, *38*, 40
as post-industrial economy,
79
prime ministers in, **45**,
50–51, 52, 53–55, 92
privatization in, 50, 79
public spending in, 80
referenda in, 62, 67, 69
religion in, 43–44, 72,
73–74, *74*, 87
Scottish independence issue
and, 85–87
as secular society, 21
service sector in, 79
society in, 72–78
South Africa and, 634–35,
640–41, 659, 663–64
special-interest groups
in, 71